LANGSTON'S SALVATION

Langston's Salvation

American Religion and the Bard of Harlem

Wallace D. Best

NEW YORK UNIVERSITY PRESS
New York

NEW YORK UNIVERSITY PRESS
New York
www.nyupress.org

"Let America Be America Again," "Suicide's Note," "Goodbye Christ," "Prayer [1]," "Christ in Alabama," "Two Somewhat Different Epigrams," "Angels Wings," "Café: 3 A.M.," "Advertisement for the Waldorf-Astoria," "The Heart of Harlem," "Personal," "Prayer Meeting," "Communion," "Encounter," and "Pennsylvania Station" from THE COLLECTED POEMS OF LANGSTON HUGHES by Langston Hughes, edited by Arnold Rampersad with David Roessel, Associate Editor, copyright © 1994 by the Estate of Langston Hughes. Used by permission of Alfred A. Knopf, an imprint of the Knopf Doubleday Publishing Group, a division of Penguin Random House LLC. All rights reserved.

Additional rights by permission of Harold Ober Associates Incorporated.

References to Internet websites (URLs) were accurate at the time of writing. Neither the author nor New York University Press is responsible for URLs that may have expired or changed since the manuscript was prepared.

ISBN: 978-1-4798-3489-1

For Library of Congress Cataloging-in-Publication data, please contact the Library of Congress.

New York University Press books are printed on acid-free paper, and their binding materials are chosen for strength and durability. We strive to use environmentally responsible suppliers and materials to the greatest extent possible in publishing our books.

Manufactured in the United States of America

10 9 8 7 6 5 4 3 2 1

Also available as an ebook

For my mother

CONTENTS

My grandmother, "Mother Pearlie," as my siblings and I called her, was a Disciples of Christ evangelist from the community of Nahunta in Wayne County, North Carolina. For many years during the summer months she would visit us in Washington, DC for extended stays. It was the farthest she ever traveled from her small, rural town, and everything she said and did made that clear. I was enchanted. Her four-foot-eleven-inch frame would fill the house with singing, preaching, and glorious stories about "heaven." She and my father, Leviticus, did not have the strongest bond, likely because she had given him as an infant to her own father to raise after her husband had abandoned them around 1918. My father, in turn, called her "Pearlie," not mother. This perennial tension notwithstanding, those visits are among my most vivid memories of childhood. They were my first introduction to God, religion, and church, and the brand of Christianity my grandmother proclaimed would have a profound impact on my life.

Every night after dinner Mother Pearlie would gather us around for a makeshift church service. (My father would keep his distance, sitting alone in his recliner, observing.) She would sing hymns with the most beautiful voice I had ever heard. I was sure that in another place and time, as well as with a few more of life's advantages, she could have been a professional singer. Sarah Vaughn and Ella Fitzgerald both remind me of her. The preaching, however, was the main event. Standing at the dinning room table with her very large and well-worn King James Version of the Bible, she would "open" her text. It was usually a verse having to do with the death of Christ in atonement for humanity's sins. John 3:16— "For God so love the world, that he gave his only begotten Son"—was a staple. Indeed, my grandmother only had one message: "Christ died for your sins and he is the only way to heaven." Salvation was through Christ alone, as he was the only means of forgiveness of one's sins. All people must be "saved" in order to go to that place where everyone will have a "mansion" and there will be "streets of gold." It was a powerful message followed always by her plea, "don't you want to go, don't you want to be saved?" With singing like that and preaching so impassioned, who didn't? It was quite compelling and nearly irresistible.

I never questioned it, but Mother Pearlie's Jesus was white and heaven was full of white people. She apparently never questioned it either. Once describing a vision she had of Jesus appearing to her in her bedroom, she said he was "dressed in a white robe with white hair and a cane." For all intents and purposes, his skin was white, too. The Jesus in her Bible was based on the Warner Sallman painting of 1940, which by the 1970s *was* Jesus for many Americans: a white man with blonde hair, pale skin, and deep blue eyes. There was not a single dark body in all the depictions of heaven in the supplementary religious literature she would show us. Some of the people even had yellow hair as if to accentuate their whiteness. Depictions of people being "caught up to meet him in the air" during the "rapture" were of white bodies destined to spend eternity at Jesus's side as reward for having made the decision to accept Christ as their "personal savior." I came to understand that accepting Christ was the most important decision anyone could make, "white Jesus" notwithstanding. Heaven was going to be wonderful, even if I had no depictions of people who looked like me actually going there.

My own conversion did not happen around that dinning room table at Mother Pearlie's urging during one of those summers, but sometime later. She had made an impression on me, however, shaping my desire to go to "white heaven." So, at the age of fifteen, with her voice echoing in my head, I became "saved." Following a long tradition in the black Baptist church, I then formally "joined" our family church, Faith Temple No. 2, and was baptized (full immersion in water) by the pastor. The church, a Freewill Baptist congregation comprised primarily of poor and working class southern migrants, placed "salvation" at the center of all its activities. Everything hinged on that, and the most important question one could ask or answer was, "are you saved?" I could now answer yes.

I soon began to notice, however, that salvation played a peculiar and idiosyncratic role in my church, as well as in many other African American churches with which I had become acquainted. Foremost, it structured what I came to understand as a spiritual hierarchy that placed a select few at the top and most in the middle or at the bottom. Those at the top were the spiritual elites, who had some title in the church—Pastor, Missionary, Evangelist, Deacon, Mother—or had been "touched by the Lord" in some special way. They were the "saints," the frequent "shouters" ("holy dancers"), and those who, according to Acts 2, "spoke in tongues," having received "the Baptism of the Holy Ghost." The lives of the middling sorts or those at the bottom were rendered marginal and, in some cases, untenable. They were always striving "to be more like Jesus," which meant, in effect, striving to be more like the spiritual elite. In this configuration, salvation was a state of spiritual authority within the church more than an expression of one's transformative experience with Christ. It was about one's status in the church, not one's relationship with Jesus. To be sure, it was *primarily* about one's relationship with Jesus, as most of the members were true believers in the "saving power" of Christ. But where one fell in the order of the spiritual hierarchy was of utmost consequence and determined how one navigated the space of the church.

Their notion of salvation was also tenuous, conditional, and unstable. You could "lose" it. My church did not embrace the biblical axiom that salvation was "fixed" by the work of Christ on the cross and that "once saved, always saved." They held that if one did not "live right"—even after the experience of salvation—one could rejoin the ranks of the unsaved. In that case, hell and not heaven would be your final destination. In the words of one of the songs the congregation often sang, "*If* you live right, Heaven belongs to you." Hell was just as real as heaven in the theological world they created. It was a place of unending torment with fires that never extinguished and bodies that burned forever, just punishment for not accepting Christ and living a holy life. Thus, the admonition to "stay saved" made very little sense from a biblical standpoint, but it was taken very seriously and was an effective means of social control. The church was a wondrous and paradoxical world based as much on the fear of hell as on the hope of heaven, and it meted out portions of certainty and uncertainty in equal measure. My announcement that I wanted to attend college, therefore, elicited concern from the "saints" about the condition of my soul and warnings that I would "fall away." They feared that I would lose my salvation.

They were right—to an extent. I say this because in (James) Baldwinian terms I began to read, and that reading generated profound changes in me and in my theological views. My deeper reading of theology, church history, and American history in college and graduate school prompted me not only to analyze my own beliefs but also the very structures of belief, particularly in the way they were often strategically deployed in many American and African American churches. And because I began to read, I also began to question. I questioned what I had been taught as biblical "truth," such as the existence of hell, for example. Other questions regarded the culture of my church. Why was that picture of white Jesus displayed so prominently in the sanctuary? Why did female authority never seem to equal male authority? Why were congregants of "non-normative" sexualities rendered invisible despite their visibility? They were right there—sitting in the pews, playing at the organ, ushering down the aisles, and sometimes even preaching in the pulpit. Mostly, however, I began to question the spiritual hierarchy that not only neatly divided the entire world into categories of saved and unsaved but also sustained a class system within the church that unequally distributed material power and spiritual authority. In many ways, I understood the logic of this spiritual class system. The church allowed those who were considered "nobodies" in the outside world to be considered "somebodies" in the sacred space of the church. Still, the system seemed to at the very least have its problematic elements. So, the "saints" were right to be a little worried about me because my reading and my questioning lead me to identify more with the spiritually marginalized and, by extension, with those who were doubtful, skeptical, or dissenters. This meant, however, that in their view I had indeed "fallen away" and had rejoined the legion of "unsaved."

I found a fellow traveler along this road in the poet Langston Hughes. Like many Americans, I had become acquainted with Hughes's poetry early in my education. And by the time I was composing my own poetry in junior high school, I was sure of his influence on my "free verse" style of writing. It was during a trip with friends to London in 1989, however, that my connection to Hughes reached a deeper level. Sneaking off alone to the city's West End one evening, I saw Isaac Julien's recently released and already controversial film, "Looking for Langston." I was spellbound by the dreamy images of a culturally sophisticated Harlem of long ago and a city within a city full of African American artists and writers. And although the biopic only ventured to make allusions to the life of Langston Hughes, I was gripped by those allusions depicting him as elusive, mysterious, and possibly gay. He was the ultimate African American urban, secular sophisticate. I was coming to see myself as that, if only by aspiration.

The film misled me somewhat, however, as I discovered during the research for my first book on black Chicago during the Great Migration. In ways that initially surprised me, Hughes kept making appearances in the documents on black religion in Chicago. Unbeknownst to me, he had spent quite a bit of time there over the course of his life and had often written about his experiences in the city's black churches and with its religious culture more generally. The Hughes I found in those documents was indeed the urban sophisticate depicted in Julien's film, but I discovered that I would have to think more carefully about his "secularity." Hughes had developed some significant bonds with Chicago's black religious community as well as some distinct religious practices. He had written extensively about religion in a way that belied his image as anti-church and wholly uninterested in religion, which was the Hughes I was taught in school and the one I thought I had come to know. The reality, however, was much more complicated; Hughes was much more complicated. I set out to understand this Hughes and discovered in him ways of acting "religiously" in the world that defied many of the conventions of religiosity that I had come to understand from my grandmother and my church. Hughes further sharpened my identification with religious marginals, skeptics, doubters, and dissenters, and I saw in his life echoes of my own. Like me, Hughes seemed to have existed somewhere between a religious past and a present that was always in flux on matters of God, faith, and the church. We both seemed to have developed our religious practices on our own terms. We also seemed to have redirected our questions and our quests into fundamentally artistic and intellectual pursuits. Salvation was still crucial, perhaps even central, but in the end the most important question was not "are you saved?" but "what does it mean to be saved?"

ACKNOWLEDGMENTS

Completing this book took much longer than I expected. Consequently, I have amassed some pretty large debts to a great many people. There was never a time during the research, reflection, and writing when I did not feel completely supported and encouraged by colleagues, friends, and family. Their warmth, humor, and insight held me up during the low points and pushed me even higher during the high times. The project would have been impossible without them.

This book took initial shape at Harvard Divinity School, where one of the most intellectually vibrant group of people I have ever encountered read, critiqued, and debated the early stages of the project. They not only gave me space to share my developing thoughts on Hughes and religion, but they also insisted that I take the path of excellence. I want to thank, foremost, the late Ronald F. Thiemann. Ron's excitement about this project often exceeded my own, and there were many times during our conversations when I simply allowed myself to bask in it. I only regret that I did not finish in time. The same is true for the late Reverend Peter J. Gomes, who was one of my biggest supporters there. I hope this book honors him in some way. Werner Sollors basically gave me the courage to write this book. He suggested that writing a book on African American literature from the perspective of American history and religious studies was a great strength, even though English literature was not my discipline. I took that to heart. Others who were influential and helpful in all sorts of ways include Lawrence Bobo, Ann Braude, Davíd Carrascso, Harvey Cox, Diana Eck, Marla Frederick, Henry Louis Gates Jr., William Graham, David Hempton, Evelyn Brooks Higginbotham, Amy Hollywood, Kevin Madigan, Anne Monius, Diane Moore, Laura Nasrallah, Jacob Olupona, Robert Orsi, Kimberly Patton, and Stephanie Paulsell.

Princeton University took over the responsibility of nurturing the project when I arrived in 2007. The rich intellectual life that I found, coupled with the friendships and collaborations that I developed, honed my arguments and assertions, and doubtlessly made it a better book. I was given numerous opportunities to present my work in invited talks and colloquia in the Department of Religion, the Religions in the Americas Colloquium, the Davis Center, the Carl Fields Center, and the Center for the Study of Religion. I am particularly indebted to the members of the "RA workshop." Over the years, members have graced me with their insights, comments, and helpful suggestions. I am particularly grateful to the graduate students (and former graduate students) who commented on the work or helped to sharpen my thinking. They include Vaughn A. Booker, Rachel Gross, Ryan Harper, Alda Balthrop-Lewis, Rachel Lindsey, Kelsey Moss, Andrew Walker-Cornetta, and Joseph Winters. A special thanks is due to Leslie Ribovich, who read every word of this book and offered invaluable critical feedback. Her help over the course of two years allowed me to finish. Thanks also to Clifton Granby, Nicole Kirk, Jenny Wiley Legath, Alyssa Maldonado-Estrada, Anthony Petro, Xavier Pickett, Irene Elizabeth Stroud, and Heather White.

The Princeton University community of scholars and colleagues has also been grand in their support and help. Thanks to Judith Weisenfeld, who never failed to have a word of encouragement and insight about the project. Her sharp skill at analysis and historical interpretation always pushed me forward. Others who have influenced the study in significant ways both professionally and personally include Leora Batnitsky, Wendy Belcher, Ellen B. Chances, Jessica Delgado, Jarrett M. Drake, Chris Eisgruber, Patricia Fernandez-Kelly, John Gager, Eddie Glaude Jr., Eric Gregory, Martha Himmelfarb, Tera Hunter, Kevin Kruse, Regina Kunzel, Elaine Pagels, Imani Perry, Seth Perry, Albert Raboteau, Carolyn Rouse, Stacey Sinclair, Jeffrey Stout, Dara Strolovitch, Moulie Vidas, Sean Wilentz, and Robert Wuthnow.

My friends from the wider Princeton community have been a source of strength in ways they may not know. I thank them for every lunch and coffee break, walk around town, dinner party, late-night talk, and outing beyond Princeton. I will remember them always. Thanks especially to Anastasia Mann, whose grace, intelligence, and generosity introduced me to a whole new world. Thanks also to Chester Czeslowski, Lisa Fischetti, Andrew Golden, Carol Golden, Jennifer Loessy, Ali Mann, Jacqueline Mann, James Mann, Lori Martin, Catherine Mauger, Dorothea von Moltke, Maria Papadakis, Michael Roberts, Eldar Shafir, Caron Wendell, and the late C. K. Williams.

I was afforded numerous opportunities to discuss this project beyond Princeton and benefited enormously from that feedback. Thanks to R. Marie Griffith at the University of Washington at St. Louis; Josef Sorett and Courtney Bender at Columbia University; Jonathan Sheehan at the University of California, Berkeley; Paul Lim at Vanderbilt Divinity School; and Marla Frederick and Jonathan Walton at Harvard University and Harvard Divinity School.

The generosity of a large number of scholars who gravitated toward this project and offered help, support, and thoughtful critique took me by surprise and continues to warm my heart. They are among the best of the best. Special thanks go first to those who taught me by example how to live this academic life with dignity and integrity: James T. Campbell, James Grossman, Nancy MacLean, and Mark Noll. Another special thanks to David K. Johnson, who read most of the chapters, giving them what I have come to call "the David Johnson treatment." Thanks also to Edward Blum, Glenda Gilmore, and Natasha Trethewey who read early versions of the "Concerning 'Goodbye Christ'" chapter and greatly improved my thinking on that material. Randal Maurice Jelks has been an inspiration to me, and he has introduced me to the wider world of Hughes scholars, including Donna Akiba Sullivan Harper, Vera Kutzinski, John Edgar Tidwell, and Carmaletta M. Williams. The magnificent Arnold Rampersad has taught, supported, and encouraged me over many years, and for all of it I could never thank him enough. For all the ways they kept me focused and on track, thanks also to Victor Anderson, K. Anthony Appiah, Jon Butler, James Cone, Jacob Dorman, Carol Duncan, Henry Finder, Marla Frederick, Steven Fullwood, Brett Gadsden, Matthew Hedstrom, Joyce A. Joyce, Derek Kruger, Kathryn Lofton, Kathryn Gin Lum, Anthony Pinn, Paul Rauschenbusch, Margret Roadknight, Eugene Rogers, Leigh Eric Schmidt, Timothy Stewart-Winter, "Cousin" Jonathan Walton, Cornel West, and Frederick Wherry.

My editor at NYU Press, Jennifer Hammer, has shown such patience and care for this project. I thank her for believing in me and in the power and promise of Langston Hughes.

There were a number of wonderful people who took me into their homes and returned my phone calls to discuss their memories of Langston Hughes. Foremost, in this category I want to thank "the Fan who knew too much," Anthony Heilbut. I spent the most time with Tony, and the stories he told me were and remain an unceasing delight. I have never met anyone with the sheer depth of knowledge about black American life, black church culture, and gospel music that he possesses. What started as an exchange between two souls interested in a bygone era developed into a genial and caring friendship that I will cherish forever. Through Tony I met Archbishop Carl Bean of Los Angeles and Barbara F. Meyer (Griner). Bean also dazzled me with stories about Hughes from the 1960s, and Griner, one of the four original producers of Hughes's *Black Nativity*, shared not only her memories of Hughes but also her immense archival collection and objects of memorabilia. They are now among my prized possessions. I also had thrilling and informative conversations with the great Carmen de Lavallade and with Madeline Bell, the first female member of the Bradford Singers.

The list of archivists, curators, genealogists, and librarians is too long to include here, but I want to express my thanks to the scores of people who assisted me at the Library of Congress, the Beinecke Library at Yale University, the Houghton Library at Harvard University, special collections at the Mooreland-Spingarn Research Center at Howard University, the Rose Library at Emory University, the Schomburg Center for Research in Black Culture, the New York Public Library, the New York Society Library, Princeton University Library, and the British Library in London. They are my heroes, so they will not go unsung.

The list of other friends who have been my "salvation" over the years is also long, but I will do my best to name most of them. They include Richard Bourré, Anthea Butler, Carolyn Chen, Matthew Cressler, Maite Conde, Kathryn L. Dawson, Gillian Frank, Dario Gaggio (Il Mio Amico), George Gonzalez, Farah Jasmine Griffin, Paul Harvey, Obery Hendricks, Tracey Hucks, Darrell Hucks, Tariq Jazeel, Reed Lowrie, Lerone Martin, Jeffrey McCune, Laura McTighe, Samira Mehta, Torri Ofori, Devah Pager, Dylan Penningroth, Alex Rehding, Barbara Savage, Michael Sherry, Bradley Simpson, José Velazco, Clarence Walker, Cicely Walton, and Jon Wolfe.

Thanks to my brothers and sisters for always asking how the book was going. They have been waiting a long time. A special thanks to my many nieces and nephews (by blood and by love) who are sources of great joy to their "Uncle Wallace."

My mother did not live to see this project come to completion, but she was always the angel in the room as I thought and wrote. This book is for her. Lastly, I do not remember much about the time before I met César Braga-Pinto and I dare not think of a future without him. He is responsible for most of what is good about my life, and he gives me hope for an even brighter tomorrow.

Introduction

Looking for Langston

"I do not consider any of my writing anti-religious."
—Langston Hughes

When the poet Langston Hughes was twelve years old, he attended the annual weeks-long revival meeting in Lawrence, Kansas, with his "Auntie" Reed. A family friend and devout Christian, Mary Reed lived with her husband, James, in the working-class eastern section of town, populated primarily by African Americans, white southerners, and Native Americans. The childless couple had taken Hughes into their home after the death of his grandmother, Mary Patterson Leary Langston. At the special meeting for children—an evening devoted to bringing the "young lambs to the fold"—Hughes sat with the other youths on the mourners' bench, waiting to be "saved." Time passed and all the other children had gone forward to accept Christ as their savior except for Hughes and his friend, Westley, son of the town drunk. Hughes was willing to wait; Westley was not. Growing impatient with the Kansas heat and the many eyes staring at them, Westley whispered to Hughes, "God damn! I'm tired o' sitting here. Let's get up and be saved." After Westley went forward, all the attention turned to Hughes. Mary Reed and the rest of the congregation pleaded with him, "Why don't you come? Why don't you come and be saved?" But Hughes kept his seat. As he remembered, "I wanted to see him (Jesus), but nothing happened to me. Nothing! I wanted something to happen to me; but nothing happened."

Following the traditions of the African Methodist Episcopal Church (AME), Hughes had been christened as a child but, at the "age of accountability," the church encouraged such children to make a public confession of faith. Reed had promised him that at the moment of salvation he would "see and hear and feel Jesus," Hughes remembered, and

1

"I believed her." But not wanting to further detain those assembled who were fervently wailing in prayer on his behalf, Hughes finally relented. "Waves of rejoicing" rose up in the church as the last "young lamb" came forward for salvation. When later that evening his Auntie found him sobbing in his bed, it seemed to confirm for her that Hughes had indeed been saved. The tears, however, were not tears of joy but of shame and disappointment—shame that he had deceived the congregation and disappointment that he had not "seen" Jesus as he had been promised.[1]

Hughes included this story as a vignette entitled "Salvation" in his 1940 autobiography, The Big Sea. With its intentionally ironic title, "Salvation" told the story of Hughes's failed salvation experience, an event he considered to be one of the three most important moments in his life. He linked it to two other crucial moments in his life—the realization in his late teens that he hated his father and the rejection by his wealthy Park Avenue patron, Charlotte Louise Van der Veer Quick Mason, in 1930. They were the moments that he divulged with the greatest care and the most obvious pain. Regarding his break with Mason, Hughes wrote, "That beautiful room, that had been so full of light and help and understanding for me, suddenly became like a trap closing in, faster and faster, the room darker and darker, until the light went out with a sudden crash in the dark. . . . Everything became like that night in Kansas when I had failed to see Jesus and had lied about it afterwards. Or that morning in Mexico when I suddenly hated my father."[2] Beginning in 1927, Mason and Hughes had developed a deep and abiding, albeit unusual, friendship until she summarily dismissed him as her protégé, cutting him off from her patronage. Hughes had ultimately failed to heed her misguided artistic demands and refused to accept the "primitive" she believed him and all blacks to be. "She wanted me to be more African than Harlem," he explained. Heartbroken, he eventually retaliated by writing about her, breaking her "code of secrecy." Doubtlessly, Mason was the subject of the poem, "Poet to Patron," which Hughes penned in 1939.[3] As for his father, James Nathaniel Hughes, who abandoned his family and his country, Hughes had never been close to him. James Hughes was unwilling to abide by American racial codes and had contempt for the poor and all black people, the major source of the conflict between father and son. As their relationship steadily dissolved, even the thought of him made Hughes sick. "I hated my father," he bluntly stated.[4]

Hughes's hatred of his father and his break with Mason have been discussed in illuminating detail, but the failed salvation experience has not been granted the same level of attention. Given the chronology of these events, however, the failed salvation experience was the foundational one among the three. Indeed, it affected Hughes's reactions to his father and to Mason. As Hughes's principal biographer Arnold Rampersad asserts, "all three moments unveil Hughes's extreme fear of abandonment."[5] Such fear, however, began that night in Kansas. Jesus had abandoned him in a spiritual or metaphysical sense, his father would do so in an emotional one, and Charlotte Mason would abandon him materially.

The central claim of this book is that Hughes's failed salvation experience profoundly shaped his approach to religion and became the crucial backdrop for much of his writing. The event set in motion his lifelong quest to understand the nature of "salvation" and the role religion plays in daily life. Indeed, one cannot fully understand Langston Hughes without a careful examination of his thoughts on God, faith, the institution of the church, and matters of ultimate meaning. These concerns permeate the corpus of his work, as Hughes wrote as much about religion as any other topic, particularly on the paired themes of salvation and sin. At the heart of this pursuit was an understanding that in Christian theology, the substitutionary death of Jesus served as the basis of salvation. Hughes heard this claim both from the pulpit and in Sunday school at St. Luke AME in Lawrence, where his family had been members since the 1880s.[6] Black Methodists had developed a strong presence in northeastern Kansas by the first decade of the twentieth century, the result of a migration to Kansas from the South that started in the 1850s and increased after the Civil War and the collapse of Reconstruction in 1877.[7] But Hughes would have also known of Jesus's substitutionary death to provide salvation from his own reading of the Bible, the book he declared to be one of his "earliest memories of written words," along with W. E. B. DuBois's *The Souls of Black Folk*. This aspect of the Christian narrative surfaced with great regularity in Hughes's writing, particularly in the late 1950s and early 1960s, including the short stories "On the Road," "Big Meeting," and "Blessed Assurance," and in what he called his "gospel song-plays," such as *Black Nativity*, a theatrical production about Jesus's birth featuring an all-black cast.[8] A Christian theological understanding of salvation from the perspective of his church in Kansas

Figure I.1. Founded in 1862, St. Luke AME Church occupied a number of spaces in east Lawrence, Kansas, before it broke ground at the corner of Ninth and New York Streets in 1863. Originally composed of free blacks, escaped slaves, and former slaves, the congregation built a permanent edifice in the Gothic Revival style in 1910.

comprised an important aspect of Hughes's personal and literary exploration of the concept.

That sweltering night in Kansas, however, took Hughes beyond the notion of individual redemption, central to his AME upbringing. It also created the space for alternative meanings and modes of salvation found in broader liberal Protestant traditions, which he encountered in New York City and in the lives and writings of Walt Whitman and his "guiding star," Carl Sandburg. What Hughes came to understand as salvation was by no means stable or fixed but shifted and changed in his life and in his work, often according to the genre in which he was writing. Moreover, for Hughes, salvation was not always a category of "religious" experience, as it also became a discursive means of articulating intellectual, artistic, and political expressions. Indeed, an analysis of religious themes in the work of Langston Hughes shows that he was "working out his salvation," to employ the rhetorical structure of Philippians 2:12, King James Version (KJV). Such "working out" was foremost and primarily an intellectual, cultural, and artistic enterprise. Failing to "see" Jesus that night disrupted the initial stirrings of belief in Hughes, as he further stated in his vignette as a response to the experience, "I didn't believe there was a Jesus any more, since he didn't come to help me." His life and artistic production, therefore, would always connote a complicated and, at times, fraught relationship with God, with the institution of the church, and with religion more broadly, as he moved unevenly between stances of belief and unbelief, frustration, doubt, and disillusionment. Hughes's pursuit to understand the nature of salvation, which began that night in Kansas, sat at the center of his thinking, forming and shaping his writing on religious topics, as well as his approach to religion as a phenomenon of human experience.

"Working Out" Salvation

Because Hughes took the initial steps to "work out" his notion of salvation in his poetry, this book draws heavily on his poetic production. It is important to recognize, however, that in a career that spanned over forty years, Hughes wrote in nearly every literary genre—poetry, plays, social commentary, novels, librettos, children's books, and short stories—and that most of his writing across the genres had some measure of religious content. Hughes, for example, collaborated with composers whose works were thoroughly religious and overtly theological. He had an extended collaboration with Jan Meyerowitz, the prolific German "composer on moral subjects" in the 1950s to the early 1960s. Born in a German Jewish family that had converted to Christianity, Meyerowitz encountered Hughes's "blues poetry" and sought him out to be the librettist for his operatic works. No real fan of opera, Hughes nevertheless wrote four biblically based librettos over the course of their decade-long, volatile, and not particularly lucrative collaboration. "The Five Foolish Virgins" (1954) was based on Matthew 25:1–13; "The Glory around His Head" (1955) was an Easter cantata; "Esther" (1956) was the story of the biblical queen; and "On a Pallet of Straw" (1960) told the story of Jesus's birth.[9] In addition to Meyerowitz, Hughes collaborated with an impressive list of American composers during this period, including Margaret Bonds and William Schumer, for whom he also wrote librettos on religious themes.[10]

Despite a high level of proficiency in other literary genres, Hughes considered himself primarily a poet. Writing poetry was his earliest passion and became for him a "sacred commitment." He declared to the poet Vachel Lindsay in 1925 that he wanted to write poetry for the "beautiful thing that it is." Poetry, he maintained, was beauty and light, the metered and measured articulation of life itself. It was never to be propagandistic, nor at the service of "this or that cause." He composed poetry primarily because he liked it. Writing in the 1950 inaugural edition of the *Free Lance*, a magazine of poetry and prose, Hughes further developed this philosophy of poetry. "Words are the paper and the string" that "wrap" a poet's experience, he declared in a brief introduction to the magazine entitled, "A Note on Poetry." All poetry is personal, he maintained, and though it varied in quality it always revealed something of the interior world and exterior experience of the writer. "Each poet makes of words his own highly individualized wrappings of life segments he wishes to present. . . . Sometimes the word wrappings contain nothing. But, regardless of quality or content, a poem reveals always the poet as a person. Skilled or unskilled, wise or foolish, nobody can write a poem without revealing something of himself. Here are people. Here are poems. Here is revelation."[11] It was as a poet that Hughes became a central figure of the Harlem Renaissance, "the Bard of Harlem," the moniker attached to him by the late 1930s as an obvious comparison to William Shakespeare, the "Bard of Avon." As Harlem's bard, Hughes became one of the movement's brightest stars.[12] Although his poetry can be described a number of ways, Hughes often described himself as a "social poet," one whose primary intent was to focus on the lives of ordinary working people. Writing for *Phylon* in 1947, he conceded that "having been born poor and also colored," his poems, particularly the earlier ones, were not about "beauty and lyricism." They were, rather, about "people's problems—whole groups of people's problems." And early observers took note. Novelist and poet Margaret Larkin proclaimed Hughes a "Proletariat poet" and "a poet for the people" in her 1927 review of Hughes's second book of poetry, *Fine Clothes to the Jew*. For Larkin, Hughes was a "new prophet" who had answered the call for poetry to "come out of rich men's closets and become the 'proletarian art' of all the people." In a retrospective on black literature published in 1932, Alain Locke, one of the principal architects of the Harlem Renaissance, described Hughes as one who "sang of his people" and "a militant and indignant proletarian reformer." By 1935 Hughes's poems were already being anthologized in collections of proletarian poetry, poetry that was, as Joseph Freeman described it, "inspired by the revolutionary working class."[13]

The characterization of Hughes's poetry as essentially concerned with the working lives of ordinary people has been dominant and he remains perhaps best known as a "proletarian" and "social" poet. Religion, however, was just as pervasive a theme in Hughes's poetry and he wrote nearly as much poetry on religious topics as he did about workers or social protest. Indeed, Hughes's religious poetry is constitutive of his proletarian and social poetry since it, too, was mostly concerned with the lives of working people and the socially marginalized. In addition to numerous poems in which he implicitly employed religious discourses, frameworks, and imagery, Hughes wrote eighty explicitly religious poems, which involved direct engagement with American religious institutions, black church cultures, Christian theology, and liturgical practices.

Poems in which Hughes made implicit use of religious language and imagery include perhaps his most famous, "The Negro Speaks of Rivers," a poem he quickly wrote on a train crossing the Mississippi river on his way to visit his estranged father in Mexico. The poem showcases the influence of free verse on Hughes's developing craft, as it has all the hallmarks of Whitman and Sandburg. It is also an early demonstration of Hughes's enduring love affair with black people, a tribute, "rich in expression and moving in its message," to the glorious black past and the dignity of black character.[14] But what is perhaps more significant, Hughes infused it with spiritual cadences: "I've known rivers ancient as the world and older than the flow of human blood in human veins. My soul has grown deep like the rivers."[15]

The critical praise for "The Negro Speaks of Rivers" highlighted its religiosity. Jessie Fauset, who was serving as literary editor of the *Crisis*, where Hughes had sent the poem for consideration in 1921, heralded it as evidence of his "great gift" and his "spiritualness," a term she confessed to having coined especially for him. That sense of "spiritualness" was "the first and greatest essential of the poet," she further elaborated. Historian Nathan Huggins concurred with Nigerian literary critic Onwuchekwa Jemie's estimation of the "transcendent essences" of the poem, asserting that in it Hughes captured "some of the force of the spiritual." The speaker in the poem identifies with "eternal forces" and "transcends" the harsh facts of existence and the "the very conditions which make the statement necessary." The river is not only a part of "God's body," as Jemie had claimed, it is also "eternity itself, with no beginning and no end." Making symbolic use of the Mississippi as a "timeless" and mysterious sustainer of life, Hughes asserted that so, too, were the "souls" of black people in that they are "deep like the rivers." "The Negro Speaks of Rivers" is a perfect example of Hughes's implicitly religious poetry in its fusion of racial and religious rhetorics and in his tendency to depict the black experience in religious or spiritual terms. Alain Locke acknowledged this in his cogitations on the poem, calling it Hughes's "mystical identification with the race experience."[16]

Hughes's frank talk of Harlem nightlife in *Fine Clothes to the Jew* overshadowed his first series of explicitly religious poems in the collection, and many readers panned the book for its greatly misunderstood title and its focus on "low life" and sexuality in such poems as "Jazz Band in a Parisian Cabaret," "Crap Game," and "Ballad of Gin Mary." The attention went to "Red Silk Stockings," where an unnamed speaker entices, "Put on yo' red silk stockings Black gal / Go out an' let de white boys look at yo' legs." Having already been granted the honorific title of "Poet Laureate of Harlem," Hughes was then dubbed the "Poet Lowrate of Harlem" by the *Chicago Whip*. Others among the black press called him "The Sewer Dweller" and the poems "trash."[17] But in the "Glory! Hallelujah!" section of the book, Hughes waxes anything but "lowrate," exploring themes intrinsic to the Christian tradition such as mercy, redemption, sacrifice, atonement, exaltation, resurrection, and the afterlife. These poems evoke the ethos of black church culture and make reference to its material world. In them one hears the rhythmic cadences of the worship service, the fiery tones of the preaching, the exalting testimonies of faith, and the spiritual frenzy of the music.

Hughes's explicitly religious poems cluster during the mid-to-late 1920s and contain all the imprints of his black Methodist upbringing, a testament to the deep impact it had on him. Indeed, two other explicitly religious poems, which appeared in *The Dream Keeper* in 1932, were also written during the 1920s and were similar in theme to those in *Fine Clothes to the Jew*. They are two of Hughes's best-known and most evocative poems in this form, "Ma Lord" and "Feet o' Jesus."[18] Explicitly religious poems surface throughout Hughes's body of work, however, including a few during his period of radical awareness in the 1930s, including "God" and "Big City Prayer." As he turned to an emphasis on patriotism and "the folk" during the 1940s and 1950s, he published such poems as "Heaven," "It Gives Me Pause," and "Communion." He also wrote a number of religious poems that he did not publish during his "gospel years" of the 1960s, such as "Christ" and "Celestial Eye."[19] They are published here for the first time.

Thinking about Religion

Despite this extensive corpus of religiously infused work, little sustained and comprehensive analysis of Hughes's religious poetry has emerged. With the exception of French literary scholar Jean Wagner, no major study has focused exclusively on the religious aspect of Hughes's poetic production.[20] This is not to say that there has been no acknowledgment of the religious *content* in Hughes's writing, or of the important, if complicated, role religion played in his life. As African American playwright, theater critic, and friend of Hughes, Loften Mitchell definitively states, "religion was important to Langston."[21] The absence of forthright analysis of his religious work, however, has marginalized one of the most percipient thinkers about religion in twentieth-century arts and letters. It has also prompted the not entirely inaccurate but misleading conclusions by Hughes biographers and literary scholars that Hughes was "secular to the bone," "notoriously reticent about matters of religion," and "as a rule . . . stayed away from religious topics and themes."[22] These depictions of Hughes have contributed to the general perception that he was antireligious, that is, he was oppositional to religion and religious people, and that his writings bear witness to this stance. Hughes rebuffed this characterization of himself and of his poetry, as he did in a testy exchange with Wagner during an interview with him in 1958. When Wagner asked Hughes to characterize his "personal religious evolution" over the last twenty years and to state if his readers were correct in "considering his anti-religious stand of the 30s" as "merely a short-lived accident," Hughes responded simply and definitively, "I do not consider any of my writing anti-religious."[23] Hughes likely warmed to Wagner's acknowledgment that his religious views had changed over time, but he rejected Wagner's implication that his more radical religious poetry of the 1930s was disparaging of religion. He implied, rather, the very opposite. For Hughes, all of his religious writing, including that which he produced during the 1930s, was generative and contributive to religion and was not antireligious.

Given that Hughes was at times staunchly evasive about his own religious beliefs, the assertions of his antireligiosity are understandable. Many of his personal and professional affiliations were with people unfalteringly antagonistic to religion, he was formally disassociated from religious institutions, and he held palpable disdain for public pietistic displays of religion. But part of the aim of this book is to draw distinctions between the lack of religious belief or nonconformity to conventional religious standards and institutions and antireligiosity. The one does not equate the other. Moreover, this book shows that claims of Hughes's antireligiosity have to do, in part, with the very limited ways in which some Hughes scholars have thought about what constitutes "religion" generally, restricting it to matters of "confession," an uncritical celebration of God and acts of devotion, and an affiliation with religious institutions, mainly the Protestant Christian church. They have also narrowly delineated what one should consider "religious" in the work of Hughes. This limited understanding of religion and the religious content in many of Hughes's poems has largely excluded him, as it has other New Negro writers of the first half of the twentieth century, from the history and the historiography of African American religion.

The assertion of Hughes's antireligiosity has not only disregarded his own declarations about the long-enduring prominence of religion in his writing, specifically his poetry, but also his seemingly balanced assessment of his own stance toward religion. When asked in an interview in 1960 if "religious faith of any kind" influenced his poetry, Hughes responded by referring back to Mary Reed and his church experiences in Kansas. "Yes, I would think very much so. I grew up in a not very religious family, but I had a foster aunt who saw that I went to church and Sunday School. . . . I was very much moved. . . . And when I began to write poetry," he proclaimed, "that influence came through."[24] Indeed, when religion becomes a primary category of analysis for Hughes's poetry, as well as his works in other literary genres, he is revealed to be a thinker about religion of notable range and depth.

Hughes as a "thinker about religion" is a key concept in the book and one that is meant to distinguish him from a "religious thinker" or someone who is "religious," that is, a believer in a God or deities and an observant practitioner of a particular religious tradition, such as Christianity, Judaism, or Islam. This book makes no claim that Hughes was religious, espoused a particular religious tradition, or made a "confession of faith." In that sense, it is not a "religious biography" or a "spiritual narrative." Indeed, the central arguments of the book do not rest on whether or not Hughes was himself a religious person. It is clear from much of his artistic production and various public statements, however, that Hughes maintained and cultivated a religious sensibility and sensitivity to religious systems, and he harbored a deep affection for many aspects of the church of his youth, mainly its worship. He also carefully articulated a set of "personal" religious practices later in his life, having to do primarily with his engagement with the wider religious world and Harlem's religious communities in particular. That engagement became more pronounced in the 1950s and 1960s, coinciding with significant redirections in the focus of his work. But this book is focused, most of all, on tracing the complicated history of Hughes's *thinking* about religion and depicts him in the broadest sense as a public intellectual on matters of religion for the way he expressed those thoughts in his art and other writings.

A significant aspect of thinking about religion for Hughes was thinking theologically. Like many other New Negro writers, Hughes often employed theological terms, discourses, and frameworks such as salvation, sin, prayer, communion, covenant, eternity, and the cross to express his ideas. His literary opus is replete with examples. But thinking about religion also had a public and social component to it. As an aspect of "working out" his salvation, Hughes's thinking about religion involved a determination to understand the role of religion in public life, and the public function of religion particularly in regard to African Americans. He sometimes spoke of religion as a "private" matter, but Hughes also strongly intimated that if there were any value to be found in religion, it necessarily had to be in the realm of the social. Therefore, to see Hughes as a thinker about religion is to understand that religion was not only *important* to him, it was absolutely central to a vast portion of his art.

Although this book makes no claim that Hughes was himself religious or religiously observant, it illustrates how and why he took decisive steps at certain times in his career to establish that he had great respect for all religious faiths and that he held those he considered to be "truly" religious in high regard. Hughes's own declarations about his sensitivity to religion and respect for religious people and communities complicate characterizations of him as antireligious or even atheist. By the early 1940s, however, Hughes went to great lengths to distance himself from any perception that he did not believe in the existence of God. "I am not now, nor have I ever been an atheist," he stated definitively and repeatedly.[25] To be sure, a principle reason for those adamant denials certainly can be attributed to extant animus toward atheists and atheism, especially among mainstream African Americans. At the same time, the Cold War period in the United States was an exceptionally difficult time for left-leaning writers and artists who proclaimed to be atheists or "agnostics"—those who were skeptical or unconcerned about the existence of God or anything beyond the material world. Hughes likely contemplated what effect even the perception of atheism would have on his career, his marketability, and the freedom to produce his work.

While mainstream African Americans and federal authorities may have disavowed atheists and atheism, however, some of the most prominent writers, activists, and intellectuals of Hughes's day were outspoken atheists or agnostics, or at the very least had complicated relationships with religion and the church, including James Weldon Johnson, W. E. B. DuBois, George Schuyler, A. Philip Randolph, and Zora Neale Hurston.[26] In his 1933 autobiography, *Along This Way*, Johnson explained his agnosticism by indicating that he had no inclination toward religion and was simply unsure of God's existence: "I do not see how I can know; and I do not see how my knowing can matter," he determined.[27] Similarly, Zora Neale Hurston, who devoted a great deal of her life's work to the topic of religion, found no personal use for it, particularly for organized religion: "It seems to me that organized creeds are collections of words around a wish," she stated. "I feel no need for such. . . . It is simply not for me."[28] When asked whether he was "a believer in God," W. E. B. DuBois responded, "If by being a 'believer in God,' you mean a belief in a person of vast power who consciously rules the universe for the good of mankind, I answer No; I cannot disprove this assumption, but I certainly see no proof to sustain such a belief, neither in History nor in my personal experience."[29] Among Hughes's contemporaries and friends, an atheistic or agnostic stance was not uncommon. So, while it is clear from the failed salvation experience that Hughes wavered between belief and unbelief in his lifetime, it is also clear that had he chosen to publicly declare himself to be an atheist, he would have been in good company.

In light of the artistic, cultural, and intellectual spaces Hughes occupied, therefore, his insistence that he was not an atheist likely had little to do with his or anyone else's negative views about atheism. Another, more significant motivation had to do with his unrelenting commitment to his own self-fashioning and his ideas about the nature and construction of identity. As a matter of principal and as an artist, Hughes eschewed the notion of fixed identities, and the only identity he unambiguously claimed was that of a Negro artist and writer, as he demonstrated in his 1926 cultural and racial manifesto, "The Negro Artist and the Racial Mountain."[30] All others were suspect and held at bay, unclaimed or unembraced in the fullest sense.

"Personal" and Public Practices

In distancing himself from allegations of atheism and rejecting characterizations that he was antireligious, Hughes carefully crafted his presentation of a "personal" religion. The existence of his religious poetry and his sensitivity to religion and religious communities did not shelter him from speculation about his religious faith and affiliations. If anything, they fueled them. Hughes and other African American artists and intellectuals often faced questions about their faith, and doubts about whether Hughes was a person of religious faith began to surface during the 1930s with the publication of such radical poetry as "Christ in Alabama" and "Goodbye Christ." These questions seemed to gain momentum throughout the mid-1940s to early 1960s, and although Hughes's answers often varied, they typically offered only enough information to trouble the question rather than to answer it outright. "Personal," a poem he published in the *Crisis* in 1933 is a perfect example. Hughes penned the poem after YMCA officials cancelled a program sponsored by the Los Angeles Civic League in which he was to be featured. They had come across "Goodbye Christ," which many took as Hughes's "dismissal" of Christ, and charged him with Communism, antireligiosity, lack of patriotism, and being "anti-Christ."[31]

> In a letter marked,
> Personal
> God has written me a letter.
>
> In an envelope marked,
> Personal
> I have given God my answer.

"Personal" is unique among Hughes's poetry because, as Mary Beth Culp observes, it is "the only poem in which Hughes spoke of religion in his own voice and not that of a persona of his people."[32] Ordinarily, Hughes and other twentieth-century black writers did not often speak in their own voices in their religious poetry. They spoke collectively, as if for all black people. This poem, however, is unquestionably about Langston Hughes in his own voice, and that was the purpose it served. Clearly meant to address the matter, the poem also was intended to complicate and perhaps even frustrate any discussion about Hughes's personal faith. Hughes did not intend it to prevent a discussion about the *existence* of a personal faith. That is precisely what "Personal" invites. But for Hughes, the contents of the "letters"—best understood as prayers—were private.

The fact that there was a mail exchange between him and God he left open for public examination, as evidenced by the poem itself.

Hughes's evasiveness about a personal religion, however, was not always a matter of deceit or disingenuousness; rather, it clearly was a strategy—a strategy, foremost, to maintain a sense of privacy. As David E. Chinitz and others demonstrate, Hughes was famously private about his personal life and rarely divulged intimacies or particularities, perhaps as a means to preserve the integrity of his approach to life as an artist.[33] But it was also a strategy to shape his own identity with regard to religion—"God has written *me* a letter; I have given God *my* answer." Indeed, Hughes's evasiveness about his own faith was consistent with his evasiveness about other "identities" he seemingly disavowed or disclaimed.

This strategy and purposeful evasiveness apply to the common assertion that Hughes was homosexual. Although in recent years Hughes has appeared in nearly every major anthology and monograph of American and African American gay literary and cultural history, whether or not he was indeed gay—in the mid-twentieth century sexualized version of the word—and harbored same-sex attraction and desire will never be fully or satisfactorily known. Indeed, the questions and the conclusions drawn about Hughes's sexuality have been the source of much contentious debate and have their own history. The views run the gamut. Some of his closest friends, including Arna Bontemps and Carl Van Vechten, insisted that they did not know if Hughes sexually desired men or women, whereas others who knew him in more professional capacities expressed no doubt that he was homosexual. Carl Van Vechten stated that after thirty years of friendship, "never had he any indication that (Hughes) was homosexual or heterosexual." Jan Meyerowitz contended that he could tell Hughes was gay based solely on Hughes's response to a photo of an "unbelievably beautiful" black man Hughes kept on his desk. "I knew he was a homosexual," he plainly stated.[34] Carl Bean, Motown recording artist, actor, and founder of the Unity Fellowship of Christ Church in Los Angeles, who met Hughes in New York during rehearsals for *Black Nativity* in the mid-1960s, argued that Hughes was never "incognito" about his sexuality. Hughes, he contended, was openly gay, as were many in the supportive arts community in which they lived. Echoing what Richard Bruce Nugent had affirmed about black life in Harlem in the 1920s and 1930s, that "nobody was in the closet, there wasn't any closet," Bean maintained that in the 1960s the black community of visual artists, writers, and gospel singers in which he and Hughes were involved freely expressed their homosexuality without "any shame," and it was never called into question. Indeed, so many gospel singers in the 1960s were perceived to be gay that jazz critic Gene Lees called the gospel world "the gospel gimmick." "What particularly tickles my funny bone," he indelicately wrote in 1964, "is that a number of the gospel singers are fags. I cannot say that faggotry is as common among gosplers as it is among ballet dancers, but it's pretty common." Bean was more delicate but just as insistent: "The idea that there is this big guessing game around Langston is ridiculous."[35]

The "big guessing game," however, has persisted long after Hughes's death, and the scholarship on him has been similarly mixed on the issue of his sexuality. Biographers, Hughes scholars, and literary critics have made contentions about his sexuality, with various levels of certainty and differing evidential approaches that range from depictions of him as heterosexual or "straight," to asexual and uninterested in sex in a "child-like" way, to simply and only homosexual. Hughes biographer, Faith Berry, for example, argues that Hughes was indisputably gay, and she questioned the integrity of all claims to the contrary.[36] None of these sexual identifications, however, likely reflect Hughes's sexuality accurately or represent his primary sexual experiences for the entirety of his life, or perhaps they applied at different times. It is also likely that Hughes practiced a form of what Jeffrey McCune calls "sexual discretion," a performance of "dissemblance" characteristic of some black men of "queer" or "non-normative" sexualities in the face of "the constraints of surveillance."[37]

Hughes's life suggests a spectrum of sexuality rather than one single, unchanging identity. He recounts in his autobiographies several romantic entanglements with women, including a high school sweetheart and a girlfriend in Paris, Anne Marie Coussey, also known as "Mary," with whom he had a tortured and, much to her displeasure, strikingly nonphysical affair. It is clear that he had a strong, intimate connection that was quite possibly sexual with Sartur Andrzejewski, his self-described "queer" "eccentric" and "funny" high school friend. He also had at least one brief sexual encounter with "an aggressive crewman" on a boat off the coast of Lagos, Nigeria, in the 1920s.[38] Although he was at various times the object of desire for other men during the Harlem Renaissance, most notably Countee Cullen and Alain Locke, who embarked on a campaign of literary, aesthetic, intellectual, and sexual seduction of the young Hughes in the early 1920s, Hughes appeared uninterested in them and manipulated their advances to his own advantage and never responded in kind.[39] One of the clearest and most cited examples deployed to suggest Hughes's homosexuality is his poem "Café: 3 A.M." from "Montage of a Dream Deferred," written in 1951. The poem is striking as much for its implicitly religious discourse as it is for its discussion of homosexuality:

> Detectives from the vice squad
> With weary sadistic eyes
> Spotting fairies.
> Degenerates,
> Some folks say.
>
> But God, Nature,
> Or somebody
> Made them that way.
>
> Police lady or Lesbian
> Over there?
> Where?

Indeed, Hughes coupled religion and homosexuality in each of his few works where homosexuality emerged as a theme, including the play "Little Ham," with its "effeminate youth" character who was a practitioner of "New Thought"; the short story "Blessed Assurance" about a young "queer" church singer; and the short story "Seven People Dancing," featuring the character "Marcel de la Smith," a known "fairy."[40] The rest of his life and work, however, was full of silences regarding his sexuality. This was intentional on his part, and the fact that questions remain about Hughes's sexuality is a testament to his success at self-fashioning, for as Shane Vogel claims, "unknowability was something that Hughes cultivated in his life and his literature."[41] When it comes to Hughes's sexuality or his personal religion, therefore, if we are "looking for Langston," to evoke Isaac Julien's dreamy 1989 fantasy-documentary, we do not really find him.[42]

"Modernist Currents," New Directions

This book is a work of intellectual and cultural history as well as a historical analysis of literature. Concerned with the history of ideas about religion as much as it is with the materiality of religion as an expression of culture, it also views literature as a viable and vital record of the American religious past. Works of American literature are historical documents in their own right. This tripartite method opens a space to read Langston Hughes religiously; that is to say, it locates him squarely within the context of the wider world of twentieth-century American and African American religious cultures. And a crucial part of that wider world was American religious liberalism. Hughes has long been regarded as one of the most important voices of the Harlem Renaissance and of literary modernism, a crucial aspect of the larger "modernist phenomenon" in the early decades of the twentieth century. Precipitated by sweeping changes in industry and the growth of American cities, modernism rejected traditional forms in art, music, literature, architecture, and social organization to embrace new ideas and approaches. Harlem was a site of "vicious modernism," in the words of the poet Amiri Baraka, and both the Harlem Renaissance and literary modernism mutually reinforced each other in the construction of an American cultural nationalism, and Hughes's work sat at the center among black writers.[43] Hughes's religious writings, however, show that he also belongs in the context of American religious liberalism, another crucial aspect of the larger modernist phenomenon. Much of Hughes's religious poetry and social commentary further elucidates his religious thought, exemplifies his theologically modernist impulses and is, at heart, an illustration of his religious liberalism.

By the time Hughes began publishing in the early 1920s, religious liberalism had been, since the late nineteenth century, a crucial part of the complex tapestry of American religion, finding institutional and noninstitutional expression in such interconnected movements as the Social Gospel, New Thought, freethinkers, transcendentalism, and humanism. Many mainstream denominations, from Baptists to Unitarian Universalists had also appropriated it and were putting into practice this new approach to religion that was largely but not exclusively Christian and theistic. Although it had become impossibly diverse and varied among this vast array of religious groups, some common elements of religious modernism from a theological standpoint included a rejection of the Protestant status quo, Christian "myths," irrationality, and dogmatism. Modernists also lauded "higher criticism" and interrogated the basic doctrines of the Christian faith and the Bible, seeing the latter as a literary source rather than a source of divine revelation. Accordingly, they redirected religious institutional priorities from the ethereal to the material, developing a decidedly social focus in American churches, with enormous political and social implications.[44] Hughes closely identified with this aspect of religious liberalism, and it had a tremendous influence on his own politics, which sought to champion the cause of workers and those lowest down and to strive for racial equality and social justice. In this regard, it is impossible to fully understand such poems as "Let America Be America Again" without some attention to Hughes's embrace of religious liberalism. Written in 1935 at the height of the Great Depression, the poem expresses the unnamed speaker's enduring hope in the elusive "American Dream" despite a list of unfulfilled promises. It speaks of a far-reaching democracy that includes all—black, white, and immigrant—and of freedom and equality as social realities, not mere ideals of the nation.

> The land that never has been yet—
> And yet must be—the land where *every* man is free.
> The land that's mine—the poor man's, Indian's, Negroes, ME—
> Who made America,
> Whose sweat and blood, whose faith and pain,
> Whose hand at the foundry, whose plow in the rain,
> Must bring back our mighty dream again.[45]

The far-reaching, all-inclusive world where everyone is a free and equal participant in democracy is as much a social vision reflective of religious liberalism as it is an American principle of government. Indeed, it succeeds as a liberal religious vision where it fails as an American political principle.

Placing Hughes and his religious writing within the context of the "modernist currents" of American religious liberalism makes several historical and historiographical interventions. It casts Hughes as an important participant in the complex flowering of religious movements and trends that were greatly shaping the entirety of American life during the twentieth century. The religious perspectives of Hughes and other New Negro artists and writers, including their critiques, doubts, disillusionment, and frustration, are revealed to be a crucial part of the narrative of American religion. It also underscores the vibrant presence of African American religious liberals during the overlapping eras of the Harlem Renaissance and the Great Migration in religious cultures that had become dominated by theologically conservative voices. An examination of Hughes's writing on religion links him ideologically with other twentieth-century black religious liberals, including Adam Clayton Powell Jr., Benjamin E. Mays, and Mary McLeod Bethune, for example. Because of their "complex" and "unorthodox" religious views, Barbara Savage identifies Mays and Bethune as part of a "Southern black religious liberalism." Bethune, in particular, was stalwartly cosmopolitan, Universalist, anticreedal, and adopted "her own theological reinterpretation of Christianity."[46] Hughes and these other African American exponents of religious liberalism have not been viewed as religious liberals in the general historical narrative of the movement, nor have they been seen as central to this history. In most cases, they have been absent altogether. But Hughes and other black artists, writers, and intellectuals similarly embraced religious liberalism and did so as a way of life and thinking, riding its currents of cultural sensitivity, artistic expression, ecumenism, cosmopolitanism, and universal secularity. As Leigh Schmidt argues, twentieth-century American religious liberalism, in addition to its reformist commitments, progressive theologies, and its advocacy of the Social Gospel, was "also a set of cultural exchanges—with art, with cosmopolitanism, and with secularism." It restructured the whole of American life and culture, or what Richard Wightman Fox calls "the broad patterns of living, feeling, and thinking" among the many who had clutched the currents of religious modernism.[47]

Ultimately, an analysis of religion in the writing of Langston Hughes disrupts fixed categories of black religiosity and presents new and alternative sources of religious authority. Prompted by the basic features of American religious liberalism, interplayed with the religion of his youth, Hughes's lifelong search for the meaning of "salvation" revealed a notion of black religion as a project of social, cultural, and theological construction, ever evolving, transfigured, and transformed. Over the course of his career, Hughes created a body of writing that sensitively reflected the cultural and spiritual dimensions of his conservative religious background, infusing it with elements of theological modernism. In doing so, he expanded the range of who can speak religiously and what constitutes African American religion. Religion as a category of analysis in Hughes's writing also lessens the force of fundamentalist modes of African American religiosity that have often policed, overshadowed, or rejected other forms of religiousness. And this, too, is both a problem of history and historiography. African American religious history has primarily been written in a triumphalist mode from the perspective of "belief," and Christian belief in particular. Stories of survival against impossible odds, of perseverance, and of God "making a way out of no way," sit at the center of that history, composing its core. The extraordinary importance of evangelical Christianity and black Protestant churches to African American history and culture in large part accounts for this. Historians of African American religion such as Albert J. Raboteau have eloquently discussed how "the gods of Africa gave way to the God of Christianity," and evangelical Christianity became the prevailing religion of enslaved peoples during the early part of the nineteenth century, embraced for its emancipatory effect on black bodies and psyches.[48] "The Negro Church," before and after slavery, became an expression of black freedom, the birthplace of African American culture, a cohesive force, and in many ways a significant bell ringer for social justice and civil rights. In his epic 1903 book of essays, *The Souls of Black Folk*, DuBois championed the "Negro Church" as the "social center" of black life, prompting sociologist E. Franklin Frazier to assert in the 1960s that Christianity and the "Negro Church" had provided a "new basis for social cohesion" in postslavery America. Announcing the "death" of Frazier's conception of the "Negro Church" for the emergence of the "Black Church" in 1970, C. Eric Lincoln affirmed that this more "radical" institution was "the spiritual face of the Black community." For all these reasons, African American culture has for the most part been viewed as a Christian culture, and this has been a significant basis for the false assumption that black people are "naturally religious."[49]

As important as the narratives and perspectives of Christian believers are, as well as the scholarly contributions of those who have chronicled their experiences, African American religious history is much broader than these primarily Protestant and biblically based tales of trial, tribulation, exodus, and deliverance. What has been lost to the historiography of black religion are the voices of the nonreligious, quasi-religious, differently religious, doubtful, disillusioned, and unsure. Their philosophical convictions, spiritual insights, critical perspectives, and historical contributions have been circumscribed, co-opted, or ignored. An entire generation of scholarship on African American religious history has suggested that nonbelievers and religious dissenters have had no say in the construction of black religious culture when, in fact, doubt and dissent, as much as faith, have always played an important role in the formation of religious traditions. Indeed, what Langston Hughes shows us is that "belief" is a process, not an accomplishment. One does not need to *be* religious in order to have certain religious practices. Being religious is not a profession. Struggle, conflict, paradox, and doubt have played key roles in American and African American religious formation. As social historian of religion David Hempton argues, "disenchantment is almost inevitably a part of *any* religious tradition, Christian or otherwise, as noble ideals of sacrifice, zeal, and commitment meet the everyday realities of complexity, frustration, and disappointment."[50]

By troubling and complicating the standard narratives and by decentering Protestant Christian paradigms, the religious writing of Langston Hughes and many other New Negro writers constitutes an important starting point for a new direction in the study of African American religious history. Hughes and his fellow thinkers about religion, in voices of unbelief, qualified belief, critique, complaint, and dissent, chronicle a fuller account of twentieth century African American religion and broaden the characterization of American and African American religion.[51] Greater attention to their thoughts about God, faith, spirituality, the institution of the church, and the role of religion in society will not only transform how we write this history but also will broaden our source base, expanding what constitutes viable material for the study of religious history. A consideration of Langston Hughes, therefore, signals a more inclusive religious history and a greatly diversified historiography. His religious writing moves us beyond the dominance of standard Christian historical narratives and beyond the superordination of narratives of confession and belief, revealing new religious cultural codes, values, signifiers, and paradigms that include survival, perseverance, exodus, and deliverance, but also uncertainty, mystery, critique, secularity, and universalism. What failed to happen on a Kansas night in 1914 played a vital part in shaping the artistic production of Langston Hughes and in making him one of the most significant writers in twentieth-century American arts and letters. It should now take its place as a moment central to a redirection in the history and historiography of American and African American religious history.

* * *

This book is arranged chronologically, but since narrating a life's work can never be done in an exact, linear fashion, each of the five chapters looks backward and forward in time even as they attempt to capture particular time periods in Hughes's life. The book covers the religious works written over the span of Hughes's career, beginning with his early poems during the overlapping periods of World War I, the Harlem Renaissance, the Great Migration, the Great Depression, and World War II, and it ends with his gospel song-plays of the 1960s. Chapter 1, "New Territory for New Negroes," depicts Hughes as the quintessential New Negro of the 1920s and the key figure among other Harlem Renaissance writers who wrote on religious themes. His range, versatility, and prolificacy made him the chief exemplar among this group, but Hughes was by no means the only New Negro writer of religious poetry. This chapter develops Harlem as both the real and the imagined space and context for Hughes's religious writing and New York generally as the seedbed of his religious liberalism. It is a religious history of Harlem for the early decades of the twentieth century and sees it as a city of religion and churches. It demonstrates the particular ways Hughes both carefully navigated and forthrightly engaged this culture, participating with various churches and religious movements and writing extensive commentary on religion reflecting that engagement with the religious world of Harlem, as well as the wider world of American religion.

Chapter 2, "Poems of a Religious Nature," continues the exploration of Hughes, as poet, by looking specifically at the large amount of poetry he devoted to religious themes. The chapter shows that Hughes wrote various types of religious poetry over the course of his lifetime, revealing religion as a pervasive theme from the 1920s to the 1960s. Hughes collaborated with two French literary theorists, Jean Wagner and François Dodat, to bolster this aspect of his portfolio, producing two original documents meant to highlight not only his religious poetry but also his thinking about what constituted religious poetry. Ironically, however, the conclusions Wagner and Dodat drew about Hughes's religious poetry are responsible, in part, for his enduring reputation as antireligious.

Chapter 3, "Concerning 'Goodbye Christ,'" is the story of one poem, which Hughes wrote in 1932. "Goodbye Christ" is one of the most important and consequential poems he ever wrote and one of the most polarizing, having a profound effect on his career as a writer. "Goodbye Christ" best represents Hughes's "racialized religious poetry" among the others he wrote during the 1930s. It is the poem most responsible for depictions of his anti-religiosity, as his exchange with Jean Wagner demonstrates. And the poem did signify a time when Hughes was honing his left-leaning political sympathies and activities and expressing most forthrightly his disillusionment with religion and the American church in particular. The poem became a flashpoint in various circles throughout the 1930s and, for the remainder of his life, the basis for opposition to Hughes by conservative Christians and nationalist ideologues. The chapter shows, however, that "Goodbye Christ" rightfully belongs to the larger context of other "proletarian" works being produced by American writers in the Depression era. Moreover, the poem aligned Hughes with other black intellectuals, ministers, and social critics who publicly expressed radical critiques of American religion and churches during this time. They comprised a culture of complaint and critique about the very nature and function of black religion in the interwar period. Hughes disavowed "Goodbye Christ," however, when he appeared before Joseph McCarthy and the Permanent Subcommittee on Investigations (PSI) in 1953, characterizing himself as someone with vastly changed political views and different ideas about the social purpose of poetry.

Chapter 4, "My Gospel Year," takes the story of Hughes's religious writing into the late 1950s and early 1960s. By that time Hughes had turned, thematically, almost exclusively to the topic of religion, making them his "gospel years." Although he was still producing work of a "secular" nature, the majority of his creative energies were devoted to works with religion as the central concern. *Tambourines to Glory*, a book Hughes also produced as a play and finally as a poem, is the centerpiece of this chapter. In telling the story of Essie Belle Johnson and Laura Wright Reed, two Harlem friends who started a church to amass wealth, Hughes showcased, foremost, his ever-expanding interest in religious themes, expressions, and institutions. The book and play, however, were essentially a culmination of Hughes's thinking about religion over the course of his lifetime, and every aspect of what he had come to appreciate in black religion and religious institutions, as well as what he had come to despise, found expression in *Tambourines to Glory*. Hughes consistently maintained that the story was about "racketeering in religion," but it was effectively much more complex than that. In addition to underscoring how and why churches such as "Tambourine Temple" were able to exploit many black and poor people in Harlem, Hughes provided a sophisticated analysis of the very nature of "good" and "bad," viewing them as complicated and constitutive parts of the other. *Tambourines to Glory* also put Hughes's religious liberalism on display in a fictionalized, embodied way. Although he set the story in a Harlem storefront, resonant with all the allusions to "pre-modern" expressions of black worship and theology, Hughes anchored the narrative on some of the basic frameworks of American religious liberalism, including the Social Gospel.

Chapter 5, "Christmas in Black," recounts the dramatic ordeal of bringing Hughes's "gospel song-play," *Black Nativity*, to life on Broadway in 1962. The last major production of his career, the play was also among his most lucrative and became an international phenomenon. Like *Tambourines to Glory* and other theatrical productions in this genre that Hughes wrote during the early to mid-1960s, *Black Nativity* emphatically signaled his turn almost exclusively to the topic of religion. More than this, however, the production expressed Hughes's confidence that black religion and particularly black gospel music were the last and most viable exponents of "authentic" black culture. All others, including jazz and the blues, had been appropriated and co-opted by white Americans. *Black Nativity* indicated a gradual yet distinct change in Hughes's views on the commercialization of black religion and gospel music and the theater as an appropriate venue for its display while it raised those same questions for many theatergoers and social observers. As a religiously themed Broadway production, with an all-black cast for only the second time in American history, *Black Nativity* generated inevitable comparisons to Marc Connelly's 1930 play, *The Green Pastures*. The two plays shared much in common in terms of their depictions of black religiosity and the controversy provoked by those depictions. Indeed, rather than a simple reenactment of the Nativity story with black actors, *Black Nativity* proved to be a complex feature in the complicated and polarized racial terrain of the 1960s. Many black theatergoers were not interested in dramatic productions that seemingly verified notions of innate black religiosity and otherness while white audiences in the United States and abroad were seemingly all too willing to do so. For all of the racial and class divisions it exposed, as well as the debates about the relationship between church and theater, however, *Black Nativity* was a worthy capstone to Hughes's long and storied career because for the last time it placed religious spaces, themes, frameworks, and discourses at the very center of his artistic production.

1

New Territory for New Negroes

"The American mind must reckon with a fundamentally changed Negro."
—Alain L. Locke

"It is significant to note that prior to 1914, one finds no ideas of God that imply doubt and repudiation. Since the War, and particularly since 1920, there is a wave of cynicism, defeat, and frustration in the writings of young Negroes where God is concerned."
—Benjamin E. Mays

"Christ would have walked in Selma, He would have marched on Washington, and He would have lived in Harlem."
—Adam Clayton Powell Jr.

Langston Hughes ascended from the subway at 135th Street and Lenox Avenue on September 4, 1921, to start a new life. With an unhappy year in Mexico and his time with a difficult father behind him, he was ready for change, he was ready for Harlem, and it delighted him. "I went up the steps and out into the bright September sunlight. Harlem! I stood there, dropped my bags, took a deep breath and felt happy again."[1] As a compromise, Hughes had agreed to attend Columbia University. His father had wanted him to attend a German university to study engineering while Hughes did not want to attend university at all. Columbia had seemed the best resolution to the conflict, but Hughes hated the place immediately. It was "too big" and "not fun," he declared, and "the buildings looked like factories."[2] Moreover, the housing policies, as well as the general university climate, were racist. The office staff of Hartley Hall nearly rescinded his reservation for a dorm room when they discovered that Hughes was black and not Mexican, which they likely assumed since his application had been sent from Mexico. However, none of this mattered as much to Hughes as being in Harlem. His studies were sacrificed to the sights and the sounds of New York City. He attended lectures, read books of interest, visited museums, and saw a great many Broadway shows, including *Shuffle Along*, the first major African American Broadway production. Indeed, he claimed that *Shuffle Along* was "the main reason" he wanted to attend Columbia in the first place, and he saw it "up in the gallery night after night."[3] Harlem had embraced Hughes, and he would make it the subject of many of his poems, including "The Heart of Harlem," which exemplifies an important aspect of Hughes's poetic take on the area and its meaning.

> The buildings of Harlem are brick and stone
> And the streets are long and wide
> But Harlem's much more than these alone
> Harlem's what's inside.[4]

The region of New York that had captured his imagination that September morning would later become Hughes's home for the remainder of his life.

Even before he arrived in Harlem and certainly after he made it his home, Hughes proved himself to be the quintessential New Negro. His youth, intellect, preternatural writing talent, boundless energy, and striking good looks made him the perfect representative of the new brand of black American writer that had emerged in the first decades of the twentieth century. There was at least a modest indication in his upbringing that he would one day become a writer of note, if not one of the leading lights in an African American literary movement. He had been born in Joplin, Missouri, in 1902 to an unstable and peripatetic family of mixed racial and ethic origin. His mother, Carolina "Carrie" Mercer Langston, loved and wrote poetry, provided him with frequent trips to the library, and insisted that as a child he recite poetry and biblical verses before their local congregation of St. Luke African Methodist Episcopal (AME) in Lawrence, Kansas. She would later attempt to discourage his aim to make a career of writing, however, thinking he was "wasting his time," but she blatantly attempted to profit from it when Hughes began to achieve a level of fame. His father disparaged it outright, consider-

Figure 1.1. Heart of Harlem map by Bernie Robynson and Langston Hughes. (Courtesy of the Beinecke Library.)

ing writing an "absurd enterprise."[5] Hughes, nevertheless, developed an early love for literature from his mother; his grandmother, Mary; and likely from his grandfather, Charles H. Langston. "Colonel" Langston, as he was called, the elder brother of John Mercer Langston, the first African American congressman from Virginia, had moved to Lawrence in 1888. He became the associate editor of the black newspaper, *Historic Times*, and founded the Interstate Literary Society of Kansas and the West in 1891.[6] Hughes also was encouraged to write poetry in grammar school in Lincoln, Illinois, and in high school in Cleveland, Ohio, where as "class poet" some of his earliest poems were published. By the time Hughes got to Harlem, his first major poem, "The Negro Speaks of Rivers," had already been published to great acclaim by the *Crisis*, "the secular Bible of black America," adding substantially to his stature as one of the New Negroes.[7]

Although the term "New Negro" predated the 1920s, it came into popular parlance during that time to connote a new assertion of blackness as a positive good and black people as important social, cultural, and political forces in the United States. Since the era of Reconstruction, every subsequent generation of black Americans hailed itself as "new," usually aligning the "Old Negro" with slavery and social stagnation and the "New Negro" with freedom and forward progress. The *Cleveland Gazette*, for example, declared in 1895 that "a new class of colored people, the 'New Negro,'" had emerged since the Civil War, "with education, refinement, and money." While not everyone cheered the coming of the New Negro, such as the editorialist in the *Washington Bee* who deemed the phenomenon as "but a passing show," others in the late 1890s welcomed "this new race" as evidence of a superiority in intelligence, values, "a strong sense of manhood," and self-respect.[8] A new grouping of black people was on the rise and making great individual advancements. For that reason, Booker T. Washington, Norman Barton Wood, and Fannie Barrier Williams titled their 1900 edited volume *A New Negro for a New Century*, claiming it was "written in light of achievements" of blacks since the slave era.[9] The "New Negroes" of the 1920s, however, viewed themselves as distinct from Washington's generation not only because of individual achievements by blacks but also because of broad changes in American society that were having a direct impact on all aspects of black life. In demographic terms, for example, the characterization of black

America was completely changing from rural to urban. As sociologist Charles S. Johnson intoned in 1925, "a new type of Negro is evolving—a city Negro." Looking back on the era, cultural critic Gerald Early concurred, calling it "an age in which blacks were transformed from a rural to an urban people with a distinct urban culture."[10] New Negroes such as Langston Hughes, therefore, were central to a New Negro movement in the 1920s that bore witness to a rapidly changing American society.

The principal feature of the New Negro movement, however, was the unprecedented transformations taking place in the black arts and particularly in black literature. The Harlem Renaissance, or New Negro Renaissance, which was central to the broader New Negro movement, took place roughly from the early 1920s to the mid- to late 1930s when a burst of creativity from a number of black artists, showcasing black self-assertion as well as black artistry, generated a cultural phenomenon and one of the most significant social moments in American history. Although artists in other media made their mark during this time, the renaissance was essentially a blossoming of African American literature. So central was the literary aspect of the renaissance that James Weldon Johnson, one of the principal witnesses and chroniclers of the movement, disavowed the term "Harlem Renaissance," preferring to call it "the flowering of Negro literature."[11] The creative energies of a group of primarily young writers, most of whom were born between 1891 and 1910, revealed and celebrated the beauty of black life while it redefined the role of black people in the wider society. And it was their ability to articulate black experiences, creating written records of what it meant to be black in America, as well as what Gregory Holmes Singleton calls the "reciprocal relationships" they established with readers, that rendered these black writers the most visible among Harlem Renaissance artists.[12]

The strategic emphasis placed on their artistic production by supporters, patrons, and African American journals also accounted for the visibility and prominence of the New Negro writers, as opposed to those who worked in other artistic mediums. Both *Opportunity*, the journal of the National Urban League, and the *Crisis*, the journal of the National Association for the Advancement of Colored People (NAACP), had established literary prizes by the early 1920s. African American mobster and New York City "numbers" titan, Casper Holstein, and "honorary Negro" Carl Van Vechten sponsored *Opportunity's* literary prize, which came to be a part of the Holstein Prizes and the Van Vechten Awards, and Amy Einstein Spingarn, wife of educator and civil rights activist Joel Elias Spingarn, provided the financial backing for the prize from the *Crisis*.[13] When first awarded in May 1925, *Opportunity*'s top prize went to Hughes for his poem "The Weary Blues." Countee Cullen, Hughes's chief rival, received second prize for "To One Who Said Me Nay," a sonnet about love and the passing of time.[14] They shared the third prize. Thanks to the stalwart efforts of W. E. B. DuBois, the *Crisis* in particular became a major forum for black literary expression. Having earlier called for new writers to write about black experiences, DuBois, as editor of the *Crisis*, took to the pages of his journal in May 1925 to proclaim its new mission. "We shall stress beauty, all beauty, but especially the beauty of Negro life and character; its music, its dancing, its drawing and painting, and the new birth of its literature." This group of black writers declared the beauty of blackness with a new literary clarity and cultural authority throughout the first decades of the twentieth century.[15]

Along with declaring the beauty of blackness and revealing black life and character, however, New Negro writers devoted a considerable amount of their writing, and particularly their poetry, to matters of faith, spirituality, theology, and the institutional priorities of American and African American churches. Indeed, Hughes was part of a significant number of black writers during the era who wrote poetry on religious topics from a variety of theological and ideological perspectives. Most of the poetry appeared throughout the 1920s and 1930s in *Opportunity* and the *Crisis*, as well as in several anthologies and the black press. Like Hughes, the writers were thinkers about religion, and their work ranged from expressions of belief and reverence to those of religious doubt, critique, and frustration. Most often, the issue of race and a concern for racial justice underpinned the poetic work. Hughes's religious poetry covered the entire span and was the most topically expansive, making him the group's leading voice. As "the Crown Prince" of black writers during this era, Hughes led the way in expressing new and daring ideas about American and African American religious cultures and religion more broadly.[16]

Literary scholars such as Gunter H. Lenz have seemingly venerated the secularity of New Negro writers, contending that they "did not devote much attention to religious life and institutions in their work." The contention suggests that New Negro writers were unconcerned about religion at best. Jean Wagner claims, for example, "all the poets of this group are united in rejecting religion of any kind."[17] To be sure, most New Negro poets maintained complicated relationships with the institution of the church, as well as with notions of the Divine. Few ever publicly professed to be "Christian," and while poets such as William Waring Cuney were overtly and conventionally pious, it was more common for them to creatively construct their own religious identities and practices with attending complexities, paradoxes, and contradictions. Albert Rice declared in 1927, for example, "despite my [political] radicalism I am religious." But Rice also alluded to his disassociation from the institution of the church by admitting his "dislike" of prayer meetings. Rather than expressing a lack of concern for religion, Hughes and other New Negro writers wrote forthrightly and extensively about religion. Religious life, discourses, and frameworks, primarily but not exclusively from evangelical Protestant traditions, played a significant role in the writing of the movement. As historian of religion, Josef Sorett succinctly states, "religion shaped the vision of many New Negro artists."[18]

During the early decades of the twentieth century, the religious poetry of Langston Hughes and other New Negro writers demonstrated an understanding of the important role religion played in black life. The Harlem Renaissance and the two decades following were times when religion was a "crucial battle ground" for debates about the very nature of American religion, and there were spiritual impetuses that bolstered much of the cultural production of these artists.[19] The works of these writers were crucial, if unheralded, components of that debate. They signaled their keen awareness of the religious currents of the day and perhaps the unique ability of the poetic form to combine racial and religious rhetoric as a means to portray the vicissitudes of black American experiences. Expressing what came to represent a fundamental philosophy about the meaning of black American poetry, Robert Thomas Kerlin asserted in 1923, "it can scarcely happen that any people or group has a vital significance for other peoples, or any real potency, until it begins to express itself in poetry." It is to poetry "that the wise will turn in order to learn the temper and permanent bent of mind of a people," he further asserted. Countee Cullen corroborated this point in his 1927 anthology, *Caroling Dusk*, which he compiled to give air to "the new voices" who

have "sung so significantly as to make imperative an anthology recording some snatches of their songs." Cullen stated, "the place of poetry
in the cultural development of a race or people has always been one of
importance."[20]

Harlem as a world of religion and churches became the primary context and territory for the flowering of African American arts and letters.
In the nineteenth century Brooklyn had been known as "the borough of
churches" because of its small yet established black middle-class population, but by the 1920s and 1930s the name rightly belonged to Harlem.
As the *New York Amsterdam News* noted, "in no other part of New York
are churches so closely clustered or varied in type." It had become, as
the Works Progress Administration (WPA) Guide of 1930 claimed, "the
Spiritual Capital of Black America." Although Baptists had always been
the largest religious group among blacks, Methodists, Catholics, Mus-
lims, Seventh-day Adventists, and a variety of quasi-Christian groups
also made their mark. Harlem, the editorial continued, was a "city of
contrasting churches, with a church for everyone."[21] For Hughes, the
quintessential New Negro, Harlem was not only the context for his religious poetry, but also the primary site of his active engagement with
its world of religion and churches. Indeed, Hughes's engagement with
religion in Harlem was the primary means by which he became a public intellectual in matters of religion, and it was also through his support and critique of black religious institutions and movements, as well
as his written social commentary. As Harlem created space for a "new
territory" of writing by Hughes and other New Negro poets, Hughes
developed a set of visible public practices in one of the most religiously
vibrant black enclaves in the United States. Hughes's work and that of
his fellow New Negro writers helped to shape Harlem, as a territory,
into what James Weldon Johnson called "the cultural capital" of black
America, and their thoughts on religion played a larger role in that shaping than previously imagined.[22]

Territory

Harlem was undeniably important as the context for the literary aspect
of the New Negro movement of the 1920s and beyond. The Harlem
one finds in the poetry of Langston Hughes and the other New Negro

writers existed, however, as both a real "place"—a territory of brick and mortar—and a symbolic "space."[23] It was, on the one hand, a geographically demarcated region of "locatedness" for the scripted and predetermined performances of daily life, to employ the frameworks of cultural theorists Michel de Certeau, Benedict Anderson, and Vivian Patraka. On the other hand, Harlem was a symbolic space created by the "multiple performances" and historical subjectivity of the inhabitants and the users of the geographical place.[24] Harlem as both place and space was critically important in allowing Hughes and other New Negro writers the spatial dimensions to situate and to stage their literary visions.

A wide range of people, including real estate developers such as Philip A. Payton Jr., the "father" of black Harlem; journal editors; and African American intellectuals deliberately constructed the "place" of Harlem, assisted by the mutually constitutive forces of migration, racial discrimination, opportunity, and opportunism.[25] Migration was the first and chief factor, laying the groundwork for all else to follow. Indeed, the history of Harlem as a territory is bound up with the history of European immigration and internal African American migration, what Edwin G. Burrows and Mike Wallace call the "more dramatic" aspect of African American migration.[26] Central Harlem, stretching from 110th to 155th Streets and bounded by Park Avenue on the east and St. Nicholas Avenue on the west were composed almost entirely of black people after years of their gradual yet steady northward migration beginning in the 1830s in lower Manhattan. The results of the migration northward made Harlem one of the largest black communities in the nation by the First World War. By the 1920s the nightlife and entertainment culture of Harlem was one of the richest in America, as the area in upper Manhattan was a full participant in the excesses of the Jazz Age.[27] Hundreds of nightclubs, speakeasies, bars, and restaurants, such as the Cotton Club, the Apollo Theater, the Savoy Ballroom, Small's Paradise, Connie's Inn, and Gladys' Clam House were dotted along the main thoroughfares of Lenox, Seventh and Eighth Avenues, between 125th and 140th Streets. A great number of political, social, and civic organizations were also headquartered in Harlem. These included the Harlem YMCA and YWCA, Marcus Garvey's Universal Negro Improvement Association (UNIA), A. Philip Randolph's Brotherhood of Sleeping Car Porters,

James Van Der Zee's photography studios, and the *New York Amsterdam News*, among countless others. Largely because of the popularity of Harlem's entertainment venues, some of which were racially segregated and attended almost exclusively by downtown whites, as well as the growing attention to "all things Negro" and the cultural and civic productions of the African American population, Hughes dubbed the first two decades of the twentieth century in Harlem as "the period when the Negro was in Vogue."[28]

The creation of Harlem as "the cultural capital" of black America was not inevitable, however, and has its roots in the squalor, poverty, and degradation of the Lower East Side of Manhattan. Thousands of people packed into the area's shoddily constructed, airless, fetid, and putrid shacks and tenements that came to characterize the area. Poverty and mortality rates were the highest in the city, and gangs, crime, and vice thrived under the careless watch of a newly formed and already corrupt police force. The lowest of the low, black New Yorkers called the Five Points area home, and it constituted the city's highest overall concentration of blacks until the ever-increasing Irish population pushed them out in the 1830s. With the exodus of blacks from Five Points it became, according the Jonathan Ellis, "the largest Irish community outside Dublin."[29] Greenwich Village became the next major stop on the migratory trek toward Harlem for black New Yorkers, and by the 1840s so many blacks lived on the intersecting streets of Minetta Lane, Bleecker, Thompson, Sullivan, and MacDougal Streets that it was branded "Little Africa."[30] A few blacks who left the Village after the murderous draft riots of 1863 went to join the long-established yet much smaller African American community in Brooklyn while the majority journeyed further up Manhattan island to the area that had become known as the "Tenderloin." The Tenderloin, originally bounded by 23rd through 42nd Streets between Fifth and Seventh Avenues, was no panacea either. Eventually expanding to include 62nd Street and Eight Avenue and, therefore, encompassing what would become Hell's Kitchen, San Juan Hill, Chelsea, and the Flatiron, Theater, and Garment districts. Also known as "Satan's Circus," the area became the entertainment and "red light" district of New York with the highest concentration of nightclubs, saloons, brothels, dance halls, and gambling joints in the city and was likely the most crime-ridden area in America.[31] By the end of the century about 20,000 blacks lived there under conditions that had become just as bad as they had been in Five Points and the Village.[32]

"German Jewish Harlem" immediately preceded "Black Harlem," when black New Yorkers again began to migrate en masse beginning around 1904 with the coming of the subway and the efforts of Payton, who took full advantage of black housing needs and white anxiety. Wealthy German Jews and Irish of more modest means had been the first to arrive in significant numbers in Harlem. By the 1840s and 1850s, waves of southern Italians and eastern European Jews, most of whom were poor, uneducated, and unskilled joined them.[33] Black residents later absorbed that imprint as a part of the literal infrastructure in the transition from Jewish Harlem to black Harlem, particularly with regard to synagogues that became some of Harlem's most prominent black churches, including Baptist Temple Church, the former Congregation Oheb Zedek at 18 West 116th Street, and Mount Olivet Baptist Church, the former Temple Israel at 201 Malcolm X Boulevard.[34] By the end of the 1920s, Harlem was a majority 97 percent black with a population of over 200,000, which constituted a 500 percent increase in three decades.[35] The transformation was complete.

The deliberate construction of Harlem as a place made the Harlem Renaissance possible. Harlem became the main territory of the New Negro movement and the "flowering" of black literature, and black writers moved in and out of it, actively engaged in the complex processes that elevated Harlem to a symbolic level by the mid-1920s. Indeed, the same degree of deliberate construction that occurred in the making of Harlem as a place was deployed to render it a "space" and a symbol through the lived experiences of black Harlemites and the artistic production of the New Negroes. The New Negro writers acknowledged Harlem as the site of the new literary movement and made it the theme of some of their writing, even though most of them were not from Harlem and did not live there. All but two of the major writers were born outside New York, and the majority of them hailed from Washington, DC, where the early stirrings of the Harlem Renaissance actually took place at the poet Georgia Douglas Johnson's weekly "Saturday night discussions" in her home at 1461 S Street, NW. Johnson, a celebrated poet in her own right and a member of what literary scholar Robert Bone calls, because of her age, the "rear guard" of the literary movement, designed the weekly literary salon to be a forum wherein black writers could premiere and discuss new work.[36] The weekly events proved enormously successful, and New Negro writers who rose to literary fame, including Hughes, Jean Toomer, Jessie Fauset, Zora Neale Hurston, Richard Bruce, and Waring Cuney, were regular attendees at the sessions.[37] However, many black poets who did not rise to literary acclaim, such as Albert Rice, Montgomery Gregory, Willis Richardson, and Marita Bonner, among many others, also attended Johnson's weekly salon. Harlem loomed large in the lives and literary imaginations of these black writers, no matter where they were actually located, as much a symbol as a real place.

In the same way that black Harlem had its "father" in Payton, the Harlem Renaissance had its "midwife" in another regular attendee of Johnson's Saturday night salon, Alain LeRoy Locke. As "midwife," the term he preferred, Locke not only infused the Harlem Renaissance with a sense of cultural purpose but also with a religious sensibility and "spiritual" discourses. A little known assistant professor of philosophy from Philadelphia, Locke taught at Howard University, was a graduate of Harvard, and the first African American Rhodes scholar.[38] Although others were clearly instrumental in initiating the Harlem Renaissance, Locke emerged as the true visionary, providing the philosophical and discursive frameworks from which it would operate and determining its immediate and long-term impact on American arts and letters. He was, for example, the first to acknowledge the potential of the group of new black writers to constitute a genuine movement. In a letter to Hughes in the fall of 1923, Locke enthused, "we have enough talent now to begin to have a movement—and express a school of thought." Locke's preeminence at the birth of the New Negro Renaissance is tied to his work as editor of the two volumes that emerged from a 1924 gala at the Civic Club in New York City that officially launched the Harlem Renaissance. They were an edition of the *Survey Graphic*, "Harlem: Mecca of the New Negro," and an anthology, *The New Negro: An Interpretation*, published in 1925. In both, Locke clarifies his vision for the literary movement, setting the terms for its structure and content and develops what is to become his "manifesto," stating in the preface to *The New Negro*, "this volume aims to document the New Negro culturally and socially,—to register the transformations of the inner and outer life of the Negro in America that have so significantly taken place in the last few years."[39]

There is little question that Locke manipulated the New Negro Renaissance to reflect his own elitist values and that he attempted to render it, as Henry Louis Gates Jr. has claimed, an "apolitical movement of the arts."[40] He expressed, for example, no affinity for the more political activist aspects of the New Negro movement demonstrated by the likes of A. Philip Randolph and Marcus Garvey.[41] Locke, rather, saw the renaissance in spiritual terms and had a vested interest in a type of cultural nationalism that involved crafting a new image of black Americans as ambassadors of "respectability." And he interpreted the struggle for racial and social justice as one that could be most effectively waged through literature, what David Levering Lewis calls "civil rights by copyright."[42] As the movement's midwife, however, Locke's impact on the Harlem Renaissance was profound not only for his mentorship of the New Negro writers, his careful shaping of the literary canon of the movement, and his key role in introducing the literature to the wider world, but also for the way in which he clearly articulated its vision, infusing it with religious implications. One of the most important declarations of the value of black culture in American history, Locke's manifesto made an inextricable connection between the "new psychology" of New Negro writers and the realm of the "spiritual," a word he used repeatedly throughout the manifesto to describe the movement's purposes and effects. Drawing on his Baha'i faith and uniquely pairing his cultural nationalism with Universalism, he saw the new writing in universal and unifying terms and as evidence of a link between mind and spirit. The Baha'i faith taught that all human persons were created in union with the Divine and possessed individual minds and spirits, which comprised what they considered the human "soul."[43] Indeed, this connection was more evident than those of "social change and progress." For Locke, the new and expansive eruption of literary creativity among black writers was evidence of transformations in "the internal world of the Negro mind and spirit," and it was tantamount to a spiritual awakening and rebirth. "Negro life is not only establishing new contacts and founding new centers, it is finding a new soul," he argued. "There is a fresh spiritual and cultural focusing."[44] The transformation in the psychology of black writers had led to "something like a spiritual emancipation," and it was with this "fundamentally changed Negro" that "the American mind must reckon." Freed from the problems of the past, they had experienced a "full initiation into American democracy," and "with it a spiritual coming of age."[45]

The territory of Harlem as "the cultural capital" of black America was the center of that "spiritual coming of age," and whatever it was in real or symbolic terms, it was "prophetic," Locke maintained.[46] The religious writing of Langston Hughes and many other New Negro writers reflected Locke's vision for the renaissance as a spiritual and cultural awakening in Harlem. The poetry these thinkers about religion produced on matters of faith, spirituality, theology, and institutional religion from a wide variety of perspectives comprised a core component of their artistic production during the renaissance and beyond. "The cultural capital" of black America was indeed at the same time "the spiritual capital of black America," and Langston Hughes, as the leading poet in the territory, left a significant imprint on the region's religious culture as he forged new interpretations of religious life and what it meant to act religiously in the wider world.

"The Same Thing Happens Spiritually . . . in His Poetry"

The "spiritual emancipation" and "spiritual coming of age" that Alain Locke envisioned found its clearest expression in New Negro poetry. Like many other witnesses to the launch of the new literary movement, he was certain of the central importance of poetry in particular. And while the poetry covered a wide spectrum of topics, religious themes emerged early and became a characteristic feature. The religious poetry of New Negro writers generally fell into three broad categories: poems of faith and reverence, racialized religious poetry (or political poems of a religious nature), and poems of radical critique, doubt, and frustration. These latter two types of poems were the most resonant with the theological constructs of religious liberalism. Some of the poetry crossed the boundaries of the three broad categories and others often represented paradoxical reflections on the artist and his or her work. Poems of faith and reverence, for example, flowed as readily from the pens of those who disavowed religious faith as it did from that of believers, and poems of critique, doubt, and frustration were not limited to nonbelievers. Poems in the first general category were the most common and echoed clearly the African American literary traditions from the seventeenth and eighteenth centuries and the works of such black Christian poets as Jupiter Hammon and Phillis Wheatley. Hammon's "An Evening Thought: Salvation by Christ," published in 1761, epitomizes the poetic declarations of Christ's salvific purpose common to the literature of the period.

> Salvation comes by Jesus Christ alone,
> The only Son of God;
> Redemption now to everyone,
> That love his holy word.
> Dear Jesus we would fly to Thee,
> And leave off every sin,
> Thy Tender Mercy well agree;
> Salvation from our King.[47]

Wheatley's Christian upbringing in Boston had a most profound impact on her theology and art, perhaps exemplified in her most famous poem, "On Being Brought from Africa to America": "Twas mercy brought me from my Pagan land, / Taught my benighted soul to understand, / That there's a God, that there's a Saviour too."[48] This poetry generally expresses a simple faith in the Christian conception of God and embraces conventional Christian themes such as atonement, mercy, sacrifice, redemption, hope for salvation, divine providence, and belief in the afterlife. Racialized religious poetry expresses religious sentiments mediated by race and racial language. It fuses racial and religious rhetoric to relay a political message as well as to elucidate the plight of black Americans. Employing Christian discourses and theological frameworks and narratives, this category of religious poetry often makes direct connections between the life of Christ and black experiences, particularly with regard to lynching. Poems of radical critique, doubt, and frustration also fuse religious sentiment with racial discourse, often for political purposes. But the main aim and effect is to express discontent and disenchantment with the Christian status quo, to satirize religious hypocrisy, and to question the very theological assumptions embedded in the poetry in the first two categories, poems of faith and reverence and racialized religious poetry. Poems in this category are the fewest in number but the most diverse in form and the most theologically

robust. They represent a radical break from prior black literary traditions and a whole new way for New Negro writers to express themselves
religiously. The content, theological structures, and political aims in the
three categories of religious poetry seemingly verify African American
social gospeler Reverdy Ransom's 1923 poetic assertion that the primary
contribution made by the New Negroes to American society is to bring
"gifts of science, religion, poetry, and song."[49]

The poetry of William Waring Cuney serves as a prime example of
the New Negro poems of faith and reverence. Cuney, a Washington, DC,
native born in 1906 and a regular attendee of Georgia Douglas Johnson's
Saturday literary salons, had achieved wide acclaim and won *Opportunity's* 1926 first prize for his poem "No Images," under the pseudonym
Ford Kramer.[50] The elegant poem about a black woman domestic with
no knowledge of her own beauty remains his most famous, having been
widely anthologized and translated into many languages. Described by
Countee Cullen as "cool, calm, and intensely religious," Cuney wrote
"No Images" at a time when the majority of his poetic production was
overtly religious, tinctured by the spirituals, and clear demonstrations
of Cuney's Christian faith.[51] In "I Think I See Him There," the speaker
in the poem wonders if he had been an eyewitness to Christ's crucifixion, would he have experienced doubt or confirmation that "what
this man speaks is true"? "The Darkness around His Throne" celebrates
God's omnipotence and mystery as being above human understanding,
while "Storefront Church" attempts to capture the ethos and cadences
of the worship services in one of the numerous small revivalistic black
churches dotting the streets of Washington, DC during the early decades
of the twentieth century. In two very similar poems, "My Jesus" and
"Troubled Jesus," Cuney again poetically chronicles the life of Christ.
Written in Trinitarian form, "My Jesus" covers the span of Christ's life
from "Conception" and "Crucifixion" to "Resurrection," when "way before the break of day, Angels rolled the rock away." "Troubled Jesus,"
which likely influenced Hughes's very similar poem, "Ma Lord," speaks
of the protagonist's sympathy for Christ's sorrow and suffering.

> Ma Jesus was a trouble man
> Wid lots o' sorrow in his breast

Oh, He was weary when they laid Him in the tomb to rest
Po' good Jesus.[52]

These poems, along with "Prayer for a Visitor" and "Say Amen,"—
"gospel poems," as Cuney called them—constitute the greater part of
Cuney's relatively slight artistic production and do much to reveal the
characteristics of his own faith journey, as well as the principle features of New Negro poetry in this category.[53] He, along with Jonathan
Henderson Brooks and Waverley Turner Carmichael, among others,
stood squarely within a tradition of African American religious poetry
dating back to the eighteenth century.

Racialized religious poetry, or political poems of a religious nature,
could be similarly reverential in tone and most often spoke from the
perspective of belief and deep attachment to Christian theology and tradition. The primary aim of this body of poetry, however, was to reveal
American religion through the lens of race and to draw links between
black American experiences and Christian narratives. The poetry of
Albert Rice, Mary Jenness, Lucian B. Watkins, and Esther Popel rival
Hughes in this category as their work also exemplifies the centrality of
race as it either reflects on the inextricable connection between race and
religion in the United States or ponders God's purposes for black people
in the world. Rice never "went forth to fame and infamy" as did those
he most admired among the attendees of Johnson's Saturday salons in
his native Washington, DC, but his most noted poem, "The Black Madonna," evinces a similar skill in lyrical form. Inspired by a visit to St.
Mary's the Virgin on a trip to Harlem where he was "lost in contempla-
tion before Our Lady," the poem reimagines Mary as black, "swarthy of
cheek and full-lipped as the child races are." The poem makes race crucial in Mary's role as the Mother of Christ and places black people at the
center of Christian history. "See where they come, thy people, so humbly
appealing / From the ancient lands where the olden faiths had birth."
Mary Jenness, who in addition to her poetry wrote many books on the
topic of religion, turns the implication of the link between Christ's story
and the black American experience on its head in her 1928 poem, "The
Negro Laughs Back." As the object of derision and laughter "like one of
Galilee," blacks are "condemned to be like God."[54]

Lucian B. Watkins not only places black people at the center of Christian history, he is also one of the first black poets to depict God as black and to place blacks in direct experiential relationship to Christ. The "New Negro," he claims in his 1921 poem by that title, "thinks in black. His God is but the same. . . . His kin is Jesus and the Christ who came humbly to earth and wrought His hollowed aim." God or Jesus as "black" became a common if controversial assertion in New Negro poetry throughout the 1920s and 1930s, demonstrated no more emphatically than by J. Harvey L. Baxter's "Paint Me a God." "Paint me a God, as black as I am black / Paint me a God in the likeness of my race."[55] Race, religion, and the "color" of God became inextricably linked in this body of African American poetry.

Esther Popel also centered race in her religious poetry but was seemingly more interested in how racism had corrupted many American religious values and practices, rendering them "blasphemous." Popel, one of only a few poets Hughes met at Douglas's salon whom he mentioned by name, had been born in Pennsylvania, where she attended Dickinson College, the first African American to do so, graduating with honors in 1919. Relocated to Washington, DC by 1920 and marrying William Andrew Shaw soon after, she worked for the Bureau of War Risk Insurance and taught in several junior and senior high schools throughout the Washington-Baltimore area. She also continued writing poetry, which she had begun to do in high school. Publishing regularly in both *Opportunity* and the *Crisis*, Popel's poetry evoked a sense of awe at God's creation, humanity's smallness in light of all creation, and a detached, if benevolent, deity, similar to seventeenth-century Deists. In one of her first published poems, "Kinship," she proclaims that the night sky and the "Sun's own life-blood" are proof enough for her that "there is a God," while "Grant me Strength," widely regarded as her most famous poem, is a prayer for "peace when weary day sinks quietly to rest."[56]

It was a poem Popel produced in the mid-1930s, however, that places her work in the category of political poems of a religious nature, as she expresses her disdain for racial injustice and the tyranny of "mob rule." Written in 1934, "Blasphemy—American Style," is an invective against lynching, which was still a blight on the American landscape. It appeared the same year as Popel's second volume of poetry, *A For-*

est Pool, and "Flag Salute," the story of a lynching interpolated with the Pledge of Allegiance. "I Pledge Allegiance to the Flag / They dragged him naked through the muddy streets." Unlike "Flag Salute," however, "Blasphemy—American Style" depicts God as a casual observer if not co-conspirator in the lynching, as a group of whites mockingly attempt to help the besieged black man recite the Lord's Prayer before he is strung up and burned.

> Look, God,
> We've got a nigger here
> To burn;
>
> A goddam nigger,
> And we're goin' to plunge
> His cringin' soul
> To Hell!
>
> Now watch him
> Squirm and wriggle
> While we swing him
> From this tree![57]

Second only to the racialized religious poetry of Langston Hughes and similar in theme, cadence, and rhythm, "Blasphemy—American Style" epitomizes racialized religious poetry, most of which was composed during the 1930s. After its publication, Popel came under scrutiny from many African Americans and never published another new poem, spending her latter years teaching, campaigning for women's rights, and writing reviews of works mostly on educational and religious topics.

To be sure, racialized religious poems or political poetry of a religious nature unsettled some observers and proved controversial. They elicited accusations of propaganda and stirred debates about the nature and purpose of black poetry, as well as questions as to whether political poetry could contain religious content. The political poetry of a religious nature, however, written by such poets as Popel, Watkins, Jenness, and Rice, in addition to Hughes, not only demonstrated the political and religious efficacy of the work but also showed the power of black poetry to disrupt and reimagine biblical narratives in the service of a greater awareness of the plight of black people in the early-twentieth-century United States.

New Territory

If the racialized religious poetry proved controversial, poems of critique, doubt, and frustration revealed a seismic shift in African American arts and letters during the Harlem Renaissance and beyond. Never before had a group of black writers used their pens to proclaim a lack of religious belief or uncertainty or skepticism about the existence of God, or to launch sharp criticisms of black religious institutions. Similar in tone to the racialized political poetry, bearing some of the same philosophical, theological, and political objectives, this group of poetry seemingly confirmed American philosopher Alfred Lloyd's contention that the early years of the twentieth century were an "age of doubt." Religious skepticism began to make its mark in the cultural production of black writers and in the black population more generally.[58]

The emergence of religious skepticism in New Negro poetry coincided with a shift in the crafting of historical narratives of black lives more generally. As Laurie Maffly-Kipp argues, "something fundamental had shifted" in the "Afro-Christian consciousness" at the turn of the twentieth century as narratives of black existence departed from the "Christian piety" expressed in the past.[59] African American journalist and essayist George S. Schuyler noted the shift in 1932 with an article entitled, "Black America Begins to Doubt."[60] Published in H. L. Mencken's *American Mercury*, Schuyler's article analyzes the state of black churches in the United States and, using statistical and census data, attempts to show that memberships in black churches were in decline relative to the increase in the black population. Schuyler, a professed atheist, claims that the reasons for the decline had to do first with the continued legacy of segregation in American churches and the low quality and immorality of black ministers, a trope in black literature and film since the early 1920s. The steady flow out of black churches and out of Christianity will continue, he suggests, because of "a growing number of iconoclasts and atheists" who are thinking, reading, and raising questions about churches and a notion of God that allows for lynching and disenfranchisement.[61]

Benjamin E. Mays, a sociologist, minister, social activist, and dean of the School of Religion at Howard University, provided an analysis of religious skepticism in New Negro writing in his 1938 book, *The Negro's God as Reflected in His Literature*, where he calls that writing "new territory." In what Edwin E. Aubrey in a review for the *Journal of Negro Education* deems "an important book on the history of American thought" and Josef Sorett heralds as unsurpassed in its aim "to make a grand claim about the religious dimensions of African American literature," Mays assumes the roles of literary anthropologist, intellectual historian, and sociologist to analyze the chief works of black writers from 1760 to 1937.[62] The book disregards the perceived division between religion and literature and expresses Mays's confidence that one can determine a racial or ethnic group's "ideas" about God through an examination of its literature. The chief purpose of the study, therefore, is to "discover ideas of God and see how the ideas have developed in the period covered." For Mays, the African American theologies and religious practices one discovers in black literature not only reflect the social, economic, and political situations of black people, they also change with those situations. Dividing the time span of black literature into "three epochs"—1760 to 1865, 1865 to 1914, and 1914 to 1937—Mays also puts those epochs into four categories that roughly correspond to the three broad categories of early-twentieth-century black religious poetry. His categories included "classical literature," "literature of the Negro masses," literature regarding "the impartiality of God and the unity of mankind," and literature on "ideas of God involving frustration, doubt, God's impotence, and His non-existence."[63] His sociological and historical formulation links the content of black poetry to particular time periods and the social and political contexts of those periods.

Phillis Wheatley and Jupiter Hammon represent the "classical" category of African American poetry during the first epoch not only because they are two of the first black *published* poets, but also due to the content of their poetry and the conditions under which they lived. Black poetry in the classical vein signified "traditional Christianity" and "traditional ideas," which include contentment with one's life situation and unfailing trust in God's providential plan.[64] The literature of the

Negro "masses" differed from the classical in form, production, and distribution rather than in content. It included ministers' sermons and other "public utterances"—prayers, spirituals, and Sunday school literature—in other words, religious material that reached the broadest audiences through various informal means.[65] This literature, which emerged between the end of the Civil War and the beginning of World War I, was, according to Mays, also "traditional" and at times "compensatory" or "otherworldly" (which was often interpreted as a religion of "escape"), as it spoke from the vantage point of belief with expressions of hope, faith, and dependence upon God.

It was with the third epoch, the new territory, however, Mays made his most significant assertions and greatest contribution. A religious liberal himself, Mays considered the new territory to be reflective of both literary modernism and religious liberalism. It also was the epoch of black poetry most clearly born from the "social situation" of black people, particularly in the aftermath of World War I. Mays elucidated three key features of new territory poetry that included a tendency to "doubt God's value" in the struggle to gain an "economic, social, and political foothold in America," while others suggested that God had "outlived his usefulness." A third feature was an outright "denial of the existence of God."[66] Of those who were beginning to question God's value to black people he cited Langston Hughes, Countee Cullen, and W. E. B. DuBois, whom Mays considered a "Deist." DuBois's 1920 collection of essays, *Darkwater*, was of particular note. *Darkwater* opens with "Credo," DuBois's statement of "beliefs," including "in God," "the Negro race," pride of self, service, liberty, the training of children, and patience. "A Litany at Atlanta," however, follows that statement, and it is DuBois's searing poetic response to the 1906 Atlanta race riots, in which he repeatedly invokes the "Silent God." "O Silent God, Thou whose voice afar in mist and mystery hath left our ears an-hungered in these fearful days—Hear us, good Lord!" God is again described as "dumb" with regard to the suffering of black people in "The Prayers of God," one of the two poems that close the collection. Written in the aftermath of the First World War and the "red summer" of 1919, "The Prayers of God" describes a world gone "mad," where "hell is loose" and "red murder reigns." In the end, the poem's subject, possibly DuBois himself, discovers that it is God who prays for help and is in need of human rescue. The roles are reversed and the human becomes the divine as the only hope for salvation, and the entire concept of God is overturned for one deemed more useful. This is the emphatic point on which DuBois concludes the book in "A Hymn to the Peoples": "Help us, O Human God, in thy Truce, to make Humanity divine!"[67]

Mays argued that in contrast to the classical and mass literature of the previous generations, the literature of black writers during this period was most profoundly cynical and doubtful, lacking the religious confidence and certainty that had characterized the previous eras. The First World War had shattered a sense of optimism among black writers, generating a sense of "disillusionment," shaping ways of "thinking about God" and a corresponding "spiritual depression and skepticism," all of which were reflected in their art. Deeply sympathetic to this literature, possibly due to his own "modernist impulses," Mays claimed that the third epoch warranted the most discussion and analysis because of the social and economic upheavals generated by the war. The radical shift in the "ideas" about God prompted Mays to consider the third epoch the most religiously significant of the three and the most transformative with regard to religious ideologies. "It is significant to note that prior to 1914," he wrote, "one finds no ideas of God that imply doubt and repudiation. Since the war, and particularly since 1920, there is a wave of cynicism, defeat, and frustration in the writings of young Negroes where God is concerned."[68] Black poets became disillusioned about social progress because of the First World War and this, in turn, prompted more racial consciousness on their parts. Indeed, the "awakened race consciousness" of New Negro writers during this period was chiefly responsible for it being the most productive period of the three, he claimed.[69]

Mays began his analysis of poems containing ideas of religious skepticism with Countee Cullen. Although Cullen's poetry crossed the boundaries between racialized poetry of a religious nature and poetry of radical critique and skepticism, his religious work most firmly belongs in this latter category. Cullen had a complicated relationship with religion in what Gerald Early calls his "ongoing quarrel with Christianity." Stylistically different from Hughes, preferring rhyme over free verse, Cullen wrote poetry on racial themes and the African heritage, and he produced a substantial body of work on religious (particularly Christian) concerns. As Early also claims, there are two things to understand about Cullen's poetry, first that most of it is "racial," and second, "all of it is Christian or could only have been produced by a Christian consciousness."[70] That Christian consciousness was on display early in Cullen's career with such poems as "Christ Re-Crucified," published in *Kelley's Magazine* in 1922. It spoke of a modern-day Christ whose sin was simply being "dark of hue." It also surfaced in several of the poems in his highly celebrated first collection, *Color*, in 1925, including "Simon the Cyrenian Speaks," "Pagan Prayer," "The Shroud of Color," "Heritage," "For an Atheist," "Judas Iscariot," and perhaps the most famous poem from the collection, "Yet Do I Marvel." The first line of the poem, "I doubt not Good is good, well-meaning, kind," is a tortured statement of belief that is often overlooked in analyses of the work in the interest of the last line regarding the poet being "made black" and bid to sing.[71] Cullen could never fully abandon his religious upbringing, possibly due to the influence of his adoptive father, Reverend Frederick Cullen, pastor of Harlem's Salem Methodist Episcopal Church. Indeed, some of his poetic production was an attempt to reconcile faith with doubt, or as Cullen himself put it, to reconcile his "Christian upbringing with a pagan inclination."[72]

The "pagan inclination" persisted in Cullen in large part because he could not accept that the Christian God, as widely conceived in America, was truly sympathetic to the black struggle. He wanted to believe in a merciful and just God, but he could not make that notion of God align with the realities of black life. Such poems as "Heritage," "Pagan Prayer," and "The Black Christ" highlight this essential conflict, and in each it is clear that Cullen is speaking in his own voice. In the all-important sixth stanza of his 1925 poem "Heritage," Cullen wishes "He I served were black" with "dark despairing features," supposing that a black God would more readily understand the pain of black life. He makes a plea on behalf of black people in "Pagan Prayer" because he is convinced that God is deaf to their own pleas, or worse, is willfully silent. Acknowledging that his own "faith lies fallowing," Cullen asks "Our Father, God, our Brother Christ" to grant safe homes, blessings, and release from sorrow to "this race of mine."[73]

In his 1929 poem "The Black Christ," his epic masterwork, written while in Paris one year after his failed marriage to Yolande DuBois, Cullen showed that he could be just as forceful about his doubts as about his faith. In the theological exchange between a black mother and her sons, we hear the mother affirming her faith in God while her sons, having seen too much of injustice, articulate their complaint and their unbelief:

> We had no scales upon our eyes,
> God, if He was, kept to His skies
> And left us to our enemies.
> Often at night from our knees,
> And sorely doubted litanies,
> We grappled with mysteries.
>
> Nay, I have done with deities
> Who keep me ever on my knees,
> My mouth forever in a tune
> Of praise, yet never grant the boon
> Of what I pray for night and day.
> God is a toy; put him away.

Cullen's piercing reinterpretation of the atoning death of Jesus not only showed the poet's doubt and frustration, it also provided one of the most vivid literary depictions of lynching, equating Christ's death on the cross with lynched black bodies, a literary theme that many New Negro writers would employ throughout the Renaissance era. The poem also revealed the plight of blacks in America as a theological problem. But as Jean Wagner observes, the tension in the poem between faith and rebellion or the Christian and the "pagan" reflects Cullen's own inner conflict. "The Black Christ," he argues, "is a masterly reconstruction of the poet's inner drama."[74]

Frustration gave way to expressions of uncertainty about God's very existence in some of the poetry of the new territory. Walter Everette Hawkins, for example, wrote poetry that was not only in direct revolt against the "otherworldliness" and creedalism common to many black American churches during the early twentieth century but also expressed his agnosticism. In what Mays considered Hawkins's "effort to set forth the true conception of religion," he devoted a fourth of the poems in his 1920 book, *Chords and Discords*, to religious themes, ranging from the whimsical—"humor" was his stated intent—to the highly cerebral.[75] "Chewing Gum," "Evolution," and "The Goody Goody Good" take aim at hypocrisy in American and African American worship cultures and antiscientific thinking among many "theologs." "Too Much Religion" and "A Festival in Christendom" are more focused and serious critiques of what Hawkins seemingly considered the deleterious effect of religion on society more broadly. In "Too Much Religion" he bemoaned that religion, as practiced, distracted from the real work of kindness and human sympathy:

> There is too much talk of doctrine
> Too much talk of church and creeds
> Far too little loving kindness
> To console the heart that bleeds.

"A Festival in Christendom" tells the gruesome account of the lynching of a black man by a "Christian mob" that happens upon him as they stride from church to the sound of church bells. They divide his body, pass out the parts as souvenirs among themselves, and throw his pregnant wife on the pyre for good measure. The second section of the poem highlights the disconnect between the act of violence "in Jesus's name" to the claims of American "civilization."

> And this where men are civilized
> Where culture is so highly prized
> Where liberty with blood was brought
> And all the 'Christian virtues' taught
> Where nations boast their God has sent
> The angel of Enlightenment.

Hawkins proclaimed his uncertainty about the existence of God and other basic beliefs of the major religious traditions in such poems as "God," in which he declared that "Islam, Buddha and Christ" all work toward the same goal, but that which unites all humankind, "this is my God." In "Here and Hereafter," he dispenses with the idea of "a future heaven or hell," and in "To the Hypocrite" he declares his "respect for the skeptic demanding his proof."[76] In a benediction or summation of thought, Hawkins ends *Chords and Discords* with what amounts to a personal credo of his agnosticism and a manifesto of rationalism and human divinity. "I am an Agnostic," he proclaims in the poem "Credo," "I accept nothing without questioning." Rejecting the laws of "state or country," he asserts his belief in liberty and freedom and proclaims, "Justice is my God." Hawkins continues this theme in "Hero of the Road," the last poem in the book. Free of the shackles of nationhood and the guilt of wrongdoing, he seeks only to "soar and sing," bringing cheer wherever possible along the road of life:

> And we see ourselves transfigured
> In a new and bigger plan
> Man transformed, his own Messiah
> God embodied into man.

Little known during his lifetime and not well known since, Hawkins and his *Chords and Discords* nevertheless are a prime example of the new territory of New Negro poetry of the third epoch and perhaps the best example of the category expressing "ideas of God involving frustration, doubt, God's impotence, and His non-existence."[77]

Doubtlessly due, in part, to Hughes's stature as the leading voice in the Harlem Renaissance and the quintessential New Negro, Mays concludes the new territory section of his book with a discussion of Harlem's bard. And Walter E. Hawkins, notwithstanding, singled out Hughes as particularly representative of the writers in this category, determining that he was the most "atheistic" among the group. The assertion previously had been made in 1934, when African American essayist and educator Kelly Miller declared Hughes a "radical, atheistic Negro" in an editorial written for the *New York Amsterdam News*. But Mays brought the characterization to a new level, presented it to an even wider audience, and directly linked it for the first time to Hughes's work.[78] In this way, Hughes as "atheist" (employed alternately with "agnostic") began with Benjamin Mays.

Mays based his characterization of Hughes on the Bard's 1930s poetry and used that work as the starting point of his analysis, particularly the poem "Goodbye Christ." For Mays, that poem was an example of the "total abandonment of the idea of God as being a constructive force in building a better world." He chose not to discuss Hughes's religious poetry of the 1920s, but noted the distinctions between the works of the two decades. He held that "faith is implicit in [Hughes's] earlier writings," but was more interested in the work of the 1930s, which represented "a radical departure." It was Hughes's contribution to the new territory of black poetry that captivated him. Although by the late 1930s Hughes had written poetry that covered Mays's entire thematic span, including some that reflected the ideas of "traditional" Christianity germane to the first epoch, Mays depicted Hughes's radical poetry as the most indicative of Hughes's "ideas about God." Indeed, this poetry bore all the characteristics of both racialized religious poetry and poems of doubt, critique, and frustration, and was born from a time in American society and in Hughes's life when he was, in the words of Arnold Rampersad, "unafraid to challenge religion."[79]

Although Mays formally articulated and systematized an interpretative trend that viewed black writers of the new territory as antagonistic to religion and Hughes as atheistic, subsequent literary scholars and biographers missed an important nuance in Mays's analysis. Mays did not disparage Hughes or the other writers for their poems of frustration and doubt, nor did he register concern about their departure from classical and mass black literature. Rather, he saw the emergence of this type of black poetry as a product of a rapidly changing American society, as well as "the findings of modern science." The religious views of new territory poets were expressions of modernity and a modern approach to religion and religious life. In this way, the poetry was more positively constructive than destructive to religion. For Mays, the new territory poets were not calling for an end to the "idea" of God or of religion but for a different conception of God and better expressions of religion. He determined that Hawkins's poem, "God of Love," for example, was just such a call for a better religion and *Chords and Discords* was "one of the finest and most constructive efforts to rehabilitate the idea of God along social lines."[80]

Modern religion also, and perhaps ironically, accommodated doubt. Mays acknowledged that doubt was "essential to real belief," reflecting the scholarship of a number of philosophers and theologians who maintained that in the "age of doubt," doubt had its place in the formation of religion. As James H. Snowden contended in an influential article entitled "The Place of Doubt in Religious Belief," "Doubt is uncertain belief. It is the borderland between knowledge and ignorance, the twilight between light and darkness." For Mays, doubt had a religious function and was religiously useful. And given the social circumstances under which many of the writers wrote, it was also understandable. If there were frustration and doubt in new territory poetry, Mays concluded, it was "not surprising" and was in response to the quotidian experiences of racial discrimination and social inequality.[81]

In the final analysis of his groundbreaking study, Mays attributed tremendous value to the religious poetry of each "epoch." He was convinced that "whatever approach or approaches to God the Negro takes in his literature, it will be of value and will shed light on the Negro's religion and theology."[82] He attributed more value to the third epoch and to the new territory poetry because of its social and contemporary relevance and the way in which those poems confronted the country's racial heritage and history of social and economic disparities. He was right to draw special attention to Hughes. What set Hughes apart from the other writers, however, was not that he was the most atheistic among the group but that he had developed a set of practices that brought him into a fuller engagement with Harlem's world of religion and churches. Of all the New Negro poets, Hughes developed the most extensive and intense engagement with the religious cultures of Harlem and became increasingly involved in that vibrant and religiously diverse world. He also became a consistently visible presence on the scene. Harlem, therefore, not only provided the real and symbolic context for Hughes's religious poetry, it also played a crucial role—second only to his failed salvation experience and the influence of Carl Sandburg and Walt Whitman—in structuring his thinking about religion and giving shape to his religious liberalism.

Encounters and Engagement

Hughes's practices of religious engagement had three crucial aspects: church attendance, social commentary on religious matters in the black press and other print media, and support for church-sponsored artistic events. His regular attendance at church dated back to his Kansas days and he maintained the practice throughout his life. Hughes, however, never joined a congregation or became a member, drawing a distinction between that and attendance. Indeed, remaining "unchurched" was a value to him that he proclaimed often, as he did in a little-known, unpublished essay he wrote in 1943 entitled, "Christians and Communists." Written to address speculation that he was a member of the Communist Party, the essay proclaimed Hughes's nonassociation religiously and politically, and his notion that both Christians and Communists left much to be desired. "I belong to no church and no party," he asserted.[83] This conviction, however, did not prevent his regular church attendance. He frequented St. Philip's Episcopal Church on West 134th Street so often that they considered him a member. And his church attendance observed no structural, theological, or philosophical bounds. He attended churches from the smallest working-class storefront churches to the most elite mainstream Protestant or Catholic congregations. He even frequented the religious spaces of movements on the margins of the religious mainstream. At a time when church attendance was characteristically high among African Americans, Hughes's practice seemed particularly pronounced.

Hughes connected his regular church attendance to his fascination with cities in general, as he explained in a 1926 article, where he elaborated on his love for New York and Harlem: "I cannot tell the city how much I love it," he declared.[84] Along with the "tremendousness of the city," its impressive infrastructure and staggering diversity, Hughes found Harlem's infusion of religion particularly captivating. Its "spiritual playthings," as he called the area's vibrant religious culture, were coequal and coeval to its material playthings. The fascination with cities and churches began in Mexico and Chicago, which he visited for the first time in 1917. During his visits to his father in Mexico, "where the old churches are so beautiful," Hughes developed a fondness for Catholic ritual. Such fondness served him well while living in Washington, DC, in the mid 1920s when for a short time he escorted "an old blind lady" to Mass every Sunday.[85] When he found himself again in Mexico upon the death of his father in 1934, he attended daily Mass. "I went to vespers with them [the Patino sisters, friends of his father] every night in the old church just across the street, lighted by tall candles and smelling of incense. Sometimes I even got up early in the morning to attend Mass."[86] Years later, while again living in Chicago, Hughes often indulged his eclectic churchgoing tastes. Writing in his dairy about the events of

Sunday, April 5, 1942, he revealed that he had attended High Mass at Corpus Christi in the morning and visited Reverend Clarence Cobbs's First Church of the Deliverance, Spiritualist in the evening. At Corpus Christi, which at the time was the "largest colored Catholic church in America," Hughes noted that it was "crowded" and singing was "good." Cobbs's church was also "packed," as it usually was. By the early 1940s, Cobbs's First Church of the Deliverance was already one of the largest and most prominent black congregations on the South Side despite its place as a "Spiritual" church outside the margins of the mainstream of black congregations.[87] Hughes held great admiration for Cobbs, who many Chicagoans knew to be homosexual, and included him in an article for the *Chicago Defender* among a group of other "colored and colorful evangelistic personalities" in Chicago, Detroit, and New York who were worthy of further and serious study.[88]

Hughes found Harlem's storefront churches, those established in commercial or residential spaces, to be most compelling, noting their ubiquity to his friend Arna Bontemps when one sprung up on his street, East 127th, called "God's Bathtub."[89] During the early years of the Great Migration, storefront churches were often the first thing one noticed in Harlem, and their growth in number was phenomenal. As journalist Jervis Anderson notes, "it was the storefront churches that multiplied the fastest," dotting nearly every major street and not a few minor ones in Harlem, including Hughes's. Many Harlemites reviled storefronts for their public piety and noisy worship practices, deeming them vestiges of a backward South. Others thought they were an indictment on what they perceived to be the staid worship practices of the larger black churches. Recalling his youth in Harlem in the 1930s, civil rights leader Bayard Rustin contended that "the big churches were too calm. Here there were these people coming in from the South. They were used to screaming and yelling at services, rolling in the aisles, and speaking in tongues. But the middle classes which supported the big churches were now beyond all these things." Rustin may have stated his case in overly simplistic terms, but most Harlemites did acknowledge distinctions between storefronts and mainstream black churches, primarily that they more accurately reflected a southern worship ethos. Indeed, by the 1930s southern religious practices had become prevalent in many churches in Harlem. Southern migrants had made their presence known and were having an impact on how church was practiced in Harlem. Hughes found storefront churches "thrilling," as he had in Chicago.

Like Chicago, storefront churches in Harlem comprised a distinctive culture and ethos, and it was from the religious worlds structured by the occupants of these spaces and this ethos that a number of high-profile and influential new religious movements emerged. Classified as sects and cults in the parlance of the day, as well as by a number of sociological studies, these movements and their leaders left indelible marks on Harlem's religious landscape. Each one was comprised of mostly poor and working-class black southern migrants and promoted religious worship that was similar to the vivacious services offered at many storefront churches. Many also sustained "this-worldly" approaches when it came to the material well-being of their constituencies. It was this aspect of their ministries to which Hughes seemed particularly drawn. Mother Rosa Artimus Horn, whom Hughes described as "shouting Mother Horne [sic]" in "Heart of Harlem," is a prime example and the most high-profile female minister among the group. Horn migrated from South Carolina and Georgia by way of Indiana and Illinois before she established the Pentecostal Faith Church in Harlem in 1930, where a young James Baldwin briefly served as a minister in his teens. He remembered her as "an extremely proud and handsome woman, with Africa, Europe, and the America of the American Indian blended in her face." A revivalist, faith healer, and religious radio broadcaster, Horn became known as the "Pray for Me Priestess" with an expansive range of social programming based in her church.[90] As the *New York Amsterdam News* reported in 1934, "Mother Horn's chief concern is with the problems of the people among whom she works." She stated her desire to see more schools in Harlem and better medical services and access to medical care by the poorest of the area's residents. She cared for the "destitute and jobless" and fed countless men, women, and children during the early years of the Great Depression, prompting some observers to remark that hers was "not only a church, but a community service."[91]

Operating in Harlem at the same time, George Baker, also known as Reverend Major Jealous "Father Divine" garnered more fame than Mother Horn and his "Peace Mission" had a stronger impact. The mysterious and diminutive man of dubious origins, who claimed to be God in the flesh, established headquarters in Harlem in 1932, bringing material relief to blacks during the Depression in a way that rivaled and eclipsed the efforts of the federal government. Divine ran his interracial and sex-segregated "kingdoms" with the precision of a skilled administrator and the spiritual ardor of a biblical prophet. The governance was socialist, the theology eclectic and liberal, and the worship (often of "Father" himself) was revivalistic. Like many Harlemites, Hughes was captivated by Divine and visited his church on numerous occasions, hoping to see him in person. He also made mention of Divine in his various writings, always in appreciation, particularly for Divine's interracialism and his efforts to meet the material conditions of Harlemites. Speaking through his fictional alter ego, Jesse B. Semple ("Simple") in a vignette entitled "Big Round World," for example, Hughes praised Divine as a religious leader to emulate. When Simple's companion asks him to contemplate what he'd do if he were "a giant in the spirit world," Simple replies that he would eradicate prejudice and war and promote harmony among the nations. "I would say 'pay some attention to your religion, peoples, also to Father Divine, and shake hands. If you has no slogan of your own, take Father's. *Peace! It's truly wonderful!*," he concludes.[92]

In a 1960 essay on the rise and influence of the "cults" in Harlem, Hughes singled out Divine for particular acknowledgment. In Hughes's view, by centering his movement on the social and the material, Divine had brought good to the society of Harlem and beyond, particularly during the 1930s. "Many a poor student in the dark days of the Depression had reason to thank Father Divine for the blessings of his ample banquet tables," he noted. Agreeing with both Carter G. Woodson and John Hope Franklin, Hughes concluded that Divine had met "human needs that older and more highly organized religious groups have not been able to satisfy."[93] He reiterated this point in a tribute to Divine upon the man's death in 1965. Hughes surmised that Divine had been "a good man" and that "many thousands of people are better people for his having lived. . . . and were uplifted by his grace and his goodness."[94] For Hughes, Father Divine represented the best that the religious worlds outside the mainstream could offer.

In Harlem's world of religion and churches, however, the middle-class mainstream black churches were no less influential in developing the region's African American religious culture. By the 1930s, Harlem's black churches, across a denominational spectrum, were being hailed as some of the most energetic in the nation. They included St. Philip's Protestant Episcopal, Abyssinian Baptist, Salem Methodist Episcopal, Mother AME Zion—the oldest black church in the city—Metropolitan Baptist, and Harlem Community Church. Hughes nurtured modest levels of affiliation with many of them, made statements of support for all of them, and frequently collaborated with them artistically. St. Philip's and Abyssinian were of particular note for their heavy emphasis on social outreach and the way in which they demonstrated the religious liberalism that was pervasive in greater New York City. The dominant ethos in New York by the twentieth century, particularly among the city's Protestants, was a liberal theology rooted in rationalism, biblical criticism, the historical method, and a religious culture given to issues of social concern. This liberal theological spirit was just as vibrant in Harlem as in the rest of the city, even though Harlem competed with an even wider variety of churches and religious expressions.[95] The histories of St. Philip's and Abyssinian, therefore, are bound up with the history of religious liberalism in New York City as a whole.

The history of these mainstream churches is also bound up with the story of the development of black Harlem in the early twentieth century. These churches were crucial to the story of black New Yorkers who moved northward from Lower Manhattan to escape discrimination and to seize opportunities for expansion and growth. St. Philip's, the oldest black Episcopal church in New York City and the city's tenth Episcopal parish, pioneered many of the values that came to characterize black churches in Harlem. Under the leadership of Hutchens Chew Bishop, it was the first black church to make the move to Harlem. In 1909 the church sold its property in the Tenderloin area for $140,000, investing the proceeds in the construction of a newer and grander edifice in Harlem. They also purchased half a million dollars' worth of other real estate, including in 1911 a large apartment complex on West 135th Street between Seventh and Lenox Avenues.[96] Real estate developers John Nail, a member of the congregation, and George C. Parker brokered the deals. Both were protégés of Phillip Payton. By the 1920s, the *New York Age* hailed St. Philip's as "the wealthiest church corporation in the country."[97]

St. Philip's was also one of the most socially active. Bishop was one of the principal organizers for the "Silent Parade," the committee for improving the industrial conditions of Negroes in New York, and the

National League for the Protection of Colored Women. The apartment complex was just one example of the social focus of St. Philip's. There were many others. Bishop also established a department of social work at the church in 1924, which became one of the church's most innovative programs, "tending to the various aspects of human life." Mrs. Mabel Bickford Jenkins, a trained social worker from Virginia City, Montana, became the department's social worker. During the Depression she worked closely with the rector to organize efforts of relief and counseling services at the church, and in 1946 she began assisting with the Lafargue clinic, named after Paul Lafargue, a Cuban "black physician, philosopher, and social reformer." Psychiatrist Fredric Wertham directed the free "mental hygiene clinic," the first of its kind in the country, under the direction of Bishop's son and successor, Father Shelton Hale Bishop, whom Hughes also mentioned in "Heart of Harlem."[98]

The move of St. Philip's to Harlem preceded and inspired many others, most notably Adam Clayton Powell Sr. and Abyssinian Baptist Church. Powell Sr. came to New York from New Haven in 1908, having been recruited to take the pastorate at Abyssinian, the city's oldest black Baptist congregation, founded in 1808.[99] By 1911 Powell had begun a campaign to urge his growing congregation to move to Harlem, regularly preaching a sermon entitled "The Model Church" as a part of his plan to convince his congregants.[100] He purchased property on West 138th Street in 1920 and began conducting services on the site in anticipation of a new and grand structure. Reporting years later, he said, "Harlem had never seen anything so religiously refreshing." The church was completed in 1923 and by the 1930s the congregation numbered over fourteen thousand.[101]

Adam Clayton Powell Sr. was one of the earliest African American exponents of the Social Gospel, along with Reverdy Ransom. Indeed, the two men worked closely during Ransom's time in New York. Powell was also one of the chief exemplars of theological modernism among Harlem's African American ministers, and his church typified the social focus of most mainstream black churches. He fully articulated his social mission in an editorial written for *Opportunity* in 1923, the year the new Abyssinian building was completed. "The Church and Social Work" amounted to Powell's declaration regarding the true purpose of the church and the right response to the influx of black southern migrants to Harlem. He first complained about those who "piously ram the Bible down the throats of people" on Sundays with little care for their daily lives during the week, and then stressed the anticreedal spirit in Harlem. Powell was convinced that the modern church should pay less attention to doctrine and creeds and more to social activity. He was also convinced that most lay members no longer cared about creeds and "very little about church doctrines" but only about those things that worked for their material benefit. Only a church that prioritized in such a way could retain its relevance in the modern world. "Christianity is more than preaching, praying, singing, and giving; it is all of these but a great deal more," he wrote. The church must be "the social center" of its community if it is to "Christianize the social order and is being called upon to give the world a Christianity of deeds as well as a Christianity of creeds."[102]

Powell's son, Adam Clayton Powell Jr., shared much in common with his father but further expanded his theological modernism and the social activist vision at Abyssinian. Hughes developed his strongest bond and association with Powell Jr. in a friendship that lasted for decades. Powell Jr. arrived in Harlem with his family as an infant in 1908, grew up in the church, and assumed the pastorate in 1937, a position for which his father groomed him. Like his father, the very real needs of Harlem motivated Powell Jr.'s agendas, and his work in both the political and ecclesial realms demanded better and safer living conditions and employment in area stores. While serving as the church's assistant pastor in 1934, he staged a boycott of Harlem stores with discriminatory hiring practices called, "Don't Shop Where You Can't Work." His commitment to and love of Harlem were legend, captured in his claim that "Christ would have walked in Selma, He would have marched on Washington, and He would have lived in Harlem." Powell's activities in Harlem as pastor of Abyssinian and on the New York City Council earned him the reputation as a "fighter" with concerns for more than "preaching" and "praying," invoking his father's 1923 essay. As one informant told WPA interviewer Vivian Morris in 1939, "Reverend Powell might be a Baptist preacher, but he sho don't believe only in preachin bout God." By the late 1930s, Abyssinian had become known as much for its charitable outreach as its music and preaching, which catapulted the junior Powell to the national political stage in 1944 when he became the first black person from

New York elected to Congress and only the fourth black congressman in history.[103] Hughes wrote the lyrics to "Let My People Go—Now" in support of his friend's successful campaign. "Adam Powell is long and tall / Words boom out like a cannon ball." And he lauded his political ascension with a mention in "Heart of Harlem." By the 1950s, Hughes openly supported all of Powell's political initiatives and favorably spoke of him on occasion in his weekly column. In a "Simple" column entitled "Black Is Basic," he praised Power Jr.'s "black blood," which made him "great," and for his efforts as congressman to block prejudicial bills.[104]

Powell Jr. was unapologetically modernist in his theology and, like his father, an avid exponent of the Social Gospel. Under his leadership the church functioned primarily as a community center and sustained some of the most progressive programming of any religious institution in Harlem. He clarified his Social Gospel beliefs in his 1949 autobiography, *Upon This Rock*, contending that Abyssinian was "not just a Sunday-go-to-meeting church but a seven-day, twenty-four-hour-a-day church." His thoughts on God, the church, sin, and the Bible reflected not only his father's influence, but also his education in religious studies at Columbia University. They also resonated with the modernist theological ethos pervasive among many mainstream Protestants in New York, such as Harry Emerson Fosdick of Riverside Church and Donald Harrington of the Community Church of New York. Believing strictly that "God is spirit," Powell eschewed any representations of God in human form. "Where there is anthropomorphism there is no God," he wrote.[105] His understanding of sin had more to do with a process by which one becomes aware of one's human weaknesses and with the propensity for "wrongdoing" and "injustice" than "original sin" or "missing the mark." There are no sins of "commission" or "omission," Powell Jr. claimed. People commit sin "by permission."[106] He rejected claims of the Bible as "the word of God," preaching, rather, from the "Jefferson Bible," the version of the Bible constructed by Thomas Jefferson that extracted most references to the supernatural. He also eschewed all outward "symbols" of the Christian faith that in his view only worked to exclude. "If we preach symbols, we are in danger of obscuring the all-important inwardness. As soon as one raises a symbol, a doctrine, a creed, then immediately there fall away, however few, those who do not agree."[107] Under Powell Jr.'s leadership, Abyssinian Baptist Church became what Powell described as "a church of old time spiritual power, of modern interpretation of the gospel and prophetic leadership for tomorrow's world."[108]

Hughes doubtlessly had St. Philip's and Abyssinian in mind when in 1945 he pinned in the *Chicago Defender* a set of resolutions for the New Year regarding Harlem's black churches. The resolutions called for blacks to support and improve black churches in light of their historical importance and social power in black life.

> I resolve to support and improve the Negro church which is the most solid and closely knit social force in most Negro communities. I will help this church to become a forward-looking and progressive force reaching out in both a spiritual and practical way into the community and taking unto itself the attributes of the modern church along the lines of social service, day nurseries for children of working mothers, recreational centers to keep young people off the streets and help cut down juvenile delinquency (and sin), and help the church to become a power and force influencing all walks of life in the human activities of each and every day of the week, not just Sunday and prayer meeting night, but all days and all nights.[109]

The set of resolutions acknowledged that not all of Harlem's churches were "modern" in outlook and socially activist, but it did much to reveal Hughes's own views about the role of religion and church in daily life, as well as what had become the religious institutional priorities of black Harlem by the 1940s.

By the 1950s and 1960s, Hughes's relationship with Harlem's world of religion and churches, particularly with mainstream black churches, centered on the arts. In addition to numerous poetry readings, he received many requests from Harlem churches to stage his plays, something he had been doing since the early 1940s. His relationship with Abyssinian and his friendship with Adam Clayton Powell Jr., in particular, blossomed throughout this period with Hughes featuring the church prominently in a poem he wrote in 1958 for a short collection he called "Gospel and Religious Poems." In the poem "Projection of a Day (Desecration)," the speaker imagines a day when class and religious distinctions, as well as those between "secular" and "sacred" will be obliterated. It will be a day when "Abyssinian Baptist Church will throw her enormous arms around Saint James Presbyterian and 409 Edgecombe stoops to kiss 12 West 133rd."[110] In March 1962, Gwendolyn Jones, program director at Abyssinian, arranged to have two of Hughes's plays, "Don't You Want to Be Free" and "The Gospel Glory," performed in the church's sanctuary. The following year in a *Chicago Defender* editorial entitled "Commissioned Music for Churches," Hughes praised the decision on the part of St. Philip's to enlist composer Margaret Bonds to write a Mass especially for the congregation. Bonds, one of the first black female composers to gain national fame, had orchestrated a number of Hughes's works up to that point, including "The Negro Speaks of Rivers," "The Ballad of the Brown King," and "Shakespeare in Harlem."[111] Hughes had attended the event in which Bonds conducted her *Mass in D Minor* and found it "an impressive occasion." The event seemed a perfect manifestation of the connection between art and religion, and in making this point Hughes drew on ancient history. "Originally all art came into being for specific purposes, usually the motivation being religious: the early cave drawings, the first music, the Greek dramas, the morality plays. During the Middle Ages the great patron saint of the arts, particularly painting and music was the Church." In that light, he understood St. Philip's to be following in an ancient tradition of unifying art and religion for the purpose of spiritual and cultural edification. Hughes was most pleased, however, that this new work was being produced by "a Negro church." "The Negro church can do no greater service to the humanities than the encouragement of the rich spiritual beauties to be found in the creativity of our own composers," he told his readers. "Investment in their talents would surely work to the musical glory of God."[112]

Hughes's comments about Bonds's concert at St. Philip's demonstrated that the eager undergraduate who had emerged from the subway at 135th Street and Lenox in September 1921 to become the quintessential New Negro poet had also developed into a seasoned observer of African American religious life and culture. An expansive body of social commentary on religious matters, as well as numerous poems that covered the spectrum of black religious poetry accompanied and animated those observations. Hughes had become the full embodiment of Locke's spiritual vision for twentieth-century black writers. Beginning in the 1930s, however, he had also developed the reputation that he was "antireligious" and that his work sought the destruction of religion and all its forms. It was a reputation he was unable to evade, despite a number of calculated attempts, and a reputation that would dominate perceptions about him and his work for the remainder of his life. What began most likely as a misreading of Benjamin Mays's assertion of Hughes as "atheistic" in the late 1930s became the standard depiction of one of the most engaged participants from among New Negro writers in Harlem's world of religion and churches.

2

Poems of a Religious Nature

"Langston Hughes as the poet of jazz was also well fitted to make himself the interpreter of the orgiastic religion of black people of the lower classes, where the spirit is less sure of a role than the heart and the senses."
—Jean Wagner

"Langston Hughes n'est pas croyant au sens religieux de terme, il l'a dit en racontant l'histoire de sa pseudo-conversion, mais s'il possède une foi, c'est la conviction profonde qu'il a dans le destin de sa race."
—François Dodat

Nancy Cunard loved all things "Negro," especially New Negro art, artists, and writers, even once declaring she could "speak as if I were Negro myself." It was her fondness for Langston Hughes in particular that led to one of his most significant intellectual exchanges about African American religion, the prominence of religion in his poetry, and what encompasses "religious poetry." Cunard and Hughes had become friends when the English writer, editor, and anarchist determined to compile an anthology of twentieth-century Negro art and literature in 1933. Hughes was one of the principal writers from whom she sought help and contributions to the project. Unique for its internationalist focus and interracial list of contributors, *Negro: An Anthology* generated little popular interest at the time but contained some of the most poignant social commentary that had ever been written on the plight of blacks in the Americas. The book was "necessary," Cunard argued in the foreword, "for the recording of the struggles and achievements, the persecutions and the revolts against" black people. She was extremely grateful for Hughes's assistance on the project, calling him a "revolutionary" and using his 1925 poem "I, Too, Sing America" as the volume's epigraph.

Years later she was still proclaiming to him, "You helped me tremendously."[1] So, in the spring of 1958 it was fortuitous that Jean Wagner, a graduate student at the Sorbonne in Paris who was doing research on black American poets, sought Cunard's help in contacting Hughes. He had proposed to write a chapter exclusively on Hughes. Having obtained the address, Wagner sent Hughes a letter of introduction, a synopsis of his project, and informed him of an impending visit to New York. Appeals for Hughes's help on writing projects were a regular occurrence, but Wagner's request seemed to resonate with Hughes, who responded almost immediately. "Dear Mr. Wagner: I am just about to leave for California but I will be back in New York before your scheduled arrival. Of course I will be pleased to be helpful in any way possible."[2]

Hughes was intrigued by Wagner's interest in "the religious element in Negro poetry" and saw an opportunity to spotlight his religious poetry. That fall he compiled a booklet of his poems, which he deemed "religious in nature" and sent it to Wagner. The booklet of thirty-one poems he cumbersomely titled "Poems of Langston Hughes on Religious or Biblical Themes, Some in the Manner of the Spirituals from Various Books and Unpublished Works of Langston Hughes" (hereafter "Poems of Langston Hughes").[3] Although Hughes was widely known for his generosity, producing the booklet was an unprecedented move on his part. At no other time in his career had he compiled a collection of his work for the sole use of a particular scholar. Never had he released unpublished poems for analysis, and this was the first time he had ever compiled his religious poetry in one collection. Creating the booklet suggested that Hughes believed Wagner's project to be important and perhaps long overdue. Hughes relished the thought that in Wagner he had finally found someone who understood that religion had always been a major theme in his poetry. His religious poetry would have its day as the centerpiece of scholarly analysis and be presented as a core component of his artistic production. Wagner's study would bolster his standing as a writer of religious poetry and complicate if not undermine his reputation as antagonistic to religion.

Hughes's response to Wagner's inquiry launched an extensive collaboration, culminating in Wagner's completed dissertation, *Les poètes Nègres des États-Unis*, in 1963 and, ten years later, the volume *Black Poets of the United States: From Paul Laurence Dunbar to Langston Hughes*.

Hughes seemed genuinely moved upon receiving his copy of the dissertation and read it with great interest in the original French. "You have
written what must perforce be called 'a monumental work.' Certainly,
your book contains the first comprehensive study of my poetry yet put
down on paper," Hughes wrote to Wagner. "I am grateful to you for so
thorough and extended a treatment of my work and for your over-all
sympathy and understanding." Reviewers agreed with Hughes's assessment of the thoroughness and the quality of the book when it was
published in English, with some modifications from the French dissertation. Writing for the *Journal of Negro History*, Naomi Madgett called
the book "a work of uncommon depth and insight" and asserted that
it was produced with "painstaking care, objectivity and thoroughness."
Ralph Willett called it "an exhaustive work of formidable scholarship."
In his introduction to the volume, Robert Bone praised Wagner for his
thoroughness and his "Olympian determination to view the subject in
the largest possible perspective."[4]

Wagner had chosen to place the emphasis on what he considered the
interdependent themes of race and religion, what Robert Bone called the
book's "most enduring contribution." Wagner contended that race and
religion existed "in a kind of symbiosis or vital union" in the work of a
select group of twentieth-century black poets including Hughes, Claude
McKay, and Countee Cullen.[5] "Such an approach may seem self-evident
in the case of a tradition deriving from the spirituals," Bone asserted,
"but before the publication of this book, the most substantial essays in
the field were rather belligerently secular in outlook and sensibility."
Bone thought Wagner had done a great job of fusing the issues of race
and religion and recognizing the concerns of "ultimate reality" that were
pervasive in most black poetry. Wagner had shown "the fundamental
importance of theology in formulating a history of Afro-American
poetry."[6]

Wagner's *Les poètes Nègres des États-Unis* would be one of two collaborations in which Hughes would become engaged in the late 1950s
and early 1960s. The other was a more modest exchange with another
French writer, François Dodat, for whom Hughes would also compile
a booklet of poetry. The importance of the two studies, as well as the
booklets Hughes compiled to assist them, rests not only in the fact that
they represented compelling evidence that Hughes considered religion

to have been a major emphasis in his poetry throughout his career but also that he had increasingly turned his attention to the topic of religion at the time of their collaborations. Wagner's more thorough study also revealed the specific ways Hughes's religious poetry covered a wide spectrum, including the three broad categories of New Negro religious poetry: faith and reverence, racialized political poems of a religious nature, and poems of doubt, critique, and frustration. Both studies provided retrospectives on an aspect of his poetic production that, much to Hughes's regret, had escaped analysis over his long career.

Hughes correctly intuited that the projects would bring increasing attention to his religious poetry. The collaborations with Wagner and Dodat, however, only partially met Hughes's expectations, as their comprehensiveness did not equate comprehension. Hughes's responses to the completed and published works, therefore, were a mixture of gratitude, ambivalence, and disappointment. He was pleased with the careful biographical aspect of the studies, as he assured François Dodat, "I love your book on me and my poetry and you have done a comprehensive job on my life story."[7] He was not pleased, however, with the conclusions drawn about the content or the representations of religion in his poetry. Wagner fundamentally misunderstood Hughes's conception of religion, as well as the range of his religious poetry. He disagreed with Hughes as to what constituted the "religious" in his poetry, limiting what he considered to be "authentically" religious poems to those he deemed representative of the "orgiastic religion" of the African American "lower classes." Following the example set by Countee Cullen, who equated Hughes's jazz poems with "spiritual exuberance," Wagner suggested that Hughes was uniquely and perhaps only "fit" to represent the religion of the lower classes because he was a "poet of Jazz."[8]

Despite their careful attention to Hughes's religious poetry, neither Wagner nor Dodat was able to circumvent Hughes's long-established reputation as antireligious. Indeed, they bolstered that reputation. Both men based their assessments of Hughes's religious poetry on the perception of Hughes's own lack of belief. Unable or unwilling to disentangle their sense of Hughes's lack of religious faith from his religious poetry, they not only established his antireligiosity as the interpretive pattern for this aspect of his work, but also for subsequent misreadings of Hughes with regard to religion and his religious poetry.

Poems of a Religious Nature

To compile the collection of poems he sent to Jean Wagner, Hughes highlighted his early work. Although he drew from all of his poetic production across the decades, the early poetry framed the document and composed its thematic core. Hughes clearly wanted to draw attention to this early work not merely for the sake of chronological accuracy but also because he viewed them as the most representative of his religious poetry and for the way they revealed his earliest thinking about religion. Beginning with the poetry of the 1920s, he named each of the four sections of the booklet and provided a date or a descriptor: "Glory! Hallelujah! (1927)," "Fields of Wonder (1947)," "Testimonial (from 'Montage of a Dream Deferred')" (1951), and "Encounters (Uncollected)." By showcasing the early poetry, Hughes wanted to demonstrate how crucial aspects of his poetic style and craft were particularly suited to the aims and objectives of his religious poetry. The poems in the first section came from his first series of explicitly religious poems in *Fine Clothes to the Jew*, perhaps his "greatest collection" and certainly the one that "marked the height of his creative originality."[9] As poems of faith and reverence, these early poems primarily represented the "traditional" and "compensatory" religious poetry of a just, impartial, and immanent God as outlined by Benjamin Mays's study, and in this way they were tied to a tradition of black poetry dating back to the eighteenth century. They were also the poems alleged to be most representative of the "orgiastic religion" of the lower classes. Almost certainly meant to shape Wagner's analysis of his religious poetry, the poems of faith and reverence and the overt Christian religiosity expressed in them indicated a particular set of ritual practices and theologies Hughes recalled from his youth in the AME church in both real and imagined ways.

An important feature of Hughes's poetic style and craft in the early religious poetry had to do with brevity. The brevity of Hughes's poetry, including the early religious poetry, fueled the contention by some critics that many of them were not actually poems. Brevity as a literary style, however, reflected Hughes's philosophy regarding the importance of simplicity in poetry, which he gleaned from the free verse style of Carl Sandburg and Walt Whitman. Simplicity in form and word choice was the signature feature of free verse and emerged as its most important quality. Sandburg extolled the virtue of "simple poems" for "simple people," and Whitman proclaimed "the art of art, the glory of expression and the sunshine of the light of letters is simplicity. Nothing is better than simplicity."[10] Hughes fully embraced simplicity as a value in poetry writing, no matter its intent or subject matter. He first made this claim shortly after the publication of *Fine Clothes to the Jew* in a speech before the Walt Whitman Fellowship in Camden, New Jersey. Hughes told the audience, "I believe that poetry should be direct, comprehensible, and the epitome of simplicity." A poem should be uncluttered in its thought and form. By the 1960s he was still making this point, stating at the National Poetry Festival, "a poem, I think, should be distilled emotion—the shorter the better."[11]

Initial critiques leveled at Hughes's early work, however, argued that his poems were too short and simple, failing "lamentably to satisfy [the] desire for a modernist literature attuned to the complexities of modern life." Amid the high praise for his artistic production and professional accomplishments, critics complained that his poems were "superficial, infantile, silly, small, unpoetic, common, jejune, iterative, and, of course, simple." Intellectual historian and literary critic Howard Mumford Jones bemoaned what he viewed to be Hughes's penchant for "vapid simplicity," and historian J. Saunders Redding quipped that Hughes's poetic simplicity did a "disservice to his art."[12] Even as Hughes continued late in his career to hail simplicity as important to his craft, his critics scoffed. In his *New York Times* review of Hughes's 1959 *Selected Poems*, for example, James Baldwin called it "a fake simplicity," asserting that Hughes employed simplicity as a device "to avoid the very difficult simplicity of the experience."[13] Other critics, of course, assessed the approach differently. Margaret Larkin asserted in her review of *Fine Clothes to the Jew* that the "simple stuff" of Hughes's poems contained a "delicate rhythmic variety through which the long ripple of the form flows boldly." And as most free verse poetry was designed to do, the poems often conveyed thoughts of enormous depth and a range of human emotions, or "distilled emotion," as in the twelve words of "Suicide's Note," first published in *Vanity Fair* in 1925: "The calm / Cool face of the river / Asked me for a kiss." For this reason Onwuchekwa Jemie commented that Hughes's poems were "stark, unadorned, crystal-clear surfaces through which may be glimpsed tremendous depths and significant human drama."[14]

Each of the religious poems in *Fine Clothes to the Jew* and thus many of those in the "Poems of Langston Hughes" booklet revealed Hughes's commitment to poetic simplicity and brevity as a stylistic and ideological choice. "Fire" comprised the most stanzas with seven and "Shout" the least with just one stanza and ten words: "Listen to yo' prophets, Little Jesus! / Listen to yo' saints!" The economy of words, however, not only tended to confirm Whitman and Sandburg's notions about the functional utility of the literary style, the brevity of the poems added a lyrical and visual strength. In a few lines Hughes captured a striking visual to uncover the theological aspirations embedded in certain expressions of African American religious culture, as in "Angels Wings."

> De angels wings is white as snow,
> O White as snow,
> White as snow,
> De Angels wings is white as snow,
> But I drug ma wings
> In the dirty mire.
> O, I drug ma wings
> All through the fire.
> But the Angels wings is white as snow,
> White as snow.

The brevity and breathlessness of the poem was at the service of very large ideas regarding moral purity, "willful sin" and culpability, and vivid depictions of relational exchanges between creatures of heaven and creatures of earth.

The poem "Angels Wings" also revealed the use of dialect speech as another important aspect of Hughes's early religious poetry.[15] By the 1920s, poetry written in "Negro dialect," or "African American Vernacular English" was rapidly falling out of fashion among New Negro poets in favor of lyric and free verse poetry written in conventional English. James Weldon Johnson, for example, took time to explain this trend in the introductions to both *The Book of Negro Poetry* (1922) and *God's Trombones* (1927). New Negro poets of the Harlem Renaissance longed to be free of the "limitations" of the literary device, he asserted, as they had been placed in "a certain artistic niche," particularly with the success of Paul Laurence Dunbar. The first African American poet to garner a national reputation, Dunbar wrote many of his poems in "Negro dialect," including those found in his first collection, *Oak and Ivy*, published in 1896.[16] Indeed, in subtitling his book "From Paul Laurence Dunbar to Langston Hughes," Wagner acknowledged the literary trajectory and transformation. Reflecting the change, Hughes employed dialect speech only twice in his first collection of poetry, in "The Negro Dancers" and "Mother to Son." All others were blues or lyric poems written in the free verse style exemplified by the collection's namesake, "The Weary Blues" and "Poem—To the Black Beloved." In *Fine Clothes to the Jew*, however, Hughes reversed this pattern as most of the poems were written in dialect with fewer blues poems and lyric verse. The shift back to dialect speech as a literary device in the early religious poetry demonstrated Hughes's concern for evoking the religious sentiments, theologies, and ritual practices of his own AME church background, as well as the black religious "folk" culture in general.[17]

The use of dialect speech complemented the folk idiomatic motifs Hughes was determined to highlight. He held great affection for African-American folk culture and peppered these early religious poems with the homey, informal, and unpretentious wit and wisdom seemingly intrinsic to it. Robin D. G. Kelley argues that the notion of "the folk" is "socially constructed and contingent," and it has been falsely pitted as the "pre-modern" counterpart to African American modernity. In Hughes's case, however, it is best to see "the folk" as an interplay between the pre-modern and the modern, and his embrace of the concept worked within that interplay. Although their lives and social situations were largely products of the modern world, the subjects in Hughes's early religious poetry were also the "simple people" of which Sandburg spoke. They were people of strong faith, living in challenging situations presumably in rural contexts in the South or the midwestern plains. Often, their only hope in this world was to patiently await the world to come. "Prayer Meeting" exemplifies such hope beyond this life.

> Glory! Hallelujah!
> De dawn's a-comin'!
> Glory! Hallelujah!
> De dawn's a comin'!

A black old woman croons
In the amen-corner of the
Ebecanezer Baptist Church.
A black old woman croons,—
De dawn's a comin'!

The reader is drawn, in a nearly palpable way, into the sacred setting where the "black old woman" awaits the ending of the troubles of this life and the glory of that which is to come. It is a black Baptist church in a rural part of the American South or Midwest. We visualize her seated in the "amen-corner," tear-streaked face, callused hands uplifted, "crooning" her mantra, "de dawn's a comin.'" It is a scene Hughes likely witnessed many times in his home church of St. Luke AME in Lawrence, Kansas, and therefore was simultaneously an expression of his art and imagination, as well as a product of memory.

As "Prayer Meeting" demonstrates, much of Hughes's early religious poetry features either a black woman as subject or was written in the persona of a black woman. The female persona in these poems normally speaks in the first person from the vantage point of her joy or sorrow, faith or despair. Author and social activist bell hooks calls this use of the female voice Hughes's "fictive transvestism," by which she means Hughes's efforts to explore his own female voice in the voice of his characters.[18] While this contention likely has some merit, given the careful attention Hughes paid to women in his writing, more to the point, Hughes's use of the female voice in his religious poetry indicated his gendered notion of black religion. And this had much to do with demographic realities and the actual constituency of most black churches during the 1920s. According to the 1926 Census of Religious Bodies, 80 to 90 percent of black church memberships consisted of black women. Or, as the report stated, "the excess of females among the memberships of Negro churches was very pronounced."[19] Moreover, the Great Migration, beginning around the First World War, was having a transformative effect on all aspects of black life and perhaps particularly on black churches. It was rapidly shifting the balance between the number of black churches in the South and those in the North and Midwest. But 70 percent of black churches were still located in the South. Accordingly, a black southern religious ethos pervaded many northern and midwestern churches during this time as a result of the migrants' presence and cultural influence. So to think and to poetically visualize a black religious setting in the 1920s was to think and to visualize a black woman of the South. Even in poems such as "Moan," for example, in which the gender of the poem's subject is not explicitly stated, one hears the voice of a southern black woman primarily because these spaces were overwhelmingly female.

The use of dialect speech also amplified Hughes's sense of sin as the primary theological preoccupation for those who populated these spaces. In what are rightfully considered Hughes's "sin poems," sinners and sinning loomed large, as Hughes explored sin both as a universal condition and as a matter of personal shortcoming. In the poem "Sinner," for example, the speaker pleads for God's mercy because she is "Po' an' black an' humble an' lonesome an' a sinner in yo' sight," evoking the long association of "blackness" with sin.[20] No doubt drawing on his experiences as a child in the AME church, Hughes frequently presented a Hamartiology or "doctrine of sin" that signified universal culpability in the Christian drama of salvation: all are sinners in need of God's mercy and atoning forgiveness. In the most basic terms, sin constitutes a "condition" of rebellion against God originating with the Fall, as in "by one man sin entered the world" (Rom. 5:12, KJV). This "condition" of sin is what both Catholic and Protestant theology consider "original sin," the notion that a sinful state exists in all humanity at birth. The doctrine is, as Tatha Wiley writes, "the pivot of Christian beliefs" and "the starting point . . . of other primary Christian doctrines." Soteriology or "doctrine of salvation" is the theological foil to the sinful condition and rooted in Christ's redemptive work on the cross.[21] It is the mercy that the "po' an' black" sinner seeks.

Sin in the poetry of Langston Hughes, however, was not only about the condition of sin, it was also and most often about social sins—personal indiscretions and worldly behaviors. Subjects in the sin poems usually articulate an awareness of their volatile situation, the impact of their behavior, a fear of eternal damnation, and the inability or unwillingness to change. In "Fire," for example, the speaker confesses that he "ain't been good" and "ain't been clean"; rather, he has "been stinkin', low-down, mean." He is guilty of rabble-rousing and general "misbehavin'," And, aware that eternal damnation is the punishment for such sin, he declares, as if in agony, that "fire gonna burn ma soul." Hughes's sinners are aware of their "condition" as those born into sin, but mostly concern themselves with the way they fall short of acceptable or respectable behavior rather than failing to live up to certain ethical standards, moral codes, or biblical mandates. They drink, smoke, and dance, among other "worldly amusements," and have too much fun doing so.

The sin poems extend well beyond the 1920s, however, as Hughes placed even greater emphasis on social sins in a number of poems he composed in the 1940s. During and after World War II, when the nation seemingly re-evaluated leisure culture and attempted to elide the excesses that followed the First World War and the Roaring Twenties, a deep sense of uncertainty collided with what Richard Lingeman calls "a conservative counter attack."[22] The sin poems of the 1940s, therefore, reveal characters with a more refined understanding of their state. Sin was seen as a conscious choice that separated one from God, the community of the righteous—the "saints"—one's family, and ultimately oneself by way of guilt. The emotional pain of guilt was on the mind of the speaker in "It Gives Me Pause," published in the *Carmel Pine Cone* in 1941, when the speaker says, "I would like to be a sinner / sinning just for fun / but I always suffer so / when I get my sinning done." In "Madam and the Minister," the Madam felt guilty after a confrontation with a visiting preacher, who had asked if she had "backslid," that is, fallen away from her Christian faith. She replied, "it felt good if I did." "Madam," the brassy, self-confident, and resourceful Alberta K. Johnson, a character Hughes created and began composing poems about in 1943, became "kinder sorry" for disrespecting the minister and so declared that she "ain't in no mood for sin today." In "Ballad of the Sinner," the speaker seems to indicate that the time is too late for him. Despite his moral upbringing and the warnings of his Christian family, his penchant for sin—"drinking licker and jitterbugging"—led him "straight down the road that leads to hell." This sinner, like many in Hughes's poetry, found the sinful or worldly life overwhelmingly compelling, making a holy life humanly impossible. Hughes's sinners throughout the 1920s and 1940s were often waylaid by the temptations of the world and found Christian living impossible or improbable at most, and uninteresting at best. The cost of these social sins was high, however, as the speaker in "Prayer for the Mantle-Piece" concedes: "All the sins I know are bad / that daily block my way."[23]

"Saints" were also a theological preoccupation in the black church world Hughes poetically created and reimagined in his early religious poetry. This community of the righteous existed in existential tension with sinners and was their antipode if not their aspiration. The lure of the world did not entice this group, nor were they given to the petty pleasures of social sin. They focused on prayer and the ultimate deliverance from this life, the eschatological hope. And an intimate connection with the Divine, a "friendship" with Jesus, sustained this hope. Indeed, saints spoke most often of "Jesus" rather than "Christ," a move that suggested Hughes understood the theological difference. The Christian tradition has made a distinction between Jesus as a person, the "historical Jesus," and Jesus in his prophetic role as Christ, the Messiah or "deliverer." "Jesus" expresses the human side of God in Trinitarian theology and "Christ," a title bestowed by subsequent followers of Jesus, suggests Jesus's redemptive, exemplary, and *agape-phileo* function. Those among this group were devout and persevering, seemingly strong in the knowledge that God, in the person of Jesus, was not distant but immanent and intimately concerned about their quotidian struggles.

The saint who speaks in the poem "Feet o' Jesus" is perhaps one of Hughes's most vivid, and Hughes considered the poem the finest example of his early religious poetry, second only to "Ma Lord." "Feet o' Jesus" exemplifies Hughes's notion of the devout saint who clings to her intimate friendship with Jesus as a means to endure this life and to gain a better life in the hereafter.

> At the feet o' Jesus,
> Sorrow like the sea.
> Lordy, let yo' mercy
> Come driftin' down on me.
>
> At the feet o' Jesus
> At yo' feet I stand.
> O, ma little Jesus,
> Please reach out yo' hand.

Originally published in the October 1926 edition of *Opportunity* magazine, the poem also appeared in Hughes's third book of poetry, *The Dream Keeper*, in 1932. Because of its brevity, Hughes alternatively called "Feet o' Jesus" a "prayer" and the "breath of a spiritual."[24] He never failed to read it at events when he had decided to include one or more of his religious poems as a part of his set list, and made it the feature religious poem of the twelve he included in the section he called "Feet of Jesus" in his 1959 *Selected Poems*.[25] He hailed the fact that Marian Anderson recorded the poem as a song and that she regularly included it in her concerts. Florence Beatrice Price, the first African American woman to have one of her compositions played by a major orchestra, also arranged "Feet o' Jesus," and it has remained on the repertoire of numerous classical music performing artists since the 1950s.[26]

Carl Sandburg most likely inspired "Feet o' Jesus." The title, content, and literary convention of the poem bare a striking resemblance to a poem he wrote around 1914 entitled "Black Prophetess." "I makes my livin' washin' / I keeps happy at the feet of Jesus."[27] The poem is a snapshot of the life of a black female domestic from Chicago who also spends her spare time as a street preacher, warning of "God's destruction" and Jesus's immanent return. As with many of Hughes's religious poems of this era, "Feet o' Jesus" is a cry for mercy. The cry for mercy in this instance, however, is not a cry for salvation from one's sins but a believer's cry for deliverance from the sorrows of this life. The narrator submits herself at the "Feet o' Jesus," fully aware of her dependence on God and full of the hope that Jesus will "reach out [his] hand." The tone is one of supplication and humility, and although one would imagine the narrator to assume a prostrate position, she is "standing" rather than kneeling at Jesus's feet, an indication of her confidence and her intimate connection to the Divine. This is precisely the image Aaron Douglas chose to use in his illustration accompanying the poem in *Opportunity*.[28] Standing "broad shouldered and strong," the narrator calls Jesus "ma little Jesus" to connote a deep level of familiarity and an intimate bond in what evangelical Christian theology would term a "personal Savior."

The notion of a friendship with Jesus the "personal Savior" emerges even clearer in "Ma Lord."

> Ma Lord ain't no stuck up man
> Ma Lord, he ain't proud
> When he goes a-walkin'
> He give me his hand
> "You ma friend," he 'lowed."

First published in the *Crisis* in June 1927 and also appearing in *The Dream Keeper*, "Ma Lord" displays the narrator's sentimental attachment to her Lord in the most intimate and tactile terms. Indeed, Hughes anthropomorphizes the Divine as a friend who "walks" and "gives his hand." The Lord is of good character and is not proud and also identifies in a particular way with the plight of the lowly, the poor, black, and the suffering, having faced, in the form of Jesus, his own share of hardship during his time on earth.

> Ma Lord knowed what it was to work
> He knowed how to pray
> Ma Lord's life was trouble, too
> Trouble ever day.

The friendship between the speaker and her Lord is based on their shared experience of trouble. It is their point of contact and basis of identification. Indeed, in evangelical Christian terms, the shared suffering is what qualifies her Lord to be "Savior." Heaven is her ultimate goal, and the last stanza of the poem expresses her eschatological hope to obtain eternal life beyond this life, and a life that is qualitatively better.

> Ma Lord ain't no stuck up man
> He's a friend of mine
> When He went to heaven
> His soul on fire
> He told me I was gwine
> He said, "Sho you'll come wid Me
> An' be ma friend through eternity."

Hughes often wrote about heaven and described it in the poem "Heaven" as simply "the place where happiness is everywhere." Heaven as the ultimate reward for this saint's friendship with Jesus both affirms biblical promises and acknowledges that life in this world for most black people is full of "trouble ever day."

Although "Ma Lord" was curiously absent from the "Poems of Langston Hughes" booklet, Hughes called it "one of my favorites among my own poems."[29] He recorded it several times and usually listed it prominently among his religious poems. He also provided an extensive explanation of its primary inspiration, something he rarely did for any of his writing. Hughes explained that as a little boy in Kansas he dutifully attended the Methodist church in Lawrence, but he was "thrilled" when his "Auntie" Reed would take him to Warren Street, the black Baptist church in town for its annual gatherings.[30] He loved "the almost gymnastic [enthusiasm] of the preacher, the old-time hymns with their swing and movement, the loud shouting and the deep moaning of the prayers." As he later wrote, "the vast primitive rhythm of the services made me wish that we were Baptist, too, instead of Methodists." Even though St. Luke's worship services were "quieter and more dignified" by comparison to Lawrence's black Baptists, they did, however, retain a few "old time Negroes" who were a source of amusement to the young people and an embarrassment to the "fashionable members" for the way they would rise, sing, and shout "when the spirit moved them."[31] It was one of these "old time Negroes" that inspired "Ma Lord."

There was one old lady in our church who was different from the rest of the brothers and sisters in that she would never sit in the amen corner where the other shouters sat, but instead she always took her place on the middle aisle way in the back of the church, and because she was poor and old-timey and strange in her ways the best people in the church wouldn't pay her much attention and on Sundays they would sweep up the aisle with their silks and satins rustling and never look at the old lady. And many a time I've seen her shake her head and say out loud, "Huh! You all gonna git so fine you won't know Jesus when he come." And somehow that has remained in my mind all these years,—that old woman believing in a simple kind Jesus who wouldn't be ashamed to notice her and be her friend,—and it seems to me that she expressed in her few words all the simple and beautiful faith of the old Negroes in a plain understandable God that they could love and who would be their friend.[32]

At times when he found himself visiting or doing a poetry reading in some "fine church" or one "built for white people," where he would be welcomed as an "entertainer" but not if he only "wanted to pray," Hughes stated that he thought of this "old colored lady." It was her courage and her relationship to her Lord that he wanted to express in the poem.

Hughes made extensive changes to the introduction of "Ma Lord" over the years, most likely to reflect the economic realities of mid-twentieth-century Harlem and black America more generally, as well as his own perceptions about class tensions in black communities. Indeed, although class disparities played a role in it, the earliest version of the introduction was primarily about intra-denominational religious differences. In the 1955 version, however, recorded for Folkways Records, the "old colored lady" becomes an "old woman" who is "very poor." In this version, *she* is the one who wears a satin shirtwaist, a high collar, and wide skirts, which indicate that she is quaint and old-fashioned. Rather than shunning the "amen corner," she always sat there, "right up in front." Her rebuke is also different. Rather than addressing "the best people in the church" for their class-consciousness, she scolds the young people of the congregation who regularly laugh at her. "That's alright, ya'll young folks can laugh if you wanna, you can be stuck up if you wanna. But ma Lord ain't stuck up." It is a touching scene, designed to underscore generational and class differences among blacks. The old-timer, as one of the "old Negroes," is much more in touch with her faith and worships a "plain understandable God" and "a simple kind Jesus" who loves her as a friend.[33] The newer Negroes of the congregation, who never look at her, possess a nominal faith, their religion overshadowed by class striving. What remains consistent in the versions of the introduction, however, is the primacy Hughes places on renderings of black religion, gendered female and deeply committed to notions of an African American folk culture of the American South and Midwest.

The "Poems of Langston Hughes" booklet by no means represented a complete list of the poetry Hughes considered "religious in nature." In addition to "Ma Lord," there were other notable absences, including the racialized religious poetry, or political poems of a religious nature from the 1930s such as "A Christian Country," "Christ in Alabama," and "Goodbye Christ." Hughes signaled to Wagner during their interview, however, that the list was not complete, declaring that "Scottsboro," "Christ in Alabama,"

"Tower," Negro Mother," and "Two Things" were all religious poems for various reasons despite their exclusion from the booklet. "Scottsboro," for example, contained the line "Christ is not dead," he declared, and "Dear Lovely Death" affirmed the existence of an afterlife.

> Dear Lovely death
> that taketh all things under wing
> Never to kill
> only to change
> Into some other thing.

The exclusions indicated the editorial choices Hughes found necessary for the purposes of space and structural flow. The number of poems he considered "religious in nature" was large and he could not include everything. His omission of the poetry of the 1930s was also likely a strategy designed to shape Wagner's perspective. Hughes wanted to place the emphasis primarily on the poems written in the 1920s to reveal the nature of his thinking about religion during that early period. That poetry clearly exemplified the primacy of religion in his poetry and vividly evoked the discursive modes, rhetorical patterns, and theological preoccupations of African American religious culture. The exclusion, however, emerged as a source of tension between Hughes and Wagner, and the poems of the 1930s played a larger role in Wagner's analysis than Hughes had expected.

"Poems of the Spirit"

In June 1963 Hughes compiled another booklet of religious poetry: thirty poems he called "Poems of the Spirit." With the same sense of urgency he had shown in 1958 to Jean Wagner, he sent the booklet off to François Dodat, who was conducting research for a short book on Hughes and his poetry. Hughes responded to Dodat's request for assistance with an offer to help "in any way that I can," pointing Dodat in the direction of particular book titles, particularly Wagner's just-completed dissertation, his own *Selected Poems*, and "Ask Your Mama: 12 Moods for Jazz," the epic poem inspired by his love for jazz and his attendance at the Newport Jazz Festival in 1960.[34]

Dodot had been commissioned for this project by Pierre Seghers, poet, editor, and former member of the French Resistance for his famous book series, *Poètes d'aujourd'hui*, a rare honor shared by only three other American writers—Emily Dickinson, Walt Whitman, and Edgar Allen Poe. Seghers held Hughes in the highest regard. Writing to inform him of his plans, he said, "Je pense que votre oeuvre mérite bien cet hommage, dans cette collection qui est diffusée dans le monde entier" (I think that your work well deserves this tribute, in a collection that is distributed around the world).[35] Dodat took to his task with great diligence and produced a volume, *Langston Hughes*, in just over a year.[36] He had been a Hughes enthusiast since 1955, when he produced *La poésie de Langston Hughes*, a collection of thirty-six Hughes poems translated into French, including "*Mon Sauveur*" ("Ma Lord").[37] Dodat's seventy-page introduction to *Langston Hughes* in the *Poètes d'aujourd' hui* series extended his 1955 biographical and literary analysis of Hughes, recounting Hughes's early life and role in the Harlem Renaissance. Dodat contended that Hughes's racial and family heritage, his experience in the wider world, as well as his affinity for the black masses served as the primary inspiration for his poetry. "*Il est certain que sa formation très particulière explique pour une large part la place très originale qu'il occupe dans l'école américaine d'aujourd'hui*" (It is certain that his very particular formation explains for the most part the very original place that he occupies in the contemporary American school of poetry).[38]

"Poems of the Spirit" differed in important ways from "Poems of Langston Hughes," compiled just five years earlier. The differences indicated that Hughes had other aims and intents for this collection and that he would use other discourses, symbols, and images to reveal his thoughts about the purposes and practices of religion. The first and most obvious difference had to do with terminology. To be sure, Hughes considered the poems in this collection to also be "religious in nature," but the decision to employ the language of "spirit" (by which he strongly implied "spiritual") over "religious" was deliberate. Perhaps anticipating the debates about the differences between the spiritual and the religious, Hughes seemingly wanted to further stake his claim as a writer of religious poetry but framed this collection in a way that expanded the conception of "religious" beyond any specific religious tradition or institution, as well as the regionally specific religious ethos of his early poetry. As Leigh Schmidt argues, spirituality in America has tended to mean a "disassociation" and "disentanglement" or a redefinition of the "Protestant habits" of organized religion in favor of a direct experience with the Divine and an emphasis on the interior life of the individual.[39] The "Poems of the Spirit," therefore, did not invoke a particular church, the African American rural South and midwestern plains states, or the folk religion of the lower classes. Both theologically and culturally, these poems took Hughes further from his AME background, and although the booklet contained many of the explicitly religious poems of faith and reverence from the early period, Hughes placed greater emphasis on the implicitly religious poetry of the 1940s through the early 1960s. These later artistic productions took center stage in the way the earlier poetry had done in the "Poems of Langston Hughes" collection.

The early religious poems were not absent or ignored in "Poems of the Spirit," but the five poems Hughes included from this era underwent a transformation and were relocated to the margins. Decentering them, however, did not entail a move away from all of the themes that animated this work. While the later poems did not contain the particular theological preoccupation with "salvation" and "sin," they nevertheless expressed a similar concern for concepts intrinsic to Christian traditions. Indeed, many of the "Poems of the Spirit" gave even sharper focus to such notions as the substitutionary death of Jesus, atonement, and redemption, emerging primarily under the rubrics of the Nativity, Christ's Passion, prayer, and testimony. At the same time, the large number of implicitly religious poems put Hughes's theological modernism in bold relief. "There," for example, contemplates the possibility that upon death the human body transfigures into "infinity, perhaps even divinity." "Pennsylvania Station," a poem Hughes revised in 1962 in tribute to the Beaux-Arts structure by the famed architectural firm of McKim, Mead, and White, which was set to be demolished that year, is reverential in tone but roots that reverence in a secular public space, granting it similar meaning and purpose to spaces designated as sacred. Pennsylvania Station facilitates the search for God, and in this "temple" it is the earth and human beings that are "glorified."[40]

The Pennsylvania Station in New York
Is like some vast basilica of old
That towers above the terrors of the dark
As bulwark and protection to the soul.
Now people who are hurrying alone
And those who come in crowds from far away
Pass through this great concourse of steel and stone
To trains, or else from trains into the day.
And as in great basilicas of old
The search was ever for a dream of God,
So here the search is still within each soul
Some seed to find to root in earthly sod,
Some seed to find that sprouts a holy tree
To glorify the earth—and you—and me.

As "There" and "Pennsylvania Station" demonstrate, another crucial level of difference in "Poems of the Spirit" is their appearance or form. They tend to be longer poems of free verse, and the shorter poems contain simple rhythmic patterns. Hughes made significant linguistic changes to the early poetry as well. Having partially translated some of the early religious poems from dialect speech to conventional English in his *Selected Poems* in 1959, Hughes stripped them of dialect speech entirely in "Poems of the Spirit." "Feet o' Jesus" became "Feet of Jesus" and the phrase "de Angels wings" from that poem become "the angels wings." There were no dialect poems in the entire collection, and the scenes were decidedly more contemporary, expressed with quotidian language or contemporary vernacular. "Vagabonds," "human faces," and "human hands" populate many of these poems amid streetlights, airplanes, and "fine hotels."

Hughes began and ended the booklet with the Nativity story and placed the Passion poems in the penultimate position. In this way he roughly covered the life of Christ from birth to Crucifixion. Likely an outgrowth of his fascination with the Christmas season, as well as the work he was doing on his gospel song-plays during the late 1950s and early 1960s, the first four poems, "Shepherds Song at Nativity," "The Christmas Story," "On a Pallet of Straw," and "Carol of the Brown King" narrated Christ's birth. All spoke of the humble circumstances of the "vir-

gin birth" and the adoration of local shepherds and the Magi, "Three
Wise men, one dark like me, part of his Nativity." The Passion poems
included "Encounter," "Gethsemane," "Road to Golgotha," and "Crucifixion" and gave graphic depictions of torture, blood, suffering, and death.
"Encounter" appeared in both booklets and was the one among the Passion poems that Hughes wrote and revised over a long period of time, beginning March 4, 1957, and ending August 22, 1961.[41] The poem recounts
Christ's walk to his death, a substitutionary death that bore the narrator's
distress and was the source of atonement and of her redemption.

> I met You on Your way to death,
> Though quite by accident
> I chose the path I did,
> Not knowing there You went.
>
> When I heard the hooting mob
> I started to turn back
> But, curious, I stood my ground
> So loud the mob cried,
> Yet so weak,
> Like a sick and muffled sea.
> On Your head You had sharp thorns.
> You did not look at me—
> But on Your back You carried
> My own Misery.

It is the "encounter" with a suffering and dying Christ that not only
explains personal pain but also makes redemption possible.

Hughes would explore the theme of Christ's atoning death in many
poems throughout this period, depicting Christ's death on the cross as
a sacrifice of "body and blood," a phrase he employed in three different
but interrelated poems. In the title poem, "My Body and My Blood," the
opening scene is of Christ on Calvary, where "on either side upon a cross,
they hung two thieves" so that he could "bring the whole world joy." A
mixture of Christ's voice and the narrator's (identified by italicized and
Roman text) ends "Ballad of Mary's Son," which told of the "awful thing"
of killing "Mary's boy," but also of its redemptive consequences.

This is my body
And this is my blood
His body and His blood divine!
He died on the Cross
That my soul should not be lost.

Hughes again used italics in "Ballad of the Two Thieves" to indicate Christ's voice speaking from the Cross.

For the sins of man I suffer
For the sins of man I die
My Body and my blood
Are the answer to your cry.

The three "Body and Blood" poems also revealed the cross as the dominant image in Hughes's Passion poems. He had been using the cross as a literary trope and metaphor since the 1920s in such poems as "Cross," which told the story of a "tragic mulatto," progeny of a "white old man" and a black mother. The parents came to vastly different ends, one dying in a "fine big house" and the other "in a shack." The last line of the poem lamented, "I wonder where I'm gonna die / Being neither white nor black."[42] In the Passion poems, however, Hughes more firmly affixed the cross to its Christian theological meanings and associations, as he did in "Ballad of Mary's Son," which stated plainly, "He died on the Cross." In "Late Corner," which Hughes repeatedly revised for an even longer time than "Encounter," he alluded to those theological meanings in that a streetlight—as "an extension of the Cross"—shares a similar fate of loneliness and abandonment. "Oh, lonely world! / Oh, lonely light! / Lonely Cross!" At the same time, Hughes rarely evoked the cross image without some reference to race, miscegenation, or black suffering. In "A Ballad of Negro History," a poem he wrote upon request in 1951, Hughes recalled the role of "Simon of Cyrene," the North African who assisted Christ with his cross on the way to the Crucifixion. "It was a black man bore the Cross / For Christ at Calvary." The poem "Crucifixion," which Hughes wrote and revised throughout the month of September 1953 but never published, evoked lynching and other forms of racial terror.

He describes the Crucifixion not as a past event or one that happened only to Christ, but as one that happens to others in contemporary times, mainly to black people and black men in particular.

> Two thousand years ago it happened?
> No! It is today they stone him dead
> It is today they nail him on a Cross
> And giggle at the blood that he has lost.[43]

Hughes included four prayer poems in the "Poems of the Spirit" booklet: "Prayer," "Rainbow Prayer," "Prayer at Midnight," and "Prayer for the Mantle-Piece." He had written many other poems about prayer and in the form of prayers during his career, including four simply entitled "Prayer" and three others with the word "prayer" in the title— "Prayer Meeting," "Prayer for a Winter's Night," and "Let All Men Pray." The first, "Prayer [1]," was written during Hughes's fourteen-month stay in Washington, DC, from late 1924 to 1926, where he was "discovered" by the poet Vachel Lindsay and was published in the Dallas-based poetry magazine, *Buccaneer*, in May 1925. Uncharacteristic of much of Hughes's religious poetry during this era, it reflects despair, lament, and existential anguish and is more a display of social commentary than an expression of faith and reverence.

> I ask this:
> Which way to go?
> I ask this:
> Which sin to bear?
> Which crown to put
> Upon my hair?
> I do not know,
> Lord, God,
> I do not know.

"Prayer for a Winter Night" struck a similarly despairing tone with a strident social critique of poverty and inequality. Written before Hughes was to set sail for Europe on the SS *McKeesport*, the poem was published fittingly in A. Phillip Randolph and Chandler Owens's socialist magazine, *Messenger*, in May 1924. It is a sardonic plea for God to "freeze the poor in their beds" as a means to hasten their arrival at "some rich kingdom of nowhere." The kingdom is "where nothingness is everything and everything is nothingness," the ironic experiential counterpart to his description of heaven, where "happiness is everywhere."

Hughes continued to use prayer as a means of social commentary well into the 1940s. Concern for the poor, particularly the poor in cities, anchored another prayer poem. In "Big City Prayer," published in *Opportunity* in 1940 and then republished as "Prayer [2]" in 1947, the speaker makes an exasperated request for God to

> Gather up
> In the arms of your pity
> The sick, the depraved
> The desperate, the tired
> All the scum
> Of our weary city.

Most likely referring to the social conditions of Harlem in the 1940s, as well as an obvious allusion to Emma Lazarus's "The New Colossus," the prayer acknowledges God's "pity" and "love" but also notes that the sick, desperate, tired, and scum have come to "expect / No love from above."

By the 1940s, however, the topic of prayer had primarily become a way for Hughes to call for peace during the Second World War. The war had become a major concern that he addressed in his poetry and prose. "Give Us Our Peace" was a prayer Hughes composed early during the war.

> Give us a peace equal to the war
> Or else our souls will be unsatisfied
> And we will wonder what we have fought for
> And why the many died.

The poem expresses a hope that the war will improve the lives of blacks and the poor by improving education and the nation's "slums." And in a keen display of humanism, the poet also hopes that a "mighty army of human kind" will rise "to work for good, to bring about a world of brotherhood." In August 1944, at the height of the war, he penned "Let All Men Pray" as a prayer for victory and "the triumph of the right." Only through prayer was there hope for "a peace that's wise / When war is through."[44] After Hiroshima, Hughes's "alter ego," Jesse B. Semple (Simple) bemoaned the state of world affairs during a time of "nothing but atom bombs and bad news, wars and rumors of wars." "If I was a praying man," he told his faithful companion, "I would pray a prayer for this world right now." When asked what kind of prayer he would pray, "Simple" responded,

> Lord, kindly please, take the blood off of my hands and off of my brothers' hands, and make us shake hands *clean* and not be afraid. Neither let me nor them have no knives behind our backs, Lord, nor up our sleeves, nor bombs piled out yonder in a desert. Let's forget about bygones. Too many mens and womens are dead. The fault is mine and theirs, too. So teach us *all* to do right, Lord, *please*, and to get along together with that atom bomb on this earth—because I do not want it to fall on me—nor Thee— nor anybody living. Amen!

Simple's companion marveled at the prayer and urged his downcast friend to "help God make a good world."[45]

Of the four prayer poems Hughes sent him, Dodat included "Prayer [2]," also known as "Big City Prayer" (*Prière*) and "Dust and Rainbows" (*Prière a l'arc-en-ciel*), which Hughes identified as "Rainbow Poem" in "Poems of the Spirit." Dodat considered "Dust and Rainbows" "*inédit*" (unpublished) in *Langston Hughes*, but Hughes had published a portion of it in *Voices* in 1955 and then as the first part of the poem, "Two Somewhat Different Epigrams," in 1957. The graphically anthropomorphized "Awe," made up the second part, which appeared again as a single poem in *Black Orpheus* in 1959. "I look with awe upon the human race / And God, who sometimes spits right in its face." The full version of "Dust and Rainbows," like most of Hughes's prayer poems, was not a petition made on the part of an individual, but one with the interest of the collective in mind.

> O, God of dust
> And rainbows,
> Help us see
> That without the dust
> The rainbow
> Would not be,
> That without night
> The sunrise
> Would have no glow:
> O, God of dust
> And rainbows,
> Help us to know.[46]

Dust and the rainbows represent earth and sky and the poem expresses the interdependence they share. The prayer is for those caught between these two necessary natural extremes to understand that necessary relationship.

"Testimony" was the fourth rubric of Christian tradition under which many of the "Poems of the Spirit" fell, and similar to the "sinners" and "saints" in Hughes's early religious poetry, subjects in these later poems often gave public testimony, rendering testimony as pronounced a feature as prayer in this body of work. Testimony in Hughes's later religious poetry, however, was unmediated by persona and dialect speech. The poems were, rather, first-person narratives spoken directly in conventional English, witnessing to the speaker's faith either in the form of praise and exaltation, resolution and surrender, or exhortation. "Testimonial" and "Tambourines" lead this group and are both hymns of praise. "Testimonial" is a section from Hughes's "Montage to a Dream Deferred," a book-length poem comprised of eighty-six sub-poems completed in 1951 in which the subject seeks the appropriate instrument of praise, wishing for a piano, organ, or drum. She ultimately concludes, however, that she "don't need none of them things / For to praise my Lord." "Tambourines," which Hughes quickly wrote in 1959 using material from his book and play *Tambourines to Glory* to fill a space in his *Selected Poems*, is a rhythmic song of praise "to the Glory of God!" "A gospel shout / and a gospel song / Life is short / But God is long!" The poems "Communion" and "Acceptance" testify to the speakers' resolution of faith and trust in "God, in His infinite wisdom" despite human frailty and the lack of complete understanding. The speaker in "Communion" only finds peace when she stops trying to understand that which she can not.

> I was trying to figure out
> What it was all about
> But I could not figure out
> What it was all about
> So I gave up and went
> To take the sacrament
> And when I took it
> It felt good to shout!

In two of the testimony poems, Hughes strikes a "preacherly" tone of exhortation. In "Selah!," the speaker reprimands those who read the Bible but don't pay it any attention. "Has been going on so many years," the poem concludes, "tain't worthy of a mention." "Not for Publication," which Hughes, ironically, did publish in the *Crisis* in 1953 and again in *Black Orpheus* in 1959, has a similar message. Imagining if "Christ were to come back black," the speaker suggests Christ would be rejected from most of the country's religious institutions, "where race and not religion is glorified." Acutely aware of how the image of a "black Christ" challenges racial conventions and disrupts the assumptions of the established religious order, the speaker, with a surreptitious nod to the poem's title, surmises that if one would say such a thing publicly, "you may be crucified."[47]

These poems of the 1950s and early 1960s set the thematic and theological tone of "Poems of the Spirit," and (with the exception of some minor overlaps) resulted in a substantively different collection than the one Hughes sent to Wagner. But just as Hughes did not include all the poems he considered "religious in nature" in *Poems of Langston Hughes*, he left as many of his later religious poems out of "Poems of the Spirit" as he included. And most of those remained unpublished and uncollected long after his 1967 posthumously published final collection, *The Panther and the Lash*. The exclusions reflect a simple editorial decision and concern for space in light of Hughes's enormous body of work in this category. The poems left out of the volume, however, are just as representative of the theological ideas pervading those that are included. "Each Soul Has Need" and "The Lord Has a Child," for example, stress the narrative feature of the testimony poems just as decisively. The speaker in "Each Soul Has Need" testifies that everyone needs help and guidance beyond what humankind can provide.

> And so I seek a harbor where
> I'm anchored in His love
> I seek a harbor where
> I'm anchored in His love.

The use of the contraction emphasizes the personal nature of the statement, and Hughes uses that device more forthrightly in "The Lord Has a Child," making generous use of the terms "I," "I'm," "me," and "my."

> The Lord has a child
> That child I know is me
> Even when I'm not all I ought to be
> His loving care
> Guides me on my way
> Every place, everywhere, every day.[48]

The poem "Yes!" is one of only two poems in this group where Hughes uses the word "saved" (the other is "Sunday Morning Prophecy"). It is the testimony of one who is happy for her salvation, for "it's something to be happy about if you're saved!" In "Celestial Eye," written in January 1963 and perhaps the last of the later religious poems, Hughes likely drew on the imagery of the well-known verse in the Gospel of Matthew about God's knowledge of the sparrow that falls, as well as Ethel Waters's heart-wrenching 1952 version of the song, "His Eye Is on the Sparrow."

> God is high
> Scans earth and sky
> And all
> Including sparrow's fall
> And me so small.[49]

"Poems of the Spirit" accomplished Hughes's goal of using different terminology, images, theological frameworks, and discourses to represent his religious poetry. Utilizing the term "Spirit" in place of "religious" influenced his selection, expanding his notion of the "religious," making the booklet also a worthy display of his theological modernism. And the booklet was influential on Dodat, who drew on it for fifteen poems to supplement those he used from published sources. Combined with "Poems by Langston Hughes," the booklet succeeded in putting nearly the entire range of Hughes's poetic thinking about religion since the early 1920s on full display.

In Defense of Religion

When Dodat's *Langston Hughes* appeared in print, Hughes seemed happy with the results, writing Dodat to thank him and to tell him that "many French speaking friends of mine have remarked on what an excellent job you did." To Segher he simply wrote in French, "*C'est beau et très bien fait.*"[50] Hughes's praise for François Dodat's treatment of his life and work was understandable and appropriate. *Langston Hughes* had its strengths as biography and as literary analysis. It was thoughtful, well structured, and beautifully produced, interspersed with photos by Carl Van Vechten, Roy DeCarava, and Sibyl Anikeeff. It is clear from Dodat's introduction, however, that "Poems of the Spirit" notwithstanding, Hughes's religious poems carried little interest for him *as* religious poems. He had a clear agenda, which was to depict Hughes as a muse of his race, someone deeply connected to the African ancestors, and whose body of work revealed a desire to accurately reflect black people in his art. For Dodat, Africa more than Harlem was the seat and center of black life and Hughes was the principle voice of a transplanted people in the strange land of "*Les Blancs.*"

Dodat considers the "Poems of the Spirit" to have more of the quality and purpose of song rather than literature. Indeed, he calls Hughes's religious poetry "spirituals"—interchangeable with and comparable to Negro spirituals and gospel songs. Seeing Hughes as a blues poet and a poet of spirituals, Dodat considers the musical aspect of these poems to be more important than their literary aspects for the way they provided black Americans with a means of resistance and the fortitude to navigate the racist terrain of America. ("Le blues est donc avant tout un chant de protestation solitaire, la prière du muezzin dans un ville qui serait bizarrement peuplé de chrétiens" [The blues, therefore, are above all a solitary song of protest, the prayer of the Muezzin in a city that strangely enough has Christian people]).[51] Arguing that Negro spirituals were the "original Christian songs" that American blacks adapted from the "ritual dances of African tribes," Dodat maintains that they were songs of "triumph." They nourished the hopes and the joys of American blacks, "hope for a better world, joy in the feeling of communion with others . . . far from whites." These same themes of liberation, uplift, last judgment, and release of the soul after death were all themes in Hughes's spirituals, Dodat further maintains. But any notion of the "religious content" of Negro spirituals or of Hughes's spirituals was nonsensical. "To speak of the subject of their faith, more or less, will result in a naïve real nonsense," he declares. For Dodat, the search for "religious content" in Hughes's poetry missed the more important musical, social, political, and cultural purposes it served.

Dodat rests his assertion that Hughes's *poèmes d'inspiration religieuse* lacked religious content on his contention that Hughes was not a religious believer. Hughes himself, Dodat argues, confirmed his lack of belief, tracing it back to his failed salvation experience in Lawrence, Kansas. As he states, "Langston Hughes n'est pas croyant au sens religieux de terme, il l'a dit en racontant l'histoire de sa pseudo-conversion, mais s'il possède une foi, c'est la conviction profonde qu'il a dans le destin de sa race" (Langston Hughes is not a believer in the religious sense of the term, as he said in the story of his failed salvation, but if he possesses a faith, it is the profound conviction he has in the destiny of his race). Dodat understood Hughes's only creed to be the profound belief he maintained in black people and their destiny. His only Christ was a black Christ who embodied all the misery of black people, and the cross was a symbol of a better life for blacks. Dodat maintains that Hughes's religious poems "seemed to have essentially retained Protestant Christianity," but the lessons Hughes drew from the Bible and other religious sources and experiences had most to do with the struggle for equality and social justice.[52] They were tools in his musical arsenal for black freedom, but religion and the religious worked to its detriment.

The racial essentialism or romantic racialism underlining Dodat's *Langston Hughes* remained unchanged from the anthology he had written eight years prior where he, as Ryan James Kernan argues, depicted Hughes "first and foremost, as a black poet who gave musical voice to U.S. black culture and consciousness." Produced for Seghers's *Autour du monde* series, *La poésie de Langston Hughes* compared Hughes not only to Carl Sandburg and Walt Whitman but also to Wordsworth and Shakespeare. The poems Dodat chose for the anthology scripted a life of Hughes that was rooted in his mixed heritage and the slave past of black Americans, and he stated to Hughes that his purpose for the volume was to topple racial oppression and injustice using Hughes's words, fighting on his behalf as a "white brother." "If I have done a bit of fighting on your side to conquer racial prejudice," he wrote to Hughes in March 1955, "then I shall feel proud of it."[53] For Dodat, Hughes was the musical poet who was the hope of his formerly enslaved people, the future of world culture.

Such romanticism in some respects accurately reflected some of Hughes's core principles as a "Negro artist" and his love for black people, but it elicited mixed critical reviews that never failed to underscore and critique it. For his part, Hughes remained, for unstated reasons, uncharacteristically silent about *La poésie de Langston Hughes* when it appeared in print in contrast to his timely response to *Langston Hughes*. But Dodat's view of Hughes as primarily a musical poet of his people at the expense of all other perspectives, particularly religious ones, persisted well into the 1960s. In an article he wrote for *Présence Africaine* in 1967, entitled "Situation de Langston Hughes," he declared Hughes a "prophet of suffering humanity" who was a fighter for his race with "robust optimism that found its source in an unalterable faith in man." This was only possible, however, after he had "torn away all the symbolic rags of the heritage of black Presbyterian and Baptist pastors." Religion had to be jettisoned in order for Hughes to release the "grand spiritual" of black people, which would allow for a "grand democracy."[54]

Jean Wagner shared Dodat's Francophone "Négritude" interest in Hughes at a time when Hughes's reputation as a "radical" poet was being sustained internationally as it waned in the United States.[55] Their studies were very much products of that literary movement among French intellectuals that focused on black writers from the 1930s through the 1960s and was rooted in Marxist philosophy, which historically had expressed negative views of religion, anticolonialism, and pan-Africanism.[56] Wagner's work on Hughes did not approach the level of racial essentialism Dodat displayed, but he did see Hughes as a larger-than-life figure with perhaps a unique ability to represent black people and champion the cause of blackness in the wider world. However, Wagner primarily honed his hypothesis regarding the "interdependence between race and religion," which he concluded Hughes was unable to "evade." When he asked Hughes to explain this interdependency in "the Negro's search for progress," which had always had "religious connotations," Hughes gave a humanistic response. "Universal harmony in human beings" was necessary to solve the problem, he contended. The interdependence of race and religion was central to Wagner's analysis and was the basis for Hughes's interest in Wagner and for his collaboration with him.[57]

For all of his appreciation, however, Hughes was not pleased with Wagner's conclusions and registered annoyance at some of them. But in his typical, discreet fashion, Hughes would not specify his disagreement in writing. "The few pages where I think your interpretations are a bit off track," he wrote, "I will tell you about when I see you—the nuances might be lost in a letter since they concern the rather tenuous (and viewpoints-variable-depending-on-who's-looking-at-what) subjects of humor and religion."[58]

Although Hughes did not state explicitly where he thought Wagner's interpretations were "a bit off track" regarding "humor and religion," Wagner's assertions about the religious nature of Hughes's poetry and Hughes's apparent lack of religious belief made it plain. Wagner confirmed the importance of humor in Hughes's work, noting that Hughes had used it as an effective literary tool his entire career, often to elucidate tragic and sober circumstances, as in "laughing to keep from crying," in the words of his 1952 book of short stories. But the presence of humor in some of Hughes's religious poetry prompted Wagner to discount its religious aspects. It was not truly religious if it was also funny, he intimated. Hughes's attempt to write a black sermon in the style of James Weldon Johnson, for example, struck Wagner as a means to caricature black preachers. Because Hughes chose to end "Sunday Morning Prophecy" with a preacher's appeal for money, Wagner claimed the poem "barely rises above the humorous."[59]

Come into the church this morning
Brothers and Sisters
And be saved
And give freely
In the collection basket
That I who am thy shepherd
Might live.

Indeed, "Sunday Morning Prophecy," which Hughes intended to be both humorous and satirical, served as one of the bases for Wagner's first major assertion about Hughes and his religious poetry. Likely due, in part, to the strong emphasis Hughes had placed on depictions of "the folk" in the early religious poetry from "The Poems of Langston Hughes," Wagner contended that Hughes was primarily a "folklorist." He grouped Hughes with Sterling Brown and James Weldon Johnson, whose religious writing he deemed merely "folklore" inspired by African American folk sermonic, jazz, and blues traditions. Religion for these writers was an "essential ingredient" of folklore because of its importance to "the American creed," but had no intrinsic religious value. He attributed the lack of intrinsic religious value primarily to either professed unbelief, religious skepticism, or lack of religious affiliation. Noting that Johnson was an agnostic, for example, Wagner found "the religious feeling he displayed in his poetry" to be "paradoxical" and could only be explained by the "strange attraction" Johnson felt for "the religious folklore of his race."[60] His ability to write such religious poetry only showed that Johnson was not "narrowly sectarian," but the "religious content" of his work carried no interest for Johnson and no meaning beyond the cultural and folkloric. Similarly, Wagner argued that Hughes's religious writing was "essentially inspired by the folk traditions," while any sense of religion as an experience of "inner life" was a "closed book to him." Contrasting him with other New Negro writers such as Claude McKay, Countee Cullen, and Jean Toomer, who "follow[ed] the paths of the Spirit," Wagner maintained that Hughes's religious writing lacked the emotional depth and religious conviction of those "spiritualists."[61]

Wagner's second major claim was that Hughes had no interest in religion beyond its political, cultural, and historical importance to black people. Religion as it has been conceived and practiced in America had only done harm to black Americans. Attributing Marxist thought to Hughes, he maintained that for Hughes, Christianity was "the religion of slavery, the opiate of the people, and a major obstacle to black emancipation," necessitating his rejection of it out of loyalty to the black masses.[62] The "slave religion" of black American Christianity had become "a device for hypnotizing the victims of oppression," and Christ's death had no effect for black people, who were compelled to "expect liberation only as the result of their own efforts."[63] In effect, despite the prominence of religion in his poetry, Hughes was antireligious for cultural and historical reasons. And like Dodat, Wagner claimed that this antireligiosity had its roots in Hughes's failed salvation experience. He further asserted, however, that it found its clearest expression in "Goodbye Christ" and the other political poems of a religious nature from the 1930s. Moreover, Hughes's Christ was a black Christ who *incarne toute la misère* (embodied all the misery) of "people of color," and that Christ's climb to Mount Calvary strangely resembled lynching in Texas and Alabama. Wagner called "Goodbye Christ" Hughes's brutal "revolt against God" and evidence of someone who had endured a "personal religious crisis" born from a feeling of "spiritual frustration."[64]

Although Hughes deliberately chose not to include his religious poetry of the 1930s in the document he prepared for Wagner, it was that poetry which generated the pivotal moment in their collaboration and, ultimately, became the focal point of Wagner's analysis overall.[65] In their only interview and in correspondence dating from 1958 to 1961, Wagner insisted on discussing this body of work and eventually included "Christ in Alabama" and "Goodbye Christ" in *Les poètes Nègres des États Unis*. It was not uncommon by the late 1950s and early 1960s for Hughes to omit this body of work from anthologies and other collections of his poetry. He failed to include it in *The Langston Hughes Reader* in 1958, choosing instead to include "Ballad of Mary's Son," "Acceptance," "Pastoral," and "Dear Lovely Death." He also omitted them from *Selected Poems* in 1959, in which a section called "Feet of Jesus" primarily showcased the religious poems of the 1920s. The omission of the 1930s poetry in *Selected Poems* has garnered the most attention, as some scholars have interpreted this as an indication of Hughes's movement toward political conservatism and away from his radical past. While it is clear that by the late 1950s Hughes had shifted in some of his political views and perhaps strategically chose not to include the religious poems of the 1930s in order to influence Wagner's study, the omission was not because Hughes agreed that they were not of a "religious nature" or had no religious value. Indeed, in their meeting Hughes used the 1930s poems—and particularly "Goodbye Christ"—to make his fullest articulation of what Wagner alternatively called Hughes's "defense of religion" and "defense of true religion." Having already declared "Christ in Alabama" to be "religious in nature," he further insisted that "Goodbye Christ" was not an example of his "anti-religious stand of the 30s," but a statement "against the commercialization of religion." Wagner indicated his skepticism on this point with question marks in his notes, however, and a record of the exchange did not appear in the final version of his dissertation or the book.[66]

Wagner's interest in the poems of the 1930s, beyond the doubtlessly intriguing fact that Hughes did not include them in the pamphlet, was not surprising. Although, in qualitative terms, they are among the least regarded of Hughes's poetic production, these poems comprised some of his most incisive critiques of the racism intrinsic to American society, the inattention of the federal government to the condition of American blacks, and the failings of Christianity and the American church. Although Hughes did not consider them to be antireligious, Wagner correctly linked them to a period in Hughes's life characterized by a heightened racial awareness, radical activism, and overt religious skepticism. Coinciding with his turn to the political Left during the 1930s, Hughes developed a political language to discuss religion and employed religious language to write about politics and American society, demonstrating with this poetry the intersection of religious imagery and rhetoric, social critique, and political commentary, as he sought to depict American religion as nonresponsive to the needs of the black poor. In an expression of one of the key features of "new territory" poetry, he also depicted God as complicit with this nonresponsive religion in striking contrast to the theologically conventional poems written a decade earlier. God was not the "friendly" deity in the person of Jesus who understood and identified with black people. In Hughes's 1930s poems, God was either unaware of those conditions or, worse, unconcerned, and was always linked to the government and the church as the institutions of power that perpetrated the oppressive conditions.

The political robustness seemed to intensify with every poem during this time in Hughes's artistic production because his class-consciousness could be as easily provoked as his racial consciousness. He responded to a *Vanity Fair* advertisement for the opening of the Waldorf-Astoria in 1931, for example, with a mocking poetic parody in the form of a three-part poem entitled "Advertisement for the Waldorf Astoria." The forty-seven-story Schultze and Weaver Art Deco hotel had been built on Fifth Avenue between 49th and 50th Streets. In addition to becoming New York's tallest hotel, it also became the city's most opulent, complete with miles of imported carpeting, rare marble, antique furniture from England and France, crystal chandeliers, and gold doorknobs.[67] Incensed by the gross materialistic display in the *Vanity Fair* piece, as well as the twenty-eight-million-dollar new hotel during a time of national economic crisis, Hughes parodied the opening with an allusion to Christ's Nativity in the last section in the poem entitled "Christmas Card." The baby to be born, however, was "the new Christ child of the Revolution."

> Call Oscar of the Waldorf—for Christ's sake!!
>> Its almost Christmas, and that little girl—turned whore
>> because her belly was too hungry to stand it anymore–
>> wants a nice clean bed for the Immaculate Conception.
> Listen, Mary, Mother of God, wrap your new born babe in
>> the red flag of Revolution: the Waldorf-Astoria's the
>> best manager we've got: For reservations: Telephone EL.
>> 5-3000.[68]

A grand hotel born from a feud among one of the country's most elite families, destined to cater exclusively to the rich and powerful during an economic depression seemed an apt occasion to underscore rampant economic disparity. Connecting the hotel's opening with a reference to Christ's birth evokes the humble circumstances under which Christ was born—in a manger with no room at the inn, according to most biblical accounts. The literary allusion provides a trenchant rebuke to the hotel's ostentatiousness. It is also, according to the speaker in the poem, a basis for revolution.

Hughes wrote another of his most daring political poems of a religious nature in response to a request from two white University of North Carolina, Chapel Hill, students. Anthony Buttitta and Milton Abernathy had spearheaded a visit by Hughes to the university—considered to be one of the more progressive among white, southern educational institutions—and wanted Hughes to write a poem, in advance of his visit, about the Scottsboro case for their underground journal, *Contempo*. The Scottsboro case involved the biased conclusions of a hastily convened, all-white grand jury regarding nine black men and boys accused of raping two white women while they were all "hoboing" on a train heading from Chattanooga to Memphis, Tennessee, on March 25, 1931. Based on the contradictory and conflicting testimony of the two women, Ruby Bates and Victoria Price, virtually no physical evidence, and horrifically inept counsel, eight of the nine were tried, convicted, and sentenced to death just twelve days after the alleged crime.[69] The injustice of the case incensed Hughes. He visited the boys in jail and composed several poems about their plight, including "Brown America in Jail," "The Town of Scottsboro," and "Scottsboro." "8 BLACK BOYS IN A SOUTHERN JAIL / WORLD TURN PALE! / 8 black boys and one white lie / Is it much to die?" Hughes penned "Christ in Alabama" and submitted it to the journal, reprinting it a year later along with three other poems that accompany his leftist verse play, "Scottsboro Limited."[70]

Christ is a Nigger,
Beaten and black:
Oh, bear your back!

Mary is his Mother:
Mammy of the South,
Silence your mouth.

God's His Father:
White Master above
Grant us your love.

Most Holy Bastard
Of the Bleeding mouth,
Nigger Christ
On the Cross
Of the South.

A firestorm of controversy and denunciations followed *Contempo*'s pub-lication of "Christ in Alabama" and Hughes's reading of it in November 1931. The reading was held without incident under police protection and Hughes's two-day visit was by all accounts successful. Many among the white liberal faculty, such as Guy B. Johnson, however, were angered by it, and the executive secretary of the university repudiated Buttitta and Abernathy for their actions, calling them "wholly reprehensible adolescents."[71] Wilton E. Hall, the editor of the *Anderson Independent*, was so angry he attempted to get the North Carolina governor involved. Two weeks after the reading, he wrote O. Max Gardner asking him to expel Buttita and Abernathy and to take control of *Contempo* because of its "rank Communist writings." He asked the governor if he had in his "long and useful career ever seen the red flag of Communism so defi-antly flaunted in the face of Southern democracy?"[72] Declining to take any action against the students or *Contempo*, however, Gardner thought Hall was "raising a tempest in a teapot." The university president, Frank Porter Graham, attempted to defuse the situation by insisting that *Contempo* was an "independent paper" not officially connected to the university. The poem and Hughes's reading, however, had clearly shaken the community.[73]

The audacious stroke in "Christ in Alabama" is the way Hughes rei-magines one of the most sacred stories in Christian history—the vir-gin birth—in order to realign the players in America's racial drama. In Hughes's "Holy Family," the encounter between God—"*White Master above*"—and Mary—"*Mammy of the South*"—is far from virginal and pure. It is rape. It is profane. And the child from this union is a mu-latto "Bastard." The firestorm that followed the poem was expected. As Hughes told the *Atlantic World* a month after the event, "anything which makes people think of existing evil conditions must embody these ideas in sensational forms. I meant my poem to be a protest against the domination of all stronger peoples over weaker ones." Thinking about the Holy Trinity in racial terms, he wondered "how Christ, with no human father, would be accepted were He born in the South of a Negro mother."[74] This was precisely what so many found upsetting about the poem. As the sheriff of Chapel Hill put it, "It's bad enough to call Christ a bastard. But when he calls him a *nigger*, he's gone too far!"[75] As it re-garded the Scottsboro case, the racial-religious translation turned the focus on the actions of the "Father"—white southern men—rather than his sons, the "Nigger Christ[s]." The sexual violence to which white men had long subjected black women far outweighed a single accusation of rape from two women that many considered to be of "questionable reputation." As William J. Maxwell contended, "the South's champion miscengenationist—'White Master above'—[had] fingered his black sons for his own sins and chastised them in Scottsboro."[76] Hughes's point was that the blame in Scottsboro did not fall on the eight young men accused of rape, nor on their white women accusers, but on a history of sexual violence enacted by white southern men on black women that produced unwanted "bastard" sons.

Since Wagner was "at bottom a religious man," as Robert Bone claimed, Wagner's own religious convictions could have played a role in his assessments of Hughes's political poems of a religious nature. He not only belittled their quality as poetry, as subsequent literary critiques would do, he also contended that there was nothing religious about them. "Christ in Alabama," for example, had "despite appearances no religious content." The poem was "shocking rather than profound" and was "above all an indictment of the South."[77] Hughes's poetry from this era was a result of Hughes's "rebellious gestures" born from his "crises of conscience." The poems could not be trusted as products of Hughes's engagement with religion and religious communities because he had "rejected the faith as absurd, ineffective, and possibly even harmful."[78] Seemingly allowing his perspective on Hughes's political poems of a religious nature to shape his views on all the religious poems, Wagner saw more humor, satire, and irony than he saw religion in the religious writing of Harlem's bard. Wagner considered the many Christmas poems "facile."[79] The poem "Heaven" he deemed a "childish" production. And although he praised the poems from *Fine Clothes to the Jew*, calling them "the best poems written by Hughes in this manner," Wagner did not see them as particularly theological, despite the fact that they were evocative of black church culture and replete with the theological language and concepts intrinsic to that culture. In such poems as "Angels Wings," "Moan," "Fire," and "Feet o' Jesus," he contended, one finds elements of insincere self-accusation rather than true belief or remorse on the part of the subjects. "This self-contempt should not be confused with the pure act of Christian humility, nor even with the avowal made in the confession of one's sins, for the individual, instead of simply admitting his faults, derives a kind of morbid pleasure from deliberately badmouthing himself." In Wagner's view, the best that these poems could offer, and Hughes's great contribution, was the way they revealed "the essentially emotional character of traditional Negro religion."[80]

Hughes's estimation that Wagner's interpretation of his religious poems was "a bit off track" was both correct and generous. In many ways, despite his thoroughness, Wagner demonstrated a fundamental misunderstanding of Hughes's religious poetry and of religion. He rightly placed the work in the context of Hughes's affinity for African American folk culture, as had Dodat. But his unwillingness to see the religious poetry as religious overshadowed his analysis and perhaps, inadvertently, authenticated the most conventional understandings of the Christian faith. The poems were "fleeting and transitory," he maintained, because they did not stem from Hughes's own experiences or his reflections on religion in any significant and theologically informed way. In Wagner's view, following "the paths of the spirit" meant following the paths of commonly espoused Christian theological frameworks like the New Negro "spiritualists" had done. He acknowledged, for example, that Countee Cullen had once been a self-professed pagan and argued that his paganism was "devoid of positive content" since it was essentially a "withdrawal from God." But once he "encounter[ed] Christ" his life and his poetry evinced one who "thirsts for the Christian ideal of perfection and self-transcendence." And even during his pagan years, some of the poems in *Color* had brought together "the elements of an authentic Christian spirituality."[81] Although he depicted Claude McKay as a religious nonconformist, Wagner considered his turn from paganism to Catholicism a type of spiritual growth. "His religious poetry is the expression of an inner growth," he argued, "and his discovery of God the result of his individual search for the truth." They were "Christians," in other words, and Hughes was not.[82]

Wagner's analysis of Hughes's poetry was both a product and a producer of the idea of Hughes's antireligiosity. He was not the first scholar to consider Hughes antireligious, but Wagner has been even more influential than Benjamin Mays on this point while missing all of Mays's important nuances. Following Wagner's work, most scholarship on Hughes has accepted the notion of his antireligiosity, largely because of the poetry and leftist activities of the 1930s. His political radicalism during that period has been accepted as a countervailing force to religion although Hughes himself did not view it that way. It has also been read back onto his life and art in the 1920s and forward to the 1940s through 1960s without regard to change over time, demonstrated by general claims that his "politics were radical not conservative, his concerns were radical and political not philosophical or religious."[83]

The extensive collaborations with Jean Wagner and François Dodat demonstrate the degree to which Hughes was determined to show the prominence of religion in his work. While both studies fell short in their analysis of religion in Hughes's poetry, the inadvertent and perhaps un-intended consequence was to mark that primacy and to show shifts and changes in his thinking about religion over the course of his career. As the booklets he compiled for them should have shown them, his think-ing about religion had been anything but static over the years and most often reflected an interplay between his past experiences with religion and the present. As a consequence, the work of Wagner and Dodat also revealed Hughes's views on the role religion played in various sectors of modern society, as the story of "Goodbye Christ" will demonstrate further.

3

"Concerning 'Goodbye Christ'"

"Kindly advise how one may secure a copy of a poem of
yours, written 12 or 14 years ago, which ran something like
this; 'Goodbye Christ, hello Lenin, burn the churches and
hang the Bishops.'"
—J. B. Simmons Jr.

"Is this the Christianity intended for us, or shall we look for
another is the question on many minds."
—Reverend M. A. Talley

"Goodbye, Hughes. All hail to Christ!"
—Reverend Reverdy Ransom

On the afternoon of November 15, 1940, Langston Hughes was headed
toward the exquisite Vista del Arroyo Hotel in Pasadena to attend a
book-and-author luncheon in celebration of his recently published autobiography, *The Big Sea*. As the car got nearer to his destination, he heard
the strains of Irvin Berlin's recently revised "God Bless America." The
music was coming from a sound-truck parked directly across the street
from the hotel, displaying a banner with the phrase "100 percent American" written in gold lettering. A large crowd had gathered in front of the
hotel with picket signs emblazoned with Hughes's name, causing traffic
and general chaos. With the car in which he was being driven unable to
move forward, Hughes got out a few blocks away and walked, unnoticed,
through the crowd.[1] In the hotel lobby the manager and organizer of the
event, George Palmer Putnam, met him and explained that Evangelist
Aimee Semple McPherson had sent about a hundred of her followers to
protest Hughes's appearance. McPherson had recently denounced Hughes
from her Angelus Temple pulpit as a "radical and anti-Christ." As she
warned her congregation, "There are many devils among us, but the most

dangerous of all is the red devil. And now there comes among us a red devil *in black skin!*"[2] Heeding her call, McPherson's supporters had come to distribute flyers denouncing Hughes as a Communist and an atheist. Called to keep the situation under control, police arrested a local Four Square Gospel pastor for resisting an officer and another McPherson supporter for advertising without a license. Embarrassed by the ruckus, Hughes withdrew from the event before it began and headed back to Los Angeles.[3]

McPherson's anger had been simmering since Hughes unfavorably mentioned her in "Goodbye Christ," a poem he had written in 1932. She took it as a personal attack and had been on a mission to malign him and thwart his efforts for nearly a decade. "Goodbye Christ" is rarely included among Hughes's most notable poetry, such as "The Negro Speaks of Rivers," "The Weary Blues," and "I, Too, Sing America," but it had a profound, lasting, and at times pernicious impact on his life and career—more so than any of his other poems up to that point. Not long after it appeared in the pages of the *Negro Worker*, the German-based COMINTERN (Communist Third International) journal, Hughes's career and the reception of his work veered off in directions irreparably out of his control, and in some respects he never fully recovered. Within a few years of the poem's publication, recognizing its deleterious impact, Hughes attempted to distance himself from "Goodbye Christ" and wouldn't allow anyone to reprint it. His efforts, however, were all for naught, and as Arnold Rampersad contended, it was "a poem that would haunt him for the rest of his life."[4] The poem, which Hughes claimed he never intended for anyone to see, is perhaps the best example of his political poems of a religious nature, written during the 1930s, and it is the clearest expression of his turn to radical politics at that time. It also showcases his philosophical alignment with Communist causes and ideology, an aspect of the poem that generated a great deal of ire and angst from the likes of McPherson. In it, he took on capitalism, the American government, the press, the Christian church, Christian ministers, a sacred text, and a civic saint.

> Listen, Christ,
> You did alright in your day, I reckon—
> But that day's gone now.
> They ghosted you up a swell story, too,

Called it Bible—
But it's dead now,
The popes and the preachers've
Made too much money from it.
They've sold you to too many

Kings, generals, robbers, and killers—
Even to the Tzar and the Cossacks,
Even to Rockefeller's Church,
Even to THE SATURDAY EVENING POST.
You ain't no good no more.
They've pawned you
Till you've done wore out.

Goodbye,
Christ Jesus Lord God Jehova,
Beat it on away from here now.
Make way for a new guy with no religion at all—
A real guy named
Marx Communist Lenin Peasant Stalin Worker ME—

I said, ME!
Go ahead on now,
You're getting in the way of things, Lord.
And please take Saint Ghandi with you when you go,
And Saint Pope Pius,
And Saint Aimee McPherson,
And big black Saint Becton
Of the Consecrated Dime.
And step on the gas, Christ!
Move!

Don't be so slow about movin'!
The world is mine from now on—
And nobody's gonna sell ME
To a king, or a general,
Or a millionaire.[5]

It was the poem's "dismissal" of Christ, however, that many took to be as un-American as it was anti-Christian, and it generated the most ire, angst, and controversy. This bidding Christ "goodbye" was, far above anything Hughes wrote during that period, the most responsible for subsequent contentions of him as Communist and atheist, as Benjamin Mays would demonstrate in his book *The Negro's God according to His Literature* in 1938 and Jean Wagner would further bolster in his *Black Poets of the United States* decades later.[6]

"Goodbye Christ" became a lightening rod and touchstone all across the United States, and in particular ways within African-American communities; it generated debates about Hughes, African American poetry, and American religion. In terms of 1930s Great Depression literature, however, the poem was not unique. Throughout the decade, leftist or "proletarian novelists" such as Jack Conroy (*The Disinherited*), Michael Gold (*Jews without Money*), and Henry Roth (*Call It Sleep*), wrote about the deleterious effects of capitalism, how the Depression disproportionately affected the poor, and about the lives and living conditions of the working class—often with a strident critique of the religious status quo. And as Morris Dickstein and Cary Nelson note, these themes also "drastically affected" the work of many poets, including William Carlos Williams, Wallace Stevens, and Edwin Rolfe, who published in leftist journals such as the *Anvil* (founded by Jack Conroy) and the *New Masses*. Examples of Hughes's more readily identifiable proletarian poetry include "Let America Be America Again," first published in *Esquire* magazine in 1936.[7]

> I am the poor white, fooled and pushed apart
> I am the Negro bearing slavery's scars
> I am the red man driven from the land
> I am the immigrant clutching the hope I seek
> And finding only the same old stupid plan
> Of dog eat dog, or mighty crush of the weak.

In "Park Bench," a lesser-known example, the poem's speaker proclaims, "I live on a park bench / You, Park Avenue / Hell of a distance between us two." In theme, literary structure, as well as social and political context, "Goodbye Christ" should take its place among his other proletarian poetry and the larger body of literature produced during the 1930s with its social commentary on the indifference of governmental powers and religious institutions, on poverty, and the juxtaposition of the "haves" and the "have nots."

It was not, however, a declaration of Hughes's commitment to Communism, nor was it a statement of his disbelief in God. More than anything it could say about Hughes himself, "Goodbye Christ" emerged as an expression of a culture of complaint and critique among fellow New Negro poets and an array of African American intellectuals and clergy. In the aftermath of the fundamentalist modernist controversy of the 1920s, the 1930s were a destabilizing time for religion in America as notions of American religious identity were being negotiated and contested. For African Americans, that negotiation and contestation took the form of surprisingly dire appraisals of the state of black churches—that there were too many of them and they were materialist and politically ineffectual. A small but vocal minority even asserted that Communism was more "Christ-like" than Christianity and made calls for a "new religion." The seemingly antireligious rhetoric of "Goodbye Christ," therefore, doubtlessly shocked many readers, but a significant body of black intellectuals and clergy, along with some white clergy and laypeople from across the nation, echoed the sentiments of the poem throughout the 1930s with ideas that were fueled, in part, by the devastating impact the Great Depression was having on the lives of the vast majority of black Americans. Indeed, in many ways, the implication of their ideas and the level of their rhetoric eclipsed those expressed by Hughes in "Goodbye Christ." This group critiqued and complained about the capitalist system, American churches' alliances with capitalism, and what they saw as an inherent insufficiency in religion itself. Hughes, perhaps unwittingly, became a crucial player in this culture of critique and complaint and his poem became its controversial and much-debated call to arms.

Make Way for a New Guy

Langston Hughes wrote "Goodbye Christ" while on a trip to Russia in 1932. Although he had written many of the poems in *The Weary Blues* when he was in Paris, his detractors immediately made much of the fact that "Goodbye Christ" had been composed during his stay in another country—and the Soviet Union at that. They were certain his audacity to "dismiss" Christ had come from his experience in the "godless" Communist state.

They were correct, to an extent. Although the ideas in "Goodbye Christ" had been percolating in Hughes since the start of the Scottsboro case and his book tour to the American South earlier in the year, the Soviet Union provided the psychological and emotional space to express them. The Scottsboro case was widely viewed as one of the worst travesties of justice in recent American history, and the racist treatment Hughes received and witnessed on the book tour compounded his disgust with the events involving the case.[8] The Communist context doubtlessly emboldened him to speak so disparagingly about key aspects of American society, namely, wealth and religion. It is also clear that the Soviet Union made an excellent comparative model. The poem in many ways is a study in contrasts, comparing two very different economic, religious, and social systems. But the Soviet Union is important as a context for another, more immediate reason. Hughes's experience there was an overwhelmingly positive one. Although the trip ultimately failed in its purpose, it allowed Hughes and his compatriots, for a few months, to have a life in Russia that they could only have imagined as black people in the United States. Hughes experienced a freedom from racial bias and a level of social acceptance unknown to him on American shores. The story of Hughes's trip to Russia, therefore, is worth recounting in some detail.

Plans for the trip were solidified in the spring of 1932 when Hughes had returned briefly to Harlem from his southern book tour. His collaborator on a musical, *Cock o' the World*, had sent him an urgent message telling him they were close to signing Paul Robeson—for whom the musical had been written—in the lead role. Hughes's presence at the meeting would likely seal the deal. After arriving in New York, however, Hughes was not only refused admittance into the building where Robeson's manager lived, he discovered that Robeson had gone back to London anyway. A few days after that fiasco, he came in contact with Louise Thompson, a longtime friend and a radical social activist who had been one of the prominent figures of the Harlem Renaissance and a founder of the Harlem chapter of the Friends of the Soviet Union. Hughes had learned that she was organizing a trip to the Soviet Union to make a film about black relations in America. Soviet authorities had reached out to James W. Ford, African American candidate for the vice-presidency on the Communist ticket, to help them find African Americans who could come to Russia to assist them in making the film.[9] Ford approached Thompson, who immediately set out to find willing participants. She convinced Hughes that his participation in the project would lend it the prestige needed to assist in the recruitment of others. During a brief stop in Harlem, he had agreed to be on the sponsoring committee and reaffirmed his commitment to going to Russia with the group.

Hughes went back on tour, ending it out west in Los Angles. Exhausted after the months-long ordeal, he set out for New York, arriving just hours before the SS *Europa* was to depart. It was doubtful they would have left without him, important as he was to the trip, and also because he had telegrammed Louise Thompson from Arizona, charging her to "hold that boat 'cause it's an ark to me."[10]

Astutely aware of Russia's renown as the "motherland of radical socialism," the trip seemingly filled Hughes with a sense of wonder and excitement. At age thirty he had already traveled extensively throughout Europe and Africa, but this trip was on an entirely different scale. In Russia he would witness firsthand the system that had seemingly eradicated social distinctions and racism. He could hardly contain his joy en route to Germany, where he and the rest of the group of twenty-two were to dock first. He spent most of his time prancing around the ship in his favorite outfit—grey flannel pants and a sailor's jersey—and studying German, a little of which he had picked up from Frau Shultz, his father's housekeeper in Mexico.

The rest of the group, which included Mildred Jones, Constance White, Katherine Jenkins, Allen McKinzie, Wayland Rudd, Henry Moon, Sylvia Garner, and Dorothy West, seemed equally happy to be going to Russia, but they made an odd bunch. They had been commissioned to make a movie but only two members of the group, Sylvia Garner and Wayland Rudd, had any acting experience. (Rudd would later be dubbed "Moscow Matinee Idol.")[11] The rest were professors, journalists, social workers, and writers. And not everyone shared the radical values of the core group. What they had in common was a near unbridled excitement about Russia, and the first few days upon arrival in Germany and Russia would exceed their wildest expectations.

Figure 3.1. Hughes and the group headed to Moscow on the SS *Europa* to make the film *Black and White* in 1932. In addition to Hughes, the group included Louise Thompson, Dorothy West, Mildred Jones, Sylvia Garner, Allen McKinzie, Wayland Rudd, Henry Moon, Constance White, Katherine Jenkins, Matthew Crawford, Juanita Lewis, Thurston Lewis, Ted Poston, Mollie Lewis, Laurence Alberga, Loren Miller, Leonard Hill, and Homer Smith. (Photo courtesy of the Beinecke Library.)

The group was treated like celebrity royals from the moment they disembarked in Bremerhaven, Germany on June 22. A representative from the Meschrabpom Film Company, which was to make the movie, welcomed them before they boarded a train to Berlin. In Berlin they were introduced to members of the Workers International Relief Organization, the film's parent body. From there the group boarded a Swedish vessel to Helsinki and then an overnight train bound for Russia. The next morning a banner that read "Workers of the World Unite" greeted them. A brass band played for them. At the Grand Hotel where they stayed they dined on "caviar, roast chicken, fresh vegetables, coffee, and ice cream." Dorothy West remembered that the waitstaff greeted the group "with such heartwarming bows." They toured the grand buildings and museums with crowds parting for them as they made their way, when they weren't being chauffeured around in luxury automobiles. They were even invited to give special appearances, convinced as they were that "all blacks can sing and dance." At one such appearance, Louise Thompson, Sylvia Garner, and Constance White sang Negro spirituals. Loren Miller gave a talk on Negro literature. Hughes read his poems. This unlikely group of African American moviemakers, immersed in, as Hughes recalled, "the fun and wonder of a foreign land," was having the time of their lives. Years later in an interview for the New York Center for Visual History, Thompson concurred with Hughes's assessment. "We were just a group of young people out on a wild adventure," she said. And Hughes, she contended, was particularly taken with the country. "Langston was received in Russia as he should have been—should be received anywhere in the world. . . . In the Soviet Union he was accorded, not only by the film company, Meschrabpom Films, but by the people of the Soviet Union, with tremendous respect."[12]

The only real problems stemmed from the very purpose for which they had made the trip, the movie itself. Entitled *Black and White* in honor of a poem by Vladimir Mayakovsky, the leading poet of the Russian Revolution, the movie presented difficulties for Hughes and the group from the very beginning.[13] The first problem was the most basic. The producer chosen for the film, Karl Junghans, was German and spoke neither Russian nor English. He needed a translator to speak to the group, which made communication extremely difficult. The more daunting problem concerned the script. First, it had not been written and was, therefore, unavailable. Waiting for it, most of the group passed the hours in local bars, with some of the men chasing Russian women, who had shown a great interest in them. Second, when the script finally did arrive, it became clear that the Russian writer had greatly misunderstood the dynamics of race in America. Hughes and the group had gotten some sense of this when on a number of occasions Moscovites had asked them if *all* of the group were in fact Negroes. The great disparity in skin tone—some of the cast "looked more white than black"—confused them.[14] Russians, as it turned out, knew very little about black people. They had theoretically identified with the plight of American blacks, but knew nothing about what it actually meant to be black. This frustrated the stated aim of the movie to "depict the actual conditions of Negroes in the United States."[15]

The script was a well-meaning yet naïve farce. It told the story of a band of African American steelworkers in Alabama who were engaged in a battle to resist the forces of racism and classism. When oppression of the group by racist southern whites intensified, they joined forces with well-to-do Alabama blacks, who used their own radio station to request help from sympathetic northern whites. Without delay, northern whites head south in defense of their southern black "brothers." It was a fantasy world where intraracial class tension did not exist and interracial cooperation trumped class loyalties. The script had more in common with the optimistic "collective effort" that characterized Russian revolutionary cinema, as well as the 1930s collectivism generated by the Great Depression, but it bore no resemblance to the realities of race in America. "At first I was astonished at what I read," Hughes later recalled. "Then I laughed until I cried. And I wasn't crying really because the script was in places so mistaken and so funny. I was crying because the writer meant well, but knew so little about his subject and the result was a pathetic hodgepodge of good intentions and faulty facts."[16]

In a sense the script for *Black and White* indicated that Russians had misjudged just how dire American race relations really were. They understood that black Americans faced much discrimination and were marginalized in American society. They also understood the degree to which blacks were considered second-class citizens with regard to the political process. What they did not understand were the social ramifications of all this and its effect on the social interactions between black and white Americans. It was *because* blacks were largely viewed as second-class citizens that certain social arrangements and political alliances were difficult, if not impossible. As Arnold Rampersad concludes, the script was "ideologically correct," it was just not plausible. Louise Thompson simply remembered it as "impossible."[17] As the most accomplished writer in the group, Hughes was called upon to rewrite the script but he refused, citing his lack of knowledge about steel mills. After a few more weeks of script problems and filming delays, the film company abruptly and without explanation cancelled the project.

Although Communism gained in popularity among some blacks in the United States during the 1930s, due in part to Soviet Russia's efforts to recruit blacks into an international revolutionary movement, the cancellation of *Black and White* confirmed the suspicions of naysayers.[18]

Some among the intelligentsia and friends of the group had expressed doubts about the project, as well as Russia's motives even before they left. Carl Van Vechten had told Hughes that he thought the movie idea was ill advised and destined for failure. Word of the cancellation spread quickly and the response from the African American community was immediate. Despite the inroads Communism had made among blacks, many suspected that there were inherent racist impulses within Russian society and that "salvation" for blacks was not likely to be found there. For those who had been monitoring the progress of the film project, its cancellation served to prove this point. An editorial published in the *Pittsburgh Courier*, entitled "Something Rotten in U.S.S.R.," typified the response from those who maintained this view.

> Misguided black folk who have for several years been worshipping the Russian Communists and lauding their absence of race prejudice will naturally be surprised to learn these pure and undefiled Bolshevists have succumbed to race prejudice and abandoned the filming of a moving picture intended to depict the exploitation of blacks by whites in America.... The Russian Communists, like the dated capitalists they condemn, are following the lines of the least resistance. They are looking out for their interest first, and to them 150,000,000 Russians are more important than 12,000,000 Afra-Americans. Some day American Negroes are going to learn that if they are to be saved they must do it themselves, and not depend on others to do it for them. History should have taught them ere this that salvation, like charity, begins at home.[19]

In reality, the issues were, in fact, more economic and political than racial. The Soviet Union was the world's newest republic and desperately in need of international recognition. It coveted recognition from the United States especially, and all the political and financial rewards that were certain to follow. When it became clear that a movie showcasing the racial disparities in the United States would be damaging to those efforts, the Soviet authorities shut it down. After a brief five-day trip to Tashkent in Soviet Central Asia sponsored by the "theatrical sections of the Soviet Trade Unions," most of the group of twenty-two would-be African American movie makers packed their bags and made for home.[20] Louise Thompson was the first to leave.

Langston Hughes, however, did not leave. He made plans to go deeper into the USSR to observe for himself the great social transformation that had happened in Uzbekistan. Before the Russian Revolution, the plight of dark-skinned Uzbeks had been comparable to American blacks. They were discriminated against because of their color and viewed as second-class citizens. After the revolution, however, they were elevated in social status, viewed on a par with other Soviet citizens. Some had even begun intermarrying with white Russians.[21] The cancellation of *Black and White* had been just as much a disappointment to Hughes as it had been to the rest of the group, but it by no means soured him on Russian society. For him, the "Motherland" was still the promised land, in stark contrast to the United States. His experience there had been delightful. No Jim Crow. No "mob rule." No color prejudice. For several weeks he moved freely throughout Russian society, treated more like a first-class citizen than the second-class citizen he was back home. He was clearly enamored.

Before Hughes departed on his grand adventure into the far reaches of the Soviet Union, however, he wrote "Goodbye Christ," just after completing another poem, "Good Morning Revolution." That poem was most certainly inspired by Carl Sandburg's 1928 volume, "Good Morning, America" and Hughes's recollection of the banner he saw when he first arrived in Moscow. It was a clear statement regarding his overwhelmingly positive experience in Russia. "Good-morning, Revolution / You're the best friend I ever had / We gonna pal around together from now on." "Good Morning Revolution" and "Goodbye Christ" were in a sense companion pieces. Indeed, at least one version of "Goodbye Christ" contained the alternate ending: "Goodbye Christ, Good Morning Revolution!"[22] While the first poem bids hello to a new system of government and a new way of life, the second one bids goodbye to an old way of life sanctioned by American religion and American churches. In both poems, Hughes was intent on exposing the differences between Russia and the United States. The contrast is even heard in the tone of the two poems. "Good Morning Revolution" is welcoming, open, and light, while "Goodbye Christ" voices disappointment, disillusionment, and possibly anger. Together they summarized his thinking about the USSR and the United States.

If *Black and White* had been successfully filmed, it is possible that neither poem would have been written. And although Hughes never explained his reasons, he always had made it clear that he had never planned to publish the poem or share it with anyone. However, Otto Huiswood, a "light mulatto" and well-known black Communist from Dutch Guiana, somehow obtained the poem and sent it to the *Negro Worker*, where it appeared in the journal's November–December 1932 issue.[23] By that time, Hughes was off on his journey to Soviet Central Asia, unaware of the gathering storm.

Goodbye, Hughes

The storm hit with great force. Just weeks after it was published in the *Negro Worker*, "Goodbye Christ" appeared in the Baltimore *Afro-American* in January 1933, which introduced it for the first time to a wider African American audience. The response was immediate and explosive, generating heated exchanges in all sectors of the black community. A true touchstone, the poem was debated in schools, social clubs, places of employment, and churches. There had never been a literary work by an African American that had proven to be so controversial *among* African Americans.

Another African American newspaper, the *Pittsburgh Courier*, did not reprint "Goodbye Christ" in its entirety until March 1933. But the debate in its pages began some time before that, and over the course of several months editorials appeared espousing pro and con views from all across the country. The two principal editorialists who most represented this divide were a pastor from Atlanta and an English professor from a historic black college in Marshall, Texas.

Reverend J. Raymond Henderson of the Wheat Street Baptist Church and Melvin B. Tolson of Wiley College began a series of responses to each other about the poem beginning in January 1933. Their exchanges set the tone for the discussion, which by the end of the summer included various voices from around the country. Clearly as annoyed at Hughes for writing the poem as at the poem itself, Henderson began his first editorial with a veiled personal attack. It was "ignorant or stupid" for anyone to rank Christ among the likes of Aimee Semple McPherson, George Becton, and Gandhi. "Any man who has no more judgment and discrimination than to link these names is surely to be pitied." As for the poem, it was "not really poetry" by any standard of measure. "Goodbye Christ" was simply an "idea" conceived by Hughes which he attempted to pass off as poetry.

Henderson, one of Atlanta's most "outspoken" black ministers at the time, probably read reprints of "Goodbye Christ" in the black press, as most people did.[24] But he knew that Hughes was in Russia when he wrote the poem and that it first appeared in a leftist publication based in Germany. His first intimation, therefore, was that being in a foreign country and publishing in the foreign press gave Hughes the courage to dismiss Christ with a "careless wave of the hand, yet stern voice." The core of his editorial responded to what he believed to be the three prevailing ideas in the poem: Christ has had his day; the Bible is a fictitious story; and Christ is in the way (of social progress). The refutations of the second and third ideas were ordinary enough. The Bible is "the greatest fact of history," proven by its sales record. It is a longstanding best seller, outselling Shakespeare. Rather than Christ being *in* the way, Christ *is* the way. With the refutation of the first idea, however, Henderson was seemingly more thoughtful. Noting first that one should not expect a poet to know church history, he argued that although Christ was born in time, he is timeless. Every generation experiences its own spiritual awakening through a fresh discovery of the meaning of Christ. "The day of Christ, instead of being over," he continued, "has scarcely begun." Echoing what others would say from both sides of the debate, he concluded that Christ is really an "untried door," who has not been given a chance.[25]

Melvin B. Tolson responded to Henderson's theological refutation of "Goodbye Christ" from a standpoint that was sociological, pragmatic, political, and perhaps prophetic. First, he addressed the personal attacks. He claimed they demonstrated Henderson's lack of familiarity with Hughes. Tolson had made Hughes's acquaintance while completing a master's degree at Columbia University, studying the Harlem Renaissance. He was particularly troubled by the insinuation that Hughes wrote the poem to gain notoriety ("So few people read Langston Hughes," Henderson had claimed) and that he was not sincere. "Nobody who knows Langston Hughes intimately can doubt his sincerity. He has always stood for the man lowest down and has sought to show his essential fineness of soul to those who were too high up—by the accidents of fortune—to understand." For Tolson, Langston Hughes was "a Catholic, a rebel, and a proletarian in his personal life and in his poetry and criticism," a characterization he would expand in his master's thesis, "The Harlem Group of Negro Writers." As for Henderson's claim that "Goodbye Christ" was not really poetry, Tolson quipped, "certain men of the cloth have a way of becoming self-styled judges on everything." A poet in his own right, Tolson has been considered the first true "modernist African American poet" and "the last of the major poets" of the Harlem Renaissance.[26]

With the personal sparring over, Tolson launched into his reasons for supporting "Goodbye Christ." The poem was a "challenge and a warning" to all American churches and all Christians, he began. It should not be laughed at, scorned, or "scandalized by the religionist." Those who did so were "illogical" and in peril. The poem spoke to the current "tragic modern conditions" as well as to the failings of the church to meet those conditions. It was an outgrowth of the church's disregard for the ills of society. "The world is in terrible condition today, and if Christianity does not do something to solve the problems of humanity, it will have hurled at it repeatedly such challenges as 'Goodbye Christ,'" he declared. The terrible social and economic conditions of the day and the church's lack of response prompted Hughes's seeming interest in the Soviet system of government. The Soviet system was, in fact, more Christlike than American churches, he argued, a point reiterated throughout the 1930s by a number of African American clergy. African Methodist Episcopal (AME) minister D. Ormonde Walker, for example, asserted in 1933 that Jesus was the founder of Communism. "Jesus gave communism to the world before Marx or Lenin, or Stalin," he insisted. In Tolson's view, "followers of Marx" carried out the teachings of Jesus with tenacity and verve. American Christians, on the other hand, involved themselves in self-serving trivialities. "The leaders of Christianity live in comfortable homes and ride around in big cars and collect the pennies from washerwomen." He continued, "Magnificent edifices are erected while people go hungry and shelterless. Preachers uphold or see not the ravages of 'big business.'"[27]

For Tolson, the issue was not so much what the poem said or did not say about Christ. Indeed, he asserted that he was not interested in "what Mr. Hughes thinks of Christ." He was more interested in "the *reason* for

the poem than the poem." And the reason for the poem was the piti-
ful state of affairs in 1930s American society. He ended his response to
Henderson by calling for radical change among American churches. The
time was past for a church unconcerned with the things of the world.
"Christianity must come down from the pulpit and solve the problems
of the day. Men will no longer listen to the echo of that beautiful, but
illogical, spiritual of long ago: 'You may have the world, give me Jesus.'"
Jesus would never sing a song like that, Tolson concluded. Jesus was
a "radical" and a "Socialist" whose "guns were turned on Big Business
and religionists" and who heralded a "new economic, social, and political power." This was apparently all too much for Henderson, who
responded to Tolson by simply restating his earlier points and calling
for an end to the debate.[28]

The debate about "Goodbye Christ," however, did not end. Though
the exchange between Henderson and Tolson ceased in the pages of the
Pittsburgh Courier, in the ensuing months the debate actually gained
momentum, prompting even deeper discussions about the state and the
fate of American religion. Henderson and Tolson had clearly framed the
discussion, leaving many editorialists either to react to or expound upon
points the two men had made. J. Edward Hines from Louisiana, an "old
personal friend" of Tolson, was the first. Hines tried to understand "just
what Mr. Hughes really means by 'Goodbye Christ.'" He asked whether
these were Hughes's personal views. Can the "guy with no religion at
all" really improve society? To this last question Hines provided his own
answer. Noting that Communism supports equality and citizenship
rights for all and was opposed to lynching and supportive of the lower
class against capitalism, he asserted, "no depressed man would abhor
that platform of the 'guy with no religion.'" Indeed, the true teachings
of Jesus and Communism share much in common. Both disapprove of
race discrimination. Both disapprove of "trials like the Scottsboro trial
and a denial of the ballot to Negroes." So for Hines, the challenge was
not to Christianity in general, but to the "living tombs" of the American
church. The appropriate title of a poem for Hughes to write, he proclaimed, would be "Comeback, Christ."[29]

The next week, James Oliver Slade, a professor of social science at
Morris Brown College, weighed in. Slade wanted his readers to understand, however, that he was also a Christian. He simply did not share the

opinion of those "hasty, unthinking and narrow-minded herd of people who profess Christian faith" by condemning the poem. "Goodbye
Christ" may be "sacrilegious," but it was not entirely wrong, and it was
a fair indictment of the church. Like Hines, Slade found Communism
to be more Christian than American churches. Communism's "altruistic
platform" showed more compassion than the American churches and
the American political system, and if Communism was "Christ-like,"
then Hughes was "not so unchristian after all." Edward Taylor followed
Slade's editorial with an impassioned one of his own in which he argued
that the American church had strayed so far from the teachings of Jesus
that many people such as Hughes were merely asking, "is it the true
religion or shall we look for another?" The religion that Jesus taught
was not circumscribed by race, creed, nation, or theological dogmatism.
It was "universal in its application and all-inclusive in its scope." For
Taylor, this was the religion to which Christians must return and the
"great furor" roused among those who vilified Hughes and his poem
only pointed to the fact that "somewhere something is wrong with the
present day concept of religion."[30]

When the *Pittsburgh Courier* finally reprinted "Goodbye Christ" in
its entirety—without comment and adding the last line "go ahead on
now"—many African American ministers reacted in anger.[31] The reactions from two black ministers in particular—Bishop Reverdy Ransom
and Reverend D. DeWitt Turpeau—demonstrated that the poem had
clearly touched a nerve and that not everyone participated in or thought
favorably of the culture of critique and complaint. Both ministers responded to "Goodbye Christ" with poems of their own that attempted
to "dismiss" Hughes for his irreverence. The reaction from Reverdy
Ransom in particular further indicated, as it had with Henderson, that
the furor over the poem did not emanate exclusively from politically
and religiously conservative circles. A bishop in the African Methodist
Episcopal Church, Ransom had long championed liberal causes in his
denomination and was among the first African American ministers to
embrace the Social Gospel.[32] He had also been a longtime supporter
of the New Negro movement and the New Negro writers in particular,
celebrating them as God-ordained arbiters of black culture in a poem he
wrote in 1923, "The New Negro."[33] He entitled the following poem "All
Hail to Christ: A la Langston Hughes."

Listen Hughes,
You are not sacrilegious—
Just silly.
You are no more profane
Than the flight of a bat
In the twilight,
Or the screech of an owl,
In the Gothic towers of a temple.
This futility great Shakespeare saw,
In the dog that bays the moon.
Stop on the brimstone, Hughes.
Go away from that mike,
And get the hell off the air.
Stop your kidding,
"Don't be so slow about moving;
Move!"
Not a religion, but a life
Of Peace and Goodwill,
Would the Nazarene give to the Ages,
While your Saints, Lenin and Stalin,
Spread violence, terror and blood.
So these are the guys,
Who are going to take charge
Of our social salvation,
Led on by a prophet like you.
Alas! And Alac!
Light breaks from the Cross
Of the Prince of Peace
While a growing world-brotherhood
Is slowly building
A Temple of Justice and Peace
According to the Plan
Of the Master–
Goodbye, Hughes.
All hail to Christ![34]

Ransom wrote the poem using the same free verse style, similar linguistic frames, and terminologies as "Goodbye Christ," as if to mock
Hughes. The central ideas were that Hughes lacked the necessary theological depth for his poem to even merit being considered "sacrilegious"
and that as literature it did not rise to the level of the "great Shakespeare."
More important, the political systems of the Communist "Saints" Lenin
and Stalin were not salvific, but were, rather, bloody and tyrannical.
Justice, peace, and brotherhood could only come from Christ, "the
Master."[35]

The poem by D. DeWitt Turpeau Jr., "Father Forgive," revealed more
compassion for Hughes than Ransom's poem. But it, too, was dismissive,
contrasting Hughes's insignificance with the significance of Christ, who
"came down through the ages." Turpeau seemed similarly perturbed
at Hughes and bothered by the implications of "Goodbye Christ." "Father Forgive" was his prayer of redemption for one he considered both
"childish" and a "self-styled philosophic crank."

> Forgive, O Christ, the poet of unlimited promise,
> For his blasphemous words like the thief on the cross,
> Open his eyes to the inevitable ending
> Crowned with disappointment, regret and remorse.
> And for this misinformed and erring young pilgrim
> May I offer a prayer, not as a priest or a preacher,
> That soon he may have a prodigal's awakening,
> And know Thee, O Lord, as his personal redeemer."[36]

Forgiveness had also been the theme of another African American
minister's poetic response to Hughes weeks earlier. Bishop E. E.
Bennett wrote "Forgive Him Christ" as a prayer for the "foolish Bard"
and his "sacrilegious" poem. He wrote as if fearful for Hughes's soul
for having the audacity to "mock his God." "How can he bid Thee
"Go"? / Refuse Thine aid, spurn truth / Reject the anguish, pain and
dreadful woe." Like Ransom and Turpeau, Bennett was intent on contrasting the supremacy of Christ to the "dust" of Langston Hughes, but
for him, "Goodbye Christ" seemed more a simple matter of a sinner
in need of redemption.

Forgive!
"Christ Jesus, Lord God, Jehovah,"
Forgive and stay Thy Rod.
Pardon, Lord, the blasphemy, sacrilege,
Of this blind, railing, son of earth
Who dares deny Thee God.
Forgive him, Christ!
'Tis lack of faith in Thee,
Injustice, wrongs done his and him
By some who own Thy name,
Which prompts his sin.[37]

Unlike Henderson, none of these ministers attempted to critically engage the poem, either to judge its value as poetry or the quality of its ideas. They seemingly operated from the standpoint that the poem was sacrilegious and its ideas, therefore, meritless. In the end, their responses seemed more akin to panic among marketing executives whose "product" had been defamed. Seen as a challenge and warning, Hughes's poem threatened the relevance not only of these ministers, but also of American Christianity.

Wore Out and in the Way

The Scottsboro case and the Great Depression bolstered a culture of complaint and critique among another set of American ministers, whose sermons and social commentary provided a striking contrast to the likes of Henderson, Ransom, Bennett, and Turpeau. These clerics expressed themselves as politically, theologically, and literarily in synch with Hughes and offered dire assessments of American religion that mirrored and at times exceeded Hughes's in "Goodbye Christ." Their complaints and critiques not only further demonstrated the extent of the poem's polarizing effect, but also revealed what was for them primarily at stake in the debate, which was the very relevance of the American church. Indeed, in their view, the failure of the church to meet the crises of the Scottsboro case and the Depression served as one of culture's key tenets. It was also one of the primary precipitators of the calls for a "new religion." The Scottsboro case seemed to be an example of how the church was "loosing ground" or had "missed an opportunity," as asserted by a Philadelphia divine who delivered the keynote address before the Baptist Seminar held in Washington, DC in July 1933. Reverend W. H. R. Powell's address argued that "thoughtful" people were losing confidence in the black Baptist church principally because of social inaction. "We are challenged to definite action by the principles involved in the far-famed Scottsboro case. As a denomination, we cannot hope to maintain the confidence and sympathies of our people, especially the young and thoughtful, as long as we refuse to be touched by these circumstances which so seriously affect us." The major problem with black Baptists, according to Powell, was a lack of vision and what he termed "progressive paralysis." Radicalism, industrialism, and the proper distribution of wealth were the issues of the day, yet black Baptists had nothing to say about them.[38]

Powell used similarly strong language to expound upon these and other points during his keynote address at a Baptist convocation in Philadelphia a few months later. Powell, a fiery and busy minister who simultaneously held a pastorate in Philadelphia while heading a Virginia seminary in Lynchburg, argued that the black Baptist church was losing its historic influence in the black community. While it had a remarkable history, had done great work in the past and retained tremendous potential, it had become unhealthy and stagnate. Certain leaders had become "pus pockets of denominational weakness," Powell contended, and constituted "centers of evil," spreading their pernicious influence throughout the entire black Baptist world, leaving it "diseased and paralyzed." Comparing the present state of the black Baptist church to the Babylonian captivity, Powell argued that the core problem was an idolatrous hold on an outdated, antimodern theology, ill-fitted for the present day. Black Baptists were faced with a choice: "stand aside and make room for a new leadership outside of and contrary to the church," or create a new leadership and a "new faith" responsive to the needs of the day.[39]

For Powell, "a new social order" was the pressing need for black Baptists. The social injustices that existed around the world—which black Baptists seemed woefully unaware of—were what had prompted the Russian Revolution in 1917, upheavals in Spain and Italy, as well as the rise of the Nazi movement in Germany. In order to face the demands of the "modern world," he recommended a "complete revision" of black Baptist creeds and articles of faith. "The principles of Jesus Christ are subject to reinterpretation at the crossroads of every crisis, when it becomes evident that old interpretations are outgrown," he contended. [40]

Speaking at the same Baptist convocation, Reverend M. A. Talley opened his address with a question he believed was on the minds of many black Americans: "Is this the Christianity intended for us, or shall we look for another?" In answer to the question—which Edward Taylor had attributed to Langston Hughes earlier in the year—Talley, a pastor of Mt. Zion Church in Indianapolis, concluded that blacks had adopted a form of Christianity from "Anglo-Saxons" that had been "de-Christianized" and no longer reflected the values of Jesus. The Christian religion had become corrupted and was merely "a wolf in sheep's clothing." No longer the "Bride of Christ," it was the "Harlot of the Nations." There was a point at which blacks had "marvelously profited" from Christianity, he asserted, but since the time of slavery and emancipation blacks began to absorb more of the "distorted" religion of whites and have since "not only lost Christ, but we have lost his power and personal life in our religion." Blacks needed to repudiate that which was handed down to them and "make a new religion."[41]

Dr. L. H. King, pastor of St. Mark's Methodist Episcopal Church in New York had an even broader message. Rather than implicating his or another denomination for current social ills, he asserted that religion itself was the problem. Speaking at a Methodist Episcopal Clergyman's conference, King argued that religion was insufficient for the "present age" and must undergo radical change if there was to be any hope for relevance in the modern world. The economic interests of the powerful, who agitated class and racial division, controlled religion in America. Like many who launched these complaints, King called for a new church free of the "myths" of Christianity: "The new church must be more than theological teaching. It must imbibe more of the immanence of God in its relations to humans. It must save the lives of men rather than seek after that elusive thing called the soul. Not one out of ten thousand persons believes in a hell, and a new religion that will bring the richest, fullest and freest experience in living will be the only thing that will meet the demand caused by the revolution in the hearts of the people against the old order."[42] Bishop E. D. W. Jones, AME Zion Bishop of South Carolina, took a similar view contending that African Americans needed a new religion of "revised beliefs." This new church and new religion should be devoid of the supernatural (the Christian myths) but be anchored in reason and experience. "We should revise entirely our religious beliefs and practices and give to our people the birth of a new church and a new religion," he told his audience. "Neither should be based upon denominational creeds, rituals and ecclesiastical ceremonies, but upon experience, reason, hope, truth and the ultimate triumph of the right." While not inciting a full abandonment of the Christian faith, King and Jones called for a new interpretation of the life and teachings of Christ.[43]

Throughout the early 1930s, these calls for a "new religion" continued from all sectors of the American Christian church. Many, like R. W. Tryne, called for the wholesale "demythologizing" of the Christian tradition. Tryne's 1933 "sermonette" insisted that science had disproved the most basic tenets of Christianity, including the fall of humanity and the infallibility of Scripture. Others, such as former Howard University president Wilbur Patterson Thirkield, merely sought changes among black preachers, reckoning that too much attention had been given to dogmatic theology and not enough to the "practical ways of life." In all, these calls for a "new religion" showed that many religious thinkers and thinkers about religion considered the church to be antimodern. The real need was for a new church with modern forms based on modern ideas. None other than W. E. B. DuBois suggested this publicly—and in a church. At the December 1932 Young People's Forum at Bethel AME Church in Baltimore, he shocked the listening audience by declaring that he did not attend church because preachers usually had "nothing to say." And when asked, "Do you believe that the present system of religion should be discarded and a new religion based on science substituted?," he simply responded, "yes."[44]

The Soviet Union indeed provided the most immediate context in which to understand "Goodbye Christ" since Hughes wrote it there and was doubtlessly influenced by his Russian experiences. The culture of complaint and critique that had developed among a few New Negro poets, black intellectuals, and some African American ministers and laypeople during the early 1930s, however, is just as significant. Hughes's daring to bid "goodbye" to Christ happened at a time when others from around the country were working toward a radical reconfiguration of the Christian tradition. Despite the furor among those like Henderson, Ransom, Bennett, and Turpeau, who dismissed Hughes and the poem as "sacrilegious," the poem was integral to an ongoing discussion that questioned the efficacy of black churches and the relevance of American religion. And at least from the standpoint of the African American church, the publication of *The Negro Church* in 1933 by Benjamin Mays and Joseph Nicholson tended to substantiate those claims. Finding that black communities were "over churched," the two sociologists concluded, "except in rare instances it ('the black church') is static, non-progressive and fails to challenge the loyalty of many of the most critically minded Negroes."[45]

Popes, Preachers, and Money

Most people came to the conclusion that Langston Hughes was an "atheist" after the publication of "Goodbye Christ." They took the poem to be a declaration of his nonbelief in God and his rejection of Christianity in particular, what German theologian Rudolf Bultmann calls "conscious atheism . . . the categorical denial of the reality of God as . . . encountered in church dogmatics."[46] There is little question that the radical poems of a religious nature, of which "Goodbye Christ" was a part, grew from and reflected a time when Hughes was furthest removed from the institution of the church, the most critical of the Christian religion generally, and perhaps his most skeptical about the church, religion, and God. He had demonstrated a capacity for this level of skepticism and doubt the night of his failed conversion at age twelve when he proclaimed that he "didn't believe there was a Jesus anymore." Aside from this moment, however, there are no instances in Hughes's entire body of work that proclaim an outright disbelief in God, or a denial of God's existence. And "Goodbye Christ" does not qualify as such for a reason that many of his detractors missed. Hughes's apparent "dismissal" of Christ necessarily implied Christ's existence and presence. Those who used the poem as evidence of Hughes's atheism, therefore, either misread it or read into it for particular political purposes. In the same way that Hughes would declare that none of his writing was antireligious, he could have also proclaimed that not even the poem most responsible for his reputation as an atheist asserted an unqualified disbelief in God.

The detractors also underestimated the power and misunderstood the role of metaphor as a literary device. In literary terms, "Christ" in the poem can be understood as a metaphor for churches in America. James Oliver Slade was among the few who made this connection when he asked, "is it not likely that Langston Hughes, although knowing the real philosophy of Jesus Christ has conveniently used His name analogous with the church that is the exterior of Christ (the interior) now that He has passed from active human life in order to awaken us so-called Christians who have abused His institution, the church"?[47] "Christ" in the poem personified the American Christian church in the same way the "guy with no religion" served as a metaphor for the Soviet Union. "Goodbye Christ" compared one religious/political system with another. So the poem was not a statement of non-belief or a call to jettison God because it made no attempt to speak of God directly. It was a call to either reform the American church or to eradicate it.

For Hughes, American churches had become inextricably tied to capitalism, and that was one of the major points of the poem. Indeed, capitalism in his view had become the true religion of America. His use of the language of the market to depict religion in "Goodbye Christ" was meant to demonstrate the corrupting impact of capitalism on his notion of true religion. For this reason, the mention of Pope Pius XI remains baffling. Although he was from aristocratic Italian roots and would emphatically state the Catholic Church's philosophical opposition to Communism as intrinsically atheistic, Pius XI was staunchly anticapitalist and a champion of the poor and working classes, as well as the racially marginalized. Seemingly he was "an autocrat through and through," as John Julius Norwich has claimed, but his pontificate is generally viewed to have been humane and progressive.[48] The assessment of Gandhi was more mixed, and Hughes appeared to be of two minds about him, producing a later poem in which he hailed the power of the nationalist leader's "fasting."[49] By the time "Goodbye Christ" was written, Gandhi had already become internationally recognized for his fight for India's independence from the British Empire. He had renounced all material possessions allegedly to devote himself to the cause of the poor and the powerless around the world. Not everyone at the time viewed Gandhi's actions as entirely selfless, politically expedient, or economically viable, however, noting the ways it tended to overburden the very people he aimed to champion. As Indian independence activist and poet Sarojini Naidu famously quipped, "it costs a lot to keep Gandhi poor." Gandhi *became* the saintly self-sacrificing anticapitalist and anticolonialist freedom fighter that not everyone believed him to be during his lifetime.[50]

The two Americans mentioned in that group of four in "Goodbye Christ" were another matter. Dr. George W. Becton, also known as "big black Saint Becton," whom Hughes had met, personified the profiteering of capitalist religion. Becton had become famous for the "consecrated dime" program he instituted in which he expected the twenty thousand primarily poor members of his church to put aside a dime a day to be given over to him weekly upon his request in exchange for divine blessing. In what must have appeared to Hughes as a disturbing if unsurprising turn of events, Becton was shot at point blank range by mobsters in Philadelphia just months after "Goodbye Christ" appeared in the *Afro-American*.[51] "Saint Aimee McPherson" was little better than George Becton as far as Hughes was concerned. During the 1920s and 1930s, Aimee Semple McPherson rode a wave of popularity previously unknown to American ministers, with the possible exception of Billy Sunday. Her five-thousand-seat Angelus Temple in Los Angeles netted her millions of dollars annually, providing her a lavish lifestyle that belied her humble Salvation Army roots. Her church services, part of the Four Square Gospel Church, a denomination she founded, were known as much for their theatricality as anything else, and McPherson's Hollywood good looks and flare for the dramatic contributed to her celebrity. As her biographer Daniel Epstein wrote, "Her years on the tent-show circuit had taught her that a religious service is sacred drama, a species of nonfictional theater, pure and simple."[52] By the time her name appeared in "Goodbye Christ," McPherson's career had already been marked by charges of charlatanism, lawsuits, a mysterious disappearance (and an even more bizarre reappearance), two divorces, and a sex scandal. The protest she staged at the Vista del Arroyo Hotel in 1940 would not be the last time she publicly attacked Hughes for naming her in the poem. Indeed, McPherson harbored a particular animus for Hughes, and until her death in 1944 regularly denounced him from her Los Angeles pulpit. For his part, Hughes made her one of the primary targets in "Christians and Communists," most likely written for his weekly *Chicago Defender* column in 1943. In it, Hughes stated that while McPherson had declared him "an enemy of religion and democracy," she had shown no interest in the betterment of black people or in efforts to "extend to us democracy." For Hughes, she and Becton were among the worst examples of the Christian religion.

A few months after the Pasadena incident and perhaps sensing a genuine opportunity to clarify his motives for writing "Goodbye Christ," Hughes wrote an article published in the *Chicago Defender* entitled, "Let's Get It Straight." It was subtitled "Poet, a little confused about all the fuss made over a poem he wrote 10 years ago, does a little explaining for those just getting around to it." The article suggested that Hughes was genuinely befuddled by the flap and struck a tone that was defiant but explicatory. Intending to reveal his motivations and the context in which he wrote "Goodbye Christ," he explained that the shock value was his initial primary intent. He wrote the poem "with the intention in mind of shocking into being in religious people a consciousness of the admitted shortcomings of the church in regard to the condition of the poor and oppressed of the world, particularly the Negro people." He disagreed with the common assumption that the Russian context played a primary role in the writing of the poem. Although he wrote the poem while in Russia, he argued, it did not serve as the primary context or motivation for writing. The true context for "Goodbye Christ," rather, were the memories he carried from a trip through the American South just prior to leaving for Russia, the Scottsboro case, and the widespread discrimination he witnessed in other parts of the United States. His impassioned description of the trip and what he saw is near poetic and has all the hallmarks of Hughes's characteristic plainspoken style:

> Just previous to the writing of the poem, in 1931 I had made a tour through the heart of our American Southland. For the first time I saw peonage, million dollar high schools for white children and shacks for Negro children (both of whose parents work and pay taxes and are Americans). I saw vast areas in which Negro citizens were not permitted to vote. I saw the Scottsboro boys in prison in Alabama and colored citizens of the state afraid to utter a word in their defense.
>
> I crossed rivers by ferry where the Negro drivers of cars had to wait until all the white cars behind them had been accommodated before boarding the ferry even if it meant missing the boat. I motored as far

north as Seattle and back across America to New York through towns and cities where neither bed nor bard was to be had if you were colored, cafes, hotels, and tourist camps being closed to all non-whites. I saw the horrors of hunger and unemployment among my people in the segregated ghettos of our great cities. I saw lecture halls and public cultural institutions closed to them. I saw the Hollywood caricatures of what passes for Negroes on the screens that condition the attitudes of a nation. I visited state and religious colleges to which no Negroes were admitted. To me these things appeared unbelievable in a Christian country.

It was not that the Soviet Union played no part in the writing of the poem, however. Coming on the heels of his experience during his America tour, the trip to Russia provided a contrast between Soviet and American societies that seemed striking and noticeably clear. With regard to the construction of an egalitarian society, Marxist Russia had accomplished what Christian America had miserably failed to do. "There it seemed to me that Marxism had put into practical being many of the precepts which our own Christian America had not yet been able to bring into life, for in the Soviet Union, meager as the resources of the country were, white and black, Asiatic and European, Jew and Gentile stood alike as citizens on an equal footing protected from racial inequalities by the law." Hughes, as he put it, was "deeply impressed by these things."[53]

He was impressed because like most Americans in the 1940s, Hughes would have been well aware of depictions of Russia as atheistic and anti-religious. Yet, in this supposed godless country he and his cohorts had been received with a hero's welcome and the country functioned apparently without regard to racial, ethnic, or class differences. The contrast was glaring and one of the principal supports for the claim from some within the culture of complaint and critique that Communism was more "Christ-like." It was in the spirit of contrast that Hughes penned the poem. But in his explanation of the contrast Hughes also revealed the central irony of the poem—a word he would use again and again to describe it. It was not only Marxists who had bid Christ "goodbye," it was also Christians, those who had forsaken the most basic principles of their faith with regard to American blacks. "In the poem I contrasted what seemed to me the declared and forthright position of those who, on the religious side in America (in apparent actions toward my people) had said to Christ and the Christian principles, 'Goodbye, beat it on away from here now, you're done for.'" "I gave to such religionists," he further explained, "what seemed to me to be their own words merged with the words of the orthodox Marxist who declared he had no further use nor need for religion."[54]

In "Let's Get It Straight," Hughes also dealt with the poem's subjectivity. He was clear on one point: he was not the "I" in the poem. Those who read "Goodbye Christ" should no more see him as the subject as they would in his other poems, where he was clearly not the subject because of time, place, gender, or social location—the blues poems, for example. The "I" in the poem, rather, was a complicated amalgam of voices. In addition to the hypocritical Christian and the godless Marxist, the voice was that of "the newly liberated peasant of the state, collectives I had seen in Russia merged with those American Negro workers of the depression period who believed in the Soviet dream and the hope it held out for a solution of [sic] their racial and economic difficulties." What he did not, and perhaps could not, say, was that among the amalgam of voices was his own, for as he would strongly imply in "A Note on Poetry" for the *Free Lance* magazine in 1950 and plainly state to James Emanuel in 1961, he was to be found somewhere in all his poems and his stories. "Of course, I am in all of them," he wrote.[55]

What most clearly annoyed Hughes about the way in which people read "Goodbye Christ" had less to do with his subjectivity and more to do with their limited perspective on the entirety of his work. They often failed to view it in light of his other work and also considered him somehow immutable. He had written "many verses most sympathetic to the true Christian spirit" for which he had "great respect," but his detractors seemingly took no notice. He had even won the Harmon Award from the Federal Council of Churches for his novel *Not without Laughter*. Perhaps more importantly in his view, he had changed as a person and as a poet over the last ten years. His political views and approaches had mellowed. Stating that he had left the terrain of the "radical at 20" to become the "conservative at 40," he insisted that he could no longer write such a poem as "Goodbye Christ." Indeed, he harbored doubts about the political efficacy of poetry. The world was long past the time when a poem could shock people into consciousness. He stated, "I would not now use such a technique of approach since I feel that a mere poem is quite unable to compete in power to shock with the current horrors of war and oppression abroad in the greater part of the world." The war had proven that humanity was in a sad state, "both Marxists and Christians can be cruel." Changes in government, therefore, must be preceded by a change in the human heart. On that note, he ended "Let's Get It Straight" with what was effectively a prayer for civic and social salvation. "Would that Christ came back to save us all. We do not know how to save ourselves."[56]

Poet and Poem under Pressure

After the publication of "Let's Get it Straight" in January 1941, it became clear to Hughes, his publishers at the *Chicago Defender* and at Knopf, his lawyer, and many of his friends that "Goodbye Christ" was a problem he needed to address in a public way with a public statement that went beyond that essay. Since the publication of the poem in 1932 Hughes had received a "mountain of mail" regarding it, making it an ever-increasing and distracting factor in his career.[57] Aimee Semple McPherson had not ceased her attacks from the previous year and the *Saturday Evening Post* had printed an unauthorized spread of the poem in its Christmas issue—without commentary, which suggested it was a "new poem." The embarrassing episode in Pasadena was damaging enough, but Hughes's publisher at Knopf and his lawyer, in particular, felt that the unauthorized reprint in the *Post* "required a comeback and explanation."[58] So at the Hollow Hills farm of his friend Noel Sullivan in Monterey, California, and desperately sick with the flu, Hughes began writing a statement he called "Concerning 'Goodbye Christ.'" He would revise and edit the statement for the next twenty years.

Hughes disliked making "statements," but he was even more averse to controversy and it distressed him that a poem from his past required any response at all. Writing to several friends throughout the months of January and February 1941 he revealed just how disheartened he had become. To Matthew Crawford, an African American labor rights activist whom Hughes had met in California in 1932, he wrote: "Golly! How I hate all this controversy! Deluged with letters from everybody left, right, colored, and Christians." To Louise Thompson he despaired, "the New Year came down on my head like a ton of bricks!!!" because of the flu, a toothache, and "Aimee and the SATURDAY EVENING POST." He enclosed a copy of the statement in his letter to Thompson and requested that she get back to him with her reactions, conceding as he also did to Crawford that the situation required "some sort of statement." "I had intended, as usual with me in controversial matters, to simply say nothing," he further stated, "but . . . GBC ['Goodbye Christ'] . . . just won't down."[59] Thompson and Hughes had been friends since the late 1920s when she arrived in Harlem after a short teaching stint at Hampton Institute. They remained close friends through Hughes's tumultuous breakup with Charlotte Mason (for whom Thompson worked for a time), his dispute with Zora Neale Hurston over the authorship of "Mule Bone," her brief marriage to the gay writer and one-time Hughes collaborator, Wallace Thurman, and the failed movie-making expedition to the Soviet Union. She was convinced that Hughes was special and gravely misunderstood. To her, Hughes was a person of "many moods," and "the things that he felt deepest about he scarcely ever talked about." Their bond was a strong one, and it was clear why he would seek her advice about "Goodbye Christ."[60]

Shifting at times between apology and defense, the various versions of "Concerning 'Goodbye Christ'" expressed Hughes's view that the poem had been greatly misunderstood and wrongfully handled by his enemies. Over the years, the poem had been reprinted (even though Hughes had taken it out of circulation) by the likes of the KKK, the Minute Women of America, and Gerald L. K. Smith and his America First Party. Smith, "minister of hate," an ultra-nationalist and "nationally known Negro-hater," who was also an anti-Communist and anti-Jewish agitator, had turned the poem into a rallying cry against Hughes and anyone who supported him.[61] Smith was also prominently featured alongside McPherson in "Christians and Communists." While most of the statement was intended to address the contention that Hughes was a member of the Communist Party, it was just as adamant that he was not an atheist, issues that most of his detractors, including Smith and McPherson, had conflated. Indeed, later versions of the statement addressed accusations of irreligion in greater detail than accusations of his alleged membership in the Communist Party.

The first versions of "Concerning 'Goodbye Christ'" struck a defiant and politically charged tone, as had "Let's Get It Straight." Hughes characterized those who used the poem to stain his reputation as "the most anti-Negro, anti-Jewish, anti-Labor, and anti-Roosevelt groups in our country." They could "hardly be called Christians," he insisted, because their actions did not honor Christ. They made democracy and religion a reactionary "evil" that masked their hatred of blacks and their anti-Semitism. Conceding that he had once belonged to organizations that supported leftist causes—as did other high-profile Americans such as Ernest Hemingway, Dorothy Parker, and Vincent Sheen—Hughes concluded the statement by asserting his "freedom of speech" and his right to oppose his attackers. The poem was "no reflection on Christ" and was not intended to be antireligious, as they had claimed. It was, rather, "a poem against racketeering, profiteering, racial segregation and showmanship in religion which, at the time, I felt was undermining the foundations of the great and decent ideals for which Christ stood."[62]

Hughes tempered the defiant tone of the statement after Joseph McCarthy and the Permanent Subcommittee on Investigations (PSI) called him to give testimony before them in March 1953. The subcommittee had been established in 1948 to continue work done by a special committee chaired by Harry S. Truman during the Second World War to investigate allegations of corruption in the national defense program. When McCarthy assumed the chairmanship in 1953 he continued the work that had been started by others to redirect the focus of the subcommittee, turning it into a tribunal to expose Communist subversives among federal employees as well as the general public. Hughes was genuinely baffled by the subpoena, as he explained in writing to McCarthy, "the space apparently provided in the subpoena to inform me why my presence is required is entirely blank."[63] Although the subpoena contained no explanation, as the hours of the interrogation passed it became increasingly clear to Hughes that "Goodbye Christ" sat at the center of the committee's interest in questioning him.

It is likely Hughes first thought the summons had something to do with rumors that he was homosexual. By the 1950s, speculation that Hughes was gay had been a mainstay of Harlem gossip for many years, and as historian David Johnson shows, in 1950s Washington, suspected

Figure 3.2. Langston Hughes before the Permanent Subcommittee on Investigations, March 26, 1953: Hughes testifies before the PSI on day two of his interrogation. He is accompanied by his lawyer, Frank D. Reeves. (Photo care of AP Images.)

homosexuals and Communists were both considered serious threats to national security.[64] The true impetus for the summons, however, was likely more personal and more sinister. Hughes had been under the watchful "eyes" of Hoover and the FBI since the Pasadena incident in 1940, and they had gathered a great deal of information about him, much of it plainly wrong, including the notion that he belonged to thirteen different Communist organizations. Indeed, if Hughes was concerned that he would face questions about his alleged homosexuality, he need not have worried. Hoover's informants not only considered Hughes to be heterosexual but also to be married to a white woman named Sonya Croll with whom he had a son and whose mother was a "known Communist operative."[65] In the information-gathering, Hoover had come across "Goodbye Christ" and had been using it across the country in a speech entitled "Secularism—A Breeder of Crime" in which he vilified Hughes and Communists in American society. When the editors at Abingdon-Cokesbury Press asked him to submit a written version of his speech for publication, he was put in the ironic and awkward position of asking Hughes for his permission to use the poem in the published essay. Specifically, Hoover wanted to say, "The blasphemous utterances of one who sought public office on the ticket of the Communist Party, as represented by Langston Hughes, in a poem entitled 'Goodbye, Christ' reflect their [secularists']true aims." The editors had refused to publish the essay without Hughes's permission. After many months of back and forth, Hughes ultimately refused. Hoover was humiliated and his anger at Hughes likely played a role when, five years later, Hughes received the summons in the mail from McCarthy.[66]

The first day of the interrogation was a "closed session" conducted by Republican Senator Everett McKinley Dirksen of Illinois. Roy Cohn served as special counsel. After a few preliminary questions concerning Hughes's age, employment, and residence, Dirksen explained that Hughes had been called before the subcommittee because of a federally funded propaganda campaign. Congress had appropriated over eighty-five million dollars "for the purpose of propagandizing the free world" with pro-American literature to be placed in libraries.[67] When it was discovered that Hughes's poetry books had inadvertently been a part of this effort, the subcommittee deemed it necessary to have him explain if his work was in fact pro-American rather than pro-Communist.[68]

Roy Cohn, who already at that early stage in his career was recognized as one of the most ruthless lawyers in the country and who would later in his life vehemently deny his homosexuality, made repeated attempts to get Hughes to confess that he had been a member of the Communist Party and that he still believed in the ideals of Communism.[69] Hughes responded by saying he had never to his knowledge attended a Communist Party meeting, and as to whether he believed in Communist ideals, "I would have to know what you mean by your definition of communism," he retorted. When Dirksen took command of the questioning he wasted no time revealing that the interrogation was rooted in the Pasadena incident and one of Hughes's poems, "Goodbye Christ." Before reading the first stanza of the poem, Dirksen stated that his "familiarity with the Negro people" led him to conclude that they were "innately a very devout and religious people." He wanted to know if Hughes thought "the Book [the Bible] is dead" and whether or not "Goodbye Christ" could be considered an accurate reflection of African American religious values. The underlying current of the question was to determine if the poem represented Hughes's atheism, and therefore, his belief in Communism.[70] Hughes responded, "No sir, I do not." Seemingly looking for an opportunity to teach his inquisitors something about literature and the craft of poetry writing, Hughes responded at length when Dirksen asked him about his "purpose" for writing poetry. "You write it out of your soul," Hughes began, "and you write it for your

individual feeling of expression. First sir, it does not come from yourself in the first place. It comes from something beyond oneself, in my
opinion." Hughes concluded by asserting the spirituality of poetry and
of life. "There is something more than myself in the creation of everything that I do. I believe that is in every creation, sir." Dirksen registered
his befuddlement that these "rather ethereal thoughts" could "suddenly"
come upon Hughes.[71]

The session intensified when Dirksen and Cohn attempted to get
Hughes not only to declare himself a Communist but also to name
names. When asked if he knew Paul Robeson, Hughes answered by saying that he knew him well before his fame but not so much since. The
answer did not please the committee, as Cohn launched into a tirade
about the consequences of "not telling the truth." Cohn was particularly keen on getting Hughes to confess to writing an article in 1949 for
the *Daily Worker* in which Hughes defended Communist leaders. He
also wanted him to implicate the *Chicago Defender* and to claim ownership of a number of other poems, including "Ballad of Lenin," "When
Sue Wears Red," and "Good Morning Revolution." Hughes claimed the
poems as his own, but sensing that admitting so was turning the tide
of the interrogation, he requested an extended time to tell the story of
his life, which he insisted would help the committee to "interpret" his
authorship of those poems. After a period of more testimony and interrogation, Cohn again attempted to get Hughes to declare at least an
affinity with the Communist Party. Hughes responded by saying that he
has at times disagreed with the Communist Party, particularly its attack
on black leaders and found himself to be "under attack" by Communists
who looked unfavorably on his "sympathy and interest and encouragement to religious groups and religion in general." Again, Cohn was not
satisfied. "Would you call this poem, 'Goodbye, Christ,' a sympathetic
dealing with religion?" Hughes held his ground. "Yes, I would."

All pretensions about the true reason for which Hughes had been
summoned before the PSI, however, were abandoned during the public
session chaired by Senator McCarthy two days later. (What happened in
the interim of the two meetings remains a mystery.) Sure in the knowledge that "Goodbye Christ" prompted the subcommittee's insistence
that he was both an atheist and a Communist, Hughes had his lawyer,

Frank D. Reeves, an African American from Washington, DC, read the latest version of "Concerning, 'Goodbye Christ.'"

> Perhaps the most misunderstood of my poems was "Goodbye, Christ." Since it is an ironic poem (and irony is apparently a quality not readily understood in poetry by unliterary minds) it has been widely misinterpreted as an anti-religious poem. This I did not mean it to be, but rather a poem against racketeering, profiteering, racial segregation, and showmanship in religion which, at the time, I felt was undermining the foundations of the great and decent ideals for which Christ himself stood. And behind the poem is a pity and sorrow that this should be taken by some as meaning to them that Christianity and religion in general has no value. Because of the publication of this poem—which more than fifteen years ago I withdrew from publication and which has since been used entirely without my permission by groups interested in fomenting racial and social discord, I have been termed on occasion, a Communist or an atheist. I am not now an atheist, and never have been an atheist. . . . I am not a member of the Communist Party now and have never been a member of the Communist Party.[72]

McCarthy did not read from "Goodbye Christ" as Dirksen had done at the "closed session," but he placed it on file, where it remains as part of the *Congressional Record*. Seemingly pleased with Hughes's denunciation of the poem, as well as his statements that he was neither atheist nor Communist, the subcommittee nevertheless pressed further:

> COHN: That poem, you no longer hold any of the views expressed in that poem? Is that correct?
> HUGHES: No, I do not. It is a very young, awkward poem written in the late 1920s or early 1930s. It does not express my views or my artistic techniques today.
> MCCARTHY: It was written at a time when you were devoted to the Communist cause and you would not subscribe to this at this time at all?
> HUGHES: No, Sir, I certainly would not.
> MCCARTHY: Thank you.

COHN: No further questions of Mr. Hughes, Mr. Chairman? Mr.
   McClellan?
MCCARTHY: Thank you very much, Mr. Hughes.
HUGHES: I am excused now?
COHN: Yes, you're excused.[73]

Hughes's answer reflected an important shift in his statements about
"Goodbye Christ," as he began for the first time to downplay the significance of the poem, understate its quality, and to emphasize that it had
long been misused and misunderstood. He had been conquered and his
exhaustion showed.

Possibly as a further means to humiliate Hughes, McCarthy and
his fellow inquisitors forced him to provide examples of his work that
showed his "pro-democratic belief" and "faith in Democracy" when
throughout the 1940s that was precisely the theme of many of his poems
and other writings. When Senator McClellan asked, "have you written
other works, other books that repudiate the philosophies expressed in
these writings that we now find in the libraries?" Hughes mentioned
"Freedom's Plow." Written in 1943 for a radio program at the request of
Lester B. Granger, executive secretary of the National Urban League in
New York, the prose poem was an optimistic social vision of America
that saw blacks and whites building the country together.

> America!
> Land created in common
> Dream nourished in common
> Keep your hand on the plow!
> Hold on!

In explaining the poem to PSI members, Hughes said that the country
had "many problems still to solve," but it was "young, big, strong, and
beautiful." Justice was for all and "all of us are a part of democracy."[74]

In addition to "Freedom's Plow," much of the work of Langston
Hughes during the 1940s, especially during the war years, expressed
confidence in the democratic process. In a striking departure from the
radical themes of 1930s poetry and prose, these works were "nationalist"
in sentiment. In such poems as "Words Like Freedom," "The Black Man

Speaks," Freedom [1]" and "Freedom [2]," Hughes seems to suggest that black people's participation in a war to spread democracy and to stop fascist tyranny would transform American race relations. In "The Black Man Speaks," the question is mostly rhetorical, stated as if the process had already begun:

> If we're fighting to create
> A free world tomorrow
> Why not end *right now*
> Old Jim Crow's sorrow?

In "To Captain Mulzac," Hughes revisits the "unity" theme he had expressed in "Freedom's Plow." Depicting America as "a crew of many races—yet all of one blood," Hughes intones that the hope of the country was in the combined efforts of its black and white citizens. "In union, you, White Man / And I, Black Man / Can be Free." At the end of "The Sun Do Move," a play he wrote for the Skyloft Players in Chicago in 1942, the protagonist, Rock, and the audience sing "The Star-Spangled Banner."[75]

Before Hughes was dismissed from the proceedings, the committee dealt him a parting insult. McCarthy asked if he felt he had been "mistreated" by the subcommittee during the interrogation. Hughes replied that he was "agreeably surprised" at how "courteous and friendly" the proceedings had been, and particularly Dirksen, who was "most gracious."[76] Not once throughout the two-day session was Hughes pressed to further expound upon his stated intent that "Goodbye Christ" aimed to address profiteering and racketeering in American religion. And then McCarthy winked. In a move that was doubtlessly given to punctuate his victory over yet another detainee before his government-sponsored tribunal, McCarthy "flashed [Hughes] a wink."[77] The ordeal was over, the humiliation complete.

The appearance before the PSI devastated Hughes. At the end of two days of rapid-fire questioning he acquiesced (as most did) by denouncing a poem he had previously proclaimed "good." Faced with McCarthy and his inquisitors, Hughes chose to give the subcommittee what they most desired—a reason to earmark "Goodbye Christ" as an atheistic piece of Communist propaganda. In doing so, Hughes employed what

David E. Chinitz calls his "ethics of compromise." It was both an artistic and political compromise, but to do otherwise would have further jeopardized his reputation and quite possibly his career. That had become painfully clear over the course of the two sessions, and he was gravely concerned about it. A few weeks after the proceedings, Hughes wrote John Sengstacke, the editor of the *Chicago Defender*, to give him assurances that "the name of the DEFENDER only came up once." Hughes had not stained the newspaper and he, as a frequent columnist, had come out "entirely in the clear." He made a similar point in a letter to Frank Reeves a month after the ordeal. "All of my publishers are pleased with the outcome of the hearings, have backed me up beautifully, and are going ahead with their publishing plans in relation to my work.[78] The real blow had been to his dignity.

By the early 1960s, versions of "Concerning 'Goodbye Christ'" made little mention of Hughes's enemies, the wrongful way they were using the poem, or of his "freedom of speech." It had transformed into a carefully constructed, nondefensive explanation of the poem and an obliquely worded statement about faith. Hughes had long been frustrated that the bulk of his religiously themed work had not suggested the possibility that he himself was religious. In the closed session with the PSI he had remarked to Dirksen, "Certainly I have written many religious poems, many poems about Christ, and prayers and my own feeling is not what I believe you seem to think [those poems] as meaning."[79] In his view, not seeing his work as religious or failing to entertain the possibility that he himself could be religious was a choice made by those who did not understand him, had little capacity to rightfully interpret literature, or sought to do him harm. Later versions of the statement attracted sharper attention to this aspect of his work and drew inferences about what it could mean for Hughes personally. As he had before the Committee, Hughes wanted to emphasize changes in his own views and those in his work. Indeed, he had made a definite shift in his work, having proclaimed to Louise Thompson as early as 1940 that he was "laying off political poetry for a while . . . and going back to nature, Negroes, and love." He had also, in his words, "gone back to the Church," although he did not clarify what that meant.[80] Hughes still claimed that his detractors had misunderstood the irony of the poem, but he devoted more space in the statement to highlight the repeated occurrences of religious themes in his poems. Religion had long been a key feature of his poetry, but his readers seemed to have ignored this, he claimed. They had also ignored the prominence of religion in his other works, as he stated in a version of "Concerning 'Goodbye Christ" sent to Jean Wagner in 1960: "In my *Selected Poems* (Knopf, 1959) there is an entire section of poems on religious themes, 'Feet of Jesus,' and Marion Anderson has sung my modern spiritual of the same title. For the theatre I have written an opera, *Esther*, score by Jan Meyerowitz, the text derived from the Bible story, performed by the Boston Conservatory of Music and at the Spring Festival of the University of Illinois." In the aftermath of his appearance before the PSI, Hughes redoubled his efforts to draw attention to his religious writings, particularly his poetry. He had produced a great deal of work on the topic of religion and was at the time almost exclusively writing religious-themed plays and other works. It was time such was brought to the attention of his detractors as well as a wider readership.

Hughes focused a great deal of attention on admirers who wrote him with their concerns about "Goodbye Christ." Excerpting heavily from the statement, he wrote a personal letter in 1961 to Harold Blake from Iola, Kansas, for example, stating that the "circulators of 'Goodbye, Christ' ignore the whole body of my work and my writing over a forty-year period, during which time I have written many poems of a religious nature." That was precisely the point he also made to a Catholic nun from Evansville, Indiana. Sister Rose Veronica of Reitz Memorial High School had written him inquiring if the poem meant that he held no belief in God. Hughes first apologized for the way she had become acquainted with the poem—through the propaganda of those who were "up to no good purpose"—and reiterated that "Goodbye Christ" was an ironic and satirical poem that should not be taken literally. He then pointed her to his works that portrayed religion in a more conventional manner. But perhaps sensing that more would be required if he were to convince a skeptical nun that he was not an atheist, Hughes ended the letter on a personal and more reflexive note. "I hope that some of the material I am sending you under separate cover will indicate to you that I sincerely believe myself to have a much deeper religious feeling than those who are circulating my long out-dated (and, I feel, misunderstood) poem."[81] Presenting himself as someone with "religious feeling" was still an evasive move, but Hughes meant to assure the admiring nun that he flatly was not a nonbeliever.

Hughes seemed especially attentive to those who wrote him expressing their concern for his soul's salvation. Gerald S. Pratt Sr. of Honesdale, Pennsylvania, wrote Hughes with concerns for his spiritual state after coming across a copy of "Goodbye Christ" distributed by the conservative radio commentator Fulton Lewis Jr. From the 1930s to the 1960s, Lewis had made his mark as a staunch opponent of liberal causes, from Franklin Delano Roosevelt's New Deal to Lyndon Johnson's Great Society. In the summer of 1960 he launched an attack on the National Council of Churches for recommending Hughes's book *The Negro American*, which he falsely alleged included "Goodbye Christ." Pratt wanted to straighten out in his own mind Hughes's "political and religious status."

> Did you write the poem entitled "Goodbye, Christ"? I have a copy of this poem and it is such a vile piece of literature that I would be ashamed to even quote from it. I understand that you are the author and the purpose of this letter is to inquire if this is true. Are you a Christian and do you claim to write literature that is helpful and conducive to Christian living? For what purpose are your writings, to make people better and lead them to Christianity or to lead them away from belief in Christ?

As a response, Hughes sent him a collection of material, including, presumably, "Concerning 'Goodbye Christ.'" He also included the transcript of the hearing before the PSI, and a copy of the poem "Prayer for the Mantle-Piece," on which he wrote at the bottom of the page, "copied especially for Gerald S. Pratt who queries my thoughts about God." Lewis renewed his attacks on Hughes months later, even after Pratt had asked him to cease because "Goodbye Christ" should be viewed as a product of a "youthful period of extreme radicalism." When Hughes learned of the renewed attacks he wrote Pratt to inform him. "I advise you of this," he said, "because you have been so kind as to be concerned in the past. And I have very much appreciated your interest."[82]

Hughes's responses to these inquiries were never unambiguous with regard to the theological specifics of his own beliefs, but he always offered assurances that he was far removed from the radicalism of his youth, drew attention to large body of his "poems of a religious nature," and depicted himself as superior morally to his many detractors. Such was the case in 1961 when Hughes wrote back to Mrs. Fern Worthington of Boise, Idaho. Worthington had come across a copy of "Goodbye Christ" and wrote to express her dismay about the poem and about what it allegedly suggested about Hughes's moral and ethical comportment. "Are you a Christian and do you claim to write literature that is helpful and conducive to Christian living?," she wanted to know. In response, after pointing out that his detractors always seem to "ignore" the presence of religion in his poetry, he strongly insinuated that *they* were the ones who lacked morality and religion, noting their silence and inaction about recent events. "They do nothing about four little six-year old girls beset by a howling mob in New Orleans last year. . . . they never lift a voice about lynchings, bombing of Negro homes and schools, or any of the problems of democracy related to race in our mutual country."[83] The tone and tenor was similar in a 1963 exchange with Raymond Konkle of Pontiac, Michigan. Konkle had written Hughes, dismayed that "anyone could have written such a blasphemous poem" as "Goodbye Christ." He urged Hughes to turn to Christ and ask to be saved from his "lost condition," including with the letter a pamphlet entitled "Facts You Should Know and Believe to Be Saved." Hughes responded within a few days thanking Konkle for the pamphlet and for his concern. He indicated, as he had done many times at this point, that "Goodbye Christ" had been circulated over the last thirty years against his will by his enemies, who were "up to no good purpose" and were "anti-Negro, anti-Jewish, anti-labor." "Personally," Hughes concluded, "I think that I have a great deal more religion than they have and that the entire orientation of my writing has been to attempt to achieve good in the world rather than evil."[84]

The Politics of Political Poetry

One of Hughes's chief detractors, Reverdy Ransom, eventually shifted positions. Although he did not change his mind about the theological implications of "Goodbye Christ," he became dismayed at the level of opposition Hughes had been receiving from those he called "narrow minded religionists." Eight years after he published "All Hail to Christ: A la Langston Hughes," Ransom wrote Hughes to assure him that he "deeply sympathized with the motives" that prompted him to write

"Goodbye Christ."[85] Indeed, Hughes received a great deal of support throughout the years from those who not only "deeply sympathized" with his motives but also wholeheartedly agreed with what he said in the poem. One of the first to do so in the aftermath of the Pasadena incident was a "militant young minister" from Los Angeles, Clayton D. Russell, pastor of the People's Independent Church. Russell preached a sermon in January 1941 based on Hughes's poem in which he blasted "modern churches and modern Christians" for their inattention to the poor and the marginalized as depicted in the poem. News of the sermon spread rapidly throughout California, and the *Chicago Defender* picked it up. Like many ministers had done in the 1930s, Russell identified the state of the American church as the problem, not Hughes or his poem. Indeed, the poem was a "challenge to the church," as it had lost sight of its mission to the world and, therefore, its "effectiveness for good." Christianity, he asserted, was "headed toward a supreme crisis," having been the one to say "goodbye" to Christ. As for Hughes, he was only the messenger and his personal religion was not in question or at stake. "'Goodbye Christ' could have been written by an atheist, an idiot, a thinker, a Communist, or a Christian," Russell concluded.[86]

The responses to the poem over many years—pro and con—demonstrated the degree to which it had become a cultural flashpoint. It generated extensive debates about Hughes, poetry, and religion in America during a time of national crisis, and it had a profound impact on the discourse about American religion and irreparably shaped the perception of Hughes's work if not the actual direction of it. Many of the professional decisions Hughes would make after the Pasadena incident and his appearance before the PSI would be in light of those experiences, as well as the continued existence of a poem over which he had long ago lost control. And despite his efforts, it would continue to serve as the basis for claims the he was Communist, antichurch, and antireligious.

"Goodbye Christ" was not a statement of Hughes's "atheism," however, nor was it an indication of his alleged membership in the Communist Party. It was, rather, a denunciation of what Hughes perceived as the corrupting influence of capitalism on American churches, which provided fertile ground for "profiteering" and "racketeering" by religionists. Far from being a remote example of antireligious sentiment, the poem was integral to the proletarian poetry of the 1930s, as well as to a culture of complaint and critique among clergy as well as laypeople who implicated American churches for social inaction. Like Hughes, who wanted to "make room for a new guy," these clergy and laypeople called for a radical redirection of American religion and a rethinking of Christian theology. J. B. Simmons shows the depth of the sentiment even as he misconstrues the contents of the poem. Having forgotten the title of "Goodbye Christ," Simmons—Toledo, Ohio's first black councilman—wrote Hughes in 1946 requesting a copy. "Kindly advise how one may secure a copy of a poem of yours, written 12 or 14 years ago, which ran something like this: 'Goodbye, Christ, hello Lenin, burn the churches, and hang the Bishops.'"[87] Hughes retained Simmons's letter but, of course, did not honor the request.

Almost certainly Hughes had "Goodbye Christ" in mind when he wrote in 1964, "Politics can be the graveyard of the poet. And only poetry can be his resurrection."[88] The poem, one that Hughes likely never intended to publish, had indeed "haunted" his career and shaped people's perception of him as an artist—far out of his control. The enduring significance of "Goodbye Christ," however, is the way it pushed Hughes to consider the limits as well as the potential of his craft, and its contribution to the discourse on politics and religion during the 1930s and beyond. The poem provided an important backdrop to his decision to retreat into the world of theater and his gospel song-plays in the late 1950s and early 1960s. But there, too, he would find no safe haven.

4

My Gospel Year

"Essie, raise your fat disgusted self up off that suitcase you're setting on and let's go make our fortune saving souls."
—Laura Wright Reed

"That part of God that is in everybody is not to be played with—and everybody has got a part of God in them."
—Essie Belle Johnson

"This church racket beats show business, baby—the way they're turning all the old theaters in Harlem into churches."
—Big-Eyed Buddy Lomax

In July 1956, three years after his humiliating appearance before Joseph McCarthy and the Permanent Subcommittee on Investigations (PSI), Hughes wrote a particularly upbeat letter to Arna Bontemps informing him that he had just written a new play entitled "Tambourines to Glory: A Play with Spirituals, Jubilees, and Gospel Songs," an "urban-folk-Harlem-genre-melodrama" he had completed in just ten days. Seemingly quite pleased with the play, he proclaimed, "It's a singing, shouting, wailing, drama of the old conflict between blatant Evil and quiet Good, with the Devil driving a Cadillac."[1] His enthusiasm for "Tambourines to Glory" was undiminished by September of that year, when he wrote to another close friend and longtime patron, Carl Van Vechten. By this time he had just as quickly developed the play into a novel, only his second novel since *Not without Laughter*, published in 1930. "Did I tell you I've just finished a little novel called *Tambourines to Glory* about the goings-on in gospel churches?" It contains "a Tambourine Chorus and two women preacher-songsters, one sweet, one naughty," and Ethel Waters and Pearl Bailey "would be ideal casting" for the play version, he continued. Van Vechten and Hughes had

Figure 4.1. Hughes at a book signing with Adam Clayton Powell Jr., Jobe Huntley, Jean B. Hutson, and Irene Fleming looking on. Harlem, New York City, circa 1958. (Photo care of the Associated Press.)

been friends since the mid-1920s, corresponded regularly, and "Carlo," as Hughes affectionately called the Manhattan "Tastemaker," faithfully read everything Hughes wrote and saw all of his theatrical productions. "I am mad to see Tambourines to Glory," Van Vechten enthused when the play was in the early stages of production in September 1958, and the very next month he replied to Hughes with his response to the novel after its publication. "Thanks for sending me Tambourines to Glory," he wrote. "It is quite a book and I read it at a single sitting with the greatest of pleasure."[2]

Although religion had been at the core of his creative energies since the 1920s, by the late 1950s and early 1960s, beginning with *Tambourines to Glory*, Hughes had turned almost exclusively to the topic of religion in his work. There were other projects that engaged him, including his second autobiography, *I Wonder as I Wander* (1956); his plays "Simply Heavenly" and "The Ballot and Me: The Negro's Part in Suffrage, an Historical Sequence" (1957); *The Langston Hughes Reader* (1958); *Selected Poems of Langston Hughes*; and "Mister Jazz: A Panorama in Music and Motion of the History of Negro Dancing" as an introduction to a one-act play by Robert Glenn based on Hughes's book of poems, *Shakespeare in Harlem* (1959). But most of Hughes's newer original work concentrated on religious themes. And by 1962 the stage production of *Tambourines to Glory* had become a crucial component to a series of gospel song-plays either in production or set to be produced. Hughes had so many of these in the works that he proclaimed to gospel artist Alex Bradford that 1962 was "indeed, my gospel year."[3]

In addition to *Tambourines to Glory*, set to open later in the fall, his "all Negro" passion play, *The Gospel Glow* (also known as *The Gospel Glory*) was opening in December at Washington Temple Church of God in Christ (COGIC), housed in the former Loews Theatre in Brooklyn for a week of shows. Ernestine Washington, "songbird of the east" and wife of the pastor, Frederick D. Washington, was in the lead role.[4] Alfred Miller directed the music and Alfred Duckett served as producer.[5] *Black Nativity*, a gospel song-play that had become a huge popular and critical success, was traveling throughout Europe and the United States to strong reviews. There were even tentative plans to combine *The Gospel Glow*, *Black Nativity*, and *The Prodigal Son*, which Hughes had completed the previous year, into one huge production to be called *Master of Miracles: The Life of Christ*. Having written a number of articles on gospel music and on Mahalia Jackson, Hughes appeared with Jackson at a Negro History Week event at Hunter College in New York City in February 1957. In introducing her, he gave a short history of gospel songs, describing them as "triumphant story telling songs" and encouraged the audience to listen with their hearts and not just with their minds.[6] He also wrote the liner notes for several albums of gospel music or "spirituals," such as Harry Belafonte's 1960 "My Lord, What a Mornin,'" where Hughes recounted the history of "spirituals," calling them "regional in origin but universal in meaning." Hughes deemed the "young lamb" Belafonte a worthy interpreter of the song tradition rooted in the American slave past but characterized by "graceful dignity, an outgoing charm and an inner assurance."[7]

Although publishers rejected them all, Hughes wrote five different proposals for "prayer books" and religious anthologies during the late 1950s and early 1960s, including *These Prayers: A Collection of Short Texts from Major Religions*; *Prayers around the World, the First Book of Ecumenical Prayers*; *Poems of the Spirit: Verses on Biblical Themes by Well-Known Poets*; *Spread Your Wings and Fly: Poems of Faith*; and *Translations on the Theme of Christmas*.[8] *Tambourines to Glory*, therefore, inaugurated what were indeed gospel years for Langston Hughes.

The emphasis Hughes placed on religion even reached beyond literature and the stage during the gospel years. Doubtlessly in acknowledgment of the increased focus on religion and church in Hughes's work, as well as a means to save the show, *TV Gospel Time* hired him to host six shows for the early Sunday morning program. It would be the first program to showcase black gospel music on TV. The show had received very bad reviews from its majority black viewers, so the producers Lenny Sait and Howard Schwartz looked to Hughes, whose charm, wit, reputation, and dignified air they believed would help to improve its image. They also reduced the amount of religious iconography, or "holy trappings," as they called them, which did not play well with general audiences, and acquired a makeup artist to work with the performers, having discovered that "Negroes don't like to see 'bad looking Negroes' on their TV screens."[9] That television appearance led to others. In 1959 he appeared with the folk artist Odetta for a TV production *Lamp unto My Feet*, and the next year he narrated the CBS series *Look Up and Live*, a gospel concert featuring a 120-voice choir from Abyssinian Baptist Church, with which he had a long association.[10] Hughes was as busy as he had ever been producing creative works on religion, participating in religious programing, writing articles and essays on religion, and becoming thoroughly engulfed in the world of black gospel music.

Hughes would always accentuate his modest intentions regarding *Tambourines to Glory*, but those intentions belied the work's larger purpose and effect. In the broadest sense, *Tambourines to Glory* was an exploration of the meaning of salvation, and salvation was the central concern of the work. It was the first time Hughes had attempted to "work out" his notion of salvation in a genre other than his poetry. As in the poetry, however, particularly the early poetry, "salvation" in *Tambourines* was a matter of changed behavior and personal piety, as "sins" were social in nature and most often sexual. The "unholy trinity" of sins, as one of the characters cataloged them, for example, was "love (illicit sex), loot, and likker." The important difference between the conception of salvation and sin in *Tambourines* and in Hughes's poetry was that for the first time Hughes explicitly connected them discursively to the issues of ethics and morality. Sin and salvation are depicted in *Tambourines* as a struggle between good and evil, or right and wrong, as Hughes stated. The consequences of sin and salvation, therefore, extended outward beyond the individual.

Good and evil, however, were not simple matters in *Tambourines*. Indeed, they were complex and often ambiguous, colliding and retracting throughout the work. Religious institutions and the people who occupy those spaces have as much capacity for immorality and unethical behavior as they do for moral responsiveness and ethical responsibility. People choose to do good or evil, but the outcomes are not always clear or what one would expect. Saints and sinners, the good and the bad share more in common than not. The saintly characters in *Tambourines* are dainty, deluded, and out of touch with themselves and others, but they are also always complicit in sin and are never truly innocent. The sinners, however, are often the sole source of the good. This theme runs throughout *Tambourines* and is embodied in the two principle characters, Essie Belle Johnson and Laura Wright Reed, as well as in the church they establish, Tambourine Temple. The women are seen principally in contrast. But often their roles are reversed. Their church also has a dualistic and contradictory capacity, being both a space of exploitation born from the most selfish and material of aims and a place of refuge and comfort to a few weary souls beaten by the daily grind of black life in 1950s Harlem. For this reason, literary scholar Leslie Catherine Sanders takes *Tambourines* to be "a social commentary on certain aspects of the black church," as Hughes wanted to reveal some black churches as places of good will *and* bad, sin *and* salvation.[11] In the cosmic struggle, however, the good and God always ultimately win, and the entire story pivots on a statement Essie makes. "Religion's got no business being made into a gyp game. That part of God that is in everybody *is not to be played with*—and everybody has got a part of God in them."[12]

In addition to establishing the ultimate triumph of the good and of God, Essie's statement also reveals a theological tension Hughes embedded in the story of *Tambourines*. In one way, the statement itself reflects the evangelical belief in God's "Omnipresence," a theology that would have been pervasive in Essie's black Baptist upbringing in her native Virginia, as well as in the storefront churches proliferating in Harlem at the time. God is everywhere and *in* all, as in Psalm 139:7–10: "Whither shall I go from thy spirit? Or whither shall I flee from thy presence? If I ascend up into heaven, thou art there; if I make my bed in hell, behold, thou art there" (KJV). But the statement also shares much in common with some aspects of theological modernism. Hughes sustains this theological tension throughout the text, juxtaposing black folk religious traditions and practices and storefront church worship with notions more akin to New Thought, humanism, and the Social Gospel. At Essie's bidding, for example, the church is eventually transformed into a community center, complete with a day nursery, meeting spaces, and a playground. And in addition to the Bible, she spends most of her time reading the works of theological modernists such as African American mystic Howard Thurman and the Reformed Church in America minister and advocate of "positive thinking," Norman Vincent Peale. Both men, she says, help her "unscramble the good from the bad" in herself and in others.

Hughes intended *Tambourines* principally to be a critique of the exploitative aspects of some black churches, particularly those he called "gospel churches." He explained this repeatedly to people who read the book or saw the play. But the effect of the play and the book was to reveal the conclusions Hughes had come to, developed over many years, with regard to the purpose of religion and the role of the church in society. While not his best play or book in terms of craft, and indeed many critics dismissed the work as an overly simplistic folk drama with an overly sentimentalized ending, *Tambourines to Glory* serves as a literary summation of Hughes's thinking about religion and churches over the course of his long career, and in this regard, as theater critic Loften Mitchell asserted, the play is "far from superficial."[13]

Similar to Hughes's first novel, *Tambourines to Glory* places women at the center of the narrative. The book and play demonstrate how Hughes's work most often centered on the experiences of black women, setting him apart from other black male novelists such as Ralph Ellison and Richard Wright, whose female characters are either invisible, one dimensional, "subordinate to male figures," or serve merely as "maternal images or sexual objects."[14] For his determination to feature the voices and experiences of black women in his art, Joyce A. Joyce maintains that Hughes was "the first black male feminist writer of African American letters."[15] Hughes offers complicated views of women's lives in both his novels, rendering them fully developed, autonomous, and multidimensional. While underscoring their relationships with men, which often involve victimization, he also highlights their strength, agility, and resolve. Similar to *Not without Laughter*, *Tambourines to Glory* features women making choices about their lives, often with difficult and tragic results, but also in ways that lead to their own self-actualization. In *Tambourines to Glory*, however, Hughes tells a story that demonstrates the close connection he drew between black women and religion (in this case urban religion), showing that, historically, black women have been known to navigate their worlds in and around religious spaces. Churches are ideal spaces to render what Joyce calls a "more balanced" view of black women's experiences, as they tend to reveal that the women are as complicated as the space itself. The women in *Tambourines to Glory* are complicated and paradoxical figures. They are not always virtuous or dishonorable, and their very lives demand complication and compromise—sometimes of their faith and the very things they hold dear. This capacity to see black women in such diverse and balanced terms reveals Hughes's empathy with the plight of black women and, as Joyce further notes, "deepens their humanity."[16]

The mixed, highly racialized, and class-based reception of *Tambourines to Glory*, however, frustrated Hughes's modest aims for the production as it prompted questions about what constituted "authentic" expressions of black religion, as *Black Nativity* would similarly do. It also generated a debate as to whether or not the theater was an appropriate space in which to enact it. Far from the simple play Hughes said he intended, *Tambourines to Glory* became one of his most polarizing theatrical productions, while at the same time was one of his most theologically astute and culturally rich works.

The Reed Sisters

Tambourines to Glory tells the story of Essie Belle Johnson and Laura Wright Reed, two southern migrants who find themselves in 1950s

Harlem, poor, unemployed, and with few prospects. They devise a plan to start a church as a means to lift themselves out of poverty and the dreariness of their own lives. The story begins with Essie having been evicted from her kitchenette apartment and sitting curbside bemoaning her fate. Laura, her faithful if wayward friend, finds her in this state and encourages her to get up and do something. "You never do nothing but set [sit]," Laura complains. Essie retorts with her determination to "ask the Lord to take my hand," a phrase she often repeats from the 1932 gospel song, "Precious Lord, Take My Hand" by gospel composer Thomas Andrew Dorsey.[17] The retort prompts Laura to list the preachers who use the church to make money, rattling off a number of names, including fictional ministers, actual extant ministers, and former celebrity Harlem ministers such as George Becton "of the consecrated dime." "You know Bishop Longjohn right over there on Lenox Avenue? That saint had three whores on the block ten years ago. He's got a better racket now—the gospel!" Laura then poses the question on which the play hangs, "why don't you and me start a church?" Pleading with her portly friend to raise her "fat disgusted self up" from the curb, Laura reminds her of Aimee Semple McPherson, the "white lady" who donned wings, "opened up a temple, and made a million dollars." They determine to start a church of their own, calling themselves "the Reed Sisters," and adopt "salvation" as their theme, stating, "We'll save them lower down than us"—which, as they saw it, was pretty low. Essie registers some disquiet about the scheme but only manages to ask, "what denomination?" "Our own," Laura tells her with some defiance.

The Reed Sisters begin their ministry on the streets of Harlem, on Lenox Avenue, one of the centers of Harlem's world of religion and churches and the obvious site to start a new ministry. They present the ministry as a church with "no doors," an allusion to Hughes's 1935 short story "On the Road," where doors on a church signified discrimination and exclusion. "Our church is this corner, our roof is God's sky, and there's no doors, no place in our church that is not open to you because there is no doors," Laura proclaims at their first meeting. The crowds begin to increase daily as the Reed Sisters make their plea with sinners to "come and accept his salvation" to the sound of stirring gospel music and the beating of a single tambourine. Both Laura and Essie are accomplished singers with fine voices, having grown up singing in their respective church choirs in the South. The success of the small congregation that had begun to gather as a result of the two women preachers eventually catches the attention of "Big-Eyed Buddy Lomax," a "good looking young man" for whom Laura instantly falls. With the financial backing of his white "fixer" Marty, he helps the two women secure a storefront church and eventually purchase an old theater, which they convert into a church. It is a "race church" by Laura's design and specification, complete with original art painted by a "refined" local artist, "refined" being coded language for homosexual. "I don't care what scenes from the Bible you paint on these windows," she instructs him, "just so you make them colored. God made us in His own image, so God must be black, or at least dark brown."

The congregation swells to about two thousand people, becoming the "biggest independent church in Harlem," due primarily to a "lucky texts" scheme Buddy devises in which Laura gives out numbers during the recitation of her sermon's scriptural passages, not an uncommon practice in 1950s Harlem.[18] They also sell "holy water"—straight from the New York tap—which proves to be lucrative beyond their expectations. "How simple can people get?," quipped Buddy, noting all the money acquired from the sales. In a short time the two women are out of poverty. Laura has the fancy car and mink coat she has always wanted and Essie has saved enough money to buy a house in Mt. Vernon, New York, and bring her daughter Marrietta from Virginia to live with her. The two women enter a whole new world and alter their entire lives by simply starting a church.

The dramatic turn in the story occurs when tensions escalate between the two women as a result of the exploitative means by which they have gained their wealth, along with conflicts over an affair between Laura and Buddy. Essie begins to suffer intense crises of conscience over the schemes and Laura's brazen charlatanry. In protest, for example, she quietly exits the pulpit each time Laura gives out the "lucky texts" or sells the "holy water." Essie's accusations of Laura's sinful ways, however, are met with Laura's assertions of Essie's complicity in a fake ministry from which she has materially benefited. "You're out here hustling just like me—in God's name," Laura snaps. The story culminates with Buddy's murder. Buddy has begun to show his true colors, becoming the "blatant Evil" of which Hughes spoke. He has tried to rape Marrietta, made a histrionic and fake public confession of faith just to win favor with the congregation, and started to openly cheat on Laura with Gloria, one of Laura's newly acquired protégés. After a heated verbal exchange in her "robing room" just before the beginning of the evening service, Laura kills Buddy while kissing him, stabbing him in the back with a knife Essie nearly always kept with her. The knife provides her with a ready opportunity to falsely accuse Essie of the crime. When she does, Essie is then escorted off to jail to be tried for murder.

Tambourines to Glory ends with scenes of confession, forgiveness, reconciliation, and reckoning. In a jailhouse encounter between Laura and Essie in which the two woman affirm their love and friendship, Laura takes full responsibility for Buddy's death, and Essie vows to assume the leadership of Tambourine Temple. The book and the play differ in the specifics of Laura's confession and Essie's arrest, but they share in common Laura's own crisis of conscience, which leads her to take responsibility for the murder in order to free the innocent Essie. Indeed, confession and testimony become the key themes in the closing scenes. In the play version, Birdie Lee, "a lady drummer" and one of the principle figures in the Temple's chorus, unbeknownst to Laura has witnessed the murder and during services that evening, while Buddy's body lay yet undiscovered in the robing room, sends a clear message to Laura in her testimony. "My testimony this evening is that I want to tell you all that it means to be a witness—I mean a witness for God, and a witness for men and women, too. Lord, lemme hold my holt! I were in a trial once, a court trial—and I lied. I let an innocent man go to jail for something he didn't do—to protect my man I thought I loved. Another man served time, innocent as a lamb." Birdie concludes by saying, "I'm going to tell the truth for the truth don't lie," after which she casts a knowing look at Laura and begins to belt the song, "I'm gonna testify." The second verse proclaims, "I did not know the strength I'd find. Thank God a-mighty, I'm a gospel lion. Things I've seen I cannot keep. Thank God a-mighty, God don't sleep."[19] In the book version Birdie does indeed report the truth to the police, which leads to Laura's confession and arrest. In the play, however, it was Laura's guilty conscience that does the work. "She prayed all night and confessed all morning—and nobody made her," Chicken Crow-for-Day (also known as Deacon Crow) informs Essie during his visit to the jail. In both versions Laura finally confesses to

Essie and asks for forgiveness as they briefly meet in the cells. "Essie, I'm sorry . . . sorry as hell for what I did to you—and with your knife, too. The law knows that I did it. I confessed." Acknowledging that Essie was one of only two people she has truly loved in her life, she asks Essie to forgive her, to which Essie simply states, "I forgive you, Laura."[20]

Essie's confession and reckoning comes in jail by way of her realization of the error of her ways. She acknowledges her complicity in the church racket and that much of what has transpired has been due to her lack of courage and inactivity. "I deserve this punishment," she concedes to Deacon Crow. "When I seen what was happening in our church—all that unholy water selling, numbers and stuff—I should have riz in my wrath and cleaned house." Instead, she concluded, "I just set and sung." The scene is more poignant in the book version as Essie's confession takes place while she is alone in her cell in a cold sweat "as she figured sweat must have popped out on the brow of Christ when He was praying in the Garden (of Gethsemane)." Speaking to the darkness she confesses that she has done nothing except receive "the Lord's blessing whilst the eagle foulest His nest," a reference to a famous recorded sermon by Detroit minister Reverend C. L. Franklin from 1953.[21] It was her inactivity and passive complicity that enabled Laura and Buddy. "I let Buddy fill the house of God with sin, and vanity of vanities take over," she exclaims, "and Laura parade her fur coat and purr in her fine car before them poor people what brought us their hard-earned money for God's work—which only such a little miteful did go." It is at this point that Essie asserts that religion is not to be a "gyp game" and proclaims her determination to turn things around for herself and for the church. She is done with just "setting" and will now be a woman of action. No longer will she allow the church to be "the devil's playground." She outlines the socially responsible programs, including sending Marrietta to school to become the church's nurse to care for the sick among the congregation. Tambourine Temple was to become "a rock of goodness in the heart of Harlem."[22]

Written in two acts, *Tambourines to Glory* was essentially a musical—a play with music—differing slightly from the gospel song-plays Hughes would write during the early 1960s. Jobe Huntley, a nurse and Harlem gospel singer and composer whom Hughes met at a gospel concert, co-wrote all the songs, and, as Hughes put it, the songs were "an integral part of a dramatic action built around the actual church rituals through which the characters move." Music was "the heart and soul of the drama, and not merely its adornment," Arnold Rampersad asserts. It was woven throughout the dramatic action of the play.[23] As playwright, Hughes's chief concern was for the most appropriate actors for each role, and he wrote very precise instructions in his author's note regarding the selection. The proper actors would set the tone for the drama, elucidate the comparative element integral to it, and enliven its eventual redemptive ending. Also in his notes Hughes acknowledged that *Tambourines to Glory* had a range of depth beyond its comic strip, folk ballad stage format. "On the surface," he explained, it was a "simple play about very simple people," but all the performers should be skilled enough to handle the "complexities of simplicity" that the play would demand. The principal character of Laura was the most important. She had to be a "compelling personality" who was not only pretty but also "capable of projecting sunlight, laughter, easy-going manner, and careless love." Essie, by contrast, was to be faithful and "solid," a salt-of-the-earth character who exuded comforting motherliness.[24] Both women were to know how to sing. All the characters were to be "lovable," except Buddy, as he was the primary source of the two women's troubles. The staging had to enhance the overall "rhythm" of the production, as it was to be a "rhythmic ballad." The "final effect" Hughes desired was that audiences be transported to Tambourine Temple to participate with the "singing, foot-patting, hand-clapping" as if a member of the church's chorus, and to witness for themselves its world of sin and salvation and its attending consequences born out in the lives of the Reed sisters.[25]

The Meaning of *Tambourines*

In *Tambourines to Glory*, Hughes's love for gospel music and the theater, his penchant for comic writing, which he had been demonstrating since the mid-1930s, and his interest in Harlem life perfectly coalesced. And it is not inconsequential that Hughes conceived of the idea for the play after attending a gospel concert. By the late 1950s he had become a black gospel music aficionado. Still a relatively new genre of music, black gospel had reached the height of its popularity, often outselling jazz and blues recordings. While living in Chicago temporarily in the early 1940s, Hughes heard such compelling artists as the Roberta Martin Singers, Mahalia Jackson, Norsalus McKissick, and the Gay Sisters, who often performed at Clarence Cobb's First Church of Deliverance, "a religious center of gospel singing."[26] Many of the top artists, including Mahalia Jackson, Clara Ward, and Alex Bradford, would become lifelong personal friends. Hughes's expertise in the new genre of music allowed him, along with Jobe Huntley, to compose the show's nine original songs in the gospel music format, "original" being a rather loose term in the early days of black gospel as many of the songs were adaptations from old Negro spirituals and standard hymns. The lyrics of the songs loosely followed the narrative of the story, as in "I'm Gonna Testify," sung after Buddy's murder. Most of the music, however, was centered on Buddy's false confession of salvation, an obvious if unacknowledged allusion to the deception tied to Hughes's own failed salvation experience back in Lawrence, Kansas. Four of the nine songs— "Devil, Take Yourself Away," "Back to the Fold," "As I Go," and "Let the Church Say Amen"—were performed during and after that scene, per Hughes's instructions but without explanation.[27]

The humor in the play was intentional, in the manner of other comic plays Hughes had written over the years, including "Little Ham" (1935), "Soul Gone Home" (1936), "Joy to My Soul" (1937), and "Simply Heavenly" (1957), a comedy about "ordinary, hard-working lower-income bracket Harlemites" based on Hughes's comedic character and literary alter ego, Jesse B. Semple or Simple.[28] As a musical comedy, *Tambourines to Glory* was funny and Hughes meant it to be funny, and that was necessary because the show was about "problems that can only convincingly be reduced to a comic strip if presented very cleanly, clearly, sharply, precisely, and with humor."[29] Hughes had been writing about Harlem life almost since the day he arrived in 1921. By the 1950s he had amassed a wealth of knowledge about life in Harlem and was one of the first to declare the end of the Harlem Renaissance and the "vogue" of the Negro due largely to the decline in living standards among blacks. Of the Renaissance, Hughes wrote in *The Big Sea*, "I was there. I had a swell time while it lasted. But I thought it wouldn't last long." He thought it would fade away because it hadn't reached "ordinary Negroes" or "raised their wages any."[30] *Tambourines to Glory* was a reflection of the world Hughes inhabited and witnessed around him in late 1950s Harlem, a story he deemed best told through gospel music and humor.

Inasmuch as black gospel music and the storefront churches where the music was being played enthralled Hughes, he suggested that charlatanry and religious exploitation, which often occurred in those spaces, also served as one of the primary motivations for writing *Tambourines to Glory*. He meant *Tambourines to Glory* to be a sharp critique of racketeering in religion, and he rarely failed to emphasize that aspect of the work in his discussions of it. The unacknowledged author of the liner notes to the 1958 cast recording contended that Hughes viewed these "small, independent, and often highly unorthodox gospel churches" as "the last refuge of uninhibited Negro folk singing." The music allowed congregants to "make a joyful noise unto the Lord" and to express themselves freely "through singing, shouting, and testimonials." Perhaps drawing a contrast with the mainstream black congregations in Harlem's world of religion and churches, it was the very free, unrestrained, and uninhibited nature of these small storefront congregations that often led to institutional corruption and exploitation. Hughes had long been aware of this potential among storefront churches and other new religious movements, and it had been a concern for him dating back to his poetry of the 1930s and "Goodbye Christ" in particular. *Tambourines to Glory*, at its core, was an incisive critique of gospel churches, particularly those where religious leaders exploited their followers for money and material gain. Hughes made this point in a letter to Jean Wagner in September 1958, two months before the book was to appear in print. "My new novel *Tambourines to Glory*, John Day, Nov. 13, is about racketeering elements in some gospel churches."[31] He was still making this point in 1965. In a sensitive and carefully worded letter to a high school student from Milton, New Jersey, who had written to inquire about the meaning of the novel, Hughes underscored the "seriousness" of the story, distinguishing the exploits of the Reed Sisters and Tambourine Temple from sincere expressions of religion, and affirming Essie's proclamation as the heart of the novel.

Dear Mr. Pakala: About *Tambourines to Glory*, it is a serious expose written in a light manner of the kinds of churches run mostly by religious racketeers (see my *Big Sea*, pages 275–278 in the chapter "Spectacles in Color" concerning a real evangelist of this type whom I knew). I have the greatest respect for sincere folks of any religious faith, but none at all for those like the late Daddy Grace, pulpit showman who died leaving almost a million dollars (so the papers said) made from the sort of activities Laura indulges in in my novel. What my book is trying to say is expressed by Essie on page 179: "Religion has got no business being made into a gyp game. Whatever part of God is in everybody is not to be played with—and everybody has a part of God in them." I'm grateful for your interest. Sincerely yours, Langston Hughes.[32]

The story of *Tambourines to Glory* was simple, told through vivacious gospel music and with humor, but Hughes wanted readers and theatergoers to understand the serious critique of religious exploitation embedded in the narrative.

Placing two women as leaders of an "open air" church, a storefront church, and ultimately a large nondenominational congregation in 1950s Harlem not only enlivened the story of *Tambourines to Glory*, it also revealed a gendered slice of Harlem life during that time. Although the voices of women are articulated throughout Hughes's work, and particularly in the work on religion, the Reed Sisters represent a demographic reality that black women were beginning to move into positions of clerical authority in these newer churches and that women comprised the majority membership in most of them. Mother Horn, the Mother Bradley in the novel who served as one of the models for the Reed Sisters, was one of the most prominent black women ministers with her own congregation in Harlem from the 1930s to the 1960s. In addition to Horn, countless other black women led churches from small storefronts to those in regular edifices. One of the most salient consequences of the rapid changes in African American enclaves during the Great Migration and after World War II was that ministry was no longer considered the exclusive province of men. Laura, at one point, proclaims herself a "she-male" minister in order to bolster her claim to authority, reflecting the "confused gender expectations" black women preachers faced during the Great Migration, even though the ministry as well as the institution of the church were becoming overwhelmingly female in some ecclesial sectors of black Harlem.[33]

Essie and Laura further represented the limited options available to black women in a Harlem that was rapidly deteriorating, far from its former glory. By the late 1950s, Harlem had become a bona fide "ghetto," in the parlance of the day. As John Henrik Clarke writes, "in the years after the Second World War, Harlem became a community in decline." There was an exodus of middle-class blacks, who moved to other Manhattan neighborhoods, Westchester County, and Connecticut.[34] In the aftermath of the Depression and riots in 1935 and 1943, work had virtually disappeared and the area had collapsed into poverty, decay, and crime— all of which disproportionately affected black women. The schools were some of the poorest in the nation. Hospitals were substandard. Over half the available housing was in some form of ruin. The unemployment rate in Harlem was among the highest in the nation, double that of white New Yorkers, and the few jobs available to women were in domestic service, often at half of the wage offered to whites.[35] Essie and Laura, like most black women in Harlem at the time, were caught in Harlem's cycle of poverty with few chances to escape it outside their own initiative.

It was the Reed Sisters' initiative that elevated them out of poverty, enabling them to avoid becoming prostitutes. For Laura, their only viable choice was between becoming a "street stander" (preacher) or a "street walker." Government relief was not an option. In Laura's view it undermined one's dignity and was never enough to meet one's needs. "The relief investigator thinks one pot ought to last a week," she complained to Essie. "I sure will be glad when we ain't no longer beholding [sic] to them people." Laura's choice to become a preacher, therefore, was a choice not to become a prostitute, and indeed it is clear that she viewed the two occupations on a par with each other. In the play version, when again challenged by Essie, this time about her mink coat, Laura responds, "Prostitutes dress well, call girls and madams. I don't see why saints [lady ministers] shouldn't." Hughes likely drew inspiration to write about prostitutes from Carl Sandburg, and he wrote as many poems about or featuring prostitutes as did Sandburg, taking a similarly dim view of prostitution. Sandburg demonstrated that dim view in such poems as "Harrison Street Court" and "Gone," in which he was unable to see "agency" on the part of women who worked as prostitutes. It was only a means of exploitation by a capitalist society that operated counter to the women's well-being. The speaker in "Harrison Street Court" for example, confesses, "I been hustlin' now / Till I ain't much good anymore / I got nothin' to show for it." These women are "soiled," exploited, and abused—"beaten by the fist of the men using them." They develop regrets, but don't develop themselves.[36] In a similar way, in Hughes's "Midnight Chippie's Lament," "Young Prostitute," and "A Ruined Gal," prostitutes are depicted as victims of exploitation rather than agents on their own behalf. The central figure of "Young Prostitute" has been "used up" to the extent that she has become like a "withered flower on a broken stem." The speaker in "A Ruined Gal" contemplates suicide because she is lonely and weary and no longer suitable for marriage. She ends her soliloquy by cursing her mother "for ever havin' a daughter."[37] Even though the Reed Sisters avoid this fate and beat the odds in Harlem, reversing the cycle of poverty, by juxtaposing preaching against prostitution Hughes further underscored his social commentary about the limited options of black women in 1950s Harlem.

For all the ways Hughes intended *Tambourines to Glory* to be a slice of Harlem life with regard to the lives of black women, a critique of the racketeering in religion among some of the gospel churches, and a showcase for his comedic writing and love for gospel music, it was also and ultimately a religious allegory and a morality play. Underlying the humor, the music, and the social commentary was a probe of the complexities and contradictions of religion on a personal and institutional level. It was a theatrical exploration of how "good" and "bad" as ethical and moral categories are rarely clear-cut and often mutually reinforcing. In this way, *Tambourines* represents two competing notions of religiosity rather than clear distinctions between a saint and a sinner, embodied in the Reed Sisters.

Hughes revealed the first indication of this deeper dimension to *Tambourines* through the name he gave the two women. The name Reed was evocative of his "Auntie" Reed in Kansas. In many ways, *Tambourines to Glory* was a tribute to Mary Reed and his memories of St. Luke AME where she belonged and where he attended as a child, "as a shining star." As Cheryl Sanders maintains, "*Tambourines to Glory* is the play Hughes wrote for Aunt Reed." But *Tambourines to Glory* was also a tribute to his "Uncle" Reed, who, as Hughes informs us in *The Big Sea*, "was a sinner and never went to church as long as he lived, nor cared anything about it." As a nonchurchgoer, James Reed would have been deemed a foil to his saintly wife in their small Kansas community. Hughes, however, made little distinction between them; rather, he saw them as two good ways of being, two good people. "Both of them were very good and kind," he explained, "the one who went to church and the one who didn't." The couple's different lives served as a lesson for Hughes, and as he put it, they were the reason he "learned to like both Christians and sinners equally well."[38] The saint and the sinner had equal value in moral terms. Indeed, the one necessitated the other.

Essie and Laura were composites of Mary and James Reed, as Hughes likely had the couple very much in mind as he wrote the play. On the surface, the two women were the foils of one another in the same way the Kansas couple were. One was a saint and the other a sinner; one good and the other bad. Laura's strength is pitted against Essie's weakness, her brains against Essie's "empty mind," her sexual appetite against Essie's lack of it, her humanity pitted against Essie's sanctimony. Laura states this clearly in her explanation to Buddy of the differences between them. "If I'm the body, Essie's the soul." Or, as Laura states to Essie in the book version, "I still got feet of clay, Essie. You're the soul." Even though good and God ultimately triumph in *Tambourines*, close analysis shows that the concepts of good and bad are not always as starkly drawn in the play and novel as Hughes intimated. Just who is performing the moral good and what exactly is good or bad is often unclear. The bad leads to good ends and moral correctness often shields hypocrisy. Laura, for example, proclaims that her motivation for starting the church actually stemmed from her need to simply be "doing something" as much as it was the desire to lift herself out of poverty. "Me, I need to be doing something—good, bad, or indifferent." "I'm active," she concludes. And it is her "activity" that leads to establishing Tambourine Temple, a church that members ultimately praise for its role in their salvation. Birdie Lee affirms on two different occasions how both Laura and Essie were instrumental in her salvation. "I heard Sister Laura preaching, Sister Essie praying," she testifies, and "they preached and prayed and sung me into the hands of God!" In the novel version, she proclaims to Essie that "in spite of Laura Reed," she was taken out of "the gutter of Lenox Avenue" and "raised . . . up to the curbstone of redemption."[39] Deacon Crow gives an even more expansive testimony: "Oh, I'm here to tell you tonight, since I started to live right, it is my determination to keep on—on the path to glory. In my sinful days, before I found this church, I were a dyed-in-the-wool sinner. . . . Now I've seen the light! Sister Essie and Sister Laura brought me to the faith." In the play version, he further asserts that no one is "without sin" and Tambourine Temple has "saved souls."[40] Essie corroborates this thought to Laura, stating, "you've done better than you know—God is in this church."[41] She even concedes that it was Laura's "activity" that brought Essie to a renewed relationship to the church and her faith from which she had strayed. In a prayer not long after they officially launch the church, Essie admits, "I got to give Laura credit, Lord, for connecting me to you. . . . Laura reached out and called Your name, and a prayer come into my mouth then and there." And although Essie increasingly retreats into a stance of "saintliness," it is her inactivity, complicity, and hypocrisy that threatens the life of the church and leads to Buddy's murder. The saint's knife, which she carried for "protection," becomes the instrument of the most heinous act in the play (and the sinner who commits it does so out of "self-defense," Hughes was careful to state). When Deacon Crow first gives testimony that he had given up the knife he'd carried for years, Essie is the first out of her seat to exclaim, "Praise God," but when Laura whispers to her that she should do the same, Essie ignores her. Later, Essie suggests that Laura not be so "bold" with her sinning, to which Laura bitingly responds that she would find it easier to be a saint than a "hypocrite."[42] Just as Hughes came to appreciate his "saintly" Aunt Reed and his "sinner" Uncle Reed, viewing them both as "good people," he constructed the characters of the Reed Sisters to disrupt and complicate notions of good and bad.

The ultimate effect of *Tambourines to Glory*, therefore, was not so much a sharp contrast between saint and sinner and good and bad, but a study of the murkiness of the categories and an exploration of two approaches to religious life. Those two approaches—embodied in Essie and Laura—had attendant consequences and both possessed modernist overtones. Laura concedes that she "ain't no saint," basing this assessment on her love for the "unholy trinity" of social sins, "love, likker, and loot." She is profane, irreverent, and has never "seen" Jesus, a clear reference to Hughes's own failure to "see" Jesus at age twelve. She is effective as a preacher and very convincing as the principal leader of Tambourine Temple but is certain that the reason she can fake religious enthusiasm is because of the gift for storytelling she inherited from her mother back in North Carolina. "Mama never saw a ghost in her life, no more than I ever saw Jesus," she explains to Essie. "But she could make up ghost stories to raise the hair on your head. That's where I get my gift of making up visions." Laura further explains that she places her faith not in visions but in her "experiences" and in herself. Her experiences are "stronger than [her] faith," and they are what inform her choices. Hers is a religion of experience over faith and one of "self-reliance," articulated through-out the text in ways that resonate with aspects of Transcendentalist poet Ralph Waldo Emerson's philosophy on the primacy of experience and the divinity of the self.[43] Laura repeatedly asserts, "I depend on myself, myself" and contends that one's own efforts must work in conjunction with faith. She is not an unbeliever. Rather, she is a believer in herself and her own efforts. "God helps those who help themselves," she informs Essie, employing the famously unbiblical yet common maxim about human agency. She does not deny God's assistance in the construction of their church but places primacy on her life experiences and her own efforts to bring it about. The church comes to be "with HIS guidance and *my* mind," she boasts to Essie. Indeed, she concludes, "everything people are talking about around here was my idea."[44]

Essie's approach to religious life involves doubting herself and her own abilities while determining to trust in God. She places her Christian faith above her own efforts and experiences, and she prioritizes piety over action. Indeed, inaction for her is a form of piety until she learns the futility of just "setting." Essie describes herself, for example, as too "lazy" to sin. When explaining why she converted, she says that she was "never much of a sinner, nohow. I can't go for sin like Laura. Fast life tires me out."[45] For Essie, sins are the social ones Laura commits and sal-vation is foremost a matter of changing one's behavior. "When peoples is under the spell of Christ," she explains to Laura, "they most in generally behaves themselves." Changed behavior is the first indication of salva-tion in Essie's approach to religion, a personal piety that is primarily about inaction, what one *doesn't* do. Essie's pious inactivity is a principal source of the tension between the Reed Sisters, as Laura consistently urges Essie to "do something." "Energize yourself, Essie!" Essie's faith of inactivity, however, plays out in *Tambourines to Glory* as the more conventional approach and the one most resonant with many African American religious traditions. Hughes makes this clear in both genres of the story, as it is Essie who most ardently clings to the theological and discursive formulations, musical traditions, and liturgical practices of her theologically conservative Christian upbringing.

The book opens with Essie's remembrance of the church she attended on Palm Sunday and Easter as a child. "I loved those songs," she mused. Essie is the one who prays about starting the church, and she resists any form of bodily "pleasure" and "temptation." Indeed, Essie spends a great deal of time condemning Laura for not conducting her life in a way she deems appropriate for a "Christian woman." Moreover, Essie aligns with certain black religious traditions by way of words and phrases that indicate their influence on her, as well as the influence of the Christian Scriptures. "I don't want to start nothing religious on the wages of sin" (Romans 6:23, KJV), she exclaims upon learning that Laura has purchased a Bible for Tambourine Temple with winnings from a policy hit. At the same time, Essie embraces notions seemingly inconsistent with the religious traditions of her Baptist past. She explains to Laura, for example, that her quest for "the good" can be described as a quest to find out "what *is* God in terms of what *we* is," a humanist worldview that puts primacy on the human experience of God rather than God as an entity separate from human experience. And in her reading of modernist theologian Howard Thurman she is confronted with someone who has been just as influenced by Quakerism and Gandhi as he has his black Baptist faith and whose "interpretation" of Jesus concludes that Jesus "belongs to no age, no race, no creed."[46] When her reckoning in jail prompts her to reject pious inactivity for social activism, it leads to a transformation of Tambourine Temple in a way that reflects the basic assumptions of the Social Gospel.

On the one hand, as composites of the Reeds, Essie and Laura embody the couple's contradistinctions as saint and sinner and good and bad. But on the other hand, they represent the murkiness of the categories. Hughes wrote the play and the novel with the modest aim of telling a story about Harlem life with wit and humor, the racketeering in the gospel churches, and to showcase his love for gospel music. The real meaning of *Tambourines to Glory* as an urban folk melodrama, however, is in the way the lives of the two women unfold as a morality play that complicates notions of sin and salvation, underscoring two equally valid approaches to religious life. As Hughes had done in his first novel and in much of his other writing, the women of *Tambourines to Glory* ultimately meet on the plain of their common humanity, despite apparent surface differences. As Hughes surmises, they were "two human pebbles in the Harlem brook" that had "begun to change the course of its water."[47] Theatergoers and readers largely missed this deeper, more serious level of meaning in *Tambourines to Glory*, as reaction to the work rarely reached beyond the surface of the fictional Harlem church with two black southern migrant women at the helm, singing, shouting, and exploiting their parishioners.

The Drama of Church and the Church as Theater

With *Tambourines to Glory*, Hughes not only explores the dramatic possibilities of black cultural expression on stage, but also the drama inherent in black religious forms and black church culture. At its core, however, and in artistic terms, the complex morality play behind the urban folk drama reflects Hughes's love for the dramatic arts and the theater. His attraction to the theater began early at his mother's behest. An amateur actress herself, Carrie Langston had introduced Hughes to the theater as a young child. His love was immediate and deep, which accounts, in part, for his fascination with *Shuffle Along* when he first arrived in New York. Although he had begun to write poetry in high school, he started writing plays soon after. *The Gold Piece*, Hughes's first play, written in 1921 and published in the children's magazine *The Brownies' Book*, gave a thematic foretaste of the dramatic works to follow. It told the simple story of a "peasant boy" and his wife in a Mexican village who sacrifice a gold coin in order to help a distressed old woman and her blind son.[48] By the 1930s he had significantly developed his skill as a playwright, evidenced by fourteen major and minor productions, including *Mulatto: A Play of the Deep South*; *Mule Bone: A Comedy of Negro Life*; *Little Ham*; and *Don't You Want to Be Free?: A Poetry Play from Slavery through the Blues to Now—and Then Some! With Singing, Music and Dancing*. Of these, *Mulatto* was Hughes's first professionally developed play, appearing on Broadway in 1935.[49] The Broadway version varied significantly from Hughes's original script, but the core idea about race and miscegenation had surfaced in Hughes's 1925 poem "Cross" and served as the basis for the libretto of *The Barrier* (1950), the opera he co-wrote with Jan Meyerowitz.[50] The story of "Cross" impressed Meyerowitz, who, as a German Jew and Christian convert, was drawn to its account of alienation and displacement. African American poet Stanley

Braithwaite, however, a Boston-bred admirer of the English Romantic poets, was not so impressed. To Hughes's great disappointment, Braithwaite awarded "Cross" third prize in the *Crisis*'s poetry competition.[51] It would become, however, one of his most cited poems about race among his early artistic productions.

Like most of Hughes's work, his dramatic plays covered a range of topics, including race, race relations, class disparity, economic struggle, urban culture, and romantic liaisons. The theater's ability to capture the lives of ordinary blacks or the "low-down folk" captivated him, and it became another means by which he could artistically display his love for black people, the "beautiful" and the "ugly," as he so elegantly stated in "The Negro Artist and the Racial Mountain" in 1926. In an application to the Rosenwald Fund in 1938, therefore, he insisted that there was a "great need for spiritually true dramas for the Negro theater," by which he meant dramas that authentically showed black life. His use of the term "spiritually true," however, revealed another dimension of Hughes's theatrical productions. In his pursuit of black authenticity via the stage, he often employed religious material, including theological language and frameworks, sacred music, and aspects of black church culture. This was not uncommon. Throughout the interwar period, African American playwrights produced hundreds of scripts with religious themes, viewing plays, in the words of Craig Prentiss, as "a vital site for conveying and contesting various theological perspectives within African American communities."[52] The first instances of this in Hughes's writing were in two plays he produced in 1937 and 1942. The first, *Don't You Want to Be Free?* was a "music-drama" written for the Harlem Suitcase Theater, one of three theater companies Hughes established during his lifetime and developed with the support of his friend Louise Thompson and backing from the International Workers Organization (IWO).[53] The play told "the entire scope of Negro history from Africa to America," Hughes suggested, and was replete with the music common to "any humble Negro church." It was a tremendous success when it first aired and he went on to stage many performances.[54] *The Sun Do Move* contained even more religious material, particularly with regard to the music and in most respects was Hughes's first bona fide religious play. Produced in Chicago for the Sky Loft Players, another of Hughes's theatrical groups, *The Sun Do Move* took its name from the famous nineteenth-century sermon by African American minister, John Jasper. The three-act play was set in the Deep South from 1800 leading up to the Civil War and depicted emancipation as an act of God and was told through testimony and spirituals. Aptly resonant with nascent civil rights struggles in the early 1940s, *The Sun Do Move* linked social justice, nationalism, and spiritual freedom. In the play, when Quakers take the core protagonists into free territory the chorus sings, "Free at last, Free at last, Thank God-A-Mighty, Free at last."[55] The religious material in these early theatrical productions not only expressed Hughes's confidence in their ability to represent the "spiritually true" with regard to black authenticity, but also to provide a platform for his religious and theological ideas.

Tambourines to Glory, however, took the search for black authenticity a step further, building on the notion that certain expressions of black church, particularly the gospel churches, were already theater. Noting the inherent theatricality of black religious worship dating back to the nineteenth century, sociologists C. Eric Lincoln and Lawrence Mamiya state, "the black church was the first theater in the black community."[56] The connection between black churches and theatricality, therefore, was not new. The connection between black church worship and the theater as a venue, however, was entirely novel, and Hughes pioneered this connection in public discourse. Indeed, *Tambourines to Glory* combined the issues related to church and theatricality, black church worship performed in theaters, and theaters converted into churches. With *Tambourines to Glory* and the gospel song-plays that followed it, Hughes had found a niche and a worthy cultural vehicle for his interest in black gospel music and his explorations of the inherent drama in black religious institutions and forms of worship, notably in a type of church deemed especially prone to racketeering in religion.

Hughes's confidence in the dramatic possibilities of black church worship and music represented a reversal of opinion on his part. A decade before penning *Tambourines to Glory* he had shifted between serious doubts and a pallid ambivalence about the connection between church and theater, theaters converted into churches, and about the commercialization and materialism of gospel artists. He saw the worlds of church and theater as separate and self-contained with no need for cross-influencing. Writing for the *Chicago Defender* in 1947 in an article entitled, "Church, Theater, and Gospel Songs," Hughes expressed dismay at the number of new theater-churches with huge placards announcing their services. The placards made the churches seem more like places of entertainment than of worship. In addition, some churches were even drawing on the world of the theater for their worship services and music. "These placards set me to thinking how nowadays the theatre has invaded the church," he bemoaned, "and the church has taken over various aspects of show business." He further wrote, "the churches have so many wonderful entertainers in their ranks that I do not quite see why they need to draw upon the theatre."[57]

In the same piece, Hughes singled out Sister Rosetta Tharpe for criticism. Tharpe, one of the fastest rising gospel artists of the 1940s, had defied her conservative Church of God in Christ (COGIC) Pentecostal upbringing to play church music in "secular" venues, particularly in nightclubs. "Although I admire Sister Tharpe's gusto and rhythms as a singing guitarist," he admitted, "I do not always respect her taste. I remember hearing her in a Broadway nightclub swing a religious song while members of the band clowned behind her. This seemed to me to be in very bad taste indeed." For Hughes, sacred music was to be played in sacred spaces only. "I do not think religious songs with their deep meanings for many people are a proper part of nightclub entertainment where folks are out for fun and drinking."[58] But performing gospel music in nightclubs was becoming a popular trend and Tharpe was not alone. The Apollo Theater began holding gospel performances in the 1950s with such artists as the Caravans, the Staple Singers, and James Cleveland. Clara Ward and the Ward Singers also notoriously performed in secular venues throughout the 1950s and 1960s, with Ward suggesting that she found the spaces "spiritually rewarding and approved by scripture." "If people won't come to hear gospel," she further asserted, "we'll take the gospel to them." Hughes, however, had his misgivings about this cross-pollination of church music and jazz and even voiced them through Jesse B. Semple, his wise and observant alter ego. When Simple noticed that some Harlem churches had begun to play jazz forms of sacred music, he proclaimed, "just like some of the bands have been jazzing up spirituals for dancing. To take church things and jazz them up is, I think, in very bad taste."[59]

By the early 1950s, Hughes began signaling some significant changes in his attitude about the relationship between church and theater, the materialism of gospel singers, and the commercialism of gospel music. Again employing the voice of Simple, Hughes acknowledged in a 1953 *Chicago Defender* column that some new trends in church and entertainment were afoot. Always the astute observer of Harlem life, Simple informs his companion, "the churches are buying up half the old movie theaters in Harlem and turning them into temples." Up and down Lenox and Seventh Avenues, he contends, "it is getting so you can't tell a theatre from a church anymore. The ministers have got their names up in lights just like the movie actors." Churches were taking over in Harlem, but not just the smaller storefront churches that had dotted the landscape in earlier decades. Indeed, "old-time store-front churches are going out of style," Simple proclaims. "From now on, it looks like you will have to call them movie-front churches—except that the box office has moved inside and turned into a collection plate, and the choir is swinging gospel songs." Church services were being advertised as "shows" and money was being made one collection after another. While his companion registers some disquiet about all this, Simple insists that he is not troubled. Recalling a recent visit to "Sister Mamie Lightfoot and her Gospel Show," Simple explains, "I were so moved." The four singers who sang that night worked those in attendance up to an ecstatic frenzy. "Folks leaped, jumped, hollered, and shouted," prompting Simple to claim that "gospel singers these days put more into a song than a lot of night club stars hanging onto a microphone. . . . The music that these people put down cannot be beat. It moves the spirit—and it moves the feet." For this reason, Simple does not begrudge them for turning theaters into churches or for their materialism. "We have some great gospel singers in this land. They are working in the vineyards of the Lord and digging in his gold mines. . . . Which is o.k. by me, as long as they keep on singing as they do."[60]

By the 1960s, the doubts and ambivalence Hughes had expressed about the merger of church and theater had completely dissipated. Hughes had completely reversed himself, affirming in a number of articles and personal appearances the theatrical possibilities of black religion, extolling its connection to the theater and to theater people, and expressing the wonders of black gospel and gospel musicians who performed inside and outside the church. A tentative and cautious statement he had made in the late 1940s that "perhaps the theater has something to bring to religion" had become a strong conviction.[61] In an article written for the *Dramatist Bulletin* in April 1963, Hughes proclaimed gospel singers a "New Asset to American Theatre." Establishing first that gospel singers were "amazing people, capable of making music from the simplest material," Hughes went on to suggest that the most effective black ministers were those who were backed by gospel choirs because the singers seemed to understand instinctively the drama of black preaching and of black church. They were masters of the dramatic arts whose sermons were infused with "highly effective religious drama." It was due to this intuitive drama on the part of black preachers and gospel singers, he asserted, that "the first plays grew out of the church," a claim he would not have made just a few years prior.[62]

With his new conviction, Hughes praised the theatricality of black religion and the presence of gospel music in theaters and other places he had previously considered unsuitable establishments and in bad taste, including nightclubs and music festivals. And increasingly he provided an explanation for his change of mind. In a short piece written for an Italian journal at the height of the popularity of *Black Nativity*, Hughes fixed gospel music firmly in American culture as the only part of black American cultural expression that still belonged to black people. "Only the gospel songs and gospel singers remain almost entirely in the hands of the negro people, rooted in the mass negro churches, the songs sung in uninhibited negro fashion, not yet subjected to formal arrangements, rigid notation, or commercial gimmicks for the sake of record sales."[63] Laura Reed expresses the exact sentiment in *Tambourines to Glory*. "These gospel songs is about the only thing the white folks ain't latched onto yet," she explains to Essie. "But they will, soon as they find out there's some dough in 'em."[64] This sense of cultural ownership had been a concern of Hughes's for a long time and was the precise point of the 1940 poem, "Note on Commercial Theatre," in which Hughes showed his ability to "tap the reservoir of hurt, resentment, and determination in the race," and lament the "shameless plundering of black music and culture by whites."[65]

> You've taken my blues and gone—
> You sing 'em on Broadway
> And you sing 'em in Hollywood bowl,

And you mixed 'em up with symphonies
And you fixed 'em
So they don't sound like me.
Yep, you done taken my blues and gone.

You also took my spirituals and gone.
You put me in *Macbeth* and *Carmen Jones*
And all kinds of *Swing Mikados*
And in everything but what's about me—

As Hughes saw it, gospel music was the last vestige of authentic black folk culture and gospel singers had a responsibility to spread it to as many venues outside the church as possible. It was the music of the black past but also of the contemporary moment and in that way it was thoroughly modern. "Musicologists state that church music is usually a half-century behind secular music," he further clarified in the Italian journal. "In gospel music there is no such lag. Although religious in mood and meaning, it is very much of today in its melodic flavors, its driving beat, its popular appeal, and its textual use of contemporary idioms."[66] By the mid-1960s, Hughes's merging of church and theater had enhanced and augmented his professional reputation, as he became just as well known for his expertise in gospel music and his gospel plays as for any of his other work. An editorial published in the *Chicago Defender* in 1965 entitled "Poets of Song" proclaimed Hughes the monarch of gospel singing insofar as its use in the theater goes" and "the [king] of the gospelers in the American theatre."[67]

Tambourines to (Off) Broadway

As a theatrical production, *Tambourines to Glory* developed from Hughes's changed attitude regarding the connection between church and theater, theaters converted into churches, and the value of gospel music and gospel artists. In getting it to the stage, however, he faced many hurdles and complications, rooted primarily in issues of aesthetics, racial politics, racial representations, and religious differences. Only his determination and resiliency kept *Tambourines to Glory* alive and helped it to make its way to Off Broadway.[68]

Hughes circulated the play first among close friends as he thought about ways to get it produced. In further describing it to Arna Bontemps, he suggested, "If Mahalia Jackson won't go into the theatre, I'd like to have Juanita Hall and Sister Tharpe for the two leads, and pretty Reri Grist (who was in Barrier) for the daughter, Dots Johnson the handsome villain." Jackson had famously resisted singing in secular venues until she relented in 1958 to sing at the Newport Jazz Festival. As to attending or performing in theaters, she stood her ground. Recommending Rosetta Tharpe for one of the roles demonstrated in the clearest way Hughes's new attitude about the intersection of the sacred and the secular. In response, Bontemps not only agreed with Hughes's casting choices but also confirmed that Hughes had been thinking about the themes manifest in the play for most of his career. "Your new play seems to be the outgrowth of an idea that's been turning in your mind a long time—something making dramatic use of the gospel music," he wrote. "Maybe that's why you could do it so quickly once you decided to actually get it on paper. The idea as you mention it, sounds like a modern day morality play, and your cast suggestions sound like solid senders."[69]

Originally, however, the play generated little interest from producers. Figuring that a novel by the same name would have greater success, Hughes wrote the novel and steadily revised it over the course of many months, making some substantive changes. It, too, received little attention at first, as rejection after rejection appeared in the mail at 20 E. 127th Street until June 1958 when the John Day Company agreed to publish it that fall. Hughes was elated, but it was not until some producers at Hexter productions expressed interest in a "dramatized" version of the novel that it got any serious attention regarding its potential for Broadway. It was the dramatization of the novel as a play that finally peaked their interest and launched its journey to the stage.[70] Hughes busied himself converting the play that had become a novel back into a play.

There are several slightly different accounts of how the play made its long trek to the stage, but in all accounts, Jobe Huntley figures prominently. Since Hughes did not read or write music, he always recruited the assistance of musicians to put music to his lyrics. Huntley, a local gospel musician and composer, seemed happy to oblige. Despite the interest of Hexter Productions, however, the theater guild strongly resisted staging *Tambourines to Glory* until finally relenting after a two-year struggle. The difficulties with staging the play was emblematic of the difficulties Hughes faced with most of his theatrical productions. The persistent frustrations prompted him to complain to James Baldwin in 1953, the year Baldwin's novel *Go Tell It on the Mountain* appeared. "If you want to die, be disturbed, maladjusted, neurotic, and psychotic, disappointed, and disjointed, just write plays." And to arts critic Paine Knickerbocker he insisted, "Dealing with the Theater Guild . . . is like handling the Queen Mary. It is not easy to dock."[71] With everything in motion, however, Hughes's hopes for the cast were unfulfilled. Mahalia Jackson would not do it, remaining true to her convictions. Efforts to get Pearl Bailey came to naught. She was under doctor's care, waiting to see if she would be able to perform or even if she wanted to do another Broadway show.[72] Hughes also wanted Sugar Ray Robinson for the role of Buddy and tried, but failed, to get him. Robinson had had a remarkable career in the boxing ring as a welterweight and a middleweight by the late 1950s, but was in decline from his glory days of the 1940s. He had aspirations to be an entertainer and was still very popular. According to Bontemps, Robinson would have been "just right for Buddy" and bound to draw a huge crowd since it would be his first play.[73] With the exception of Hazel Scott and Clara Ward, Hughes had to settle for lesser-known actors to complement the relatively well-known co-composer he had in Huntley.

By the summer of 1960, *Tambourines to Glory* was finally in rehearsals with Hazel Scott, Nipsey Russell, Georgia Blake, Joseph Attles, Olga James, and Clara Ward. African American choral conductor Eva Jessye had been hired as musical director. The wait to get gospel artist Clara Ward proved well worth it. In her role as the feisty "lady drummer," Birdie Lee, she was already developing into what many thought would be the star attraction. "At the moment, it looks as if Clara Ward might steal the show in her character-comedy role of the little old drum playing lady, Birdie Lee," Hughes enthused to Bontemps. "Every time she opens her mouth to sing or speak *something* happens. She seems a 'natural' and is certainly authentic."[74] Hughes had long been an admirer of Wards', which he told her when he made his first tentative steps to ask her to join the cast: "I would very much like to meet and talk with you as I have long been an admirer of yours and your singers and often listen to your records which I have in my collection."[75] By the time of the rehearsals and tryouts, they were on such a rapport that Ward was offering Hughes friendly (unheeded) artistic advice, including the suggestion to add "a white 'Laura' somebody like Shelley Winters" to the cast and use more of *her* songs.[76]

The first sign of trouble with casting came at the rehearsals and initial trial run at the Westport Country Playhouse in Connecticut. Although Clara Ward as Birdie Lee was particularly good, Hazel Scott as Laura was not. The young and beautiful pianist, actress, and singer had already had a stellar career by the late 1950s. Born in Trinidad and having studied at the Juilliard School, she was a popular jazz performer and the first black woman to have her own variety TV program, "The Hazel Scott Show." By the time of rehearsals for *Tambourines to Glory*, however, Scott was headed for divorce from Adam Clayton Powell Jr. of Abyssinian Baptist Church and soon to become an expat in Paris. She never took the production seriously and often appeared bored and distracted. As her biographer, Karen Chilton, wrote, "at the start of rehearsals, Hazel approached the work with a great deal of focus. But as rehearsals continued she became distracted, losing interest in the sometimes arduous process that went into mounting a new play—script rewrites, repeated changes in stage blocking, lighting, movement."[77] Her interest in the play and its subject matter did not match her large talents as a singer and actress, even though Hughes and the producers were initially happy to have someone of her stature on board. Hughes praised the "humanity" she brought to the role but recognized that she was not right for the part. "Hazel Scott is creating a warm and very human portrayal—not as funny, of course, as Pearl Bailey might have been—nor as earthy," he wrote to Arna Bontemps, "but more believable and *human* and sort of lovable."[78] This all changed, and even Hughes began to view her as weak. "Definitely weak, beautiful, but generally unconvincing" he concluded. Only a few weeks into rehearsal, she was "quietly dropped" from the production.[79]

The difficulties acquiring the right cast and Scott's departure, however, were only surface problems compared to the deep artistic, theological, ideological, and political ones that dogged the show. After the trial run at Westport, the show received decidedly mixed reviews. Hughes, as ever, remained optimistic, even informing his friend Reverend Frank

Mitchell of Pinn Memorial Church in Philadelphia that "it went well in its Westport tryout, all good reviews," and everything went smoothly "except for a few minor blowups."[80] In actual fact, the reviews were not good, leading the nervous theater guild to stall its progress to Broadway when Hughes wanted to continue. *Tambourines to Glory* would finally make it to Broadway, opening at the Little Theatre, a venue established by American theater producer and playwright Winthop Ames. The final cast included many who would go on to great acclaim in television, movies, and the stage, including Hilda Sims, Rosetta LeNoire, Louis Gossett, Robert Guillaume, Micki Grant, Anna English, Joseph Attles, and, of course, Clara Ward. The talent of the players, however, could not fix the play, and the reviews were again mixed.[81] Lawrence Langner and the guild's responses were indicative and telling. They wanted to disassociate themselves from a production that some theatergoers and critics considered "Uncle Tommish and generally demeaning to blacks."[82] Langner, a powerful Welsh-born producer and playwright, had established both the theater guild and the Westport Country Playhouse and had a lot at stake in the production. Some African Americans took exception to the portrayal of black urban life in general and black church life in particular. And that view was widely shared. As Arnold Rampersad has written, "on religious, moral, and political grounds, several observers found the play in appalling taste."[83]

As the first series of responses indicated, the critiques of *Tambourines to Glory* generally fell along racial and class lines. They were also rooted in the question as to whether a display of black "folk" religiosity was appropriate for the stage, a question Hughes had already affirmatively answered for himself personally. Additionally, there was a concern that the show was politically regressive at a time of great social change for black people. This was precisely the point cookbook author and South African–born second wife of Walter White, Poppy Cannon White, made in a short 1963 review of the show entitled, "Too Late—Too Soon." White praised the "unusual musical" and the "extra ordinary singers," but stated that something had gone wrong with the stage production. It was out of step and out of time. "Definitely and obviously, the play does not belong in the present," she contended, "and the past is not distant enough. The feeling is not so much past as passé." For White, the show was riddled with "outworn stereotypes" and clichés about black worship and about Harlem. These would have been funny twenty years ago, she continued, but the times had changed and so had Harlem and Harlem's churches, which were on the forefront of social and political transformation. "At long last, our churches—white and coloured—are taking the lead in the civil rights battle. Ministers of the gospel are going to jail . . . but not in shame! Proudly and willingly for freedom-marching." White strongly intimated that in *Tambourines to Glory* Hughes had drawn a portrait of the old Harlem, not the "new Harlem." She was not alone in this view. Murray D. Morrison, who identified himself as "white—without any extra pride" from the Bronx, wrote to make a similar claim about the show being politically antiquated. Morrison more than disliked *Tambourines*; he found it disappointing. As a play it was "dreadful" with "pathetic staging," countered only by the singing, which he found "superb." What "puzzled" Morrison was why Hughes would produce a play replete with stereotypes and caricatures when blacks were "making advances—socially, economically, education-wise." "Why at *this* time particularly, does a group of talented people want to present the Negro in the worst light?—a phony church, phony Holy Water, knife-carrying—all the miserable clichés of which the Negro has been charged by the prejudiced, ignorant non-Negro people." Why "invite" laughter and risk giving whites justification for their prejudices toward blacks? In a way that both reflected and seized the current politicized climate, Morrison wished Hughes would write a different play. "Write us a play of nobility and poetry—about the negro as a *person*, a human being—as an equal brother in God's world!," he charged.[84]

Some African American civil rights advocates were equally concerned about *Tambourines to Glory*. After the show made its debut at the Little Theater, Anna Arnold Hedgeman wrote Hughes to complain. Hedgeman was a college-educated political activist who had been a key member of a national council working for a permanent Fair Employment Practices Commission, dean of women at Howard University, and columnist at the *New York Age*. She had also served as a cabinet member in New York City Mayor Robert Wagner's administration and was a principal organizer, along with A. Philip Randolph and Bayard Rustin, of the March on Washington. Hedgeman reported to Hughes that she had given a full presentation on her objections to the play at St. Mark's Methodist Episcopal Church in Harlem and expressed her regret that

Hughes was not in attendance. The presentation suggested that *Tambourines to Glory* was out of step with the times politically and frustrated the efforts of those working at "the grass roots" for social change. "You are part of the talent of our time and it seemed a tragic irony indeed that you should be presenting *Tambourines to Glory* when we so much need the truly significant religious story of the Negro to be presented as I believe you can do it." "I used your early poetry to illustrate my point," she further explained. Hedgeman's letter quoted heavily from a statement Hughes had recently made in the *Pittsburgh Courier*, wherein he justified his depictions of black "folk" expressions, noting the "wonder and beauty to be found in the basic creations of the Negro." Hedgeman turned the statement against Hughes, however, suggesting that "wonder" and "beauty" were precisely what *Tambourines to Glory* lacked, particularly when it came to representations of black Harlemites and black churches. "Your quote is very revealing, for all I am really asking of you is that you present the 'wonder' and 'beauty' of the basic creations of the Negro, past and present." Hedgeman took issue with the depiction of storefronts as spaces of exploitation. For her, these smaller spaces are "essentially the story of the loneliness of the refugee." Echoing the sentiments of her friend and fellow worker, Bayard Rustin, she argued that storefront churches were spaces that "brought warmth and friendliness when the larger churches seemed too formal and/or too unaware. There are wonderful stories there." *Tambourines to Glory* was a play that underscored the problems with these spaces while failing to see their "beauty" and "wonder." The real danger, she concluded, was how *Tambourines to Glory* would be received by white theatergoers. As it stood, the play only showed the white public "the noise of the singing without the comprehension of the beauty and wonder."[85]

Artists and writers who critiqued *Tambourines to Glory* were also concerned about the religious aspects of the play, but they concentrated primarily on issues of craft, character development, and aesthetics. A few days after the Westport tryout, Loften Mitchell wrote Hughes to express his thoughts. Mitchell was a longtime Harlem resident and by 1960 had staged a number of plays in New York. He had his most successful production in 1957 with "A Land Beyond the River," which played for ninety-six shows at the Greenwich Mews Theatre. Mitchell reported, "there were times when I roared with laughter and times when I cried out loud," but he wanted to offer his "critical two-cents." He assured Hughes that he should not worry about the inevitable criticism about "stereotypes." Stereotypes are more often disagreements about "craft" than anything else, he contended. He did, however, have two central concerns. One, he felt the character of Buddy needed more "finesse." For Mitchell, Hughes did not seem to make the most out of a character that certainly was more complicated than depicted. "I believe he has more veneer than met the eye on the stage." Like many other lay critics and professional reviewers, Mitchell also disliked the ending. He did not object to the sensationalism of Buddy's killing; rather, he thought the implications of the murder for Laura and Essie were misdirected. Instead of a story of accusation, guilt, confession, and deliverance, Mitchell saw an opportunity to demonstrate religious evolution. Mitchell came as close as any of the critics to recognizing the more complex story about the religious differences embodied in the two women, even recognizing that Essie makes a move from storefront religion to the Social Gospel. For his tastes, however, this could have been made even more explicit. The biggest change should occur with Essie, he surmised. The lesson she learns in the end is that the church should be a social force. "And I'd end the play with the jail scene—with Essie's realization of a social gospel, that money-changers must be chased from the Temple, that day nurseries and the abundant life must be brought to this earth, and that God is in all of us, not out there where we reach frantically for Him and go into ecstatic numbers." Unlike Anna Arnold Hedgeman, however, Mitchell took issue with the title and the ethos of *Tambourines to Glory* insofar as it conjured images of storefront religion. He wondered why there had to be a presentation of storefront religion at all since ultimately the play was a critique of this culture, and the principal characters moved from it to a more socially aware religion. Storefront religion was a thing of the past: "Essie has moved beyond this type of stuff and so have the others," he concluded.

Jan Meyerowitz and James Emanuel expressed similar appreciations but divergent critiques. Meyerowitz liked the music but thought it suffocated the play and in the end muted the critique of black churches. "I enjoyed your show—but of your play there wasn't enough, I think. But of that remarkable music, there was too much." He saw *Tambourines to Glory* as "an immense indictment of Protestantism" and the music, however good, took away from that. The play did not do justice to the novel, which was destined to be "a solid classic, as a work of art and as a document."[86] Emanuel, who was writing a book about Hughes at the time and maintained a long and detailed correspondence with him, wrote Hughes shortly after he and his wife, Etha, saw the production. They thought the music was the high point but agreed with the critiques of the ending. He wondered, however, how reviewers could miss the larger point about "authenticity" Hughes was attempting to make. "Both of us liked 'Tambourines' very much; and the audience as a whole, if one might judge from the applause and participation in the gospel beats, was enthusiastic." He thought the play to be well cast and especially liked the gospel songs performed by Clyde Williams and Clara Ward. And while he agreed that some of the melodramatics were excessive—"I refer particularly to the knifing and death"—he thought the negative reviews had woefully missed the point. "I have seen no reviews that revealed appreciation of the authenticity of the gospel setting and its possibilities as a new kind of dramatic art," he contended. In the end, Emanuel was sure that all theatergoers could at least agree that *Tambourines to Glory* was "good entertainment," and noting that it had been set to close early, deserving of a longer run at the Little Theater.[87]

Some of the sharpest and most unflinching reactions to *Tambourines to Glory* came from the general public. Theatergoers complained that it was "the worst thing" they'd ever witnessed on stage and simply bemoaned, "I thought we'd gotten away from that kind of thing." A letter he received from David Litt of Freeport, New York, was emblematic. Writing Hughes in October 1963, Litt informed him that he had seen the play recently and "enjoyed it in spots." Though the gospel singing was thrilling, the story itself was "banal and trite." For Litt, the "basic flaw" with the play was that the satire was not sustained. What started as a satire of the church became in Litt's view a boring love story, one that had been fodder for Broadway "a hundred times over." To him Laura was "undeveloped." She would have been more interesting if her badness had been sustained as a satire throughout, from the church to love to life. Her change at the end was unconvincing and lacked theatricality. She is an exploiter and should just be that way throughout. She exploits the church because at its core, the church is also bad. Its only value was to generate entertainment and enjoyment for its congregants. Laura understands this and exploits it. For Litt, Essie was not the innocent she appears in the play. She, too, is bad and worldly wise. "She realized that to want to be good you have to sometimes be bad." In a curious move of abject hubris, he asked Hughes to allow him to rewrite *Tambourines to Glory*. "I'd like to take a crack at re-doing your play, if I may. Please let me know."[88] He would not be the last person to make such a request.

The book version of *Tambourines to Glory* fared better in public critique, but it, too, exposed large fissures among readers and provoked debates about black religion, the arts, politics, and aesthetics. And there were those from among this group who also wanted to provide Hughes with a little instruction in the craft of writing. Hughes's friend Elmer Rice was one of the first to read it and provide him with a few pointers. "I enjoyed reading *Tambourines to Glory*, and I think it could be made into a very interesting stage production. If you don't mind a little constructive suggestion, I think you make too little of the dramatic possibilities of the murder. You go to great pains to have suspicion pinned on your heroine, and then, immediately following her arrest, you release her from her jeopardy."[89] Rice then offered what he thought would be a much better and more effective conclusion to the book. On the whole, however, those who read the novel and reported back to Hughes primarily connected to it as humor, viewing it as a "comedy" in the way Hughes had billed it and the publishers ultimately promoted it. Mary Douglas, an actress whom Hughes had written tentatively regarding a role in the play wrote him, saying, "thank you for the enjoyment I received reading the delightful 'Tambourines.' It was indeed the most hilarious book I've read for some time. As for my doing the role of Marietta (if it is produced) I can only say it would be a real ball. For I believe it's a winner, a real fun show."[90] Joan C. Jackson of Chicago concurred: "Tambourines to Glory is the only book I have lately taken time to read in quite a while and I thoroughly enjoyed it from start to finish. I found it very humorous in parts and very true to life."[91] For these readers, the laughs generated by Hughes's self-described satire about "the goings-on in the gospel churches" was all that mattered.

In the end, *Tambourines to Glory* was not a critical success for Hughes. The journey from book to play over the course of seven years had been arduous and neither became commercial successes. Some of the relationships he developed grew into great friendships and many of the players and musicians used it to jump-start fairly successful careers in theater and film. The production, however, had cost him something in terms of his reputation as a writer, and it stoked the fires of those who were inclined to view him as an enemy of the church, and perhaps black churches in particular, as well as those who were coming to view him as politically out of step with the times. But the time and energy Hughes spent on it, developing it first as book, then a play, and finally as a poem, indicate that *Tambourines to Glory* mattered greatly to him. The fact that he seemingly kept all of his personal and professional correspondence about the production is also an indication of its importance. He paid close attention to the criticism contained in that correspondence, and he even incorporated some of it. This accounts, in part, for some stark differences between the book and the play, as well as the various versions of the play on the way to the final version in 1963. In the final version, for example, Buddy Lomax is a much more complex portrayal, alternatively depicted as both a man and the actual "Devil." During the prologue, he enters the stage to address the audience directly. "You think I'm who you see, don't you? Well, I'm not. I'm the Devil. . . . Big-Eyed Buddy is just *one* of my million and one names. . . . Hitler, for example. . . . Katherine the Great—I put on drag sometimes. . . . the Devil comes in various guises—and disguises. . . . Sometimes I'm white." And in response to a common critique about the character, his murder (as a man) in this final version was decidedly less sensational while it was also much clearer that it was an act of self-defense against attempted rape. "God damn you, I'll kiss you! Or I'll kill you, one!"[92] Buddy was evil personified. In that case, the line between good and evil had to be clear.

Of all the critical responses Hughes received about *Tambourines to Glory*, the one from Anna Arnold Hedgeman in particular must have stung acutely. And it was not because it was coming from an African American civil rights community that was becoming increasingly more activist in the late 1950s and early 1960s. By this time Hughes had developed a fraught relationship with the political Left, and he had been implicated in what appeared to be changed, more conservative political views. But her claim that *Tambourines to Glory* lacked the "wonder and beauty to be found in the basic creations of the Negro" called into question not only the integrity of the production but also Hughes's most basic philosophy as a Negro artist, which was to showcase the beauty (and ugliness) of blackness. This had been his highest aim in all his writing since the 1920s. Although Hughes wanted to expose the dangers of racketeering in religion, as he had also attempted with "Goodbye Christ," he by no means wanted to suggest that black people and black religion lacked "wonder and beauty." If anything, the simple melodrama and slice of Harlem life with its underlying exploration of the paradoxical nature of good and bad, sin and salvation were meant to highlight an aspect of Harlem's world of religion and churches and the people who occupied those spaces in all its wondrous humanity and complexity. It was the same aim and intent he expressed for all his religious plays and gospel song-plays. But the polarizing conflicts about race, racial representation, religion, and aesthetics that *Tambourines to Glory* exposed were even more pronounced in Hughes's culminating work in that genre, *Black Nativity*.

5

Christmas in Black

"This church where you see us gathered—this gospel church
where His word is spread—is but an extension of His manger.
Those gathered here are His worshippers who have come tonight to make—as the Bible says—a joyful noise unto the Lord."
—Langston Hughes, *Black Nativity*, act 2

"Many of the singers are not striplings, and the attitudes they
represent are not far removed from those of Marc Connelly's
faux-naïf tract, 'Green Pastures'—a simple, childlike white
man's view of the simple childlike Negro's faith."
—Kenneth Tynan

Langston Hughes was in the midst of his "gospel years" when he sat
down in 1961 to write "Wasn't It a Mighty Day?," the title of which was
almost certainly taken from the traditional Christmas spiritual "Wasn't
that a Mighty Day." Gary Kramer, a young executive at Atlantic Records,
commissioned the project after having been introduced to gospel music
a few years earlier by a Queens College undergraduate named Anthony
Heilbut. Playing for him Marion Williams's 1959 recording, "O Holy
Night," Heilbut recalled that Kramer "fell in love with Marion and the
record," particularly the track, "O Come All Ye Faithful." Kramer, who
became what music critic Robert Shelton called a "gospel missionary,"
was so taken by the music that he soon set in motion plans to produce
a Christmas play that would feature all of the major gospel artists of
the day.[1] By the summer of 1961 he had founded a production company, Jubilee Artists Corporation, and enlarged the idea into a full
Christmas musical and theatrical production. To perform the music he
contracted Marion Williams and her Stars of Faith and Alex Bradford
and the Bradford Singers. Like Williams, each member of the Stars of
Faith, including Henrietta Waddy, Esther Ford, Frances Steadman, and

Kitty Parham, were former members of the the Famous Ward Sisters, the pre-1958 iteration of the Clara Ward Singers. The Bradford Singers were composed of Kenneth Washington, Calvin White, Bernie Durant, and Madeline Bell, the group's only female member. Kramer and Bradford had also recruited the blind soloist Princess Stewart, with whom Hughes had become acquainted years earlier, declaring her as one who could "move your soul." Although plans to include the Staple Singers never came to fruition, acquiring the others was not a problem because of Hughes's close relationships and alliances with many of the top artists. He quickly agreed to write the libretto and went to work on it, and as Arnold Rampersad states, "worked so long and hard that a two-toned beard blossomed on his cheeks."[2] The fervor signaled that the project was of great importance to him.

What emerged from Hughes's long hours of labor was the "gospel song-play" that in many ways was the artistic capstone to his long and prolific career. A genre of theater that Hughes invented, the gospel song-play combined black gospel music with stage performances of biblical narratives and was essentially a gospel concert supported by a thin layer of dramatic action. The format proved to be very popular, and when Hughes and the producers renamed *Wasn't It a Mighty Day* to *Black Nativity* in November 1961, it became only one of four gospel song-plays Hughes wrote in the early 1960s. The others included *The Gospel Glow*, *Master of Miracles*, and *The Prodigal Son*. *Black Nativity* was the most successful of these and his first major artistic and commercial success since *Street Scene*, an "opera" developed with Kurt Weil and Elmer Rice in 1946. *Black Nativity* even eclipsed the modest success of *Tambourines to Glory*, which differed from the gospel song-plays in that it was a play with music, a "musical," and was based on a contemporary narrative with more emphasis on the acting. While *Black Nativity* was not the first of Hughes's plays to make it to Broadway, it was the first of his theatrical productions to generate any real income. The show by no means made Hughes rich, and it would later fall into arrears, but proceeds allowed him a level of consistent financial comfort for the first time in his life. With performances being staged throughout Europe, Africa, and Australia, in addition to the United States, *Black Nativity* generated international acclaim and relatively substantial box office receipts. And it has become the one among Hughes's gospel song-plays with the most en-

"The music they create is a moving experience, one that has so many compelling appeals—rhythm, color, intensity of emotion—that the listener can hardly fail to be caught up in at least one of them." *NEW YORK TIMES*

A CONCERT OF GOSPEL SUNG BY MARION WILLIAMS AND THE STARS OF FAITH, THE ALEX BRADFORD SINGERS, AND PRINCESS STEWART

HALLELUJAH!

Figure 5.1. *Black Nativity* cast photo, circa 1962: The original cast of *Black Nativity*, including Marion Williams, Alex Bradford, Princess Stewart, Madeline Bell, Frances Steadman, Kitty Parham, Henrietta Waddy, Mattie Williams, Alberta Carter, Willie James McPhatter, Calvin White, Kenneth Washington, and Bernie Durant Jr. (Langston Hughes Papers, the Beinecke Library, Yale University.)

during legacy. In some form and in many places around the world, *Black Nativity* has been in production ever since it premiered in 1961. This is especially true for the United States. As Cheryl Sanders has remarked, "Black Nativity in fact has become a Christmas staple in black churches all over the United States."[3]

As his last major theatrical production, *Black Nativity* represented yet another example of Hughes's return to the sights and sounds of the religion of his youth. All the elements of the African Methodist Episcopal (AME) church were there: ecstatic worship, revivifying music, unbridled faith, and expectant hope. In other words, "the preacher, the music, and the frenzy," as W. E. B. DuBois would have it. This immersion in the religion of his youth made the gospel song-play appear to be untouched by the religious modernism that had infused much of his other works on religion. But the very concept of the play—the story of the Nativity with an all-black cast—sprang from Hughes's ability to think expansively, creatively, and even subversively about religion, and American and African American religion in particular. There was a subversive aspect to *Black Nativity* as thousands flocked to theaters in many places around the globe to see black American bodies in those iconic roles. As Joseph McLaren contends, *Black Nativity* was "essentially a radical treatment of religious iconography because it rewrites the conventional Eurocentric imagery associated with the Nativity." Hughes's use of black bodies in these roles was not epiphenomenal but deliberate and intentional, and they were playing on "Hughes's faith in the importance of a black racial sense."[4] The fact that it was an all-black cast portraying the story of the Nativity already made it "modern," and the gospel song-play owed its existence to Hughes's religious liberalism. Indeed, *Black Nativity* constituted an interplay between religious modernism and the old-time religion he first confronted as a child in Lawrence, Kansas. It was, therefore, a perfect capstone to a body of work on religion that was largely characterized by this very interplay and exchange.

With *Black Nativity*, Hughes, in the twilight of his career, took further refuge in black religious culture, most likely a fulfillment of his earlier claim to Louise Thompson that he had "gone back to church." His retreat to the theater in the 1960s, beginning with *Tambourines to Glory*, was in large part an attempt to provide a platform for what he had come to understand as the last vestige of black "authenticity": black churches and black gospel music. The play was to be a display of black artistry and religiosity with the power to expand the place of black culture within the wider American culture. Any hopes that *Black Nativity* would bridge racial and cultural divides in 1960s America, however, were met with disappointment. While according to Hughes it may have been an "authentic" rendering of black religious worship, at its best *Black Nativity* demonstrated the seeming impossibility of some forms of cultural production to bridge entrenched divides. Indeed, *Black Nativity* seemed to have widened them. It widened the gaps of racial difference, confirming notions of "blackness" while reifying "whiteness" in oppositional tones and textures. *Black Nativity* shared a similar fate as *Tambourines to Glory* in that it seemingly confirmed some racist notions of black religiosity, and critical responses fell squarely along racial and class lines. Despite Hughes's authorship, the all-black cast, and the African American director, *Black Nativity*, ironically, was largely a "white" affair. White producers produced it, and throughout its initial four-year run, white Americans and Europeans were its primary audiences. *Black Nativity* may have represented Hughes's retreat into the refuge of "authentic" black culture, but it became a vehicle by which white Americans and Europeans further accentuated notions of racial and religious difference.

The sheer novelty of the show and the emergence of "race theater" in the 1960s accounts for some of *Black Nativity*'s popularity among whites. But it was clear from the beginning that the enthusiastic reception Hughes's gospel song-play received from white audiences signaled something deeper than simple enjoyment. Audience responses, countless reviews, and extensive commentary on *Black Nativity* revealed that most whites viewed the cast as "primitives" who had not only recaptured something genuine about black faith, but also something whites and Europeans had seemingly lost in their own. Not since *The Green Pastures* had a Broadway production so successfully underscored perceived differences in black and white American religion. Indeed, *Black Nativity* emerged in the shadow of *The Green Pastures* and inevitably drew comparisons for what the two productions shared in common, namely, having all-black casts in a religiously themed Broadway production. First appearing on Broadway in February 1930, Marc Connelly's play featuring a set of Old Testament biblical scenes as imagined by a black school-aged child in the Deep South became a touchstone in American culture. Richard B. Harrison playing God as "De Lawd," headlined the cast, which would eventually perform the show nearly two thousand times. Connelly won the Pulitzer Prize for drama that year and *The Green Pastures* garnered critical and vast popular acclaim, particularly among white audiences. African American critics, however, skewered Connelly for his portrayal of black religiosity and bemoaned the fact that the play supported white claims of the "quaintness" of back religion and only served to perpetuate racial stereotypes. Connelly's stated aims for the play did not help. *The Green Pastures*, he explained, was "an attempt to present certain aspects of a living religion in the terms of its believers. The religion is that of thousands of Negroes in the Deep South. With terrific spiritual hunger and the greatest humility these untutored black Christians . . . have adapted the contents of the Bible to the consistencies of their everyday lives." It was their "simple faith," he concluded, that he had attempted to "translate into a play." Nick Aaron Ford was among a chorus of voices that took Connelly to task for, among other things, his audacity to stage a play about black religion and in turn "misrepresenting" American blacks, their faith, and their conception of God.[5] But the comparisons between *Black Nativity* and *The Green Pastures* also showed that the country was in a similar mood about the cultural importance of racial art and a particular perception of black religion as passive and benign. At the height of the civil rights movement, with its promise of a more radicalized and politicized black church, many white Americans found solace in a notion of black religiosity that was simple and unchallenging. English drama critic Kenneth Tynan made precisely that point in the *Observer*, where he suggested that just like *The Green Pastures*, *Black Nativity* was at best "a simple, childlike white man's view of the simple childlike Negro's faith."[6]

"Race theater" of the 1960s, of which *Black Nativity* was a part, also gave whites the opportunity to acknowledge their "otherness" and, therefore, their progression with regard to racial issues. It was an opportunity to play the racial and religious other in observation, imitation, and seeming solidarity. This imitation and observation of black worship and song, however, represented a limited understanding of black history and evinced little sympathy with the daily struggles of black people. This was imitation and observation, but it was not solidarity. Additionally, this attempt at "cross cultural knowing," as William Sonnego also contends, appeared to "maintain the hierarchies of white privilege rather than contest the social and economic inequalities on which they are based."[7] Similarly, *Black Nativity* uncovered and agitated class tensions among black Americans that were bubbling just beneath the surface, generating debates about the nature and character of black religion and the proper venue for its display. The response from the few blacks who saw *Black Nativity* ranged from mild appreciation and indifference to embarrassment. If it was an "authentic" example of black religion, to them it was embarrassingly so. Ultimately, rather than being a straightforward example of authentic black cultural expression as Hughes had intended, *Black Nativity* substantiated white notions of black religious primitivism and uncovered ruptures among blacks about representations of black religiosity as well as about what constituted "blackness" in 1960s America.

Gospel. Song. Play.

Similar to *Tambourines to Glory*, *Black Nativity* represented Hughes's
assertion of black "authenticity" by way of the theater and black gospel
music. It was rooted thematically, aesthetically, and theologically, however, in his love for Christmas. Hughes enjoyed everything about the
season and was an avid follower of all its traditions, including faithfully
mailing hundreds of Christmas cards annually to friends and associates.
Most of his ten Christmas, or Nativity, poems either began as or became
Christmas cards, including "Carol of the Brown King," and "Christmas
Time," which were both included on the "Poems of the Spirit" list sent to
François Dodat. The most notable and enduring of this group, "Carol of
the Brown King," written in 1954, told the story of the Magi who visited
the Christ child after his birth. One of the visitors, Hughes proclaimed,
was "dark like me." "Of the three Wise Men / Who came to the King /
One was a brown man / So they sing." He often designed his own Christmas cards as he did that same year when Aaron Douglas provided the
illustrations for them.[8] Douglas and Hughes had been collaborating
since 1926, when a drawing by Douglas accompanied Hughes's "Feet
o' Jesus" on the October cover of *Opportunity*.[9] Perhaps because most
became Christmas cards, the poems were cheery and conventional.
"Madam's Christmas (or Merry Christmas Everybody)" ends with the
word "howdy." And Hughes did not stray far from the narrative script:
Mary and Joseph journeying to Bethlehem; a star in the sky; three wise
men bearing gifts; a child born in an animal stall and placed in "swad-
dling clothes." All of the Nativity poems, however, placed particular
emphasis on the uncharitable reception of Mary and Joseph. "We have
no room," the innkeeper proclaimed in "On a Christmas Night." "So the
glory fell where the cows were stalled." In "The Christmas Story," Christ
was "born on earthen floor" because "only men of means get in by a
door closed to the poor."[10]

Hughes wrote several commentaries on Christmas for the *Chicago
Defender*, hailing the glories of the season. In each one he was particularly careful to remind his readers of "what the Christmas season
means" and to recount the Nativity story. "And if you want to refresh
your memory about Christmas and the origin of gift giving," he wrote
in 1953, "open your Bible and read again the beautiful story of the birth

of Christ and of the Three Wise Men who came bringing gifts to the manger."[11] He produced at least one short story with Christmas as its theme, and from the early 1950s to the mid-1960s, numerous poems appeared on the subject, many of which were never published or collected. "The Christmas Story," "On a Christmas Night," "On a Pallet of Straw," "Christmas Time," and "Christmas Eve: Nearing Midnight in New York" are just a few examples. In 1958 he compiled a collection of stories, poems, sketches from his *Chicago Defender* columns, reminiscences from his time in Asia, and spirituals for a possible "gift book" on Christmas. Although "A Christmas Sampler" never appeared in published form, the collection gives significant insight into Hughes's affinity for his favorite time of year, showing it to be about sentimentality, racial aesthetics, literary traditions, and Christian theology. In an early section of the collection, entitled "Memories of Christmas," Hughes spoke of his first Christmases in Kansas, "the very center of the U.S.A.," where cotton snow, candles on trees, and pot-bellied stoves were "all mixed up in these memories."[12] And race sat at the center of those sentimental memories. In "Christmas Song," Jesse B. Semple explains that he always gets emotional around Christmas time and that if he were to write his own song of Christmas it would be about "the black Wise Men who went to see the Baby in the Manger." It would be the most beautiful music ever heard and would certainly make people cry. "I don't know, but something about that black man and that little small Child—something about them two peoples—folks would cry," Simple says.[13]

Beyond the sentimentality of the Christmas season, however, Hughes was drawn to the theme of crucifixion and sacrificial atonement and found the concept of the birth of Christ for those purposes both theologically and literarily compelling. In a section of "A Christmas Sampler" called "Poems for Christmas," he lauds the poetics of Christ's birth and why as a poet he finds the subject beautiful and captivating: "The story of the Nativity is so beautifully told in the Bible that it would be very hard indeed for any living poet to equal that telling. Mary and Joseph turned away from the Inn, the birth of the Christ Child in the Manger, the Angel's song, the shepherd following the Star, and the coming of the Three Kings to bow down before the Babe—what greater subjects for poetry could there be? No wonder poets over the centuries have been drawn to the Christ story as material for poetry. I, too, have been drawn to that material."[14] Staying true to this statement, Hughes prominently featured each of the above-mentioned aspects of Christ's birth in *Black Nativity*. He would do so again in an unpublished and unproduced gospel song-play he completed in the fall of 1962 called "Christmas with Christ," for which he wrote an original song, "Such a Little King."[15] So when Gary Kramer commissioned Hughes to write *Black Nativity*, Hughes was able to draw on a deep well of childhood memories, as well as knowledge about the biblical story of Christmas and all of its sights, sounds, and symbols.

Hughes's knowledge and deep affinity for the story of the Nativity explains in part why in its retelling he made few narrative or structural alterations to Mary and Joseph's journey to Bethlehem, their rejection from the inn, Jesus's birth in a manger, or the visitation of the Magi. In substance, content, and chronology it was the same story. Early reviews of the show took note of this. A week after its premier, the *Chicago Defender* declared, "Black Nativity recreates the age-old mystery of the birth of Christ in a setting of Negro Christmas spirituals and gospel songs."[16] Hughes did, however, update the narrative by using contemporary language and settings. The inn was a "hotel" and a dejected Mary sat on the "curb." An early draft of the play had a character named "Mrs. Waddy" (a reference to Henrietta Waddy, one of the Stars of Faith) exclaim "prejudice, prejudice" upon hearing that there was no room in the "hotel" for Joseph and Mary while the rich and powerful were accommodated.[17] The song developed for this scene, "No Room at the Hotel," echoed Hughes's concerns about race and class discrimination that he underscored in "Advertisement for the Waldorf-Astoria" and was, in Anthony Heilbut's view, "a masterpiece." The most striking difference, however, had to do with the absence of the key character in the story, the baby Jesus. Although *Black Nativity* is the story of the birth of a child, no production ever featured a baby, real or artificial. As Barbara Griner, one of the show's three producers recalled, the actress playing Mary "mimed the birthing process" and photos of the cast show Mary "adoring the unseen child," but there was "no baby."[18] The logistical difficulties of having an actual child on stage certainly played a part in the decision. But more likely, the complete absence of a child was a concession to the limits of white liberality and African American religious aesthetics in the 1960s. Like many writers of his generation, Hughes had more than once explored the notion of a black Christ in his work and knew all too well how fraught the very idea was to most Americans. Joseph, Mary, and the entire heavenly host could be depicted as black with no objection. And as *The Green Pastures* had proven, even God could be depicted as black as long as the notion of God was mediated through the nonthreatening and culturally specific concept of "De Lawd." But the very suggestion of a "black baby Jesus" would likely have killed *Black Nativity*, Griner intimated.[19]

Theologically, *Black Nativity* signaled Hughes's return to some very familiar territory. The gospel song-play showcased some of the same theological language and constructs found in many of Hughes's early religious poems, including the notions of sin and salvation and the redemptive purpose of Christ's birth. The conceptions of sin and salvation in *Black Nativity* differed, however, from some other works, such as *Tambourines to Glory*, in that sins were not social sins, nor were they matters of ethics and morality. Perhaps due to the perceived universal implications of the Nativity story, in *Black Nativity* Hughes reverted back to a traditional evangelical concept of the "condition" of sin at birth and of universal culpability. It was a notion of sin that implicated all of humanity, according to Romans 5 (KJV), decidedly removed from a concentration on individual behavior and personal conduct and having more to do with Christ's salvific actions. Hughes had originally intended the play to focus on sin in both aspects (the personal and the universal) but shifted directions during the rewrites. "No-Good Shepherd (That Don't Know God)" was the only song among the twenty-seven in the production that contained glimpses of the social sins emphasis found in some of his other work on religion. Most likely based on Ezekiel 34 and John 10, "No-Good Shepherd" told the story of an irresponsible shepherd boy who failed to care for his sheep. In the Bible shepherds and sheep are metaphors for pastoral leaders and their congregants. The "No-Good Shepherd"—clearly a contrast to Jesus, who called himself the "good shepherd"—had given himself over to vice. He was "lazy," "sleepy-headed," "raggedy," "jive talking," and a womanizer, and because of all this was bound for hell.

No-Good Shepherd!
Sin-loving Shepherd!
No-Good Shepherd Boy!
You can't dance and ball
And holler, *Huh! Come Seven!*
Then when death comes by,
Expect to go to heaven.
No-Good Shepherd!
No-Good Shepherd!
No-Good Shepherd Boy![20]

Salvation as deliverance from the condition of sin, however, was the major theme of *Black Nativity*. A climactic scene has one character exclaiming, "one day when I was lost Jesus bled and died upon the cross. That's why I know it was his blood—yes, it was—that saved me."[21] Indeed, this notion of sin as a condition from which humankind needs deliverance is pervasive in all of Hughes's gospel song-plays. In the Passion play *The Gospel Glow* (also known as *The Gospel Glory*), which Hughes wrote in 1962, he placed heavy emphasis on personal testimonies regarding Christ's actions as the salvific point of contact. A deacon declares, "He came into this world to save poor me." The elder proclaims, "I know that my redeemer lives. Christ by his death, sweet blessing gives" and "His love come trickling down to all mankind." His words conclude the play, giving the full range of "the narrative of the life of Christ" as Hughes intended. "The Gospel Glory! Thank God for Jesus. Thank Him for His life, His Crucifixion. His Resurrection. Thank God for His salvation. Thank God for sending his son into the world that we might be saved." In *Master of Miracles*, also written in 1962, the words of another elder simply state the theme of the entire production: "Christ was sent to save." It was the "old, old story" as told in A. Katherine Hankey's nineteenth-century poem of Jesus as "that wonderful redemption, God's remedy for sin."[22]

Telling the "old, old story" accounted for much of the popularity of *Black Nativity*, but the innovation, racialized theatrical presentation, and its particular use of religious iconography are what made it particularly notable. The story may have been old, but how it looked and where it was presented were completely new. While there had been all-black casts on Broadway and in film before, *Black Nativity* was the first time an all-black cast had been used to depict one of the most sacred dramas in Christian history. For the first time in the history of the American theater, an all-black cast of professional actors and singers performed a stage drama of the Nativity story with gospel music. The black press took note of this as well. In its coverage of the premiere, the *Afro-American* announced, "Black Nativity marks the first time that professional gospel singers have been integrated into the action of a play." As the liner notes to the original cast recording asserted, Hughes "was very much aware of the fact that his rich use of Negro Christmas spirituals and gospel songs through-out the play, and his placing them into the hands of authentic church singers, was a daring, pioneering gesture."[23]

Working closely with his director, Vinnette Carroll, Hughes designed *Black Nativity* to have four basic elements: "music, dance, mime, and text." The play comprised two acts: act 1, "A Child Is Born," and act 2, "The Word Is Spread." In addition to the two singing groups and Princess Stewart, two dancing mimes played the roles of Mary and Joseph, and a narrator read Hughes's sparse text at intervals and between the two acts. Howard Sanders was the first to serve in the role of narrator. Vinnette Carroll followed him doing double duty as director and narrator on the first European tour. When the show came back to the United States in 1964, Ed Hall took over. Act 1 is set in Bethlehem on the night of Jesus's birth. The minimalist set per Hughes's instructions included "only a platform of various levels and a star, a single glowing star high over a place that might be a manger." The music in act 1 consisted mostly of Negro spirituals, Christmas standards, such as "Joy to the World" and "Go Tell It on the Mountain." During act 2, however, the stage transformed into a black church holding "camp meeting services," and the singers who had been playing the roles of the angels, three wise men, and shepherds took the stage as an elder (Alex Bradford), townspeople, and as gospel singers. They performed the entire second half as a concert, singing contemporary songs penned mostly by Bradford in addition to Donald Love's "Packing Up," a tune made famous by Clara Ward. It was ensemble work in every way—"structure, composition, and execution"—much like Greek theater. Indeed, reflecting years later on her time with the production, Carroll concluded, "a song-play is really Greek theater."[24]

The innovation, racialized theatrical presentation, and the use of religious iconography explain the immediate comparisons between *Black Nativity* and *The Green Pastures*. For only the second time in the history of American theater an all-black cast had taken to the stage to perform a religiously themed major production. But the similarities went even further. There were similar disconnects between artist intent and audience reception, accusations of artistic impropriety, and a sense that both productions offered adaptations of biblical narratives that few could take seriously as accurate historical accounts. As perhaps the absence of a black baby Jesus accentuated, audiences and critics no more took *Black Nativity* to be a viable representation of the birth of Christ than they did *The Green Pastures* to be a viable depiction of heaven. It was something out of the black artistic imaginary with little attention to historical accuracy. The imaginative aspect of *Black Nativity* was perhaps inadvertently revealed in the liner notes to the cast recording when it described the show: "Simply and beautifully as the story of the birth of Jesus is told in the Bible, no people or race that has come to know and love it has been able to resist embroidering it with characters, settings and songs of their own. And this has been particularly true of Bible-loving people like the American Negroes." Barbara Griner was even clearer. Speaking to the *Chicago Defender* about *Black Nativity* a few months after its last performance, she asserted, "Black Nativity is a warm, tender version of the Christmas story as seen by its author. Beautifully interwoven throughout with music and lyrics, the play is a folkloric x-ray into the heart of the Negro."[25] Most who saw *Black Nativity* during its four-year run agreed that it was "authentically" black, but what that meant for everyone involved—writer, actors, director, producers, critics, and theatergoes—varied widely. Getting to the "black" in *Black Nativity* was difficult terrain, complicated by a history of white sponsorship of black art, extant discourses on race, racial essentialism, and intraracial class conflict.

Getting to "Black"

Getting *Black Nativity* to Broadway took the work of three white producers, "two of whom were Jewish," as Barbara Griner clarified. Not long after Kramer conceived of the idea, he became determined to find a way to get it onstage. He contacted Michael R. Santangelo, who at the time

was a television executive for Westinghouse Broadcasting Company
(WBC) in New York. Santangelo, young, energetic, and "unbelievably
good looking," loved the idea immediately. He had recently become
a fan of gospel music through Sam Cooke's work with the Soul Stir-
rers and started spending considerable amounts of time promoting
gospel artists. His attempts to persuade Cooke to join the cast failed,
but Jess Rand, Cooke's manager, remembered Santangelo as "brilliant."
He was "erratic," "unbalanced," and emotionally unstable but a genius
nonetheless.[26] Santangelo wanted a legitimate theater for *Black Nativity* and set out to search for one. Learning of the 41st Street Theater, a
small Off Broadway venue, he called its young owner, Barbara Griner,
who not only agreed to allow the production in her theater but also to
become one of its producers. "Three minutes of conversation later, a
partnership to produce the venture had been formed," Griner cheerily
recalled.[27] Having much to learn about black church worship practices,
the three producers—Kramer, Santangelo, and Griner—began visiting
gospel churches in Harlem. The church visits would not only grant them
some semblance of legitimacy but also deepen their understanding of
the theologies at work in the gospel song-play and the motivations of
the performers, all of whom were Christian believers. In the end, the
producers asserted that their attitude was "to take the gospel out of the
church but not the church out of the gospel," a common refrain among
some black gospel artists in the early 1960s.[28]

The troubles with getting *Black Nativity* to Broadway, however,
erupted almost immediately. From the start, Kramer assumed co-
ownership of the song-play and considered himself chiefly responsible
for its creation. In the only known correspondence between him and
Hughes, he refers to *Black Nativity* when it was still called *Wasn't It a
Mighty Day?* as "our Christmas production."[29] The other producers
found him overbearing and controlling and amid the first rehearsals
got rid of him; he in turn made it clear that he was "forced out." To
replace Kramer, Santangelo and Griner recruited Eric Franck, a twenty-
five-year-old Belgian whose wealthy parents had sent him to the United
States to learn the banking industry. Santangelo, who was principally
responsible for bringing Franck on board, also got him to put up half the
necessary money. Franck had become interested in gospel music after
hearing Marion Williams and the Stars of Faith at the Apollo Theater

in Harlem. It is not entirely clear if Hughes supported Kramer's ouster. He seemingly attempted to assure Kramer's "continuing proprietorship in the show," but his ultimate failure to do so perhaps signaled that Hughes was not overly determined to retain him.[30] Theirs was not the most congenial relationship either. In a letter explaining the situation to his agent, Marion Searchinger, Hughes confided that he had not been aware that there was "dissension among them" and found out after the fact that Kramer was "seemingly entirely out of the picture." Although he expressed concern about Kramer and refused to strike his name off the contracts as Santangelo had asked, he was equally concerned that *his* contracts for *Black Nativity* remained valid whether Kramer was a part of the production or not.[31]

Hughes suspected that all the producers wanted to bolster their roles in the show's production and minimize his. In a letter to Arna Bontemps, Hughes quipped that he was "getting ready to do another script for the producers of *Black Nativity*, who have all kinds of plans, and think *they* discovered the format of dramatizing the gospel songs *themselves*."[32] In a rare display of indignation, Hughes fired off a memo to Santangelo, Griner, and Franck regarding the billing of *Black Nativity*. Drawing his own comparisons to *The Green Pastures*, Hughes insisted *Black Nativity* was not simply a "narrative by Langston Hughes" as they implied in printed advertisements. "I am sure all of you know, there was no *Black Nativity* before I conceived it—wrote the script, selected the songs, suggested Vinnette Carroll as director, and sat in on rehearsals giving my suggestions as to cuts or additions that molded it into final form. Just as *The Green Pastures* was billed 'by Marc Connelly' . . . so *Black Nativity* should be billed 'by Langston Hughes' without any other qualification."[33] Doubtless in response to Hughes's request, his agent, Marion Searchinger, got involved. "I know that you will take care of this. Let's spend our time and effort on more productive matters," she wrote to Barbara Griner.[34] The producers made the change.

The shake-up among the producers seemed minor by comparison, however, to the differences regarding race, racial terminology, and religion that also emerged early in the production. Carmen de Lavallade and Alvin Ailey, who were both early in their careers in 1961, made swift exits just before the show went into final rehearsals. Ailey, who had worked with Hughes before on *Ask Your Mama* and with Vinnette

Carroll on *Dark of the Moon*, had been hired to choreograph the play, and he and de Lavallade were to be the two principal dancers "miming" the roles of Joseph and Mary.[35] This all changed when the name was changed to *Black Nativity*. Hughes and the producers deliberated among themselves with Santangelo taking the lead, but they did not consult the cast.[36] Barbara Griner, who talked to the *New York Post* just days after the change, even indicated that the name *Black Nativity* was suggested to them by "someone from the UN." She also said that the producers found it "sharper and to the point" and found "nothing offensive in it."[37] De Lavallade and Ailey took a different view. De Lavallade quit first and Ailey's exit immediately followed. Ailey had known de Lavallade since high school and she was principally responsible for introducing him to dance. He was fiercely loyal to her, the woman whom he considered dance to be "impossible without."[38] De Lavallade claimed that she lost her enthusiasm for the play after the name change, which to her thinking undermined the "religious significance" of the production and was "out of place," so she wanted "no part of it." The original title to her was in "much better taste."[39]

The news of the exits captivated the local as well as the national press. It seemed a bad omen for a show that Hughes and the producers hoped would be a great success. It also seemed to highlight a scintillating backstory to a theatrical production. But while most of the reportage depicted the story as one about differences over racial terminology, de Lavallade insisted years later that it was about much more than racial terminology and mostly about artistic freedom and appropriate expressions of religion, clearly showing that the issues were intertwined. When the producers changed the name without consulting the players, "something rebelled in me," she contended. And it was their insistence that the new name was "sharper and to the point" that tipped her over. "To the point of what?," she remembered thinking. The original name was "charming," but the new one offended her artistic sensibility. The name *Black Nativity* lacked the "artistry" of *Wasn't It a Mighty Day?* But the new name also offended her racial sensibility. Although she had joined an all-black cast, de Lavallade came from a mixed heritage where race was loosely defined and never emphasized. "I've been around all different people since my childhood," she explained. "That's my world." And in that world, "you don't put a color" on religion, she asserted. "All are one color as far as God is concerned." And one would not think of a "black Nativity" any more than one would a "white Nativity." Ailey denied that the name change prompted his decision but maintained that *Black Nativity* was "not the best title in the world."[40] Insisting that she meant no disrespect to Hughes, the other players, or the producers and that her exit was not "political," de Lavallade asserted that religion was the core motivation. "Religiously speaking," she declared, a production about the Nativity should not emphasize color, which is inherently divisive. What should have been a play about "praising the birth of Christ" became for her one about race and racial division. "How can you praise God and separate yourself," she queried.[41]

The term "black" doubtlessly played a role in the exits of de Lavallade and Ailey. Since the nineteenth-century, racial nomenclature had revealed deep social, political, and class tensions among African Americans, and the responses of de Lavallade and Ailey were in sync with millions during the early 1960s when the term "Negro" was the commonly accepted racial identifier. Before "Negro," most Americans used the term "colored" until leaders such as W. E. B. DuBois successfully campaigned against it in the 1920s. "Black" had not yet come into common parlance and did not reflect the political or cultural sensibilities of most African Americans. It was not seen as a positive term, and de Lavallade and Ailey were not alone in their perspectives, as a furor erupted in the black community over the name change, prompting some to contact the producers with their thoughts for and mostly against it.[42] One rare affirmative response came from Wyatt T. Walker, executive director of the Southern Christian Leadership Conference (SCLC), who informed Santangelo that "as involved as I am here in the deep south, the word 'Black' is inoffensive to me."[43] Hughes had been using "black" in a positive light and asserting notions of "black is beautiful" long before it emerged as an outgrowth of the Black Power and Black Arts movements in the mid- to late 1960s. Indeed, Hughes's strong belief in the beauty of blackness played a crucial role in the development of the "Negritude" movement, a spirit of "black soul and feeling" in France during the 1930s.[44] In a *Chicago Defender* column in the early 1940s, Hughes employed the voice of Jesse B. Semple to comment on "That Word Black." After a spirited exchange about the "odium attached to the word black," Simple announces his reclamation of the word as something good, beautiful, and God-given. "I am black. When I look in the mirror, I see myself, daddy-o, but I am not ashamed. God made me. . . . The earth is black and all kinds of good things comes out of the earth. . . . I am black." "What's wrong with black?," he asked conclusively.[45] Nevertheless, Hughes was cautious about "that word black." In a 1953 letter to fellow poet Waring Cuney, with whom he was writing an anthology to be titled *Poems of the Negro Renaissance*, Hughes warned, "Cullud don't like the word 'black' much, particularly applied to women, I've learned from long experience." The anthology was never published.[46]

After the name change, the exits of de Lavalade and Ailey, and the choosing of replacements (Clive Thompson and Cleo Quitman), *Black Nativity* was ready for its premier. The show opened on December 11, 1961, and the response was nothing short of phenomenal. As Arnold Rampersad asserts, "the response was extraordinary. The audience could hardly be contained, nor could the performers. Aroused by the musical and religious fervor on stage, the capacity audience yelled and cooed ecstatically."[47] The audience responded as if they had never seen anything so vibrantly exciting in their lives. In particular, people jumped and screamed during act 2. One woman fainted. It was as if the producers had accomplished their goal of "taking gospel out of the church but not the church out of gospel." It was a good and hopeful start.

The success of opening night can be attributed, in part, to the emergence of modern black gospel in the early 1960s, the high quality of the singers, particularly Marion Williams and Alex Bradford, as well as the expert direction of Vinnette Carroll. Although black gospel had been around since the 1930s, having been given shape by composer Thomas Andrew Dorsey, innovation in recording techniques, the proliferation of gospel groups, recognition by the recording industry, and the rise of bone fide gospel "stars" in the early 1960s ushered in the modern era of the genre. Many in the audience were hearing it for the very first time, and it was thrilling. Everyone involved with *Black Nativity* gave Marion Williams and Alex Bradford enormous credit for the show's success. Already stars in the gospel world before joining the cast, Williams and Bradford got new life pumped into their careers because of *Black Nativity*, and it became the basis of the fame they would enjoy for many years following. They were by all accounts tremendous and indefatigable performers and as Barbara Griner recalled, "They were perfect for Black Nativity."

Figure 5.2. Photo of Marion Williams, Clive Thompson, and Cleo Quitman: Marion Williams with Clive Thompson and Cleo Quitman playing the roles of Joseph and Mary in *Black Nativity*, circa 1962. (From the Barbara F. Meyer (Griner) Collection. Collection in possession of author.)

Marion Williams was born in 1927 in Miami, Florida, where she started singing in her home church at the age of six. In 1947 she joined the Famous Ward Singers and established herself as a vocalist of unusual power and stamina. Her talents provided engagements at Carnegie Hall, Madison Square Garden, and the Apollo Theater. She left the Famous Ward Singers to form the Stars of Faith in 1958 after a dispute over money with the notoriously tightfisted Clara Ward. Born in Bessemer, Alabama, in 1927, "Professor" Alex Bradford had already had significant success as a gospel singer, composer, and arranger by the 1960s. After a move to Chicago in 1947, he worked with Roberta Martin and Mahalia Jackson. His hit "Too Close to Heaven" generated significant attention from the wider music community in 1954, as such artists as Little Richard and Ray Charles emulated his flamboyant style. Charles's biographers credit his deliberate use of gospel inflections in his music beginning in the 1950s to the rise of his popularity during that time. And he freely "borrowed" from many of the gospel acts of the time. His 1954 hit "I've Got a Woman" was likely based on multiple influences, including Bradford's "Jesus Is All the World to Me," Alex Brown's "I've Got a Savior" as sung by the Bailey Gospel Singers in 1950, and "It Must Be Jesus," by the Southern Tones. When he joined the cast of *Black Nativity*, Bradford had left Chicago and was serving as minister at Greater Abyssinian Baptist Church in Newark, New Jersey, joining the vibrant world of gospel singers who lived and performed there.[48]

Williams and Bradford shared much in common in terms of their careers as gospel singers, but they could not have been more different in their personal lives. Together they perfectly represented all the ambiguities and paradoxes prevalent among gospel musicians during the 1950s and 1960s. Marion was deeply religious and never strayed too far from the influences of her Pentecostal background. She had a piety about her and was not worldly wise or well versed in the music business. She would have made a fine Essie from *Tambourines to Glory*, and Hughes likely considered her for the part along with the many others. But like many of her contemporaries, Williams could also be naïve and materialistic, known for her gold tooth, a penchant for fancy and expensive dresses, and an abundance of wigs, particularly ponytail wigs. "Always, the wigs," exclaimed Barbara Griner. Although Bradford was an ordained minister, he was not at all pious. Indeed, some of his closest associates were unconvinced of his religious sincerity. He was what many in the gospel world and the world of evangelical black churches considered a "worldly" Christian. At times it seems that money was his primary motivation, and he was, in fact, a shrewd businessman. When Hughes asked him to take part in the 1965 production of "The Prodigal Son," Bradford agreed, but insisted, "only if the money is right."[49] Madeline Bell recalls that during the first European tour, the singers went on strike over a wage dispute. They discovered that before they left New York the producers had raised their pay from seventy-five dollars a week to one hundred dollars. Bradford and Williams, who uncharacteristically paid their singers directly, failed to mention it, keeping the surplus for themselves, amounting to hundreds of dollars extra per week for themselves.[50] Bradford drank heavily and by the end of his life suffered from alcoholism. In 1970 he justified his drinking, declaring, "sure I drink, the rabbi drinks, everybody drinks. It's a better thing than shooting dope, *I* think. There's some folk who like both of them. I think in this world, people ought to do what they want to do."[51] Bradford was also openly homosexual despite being twice married to women. His flamboyant mannerisms and "swish," as Carl Bean called it, left little question as to his sexuality, and he was not particularly discreet, having been arrested at least once for solicitation.[52] Like most in the black gospel world in their day, Williams and Bradford were flawed individuals, yet they were also consummate performers.

Signing Vinnette Carroll as director of *Black Nativity* was a stroke of genius on Hughes's part from an artistic standpoint, but her presence also became emblematic of the interracial tensions and the intraracial class disparities that would characterize the show throughout its run. Carroll's work ethic, artistic philosophy, and uncompromising pursuit of perfection had also helped to make the opening night the grand success that it was. She and Hughes had known each other for a number of years, as she had performed some of his work in her one-woman shows, including some of his religious material. A native New Yorker from the black middle class, Carroll worked hard and expected the same from the cast. She was known to encourage fellow actors to "work until you drop if you want to be successful." She maintained that this was especially true for black actors, who were often wrongly described as having "natural song, dance and acting talent and are natural born entertainers." With only a few opportunities to run through the entire show before opening night, Carroll demanded discipline, punctuality, order, and perfection. The producers acknowledged that it was she who "imposed professional discipline on the singers while creating freedom for their spontaneous movements."[53] The discipline paid off.

Carroll, however, absolutely hated the producers and, in her words, "refuse[d] to acknowledge their existence in the world." In private correspondence to Hughes spanning several months in 1961 and 1962 she unleashed verbal venom about them that would certainly have made Hughes uncomfortable. She based her objection to them mostly on professional disagreements about money, staging, and venues, which would not have been unusual for 1960s Broadway. But the language made it clear that her hatred of them was also personal and racial, calling them alternatively "pigs" and "SOBs." The personal and vitriolic nature of the discourse would seem to suggest that she resented the all-white leadership of the production. Well acquainted with the racial and gender dynamics of the theater, Carroll was likely aware that it was a business dominated by white and European men, the presence of Barbara Griner notwithstanding. An event that occurred a few years after her time as the director of *Black Nativity* bore this out. Particularly sensitive to the dominant role of whites in the theater, she quickly returned to New York in 1967 after a short stint in Los Angeles as associate director of the Inner City Repertory Company, a government-sponsored program designed to "ease racial tensions." She was dismayed that the company, which was meant as an interracial effort, was staffed almost entirely by whites, and the majority of the actors were also white. As she told the *Los Angeles Times*, "I have had a great deal of hurt in the theatre both as a Negro and as a woman."[54] Carroll seemed to reserve the most venom for Michael Santangelo, lamenting to Hughes in September 1962 that even if it meant she never worked in theater again, she would "never have anything to do with that Santangelo." Exasperated, she concluded, "Why the hell doesn't somebody bump him off?"[55] Always the diplomat, Hughes apparently attempted to defuse the situation, once informing Carroll, "Barbara says you are invaluable to *Black Nativity*, and all sorts of other nice things about you." Carroll's muted response indicated that Hughes's efforts were in vain.[56]

Vinnette Carroll's upbringing, class status, education, and personal demeanor also separated her from the rest of the black cast. Her Caribbean born parents revered the British monarchy, which perhaps explains why Carroll was a self-proclaimed Anglophile. Highly educated, Carroll had degrees from Long Island and New York Universities and had worked as a psychologist for the Bureau of Child Guidance. While producing plays she also taught drama at the High School of Performing Arts in New York. She learned directing from none other than German director and producer Erwin Piscator at his dramatic workshop at the New School. Her dentist father wanted her to become a doctor and wept in disappointment when Carroll announced that she was dropping out of a PhD program at Columbia University to pursue a career in acting. The breach in their relationship never healed.[57] Anthony Heilbut and Barbara Griner remembered her physical presence as "very grand" and "very impressive." With a penchant for heavy African jewelry, Carroll appeared regal and refined and was to some people reminiscent of a "black Tallulah Bankhead," with whom she had worked in a production of *A Street Car Named Desire* in 1956 playing the "Negro Woman."[58] In a production that included several homosexuals, some "openly" and others not, Carroll was known to be a lesbian who was, as Anthony Heilbut asserted, "as out as she could be," given the circumstances of her birth and social class. Indeed, as Carl Bean, who became a close confidant, maintains, Carroll chose to be discreet about her sexuality in light of the indiscretions (sexual and otherwise) of members of the cast. When messes were made, she had to clean them up and supervise bad behavior. She felt she "had to walk a thin line, a tight rope," Bean maintained.[59]

A profile of Carroll in the *New York Amsterdam News* in 1963 toyed with perceptions of Carroll's homosexuality, clearly aligning it with her Bohemian lifestyle. The feature did its best to characterize Carroll as unusual and masculine, making its title, "Today's Woman," as subversive as it was ironic.[60] The article portrayed her as a Bohemian who lived in the West Village with only her black poodle, Jolly, and who did the wood paneling in her apartment, as she was a "do-it-yourselfer." She drove a German sports car, wore pants, and was generally inattentive to dress. "She likes to work in slacks and sweaters and admits her sister must keep after her about needed wardrobe changes."[61] Carroll was indeed different from the other African American members of *Black Nativity*, as the article intimated. Having grown up in the fashionable Sugar Hill section of Harlem, she lived downtown among the avant-garde when the majority of black New Yorkers lived in Harlem or Brooklyn. She ran in exclusive theater social circles and never lost the cultured comportment that was instilled in her by her upbringing. Carroll's disapproving and elitist parents refused to see *Black Nativity*, dismissing the cast as a bunch of "maids." It was a sentiment that both Heilbut and Griner insist Carroll shared.[62]

Despite her upbringing, class status, and her parent's disdain of the production, Carroll seemed to genuinely love *Black Nativity* and the members of the cast. She had high praise for Hughes's libretto, the staging, the dancers, and particularly the singers. Writing Hughes in advance of a series of shows in Paris, she reported that "The show is in marvelous shape and Marion and Alex are growing in presence and theatricality."[63] She repeatedly thanked Hughes for hiring her as director and remarked how proud she was to be a part of *Black Nativity*, despite her growing weariness with all the traveling. The enthusiastic response of the audiences touched her deeply, as did the show itself, and she was once spotted weeping during a performance in Spoleto, Italy.[64] Carroll's praise for the play and cast, however, was tinctured with an obvious class bias and essentialist understanding of race. She was different from the cast; they knew it, and she knew it, too. Her self-appointment as moral arbiter and disciplinarian indicated she understood that she was different, that she was set apart from the largely uneducated and working-class members of *Black Nativity*. She clarified this attitude years later while reflecting on her years of working with black actors, describing herself as "an earth mother who gives her children a discipline that will make it possible for them to survive."[65] Echoing the language of many white theater critics, Carroll lauded the show for its genuineness and folksy aura, and the singers for their simplicity. Marion, she proclaimed, was "simple and marvelous." Her answer to *Newsweek*, which had described Marion as "a huge Negress wearing a gold front tooth," as to why the show had two contrasting acts was telling. "One couldn't let the *natural exuberance* of the gospel singers take command," she said, "we had to walk a thin line between good taste and religious heresy."[66] For Carroll, *Black Nativity* was an example of authentic black religion on display, which for a moment both highlighted and bridged racial and class differences. Remarking about the London audience's response to the show, she reported to

Hughes that they "stomp and scream like 'colored folk.'" When it was announced that Princess Margaret was to attend one performance, she predicted, "it will also set at ease those stuffy people who resent this joyous way of worshipping God."[67]

Theater critics also praised the opening night of *Black Nativity*, but their exuberance was infused with racial exoticism, as they praised the singers' "natural ability," innate religiosity, and physicality. Separated by thirty years, it was *The Green Pastures* all over again, and the initial critiques set the tone for how the show would subsequently be received in Europe and elsewhere in the United States. Howard Taubman's review in the *New York Times* typified the responses from American theater critics. "If there is any justification for 'Black Nativity,'" he contended, "it is in the singing." The importance of the show was in the music and the singers. "How these singers can belt out a religious tune!" They could do this, from his perspective, because they were black. In a way that would be repeated throughout the run of the gospel song-play, Taubman employed terms that emphasized the perceived natural talent of black people, their religiosity, and both the ethereal quality and physicality of black worship. "They sing with the afflatus of jazzmen in the frenzy of improvisation. [Their] rhythms are so vibrant that they seem to lead an independent existence. The voices plunge into sudden dark growls like muted trombones and soar in ecstatic squeals like frantic clarinets." "For the most part," he insisted, "the singing has a kind of wild pounding rapture," offering a "singular kinetic experience." The production was "not always art," he concluded, but it overflowed with "fervor."[68] John Beaufort, writing for the *Christian Science Monitor*, agreed with Taubman that *Black Nativity* was not much of a play, calling it "unconventional" but falling "considerably below the level of its best." And he also considered the music and the singing to be the strongest aspect of the production. The singers sang from "a base of musically liberated devoutness" that achieved "an infectious gaiety." The "prevailing mood is innocent merriment" in the way that only blacks can show. "Nobody conveys elation like those who have known oppression."[69] These early reviews from American critics provided a foretaste of what was to follow in Europe as the audience response and critical reviews there at times strikingly eclipsed the essentialist tones of the Americans.

Spoleto, London, New York, Chicago

Black Nativity seemed destined for a longer life than the fifty-seven performances at Griner's 41st Street Theater and indeed the opportunity to extend its run presented itself on the night of the final performance. Composer Gian Carlo Menotti offered to present the gospel song-play at Festival dei Due Monde (the Festival at Two Worlds) in Spoleto, Italy, outside Rome. Menotti had founded the three-week festival of music, theater, and art in 1958 as an annual event to promote the arts produced in Europe and the United States. It was an opportunity that would also take the company on to London, the initial leg of a tour of Europe, and to a triumphant return to Lincoln Center in New York. On the night he attended, Menotti had been on his way to dinner when a friend convinced him to cancel his plans in order to see *Black Nativity*. He did and was emotionally stirred by the entire performance, particularly by Williams's rendition of "When Was Jesus Born?" Indeed, he was so moved that he sent a special request that it be sung again before the end of the show. The troupe happily complied.[70] After the performance, he congratulated the producers and, "while standing in the theatre's isle," made the invitation. Menotti had his own fascination with the Christmas season, which may explain his emotional reaction to *Black Nativity* and the immediate and enthusiastic invitation to Spoleto. He brought that fascination to bear on his 1951 opera, *Amahl and the Night Visitors*, the first opera ever to be produced for network television (NBC). The story of a crippled boy who gives his crutch to the baby Jesus as a gift in thanks for being miraculously healed, the opera had been an annual television event for a decade by the time Menotti saw *Black Nativity*.[71] The joyous troupe made their way to Italy, most for the first time, and Alex Bradford's arrest there for solicitation notwithstanding, had an extremely successful run at the Festival.

The four-week run in London was even more spectacular. At the Criterion and Coventry theaters, *Black Nativity* played before thousands, including British royalty, and received some of its strongest reviews up to that point. The *New York Times* reported that the singers "were greeted with an ovation seldom granted to companies from abroad."[72] Michael Dorfman, an English theater impresario, had seen the production in Spoleto and invited the cast to perform in London. Carroll reported to

Hughes that the show received "absolutely superlative reviews at Coventry. It seems as if each set of reviews surpass the others."[73] Hughes wrote his agent, Marion Searchinger, in September 1962 to tell her that in London "the reviews are all amazing." The people in the audience leaped and jumped "as if beset by Pentecostal fire." Germany was no exception. One reviewer called it "the most refreshing uninhibited musical in ages," and Anthony Heilbut recalls that Marion Williams was told that while in Germany the troupe received "the loudest crowd roar since Hitler."[74]

The European reviews may have been "superlative," but they also accentuated notions of racial, class, and physical differences between the performers and the white audiences. For the reviewers, *Black Nativity* was chiefly about an uninhibited black form of worship and the singers were "other." The *Evening Standard* hinted at this in an article entitled "Religion Put to a Jazz Beat," in which it described the gospel song-play as "somewhere between a revival meeting and a Harlem morality play."[75] Other write-ups were more direct. In what was meant as his praise for the show, Herbert Kretzmer of the *Daily Express* noted that *Black Nativity* was "naïve, primitive, and amateur."[76] In his view, the largely white audiences recognized and celebrated the differences between them and the singers. He demonstrated this point by relaying a quick conversation he had with a woman sitting behind him in the theater on opening night. The woman, whom he identifies as "white," whispered to him, "What a joy to find someone actually having fun with their religion." Few of the reviews failed to mention the singers' bodies, noting that they were different in some way or representative of "Negro" features. Eugenie Soderberg, writing for the *Stockholms-Tidningen*, described Kitty Parham as a "splendid café-au-lait woman" who sang with "delighted enchantment." (Parham would swing her ponytail wig furiously during performances.) Peter Lewis of the *Daily Mail* employed overtly racist language in his description of the singers, who were "massively built Negroes in severe full-length smocks with smiles as wide as slices of melon." Marion was a particular focus. Of all the "gaily uninhibited" performers, Marion stood out to the *Times of London*. She was a "cheerfully beaming archangel" with a personality that "fills the theatre."[77] Commenting both on her size and her wide smile, the *Daily Mirror* called Marion "a great jelly wobble of a woman with horseshoes of smiling teeth."[78] To Milton Shulman she was "a substantial chunk of black rhythmic dynamite."[79]

By December 1962 *Black Nativity* had become what the *Chicago Defender* called "one of the hottest shows on the continent."[80] With things going well in Europe and the buzz reaching back to the United States, it seemed only fitting to accept an invitation to interrupt the tour for a one-week engagement at Philharmonic Hall at the newly built Lincoln Center. *Black Nativity* became the first dramatic production at the hall, which had been completed amid great controversy the past September. The *New York Times* published the announcement, marking the historic occasion. "Black Nativity, Langston Hughes's gospel song-play, is interrupting a successful European tour to give 10 performances in Philharmonic Hall during Christmas week. This is the first time that Philharmonic Hall has booked a dramatic event." As Barbara Griner proudly remembered, "we opened Lincoln Center."[81] The event came about largely through Santangelo's connections. Donald H. McGannon, president of WBC, agreed to sponsor the event, deeming it integral to his company's commitment to present events that made "cultural contributions." "The presentation of this week of gospel drama in the nation's newest and most significant arts center will enrich the musical fare available to the public and perhaps stir further interest in one of our American art forms," he told the *New York Amsterdam News.*[82]

The show was a huge success, having quickly sold out for the entire engagement. "End of week *Nativity* began to sell out in the ENORMOUS Lincoln Center," Hughes boasted to his friend Arna Bontemps. "Last-night-Sunday seats all gone, and there's no standing room."[83] The show also set a box office record, grossing nearly $48,000. Hughes's 5 percent take of the total was a big boost to his own personal bottom line.[84] The simultaneous television broadcast was as well received as the seven-day run at Lincoln Center, with one reviewer calling it "an artistic masterpiece in music and movement." Echoing some of the body emphasis prevalent in the European reviews, he praised Williams in particular: "As lead singer, the plump and ebullient Marian [*sic*] Williams virtually sang with her whole body, driving cohorts into a contagious fit of religious frenzy." Ossie Davis expressed his appreciation, saying it was a great example of the fun Negroes have "when nobody's looking . . . except that this time, everyone could look, and enter, for a while, a very special world."[85] The TV broadcast went on to win the Silver Dove Award in February 1963 from the International Catholic Society at the Festival de Television de Monte-Carlo, founded by Prince Rainer III of Monaco to "encourage a new art form, in the service of peace and understanding between men." Marlene Dietrich handed out the award.[86]

Most of the reviews after the Lincoln Center engagement intensified the focus on religious difference and the perceived separation between blacks and whites. They also spoke of the gospel singers and their performances as if they were especially and innately uninhibited. As black people, they were uninhibited and free, unfettered and unrestrained. And it was this that cast a "charm-like" spell on white audiences, who were compelled—often against their will—to respond. Whites experienced a loosening of their dignity when confronted with the singers in *Black Nativity*, who shared no such particular concerns in their worship. One of the first to do so, Melvin Maddocks, proclaimed *Black Nativity* "an act of worship," a genuine expression of religious sentiment of black people, and in keeping with the "cultural" aims of the show, he noted, "it was as if all the cultural resources of the American Negro were being mustered in one exuberant, mystical hymn." He drew a sharp distinction, however, between black worship and white audience response. *Black Nativity* may have been an act of genuine worship for the gospel singers, but it could never be so for the white audiences. Whites, rather, were for an evening confronted with a foreign form of worship and one that required a temporary loss of comportment in order to take part. It was the only way to experience unity with the singers. Describing *Black Nativity* for the *Christian Science Monitor*, he said, "its power is the power of uninhibited celebration. Before this power audiences suspend their ordinary habits of taste and finally—losing their separated identity as audiences—participate."[87] The sentiment would be echoed throughout the United States and Europe over the next several months.

Hughes and the producers did not focus on the racial essentialism in the European reviews but on the good reviews and the goodwill the show was allegedly spreading along its path. By the time the European tour resumed in Paris in January 1963, for example, Santangelo had dubbed *Black Nativity* "a means of transmitting American goodwill overseas" by way of gospel singing, which was "an exciting new trend in American music."[88] The enthusiasm about how the show was being received was at its highest. After an opening night at the Théâtre des Champs-Élysées, *Black Nativity* received some of its strongest critical reviews. Hughes was so thrilled that he sent condensed copies of them to Arna Bontemps, noting that they were "all absolute RAVES." *Le Monde* called it a "flood of purity and beauty." The review printed in *Paris Presse* especially thrilled him, as the headline read, "A Dozen Black Angels Invade Paris": "Their wings rustling with gentleness and love causing the opening night audience to explode with joy," the article stated.[89] The responses were repeated on the show's second stop in Paris during a second European tour in 1965. Edgar A. Wiggins exclaimed, "nearly 2,000 spectators were in a frenzy. The 'spirit,' generated by the soul-stirring music and singing of Gospel songs, had touched not only the spectators and ushers in the Theatre, but also the stage-hands, electricians, dressers, firemen and guardians of the peace, backstage. All gave vent to their emotions by clapping hands, stomping feet and swaying their heads and bodies in perfect harmony with the music."[90] *Black Nativity* had captured and captivated Europe.

Joyful. Noise.

One of Hughes's highest aims with *Black Nativity* was to draw attention to black artistic expression, the glory of black gospel music, the drama of black religion, and the place of African Americans in the theater. In this way, he attempted to incite racial unity with the celebration of black religion in the theater, displaying "reverence, awe, joy and jubilation."[91] It was not an exhibition of hubris as *The Green Pastures* had ultimately been for Marc Connolly. The effect of *Black Nativity*, however, was to reveal deep divisions regarding the representation of African Americans, black culture, and black religion. And the very different racialized responses from audiences indicated just how entrenched those divisions were. Typically, to white and European audiences, *Black Nativity* was indeed "joyful." To many blacks it was just "noise." A huge aspect of the "goodwill" that Michael Santangelo hoped the show would spread had to do with the releasing of the audience's inhibitions in the manner in which Melvin Maddocks spoke. Europeans, in particular, reveled in a lack of inhibition that the gospel song-play seemed to invite, as they witnessed the "uninhibited" performance of the gospel singers. It was as if the cast of *Black Nativity* helped European audiences get in touch with their humanity and spirituality by way of a religion not their own. Tony Buttitta reiterated this point in a letter to Hughes in 1965. Hughes had kept in touch with Buttitta since 1932, when Buttitta had invited him to contribute to *Contempo*, for which Hughes wrote "Christ in Alabama." Buttitta wanted to recount his experience in the theater when he saw the show in 1963. "Two years ago my gal and I were in Rome for *Black Nativity*—and the audience went wild," he proclaimed. "Those elegant ladies and gents were stripped of bored sophistication and veneer to show there was a warm humanity still alive in them."[92] *Black Nativity*, he intimated had given them permission to get in touch with something within them that was more free and more primal.

Throughout much of *Black Nativity*'s European run, Hughes received a number of personal confirmations from friends that the show was taking Europe by storm and seemingly providing a fresh infusion of a black worship sensibility. Elmer and Viv Simms Campbell, for example, corroborated the popularity of *Black Nativity* in Switzerland and the enthusiastic response of the Swiss to the show. Hughes and Elmer, who signed his work as "E. Simms Campbell," had been friends since their Lincoln University days. Before moving to Switzerland, the St. Louis native had become the first African American syndicated cartoon artist with work appearing in national and international journals, including *Esquire*, *Playboy*, and the *New Yorker*. He also collaborated with Hughes and Bontemps on their children's book, *Popo and Fafina: Children of Haiti*, in 1932. Having intended to catch the show during its Spoleto engagements, Viv Campbell wrote Hughes to express her hope that it would eventually make it to Zurich. She anticipated that it would be well received because "Zurichers are nuts over niggers," she explained.[93] When *Black Nativity* arrived in Zurich in April 1963, the Campbells attended with Swiss friends and reported back to Hughes that they "tried to keep up with the Baptists in the audience." Ordinarily, they maintained, Swiss audiences are nonresponsive and staid, "painted on the wall," as they put it. "But 'Black Nativity' brought out the William Tell in them. They clapped, (as you would expect) on the one and three beat, in spite of my two and four stomp, but everybody was happy."[94]

When Europeans objected to *Black Nativity*, however, it was precisely on the basis of perceived racial and religious differences, as they considered the production to be foreign to their religious and cultural sensibilities. Television producers Friedrich Hansen-Loeve and Gerhard Freund from Vienna, Austria, discovered this when they chose to air the film version of the gospel song-play in their country on Christmas Eve 1963. News of the proposed airing was met with "threatening letters" at the station, and Freund had to be put under armed guard. Some Austrians complained about the prospect of turning on their TV sets to see black people singing on Christmas Eve, rather than an "indigenous" program. As one story intoned, "It is quite enough when one has to frantically try to make the Negroes appetizing the whole year round." On Christmas Eve at least, it furthered, one should at least be favored with programs "indigenous with our own culture." Undeterred by the complaints, Hansen-Loeve and Freund aired *Black Nativity* and defended their choice by stating that they wanted to show "that God is not only for the Europeans."[95] The lack of "indigeneity" was also the complaint some Germans lodged at "The West Berlin Festival" in October 1964. Although the festival's theme that year was "the influence of Africa on European and especially American Negro culture," the performance of *Black Nativity* seemed to suggest for some that "the many exotic imports of the 1964 festival tended to push Berlin's own offerings into the background."[96]

Opposition of a more political nature arose when *Black Nativity* returned from Europe for its extended U.S. tour, giving a foretaste of the difficulties with regard to race and religion that would follow. Soon after it was announced that the gospel song-play would open in Chicago "under Roman Catholic auspices," unsigned letters began to appear at the Catholic Archdiocesan Chancery office and the Catholic Adult Education Center renouncing Hughes as a Communist sympathizer. Although general anti-Catholic sentiment likely played a role, once again "Goodbye Christ" sat at the center of the opposition. For some Chicagoans, Hughes's authorship of the poem was proof enough that he and the poem were "anti-Christian" and reason enough to boycott *Black Nativity*. As the *Chicago Defender* reported, "The attack, which centers on Mr. Hughes's authorship of a poem 'Goodbye, Christ,' alleges that the work is anti-Christian." The sponsors of the event, however, waxed defiant, refusing to let the "letter writing campaign" stop the event or cast a shadow over Hughes's gospel song-play. Monseigneur Daniel M. Cantwell of the Chicago diocese wrote an editorial in the *New York Times* in November 1963 to defend his organization's sponsorship of *Black Nativity*. "We are sponsoring this play because it is a good play and a [*sic*] good theatre," he contended. He further claimed that the issue of whether or not Hughes was Communist had been settled in 1953 when "the McCarthy Committee" gave him clearance. If Hughes was a Communist, he asserted, that did not mean that all of his artistic production should be rejected. Echoing the pro-Hughes voices from the 1930s, Cantwell stated that it was arguable whether "Goodbye Christ" was actually anti-Christian.[97] What the poem actually argued, Cantwell maintained, was that "Christians had abandoned Christ." In any case, "poetry must be read with imagination." Cantwell had been an advocate for civil rights and racial justice since the late 1940s. He was the founder and the chaplain for the Chicago Catholic Interracial Council.[98] His statements in favor of Hughes, "Goodbye Christ," and *Black Nativity* were consistent with his sustained focus on bringing his Catholic faith to bear on a range of pressing social issues.

In agreement with Monseigneur Cantwell, the *Chicago Defender* also came to the defense of Hughes and *Black Nativity*, stating that it had been "harped upon as an occasion for deleterious criticisms of the author's political views." But, the paper concluded, "the play has nothing in it to suggest a thesis for leftist causes." It was, rather, "cleansing and edifying." The letter writing campaign failed and the show went on successfully.[99] The reputed "Father of Gospel Music," Thomas Andrew Dorsey, caught the show during its Chicago run and wrote Hughes to tell him that he "enjoyed every minute of it."[100]

Thomas Dorsey, notwithstanding, African Americans for the most part shunned *Black Nativity* and expressed deep reservations about it as a work of racialized religious theater. Alex Bradford concurred with Barbara Griner's contention that *Black Nativity* was only able to survive because of white theatergoers but chose to see the white audiences as a response to the growing popularity of gospel music beyond its most noted stars. "We're playing to predominately white audiences for the first time," he told the *New York World Telegraph and Sun.* "White people just wouldn't come to see gospel singers unless maybe Mahalia was on the program."[101] Hughes, however, kept a record of the negative responses he received from blacks about the show. He copied and duplicated several times a particularly biting letter sent to him by Mrs. Eleanor Owens of Cleveland, Ohio, after *Black Nativity* aired on television in that region in December 1962. "If the time has come that you must lend your name to such nothing as appeared on our home sets Tuesday the 11th, 'Black Nativity,'" she wrote, "then it is time you covered your typewriter for a while." The "act," she concluded, "went around the nation to the shame of millions of Negroes."[102] Legendary publisher of Cleveland's *Call and Post*, William O. Walker, agreed with the woman from his city. In a piece entitled "The Editor Expresses Himself on Black Nativity," Walker wrote, "Black Nativity has produced quite a bit of comment. From Negro viewers, most of it was bad. And what I saw and heard was bad, too."[103] Some African American reviewers expressed concern that *Black Nativity* did not put blacks in the best light and was at its core exploitative. Writing for the *Call and Post*, African American journalist Earl Calloway agreed with those who thought the show was "exhilarating, stimulating, and jubilant." But he wondered "if our religious manners and customs should be exploited in the theatre." Members of the Youth Forum at Cleveland's St. James AME Church had a similar response. When asked for their reactions to the televised version of *Black Nativity* and if religion should be "entertaining," one young participant responded, "I disliked it because it was not suitable for TV and because it showed only one concept of Negro religion."[104]

It was not only that *Black Nativity* put a negative spotlight on one aspect of "Negro religion," but it was also the way it suggested negative aspects of black life in general that troubled other African Americans. Journalist Lillian S. Calhoun was pointed in her critique of the performance. "The first act . . . had a rare dignity and deep religious feeling. The second act (the concert) was tacked on by the producers who let the gospel singers run riot and there was just a hint of exploitation about it. If that's racial integration so be it."[105] In answer to the question of whether *Black Nativity* was good or bad, Louise Peacock offered an unambiguous answer and suggested that the fault lay not only with the singers but also with African American life. Counting herself among those who considered the production a "disgrace," she continued, "as I see it, 'Black Nativity' did nothing more than show some of these modern day gospel singers just how ridiculous they appear before the public. None of us can really see ourselves as others see us." "If we want better drama," she contended, "then we better live better lives."[106] Only rarely did *Black Nativity* seem to evoke feelings of racial pride among African American theatergoers and reviewers, as it did in Louise Davis Stone, who declared, "as I left the theatre, a whisper of racial chauvinism hit me and I thought, 'my people may they always be right, but right or wrong, my people.'" She hoped that blacks would not lose the art of gospel singing "in the process of assimilation."[107] Stone's sentiments were not widely shared.

The features of Black Nativity that seemed to give African Americans disquiet—the theatrical expression of black worship and religiosity—were precisely the ones that seemingly thrilled white theatergoers. But it was not that no one extolled the aesthetics and claimed to be genuinely moved by the production in light of the highly racialized responses to it. Indeed, despite varying opinions about its value, some theatergoers found Black Nativity pleasing to watch and seemed to be deeply touched by it. The show's theme of Christmas, its originality, and the power of the singers' voices proved a perfect recipe for dramatic effect and emotional response. Some who saw the show reported "changed lives" and having been "touched" by the display. Writing to his a friend in London in January 1962, a prominent New York psychiatrist declared that Black Nativity had changed him "utterly" and thus his entire "way of life."[108] Mrs. Florence Graham of Boston wrote Hughes in 1963 to thank him for the show, which she found "marvelously conceived" and "beautifully executed." She was particularly taken with "the Negro exhilaration and ecstasy" expressed in the gospel song-play. One of the dancers reminded her of the "angular figures one sees on Egyptian friezes."[109] Carl Van Vechten, one of Hughes's closest friends and a professional "Negrophile," also reported that he loved the show. Writing to Hughes after a performance in New York in January 1962, Van Vechten said, "the jammed house today clapped all through it and one colored lady waved her arms and shouted and then got up and danced down the aisle, overcome by religious excitement." The audience, he asserted, "adored it." Hughes wrote back, "I thought you'd like it."[110]

The Negro Spoke of Nativity

Hughes had every reason to be proud of Black Nativity. As one of his last major artistic productions, it was one of his most innovative, most monetarily successful, and most extensively reviewed. It had also become an international phenomenon. And it seemed to be special to Hughes.

Although he was meticulously involved with the production of all his gospel song-plays, he kept watch over every major and minor aspect of *Black Nativity*. This indicated that the show was never mere entertainment for him. It had a higher purpose, and that purpose was to present and preserve his view of authentic black culture and religious worship. He had long abandoned his misgivings about the mixture of church and theater, proudly dubbing *Black Nativity* "a Gospel for Broadway." And he both applauded and supported the producers' stated aims to bring the "church to the theatre."[111]

Hughes was aware, however, of the pitfalls of bringing the church to the theater and wanted to maintain a reverent air and not compromise it. This became clear in a series of early exchanges with the director and producers. Hughes disliked, for example, the "cute" way the narrator orated at the Lincoln Center performances because they gave "not quite the proper framework to the production, therefore, throwing it a bit out of key and adding to its presentation a more 'childish' quality than necessary."[112] Since the narrator's role set the tone for the production, Hughes argued that the role called for "an actor of dignity and presence who can give the narration the simple, straightforward, yet poetic feeling of reverence and wonder which its performance should have."[113] Hughes was equally displeased at times with the showmanship of the singers. Though all of them came from the culture of black churches, they reveled in the acclaim and notoriety of the stage. In Europe, where they had become bona fide stars, they had taken to responding in kind, taking bows after each song. Hughes fired off his displeasure to Vinnette Carroll after having caught one of the London shows. "The Cast (in Act 2) must not be allowed to take bows after each number as they did in London. They are portraying a revival meeting or church meeting, NOT giving a concert."[114] This was an ironic response in some ways, as Hughes had from the beginning designed the second half of *Black Nativity* precisely to be a "concert." Clearly, his displeasure was directed at the blatant showmanship, not the concert itself, but he feared that the antics of the singers, which had become intrinsic to their performance, would prove to be a distraction. For Hughes, *Black Nativity* was not a casual undertaking. There were serious issues at stake.

Despite all the care Hughes gave to the show, *Black Nativity* fell short of his lofty aim that it represent "authentic" black culture and religion.

More than anything, the highly racialized and romanticized reactions to it indicated just how divided the country had become about black culture in the 1960s and how fraught issues of class were within African American communities. And although Hughes had had a conversion of sorts concerning the relationship between church and theater, it showed how commercial theater was ill-equipped to authenticate any particular cultural form. To showcase black religious worship in the theater was already an act of compromise and inauthenticity.

Hughes's most famous gospel song-play went through many iterations and cast changes throughout the mid- to late 1960s, but the varied experiences of triumph and tragedy of the original cast and producers seemed to be illustrative of the show itself. By the mid-1960s, he had moved into place as an elder statesman and an ambassador of sorts of American and African American culture. Though still not rich, his work had become a consistent source of income, and his stature as literary icon garnered many opportunities to travel and speak. He traveled extensively throughout Europe and Africa, once for the U.S. State Department on a "cultural tour," taking a fledgling writer, Paule Marshall, with him. Remembering that trip and the friendship she developed with Hughes, Marshall wrote in her memoir that Hughes was "a loving taskmaster, mentor, teacher, griot, literary sponsor and treasured friend."[115]

Marshall need not have been surprised that Hughes extended to her the invitation to travel with him. By this time in his life, Hughes was spending an extraordinary amount of time mentoring young literary talent. Alice Walker credits him for launching her literary career by publishing her first short story. In return she gave him her adoration, typifying the unabashed reverence for Hughes by many young black writers then. "By the time I met him," she wrote for the journal *Callaloo*, "Langston Hughes had turned into love." His face had become "exactly like the human sun."[116]

For his part, Hughes kept busy writing and encouraging the younger generation to do the same. He developed a number of proposals for books, many of them for children, including *Spread My Wings and Fly*, a collection of lyrics from Negro spirituals. And although many black radicals viewed him as distant from their cause, Hughes titled what would become his last collection of poetry, *The Panther and the Lash*. The title most likely reflected the founding of the Black Panther movement in

Oakland, California, in 1966 and the historic instrumentation of black punishment and motivation for revolutionary action. He meant the volume to be yet another statement regarding his philosophy of poetry and his connection to his art, but also his connection to "the struggle." Speaking in the third person, he wrote:

> There is no poem in *The Panther and the Lash* with which Langston Hughes does not have some direct or indirect, personal and emotional connection. They are not purely imaginary or contrived poems for the sake of form or word music. They are poems that come out of his own memories and his own life, and the lives of people he has known, loved, and cried for, and the continual pall of racial smog that envelops America. As a contemporary creative writer living in Harlem, the world's largest Negro city within a city, it is impossible for him to be 'above the struggle' or for his art to fail to reflect the vibrant circumstances of life.[117]

Hughes dedicated the book to Rosa Parks, "who started it all." Of his explicitly religious poetry, he included "Who But the Lord?" and "Not for Publication," renamed "Bible Belt" and first published in the *Crisis* in 1953. More important, he also included "Christ in Alabama," one of his racialized religious poems from the 1930s, the first time Hughes had ever anthologized a poem from that group.[118] He did not live to see the volume in print.

Vinnette Carroll went on to have a stellar and award-winning career, based in part on her experiences with Hughes. Some of her success, however, predated her time with *Black Nativity*. After making her Broadway debut in 1957, she won an Obie Award for her role in Errol John's *Moon on a Rainbow* in 1962, and in 1964 she won an Emmy Award for *Beyond the Blues*. In the 1970s, however, she adapted the gospel song-play format, creating and directing several vastly popular musicals. Carroll became the first black women to direct a Broadway (not Off-Broadway) show in 1972 when she developed with Micki Grant the musical *Don't Bother Me, I Can't Cope*, which garnered four Tony Award nominations. She followed that up in 1976 with the musical *Your Arms Too Short to Box with God*, based on Matthew's Gospel in the New Testament. Undoubtedly inspired by her time working with *Black Nativity*, Carroll incorporated several features from the show into both *Don't Bother Me* and *Your Arms*. The latter production included an all-black cast that portrayed the life of Christ from the biblical narrative. The show was a great success, and as Warren Burdine insisted, reflected a "deep and abiding faith in Christianity, and black pride and awareness."[119] It received three Tony Award nominations.

Marion Williams also went on to further fame and recognition. Although her career never quite matched the popularity she experienced with *Black Nativity*, she continued recording and giving concerts. Anthony Heilbut would produce her most acclaimed recordings and be largely responsible for her receiving a "genius grant" from the McArthur Foundation in 1993. She had never heard of the award and died the next year. Madeline Bell became an ex-patriot, relocating to Europe, where she refashioned herself as a "soul singer" and developed an impressive career as a solo singer, background singer, and stage performer. *Black Nativity* had been a "major step" in her career, for which she felt "blessed."[120]

The other singers were not so blessed. They either died in relative or total obscurity, two of them from alcoholism. Princess Steward died of cirrhosis of the liver due to a heavy drinking problem that was well known within gospel circles. Her death occurred three months before Hughes's in 1967, and she left a husband and five children.[121] Allegedly distraught over what he deemed mistreatment for his work on *Your Arms Too Short to Box with God*, Alex Bradford began to drink even heavier. Vinnette Carroll had commissioned him to compose most of the music for the production, with additional original music being supplied by Micki Grant. Bradford collapsed after a night of drinking in 1978, suffered a stroke, and died at the age of 51.

Barbara Griner fared the best of all the original producers. She left the world of the theater to reinvent herself, first as a cook and cookbook author, and then as a psychoanalyst. Kramer had committed suicide not long after being forced out of the show, likely battling alcoholism and depression. He had been a rather tortured gay man for much of his adult life, with a particular penchant for "street boys." Michael Santangelo left Westinghouse not long after the TV production of *Black Nativity* aired. He married a wealthy heiress, Susan Phipps Cochran, in 1971 and moved to Florida. He took up painting but became increasingly depressed and committed suicide in 1983. However, he was still given a Catholic funeral because of the powerful connections of his father, Robert V. Santangelo of the First District Municipal Court of Manhattan.[122]

For all the drama it took to get *Black Nativity* to Broadway and the personal dramas that occurred in its aftermath, there could not have been a more fitting way for Hughes's career in the theater to end than with his most famous gospel song-play. It had exposed some deeply entrenched racial, class, and religious divides both in Europe and the United States, and it proved to be a problematic representation of black religion. It resonated, however, with themes Hughes had been thinking about his entire career, and it returned him to one of the first concerns for New Negro writers and the one promoted by W. E. B. DuBois in the 1920s, which was to reveal the beauty of blackness. Indeed, *Black Nativity*, even with all of its problems, perfectly complemented Hughes's initial thoughts about the beauty of black life and history that he expressed in "The Negro Speaks of Rivers" in 1921. And he poured his life into the production and into the world of black gospel music as one whose soul had "grown deep like the rivers."

Conclusion

Do Nothing till You Hear from Me

Many of those who attended Langston Hughes's funeral on May 25, 1967, at Benta's Funeral Home on St. Nicholas Avenue were confused and bemused. It was not like any funeral they had ever attended. It was being held in a funeral parlor and not a church, there was no preacher, and the music was mostly jazz and blues. The actress and singer Lena Horne, who was among the many artists and entertainers in attendance, reported, "I didn't know whether to cry for Langston or clap my hands and laugh!" They had expected the occasion to be solemn and sad. Hughes had taken ill only a few weeks before and had swiftly deteriorated after prostate surgery. It had all happened so fast and so unexpectedly. The Bard of Harlem was dead, and it was a great loss. But there was also something joyous, even funny about this funeral. The music was upbeat and cheery, and Hughes lay in his coffin, arms folded, as musician Randy Weston claimed, seemingly "laughing at us, I'm sure, cracking up."[1]

What Hughes wanted and what actually happened at his funeral are eerily similar, even though his instructions were not found until May 26, the day after. They were also dissimilar in ways Hughes likely would not have appreciated. He had been very specific. In a document he entitled "Last Rites," Hughes insisted on what should be done with his body. "Immediate cremation. There shall be no display of the remains or funeral services of any sort before cremation. If afterwards a memorial is desired, it shall consist entirely of music, with no speaking whatsoever. The music should be performed in the following manner, with two soloists, a man and woman." Thomas A. Dorsey's "Precious Lord, Take My Hand" was first on the list. He then wanted Oscar Brown Jr.'s "Plain Black Boy (Elegy)" to be sung by a soloist or the recording played. The song was a musical adaptation of the Gwendolyn Brooks poem, "Of

De Witt Williams on His Way to Lincoln Cemetery." "He was born in Alabama / He was bred in Illinois / He was nothing but a plain black boy." Rounding out the music was to be "The Saint Louis Blues" by W. C. Handy, "played by a jazz combo"; "Caravan" by Duke Ellington or "Blues Sands" by Buddy Collette, or both; and finally, "Do Nothing Till You Hear from Me," also by Duke Ellington. This was to be played as an instrumental and "without a singer." He wanted the names of all the artists and performers, who were "to be paid union scale or above," to be printed on cards or a program because there was to be "no Master of Ceremonies." The whole affair, he insisted, "should have the air of an enjoyable concert." As for his ashes, they were either to go to Yale University, where he had been sending materials to the James Weldon Johnson collection since the early 1940s, or "perhaps they might be integrated with the wind."[2]

The three in charge of Hughes's funeral, his lifelong friend, Arna Bontemps, his current secretary, Raoul Abdul, and the executor-trustee of his estate, George Bass, had to draw from their memories, as well as their understanding of Hughes to create something he may have wanted. The first thing they got wrong was the funeral itself. Hughes did not want one. They did arrange to have him cremated, but not immediately. His body was on view for two days at Benta's in a casket bedecked in large white flowers, stirring echoes of his 1942 poem, "Funeral." The poem, which Hughes meticulously revised, gave some indication of his distaste for such display. "Carried lonely up the aisle / In a box without a smile / Resting near the altar there / Where folks pass by and stare." When he was cremated, the small group that had gathered at the crematorium recited Hughes's first major poem "as attendants rolled away the body, toward the flames."[3] It is unclear what immediately happened to his ashes. Likely, they did go to Yale to be among his papers there. (Apparently George Bass kept some on his desk.) But years later they were interred under the cosmogram entitled "Rivers" in the Langston Hughes lobby area of the Schomburg Center for Research in Black Culture.

At the first of two services (a memorial service was held a few days later), there was no preacher and the only music was jazz and blues, played by the Randy Weston Trio. After rendering a number written just for the occasion, "Blues for Langston," the trio indeed played "Caravan." Against Hughes's wishes, however, there was speaking. An unidentified "young writer" read several of Hughes's poems, including "At the Feet of Jesus," "Prayer [2], "I, Too, Sing America," and "Wake." "Tell all the mourners to come dressed in red, cause there ain't no sense in me being dead," stated one version of the latter poem. Arna Bontemps gave some somber remarks about death and also read a number of Hughes poems on the subject, including "Dear Lovely Death" and "Night Funeral in Harlem." Marion Williams sang a solo. But then the atmosphere cheered again. As Margaret T. G. Burroughs recalled, "a ripple of chuckles" erupted from the mourners as Randy Weston and his trio began to play "Do Nothing till You Hear from Me." Although it was being played without a vocalist, everyone knew the lyrics and the implication of playing the song at a funeral. It was a song about someone pleading with their lover for trust, despite alleged and actual infidelities. The last line punctuated the plea. "Some kiss may cloud my memory and other arms may hold a thrill, but please do nothing till you hear from me, and you never will." For Burroughs, that was Hughes "having the last word."[4]

Burroughs was correct in her analysis that Hughes's funeral was his way of having the last word. Everything about the "Last Rites" document and the content of the funeral and the memorial service (if not the events themselves) had Hughes's distinctive mark on them regarding the beauty of black culture and identity formation. The memorial service was held at St. Mark's Methodist Episcopal Church at 138th Street and Nicholas Avenue, and although there was an invocation by Dr. John J. Hicks, there was no preaching. Those in attendance sang "Lift Every Voice and Sing," and a number of artists, writers, actors, and activists gave "remarks" and read poetry, including Sidney Poitier, Micki Grant, Loften Mitchell, Ruby Dee, Ralph Ellison, and Roy Wilkins.[5] The unusual nature of the funeral and memorial was consistent with Hughes's approach to the construction of identity. Having lived most of his life evading static depictions of who he was, his death was not a time to settle. He was going to be as evasive, ambivalent, and paradoxical as ever. His "last rites" would further display his life as an artist and writer, a life of his own making, revealed in a memorial of his own design.

Hughes was also having his "last word" about religion. Indeed, Hughes brought all of his thinking over the course of his lifetime to bear on the "Last Rites" document. He wanted to remain religiously unaffiliated and "unchurched" to the very end. Although he had been thoroughly immersed in Harlem's world of religion and churches, he did not want his body in a church, nor did he want preaching or praying at his funeral, St. Mark's and Hicks's invocation notwithstanding. As Alfred Duckett contended in his moving tribute to Hughes, "he wanted no praying man praying over his body." One of the consequences of his failed salvation experience at age twelve was a deep skepticism about the institution of the church and preachers. He consistently maintained that he was a "member" of no church and always railed against those ministers he felt to be injurious to Christianity, such as Aimee Semple McPherson and George Becton "of the consecrated dime." And although he expressed great respect for the likes of Father Divine and Adam Clayton Powell Jr., he attributed his reticence to actually join a church to ministers. "I'm not a church member because I don't always understand ministers," he bluntly stated in his essay, "Christians and Communists."[6] More than this, however, Hughes's "Last Rites" and his funeral underscored the interplay between his past experience with religion and a present that was always in formation religiously. "Precious Lord, Take My Hand," for example, resonated with his upbringing in the AME Church. Cremation, however, was decidedly not a part of it. Also, in designing an end-of-life ceremony that appeared secular to most people, he was actually asserting an aspect of religious modernism, seeing religion as integrated with the whole of life and drawing no distinction between the secular and the sacred. Black gospel, jazz, and the blues would share equal billing at his ceremony, being of equal cultural and religious value. Hughes had spent most of his adult life honoring the religious traditions of his past, as evidenced by his "poems of a religious nature," which cover the entire span of his career, as well as by his gospel song-plays, written during his gospel years. He spent just as much time, however, disentangling religious practices from any one specific religious tradition. For Hughes, there was a difference between espousing certain religious practices and being religious. He did the one, but he was not the other.

This paradoxical display of religious subjectivity and religiosity is why the long-lasting claims that Hughes was antireligious have not only been misleading, they also have been destructive and obscuring. Langston Hughes was never antireligious in a sense that he was unconcerned for or antagonistic to religion, and to think so is to fundamentally misunderstand him as a person and as a writer. As a thinker about religion,

Hughes wrote as much about religion as he did any other topic, and one can only understand him fully through an analysis of his thoughts about God, faith, the church, and matters of ultimate meaning. He often made efforts to clarify his "ideas about God" and his thinking about religion from both a personal and communal standpoint. Nowhere is that more clearly demonstrated than in a little-known series of essays he wrote for the *Chicago Defender*, entitled, "The Meaning of Faith." He would come as close as he ever had to settling the matter regarding his personal religion and whether or not he had one.

The series, interchangeably titled "The Meaning of Faith" and "The Meaning of Our Faith," lasted from November 1959 to January 1960, further revealing Hughes's cosmopolitan and ecumenical inclinations as he explored the traditions of most major religious groups found in the United States, including Catholicism, Judaism, and various denominational expressions of Protestantism. Hughes had nurtured an interest in comparative religions since the 1920s when he read Lewis Browne's text, *This Believing World* to "get a better background for writing and for understanding the world."[7] Each essay included a substantial amount of statistical information about the size of denominations, the number of members, and the organizational structure. But Hughes determined to transcend this level of basic information, hoping to explicate the "meaning" of each religious expression, declaring in the introductory essay, "in a country like ours with such variety of religious sects, it would seem wise if we all knew what the fundamental differences are between America's main religious bodies." Proclaiming his great "respect for all religious beliefs," he pledged to objectively characterize and forthrightly explain everything from the systems of governance, liturgies, ritual practices, and theologies of each one. With Protestants, Catholics, and Jews, for example, Hughes contended that the concept of "One God" unified them all. "It is this concept, and the use of moral precepts stemming from the Old Testament, that link by their similarities America's three major religious faiths," he wrote.

Hughes acknowledged that he had read a "great many books, essays, pamphlets, and newspaper and magazine articles" in preparation for the "Meaning of Faith" series and that he had learned a great deal about the wide-ranging expressions of religion in the United States. So perhaps it seemed only fitting to end on a personal note. Hughes entitled the last essay in the series, "The Meaning of Faith: Personal," and it was indeed personal. It was as much about content as it was about practice, a move he had been unwilling to make in the 1930s, as the poem "Personal" demonstrated. The essay was by no means a full disclosure, however, as Hughes made his case on his own terms, drawing a distinction between a statement of belief (or a statement *about* his beliefs) and a confession of faith. "The Meaning of Faith: Personal" was the former while it was decidedly not the latter. Although it illuminated in greater detail Hughes's personal beliefs and practices, the statement was in essence yet another display of his engagement with religion and religious communities more broadly and a clear articulation of his "respect for all beliefs" in what he called his "sermon about God."

Hughes began his "sermon about God" with the claim that there has rarely been consensus among people of faith. Even people who share a religious tradition disagree on "interpretations of that faith," he asserted. And historically, "in no other field can divergent ideas clash more violently than in the realm of theology." Although he admired those who could stand "firmly for their faith" despite differences, "sure of the ground on which they stand," his approach was different. For Hughes, the subject of religion must be approached with "humility," not certainty, seemingly confirming what a number of philosophers and theologians had maintained since the early twentieth century—that doubt and uncertainty often necessarily precede faith.[8] "I would have to begin by saying that I don't know very much about God," he wrote. Rather than knowledge or certainty, what Hughes claimed to have was an intuitive "feeling" about the universality of God. "I have a feeling that God is related to everything and everybody on earth." That sense of universality worked in concert with his ecumenism as he again affirmed the view that all religions have equal value and worth, despite differences. "I respect each and every one of them," he further proclaimed.[9]

His next move turned Genesis 1:27 (KJV)—"God created man in his own image, in the image of God created he him"—on its head. Following the logic of "process theology," whether knowingly or not, Hughes contended that God was a human construction. "If man is made in God's image, the reverse must also be true." Formulized by English mathematician and philosopher Alfred North Whitehead, process theology is a philosophical branch of theology that holds that "all actuality is process," and creative change or "evolution" is the core of human experi-ence. God and religion, therefore, are not fixed or immutable entities but subject to change and are consequently created by humanity rather than born from divine "revelation." Whitehead viewed humanity and God in a co-creating relationship, and God as "both engaged and af-fected by the world." "It is as true to say that God creates the world, as that the world creates God," he postulated in 1929.[10] Social construc-tionist in framework and shot through with striking anthropological and cultural underpinnings, the assertion also rendered the practice of one's religious faith an issue of "natural rights" and religious freedom. As Hughes asserted, "certainly each man on earth has as much right as I do to conceive of God in his own way and believe in Him. I do not have the audacity to say that I alone know God. Whoever you are, I believe you know Him, too, whether you be Baptist or Methodist, Church or God or Church of Christ, Catholic or Jewish, Presbyterian or Lutheran, Chris-tian Scientist or Moslem, colored or white."[11] Hughes's "sermon about God" likely gave little satisfaction to those wanting him to state a spe-cific religious identity to counter his "atheist" reputation, but it offered a full exposition of his thoughts about the social function and purpose of religion, as well as his individuated beliefs and practices.

Further explicating those specific beliefs and practices, Hughes in-sisted that God transcended both race and creed. He had often taken stances against religious creeds and dogmas in his poetry and other works on religion, granting substantiation to Arnold Rampersad's con-tention that "the drama of religion appealed to him, not its dogma. Jesus was dead, ritual was alive."[12] Although the series was designed to appre-ciate and understand the "meaning" of different religious organizations and movements in the United States, Hughes held creeds responsible for those differences, as well as for the "violent" theological clashes among those he mentioned in the first essay. Moreover, Hughes positioned his stance against religious creeds as the logical and rational conclusion to his notions of universalism, ecumenism, and antiracialism. In Hughes's view, God was above all humanity and all of humanity is equal because God cannot be defined or confined by a particular race. Stating that God was above creeds, therefore, equalized the world's religions and evapo-rated the separations among all religious believers, regardless of race. And he proposed prayer as that great equalizer. God hears the prayers of all, Hughes declared, "even the least among the children of men—even the Atheist and the heathen who do not call His name.[13] To further illuminate this position, Hughes tendered another central tenet of process theology. Insisting that all people have a right to conceptualize God in their own image, he further claimed that no one has a monopoly on God and no religion can adequately portray God. Indeed, "no single word or language is big enough to contain God"; therefore, no name for God is adequate and all names for God are equally valid. "Maybe another name for God is Mystery, or Love, the Holy Spirit or Father Divine, Unity or Universal Power, Buddah [sic] or Allah, or Jehovah, or names I have never heard of," Hughes wrote. "I claim no exclusive patent on my phrasing of the word God."

Hughes ended his "sermon" with the dramatic flair evocative of the sermonic tradition of his youth in the AME Church and which certainly was common in many of Harlem's African American churches at that time. But while the structure and tone looked to his past, discursively and thematically, his closing comment was theologically modern and steeped in his awareness of the vagaries of American religious cultures.

> Can I say that there is no God in Georgia simply because Jim Crow makes more headlines? God may keep silent for a long time, but when He speaks the map of history is changed. When He speaks, the slate is wiped clean. When He speaks, sorrow runs like a river to the sea and the land is cleansed again. Do you think that God is gone just because He is banned somewhere? Who can ban God? Or you, His child? Or me, the least of His children? Try to step between me and God—and you will be thinner than a shadow and less of a wall than the evening fog.[14]

There are echoes of the strategic evasiveness of "Personal" in the last line of the sermon, as Hughes again affirms his "unknowability" and his commitment to his own self-fashioning with regard to his personal religion. Calling himself "the least" of God's children, he acknowledges a relationship with God as "Personal" had done, a relationship so tightly bound that only thin shadows dare permeate it. "The Meaning of Faith: Personal," however, revealed more than it veiled, particularly with regard to Hughes's actual practices and his views on the meaning and social purposes of religion.

Writing "The Meaning of Faith: Personal" was itself a demonstration of a type of religious practice on Hughes's part, as his religious poetry, his church attendance, and his engagement with Harlem's world of religion and churches had also been. But the great value in the essay was not that it marked him as religious, but that it indicated that one did not have to be religious to have religious practices. That is the essence of the essay. Along with Hughes's other works on religion, the essay tends to disrupt categories of religiosity and instate new means and modes of spiritual and religious authority. Hughes's lifelong search for the meaning of salvation began that night in Kansas when he failed to see Jesus. The results of his exploration and his attempt to work out his salvation after that disappointing night, has yielded some of the most prescient thinking about religion in twentieth-century literature. Hughes and his works on religion suggest a much broader reach for the history and historiography of American and African American religion. They became untethered from the conventional Protestant narratives of Christian belief and practice, making room for the perspectives, insights, and practices of the doubtful, the skeptical, the disillusioned, and the unsure, recognizing that each play a role in the structure of belief. A look to the life and work of Langston Hughes, therefore, broadens and deepens our conception of religion itself and shines a clear light on other ways we seek and sometimes find salvation.

NOTES

INTRODUCTION

1 *Embattled Lawrence: Conflict and Community*, ed. Dennis Domer and Barbara Watkins (Lawrence: University of Kansas Continuing Education, 2001); Langston Hughes, *The Big Sea* (New York: Hill and Wang, 1940), 18–21; Langston Hughes, "The Meaning of Our Faith," *Chicago Defender*, November 21, 1959, 10. Mary Reed would have been in her mid-fifties and her husband James close to seventy when she took Hughes into her home. Although she had had five children, by 1910 all of them had died. The childless couple likely relished the idea of having another child in the home. See 1910 U.S. census.

2 Hughes, *Big Sea*, 325; Arnold Rampersad, *The Life of Langston Hughes, vol. 1, 1902–1941: I, Too, Sing America* (New York: Oxford University Press, 2002), 377.

3 Langston Hughes, *I Wonder as I Wander* (New York: Hill and Wang, 1993), 5. There have been many theories suggesting what exactly caused the break between Hughes and Mason. While seeing it as fundamentally about Hughes's unwillingness to heed her demands and be "primitive," Carla Kaplan has also suggested that the Depression had depleted Mason's fortune by half, forcing her to make more streamlined choices as to which projects and protégés she would financially support. Those financial constraints perhaps added to her growing discouragement with the overall project of assisting blacks to be the "salvation" and racial "cure" for America. Lastly, Kaplan suggests that the true motive for cutting Hughes off so completely was her desire to keep him away from Zora Neale Hurston, whom she came to see as her "last hope" in her grand racial project. See Carla Kaplan, *Miss Anne in Harlem: The White Women of the Black Renaissance* (New York: Harper-Collins, 2013), 193–254.

4 Hughes, *Big Sea*, 49.

5 Rampersad, *Life of Langston Hughes*, 1:377.

6 In an interview conducted in 1977, Martha Chieks recalled Hughes both as a fellow schoolmate and a member of the Sunday school at St. Luke AME Church.

7 For general histories of the migration to Kansas after reconstruction and its aftermath, see Nell Irvin Painter, *Exodusters: Migration to Kansas after Reconstruction* (New York: W. W. Norton, 1992); "Millenarian Aspects of the Exodus to Kansas of 1879," *Journal of Social History* 9, no. 3 (Spring 1976): 331–38; Joseph V. Hickey, "'Pap' Singleton's Dunlap Colony: Relief Agencies and the Failure of a Black Settlement in Eastern Kansas," *Great Plains Quarterly* 11, no. 1 (Winter 1991):

23–36; Brent M. S. Campney, *This Is Not Dixie: Racist Violence in Kansas, 1861–1927* (Urbana: University of Illinois Press, 2015); Jacob S. Dorman, *Chosen People: The Rise of American Black Israelite Religions* (New York: Oxford University Press, 2013), 24–28.

8 Langston Hughes, "Du Bois: A Part of Me," in *Collected Works of Langston Hughes: Essays on Art, Race, Politics, and World Affairs*, vol. 9, ed. Christopher C. De Santis (Columbia: University of Missouri Press, 2002), 556.

9 Arnold Rampersad, *The Life of Langston Hughes, vol. 2, 1941–1967: I Dream a World* (New York: Oxford University Press, 1988), 175–77, 326; Allan Kozinn, "Jan Meyerowitz, 85, Composer on Moral Subjects," *New York Times*, December 26, 1998.

10 Rampersad, *Life of Langston Hughes*, 2:250, 266.

11 Ibid., 1:117–19; Arnold Rampersad, David Roessel, and Christa Fratantoro, eds., *Selected Letters of Langston Hughes* (New York: Knopf, 2015), 53–54; Edgar Lee Masters, *Vachel Lindsay: A Poet in America* (New York: C. Scribner's Sons, 1935); Langston Hughes, "A Note on Poetry," *Free Lance* 11 (1967): 36. The 1950 introduction was reprinted in the Langston Hughes memorial issue a few months after his death in 1967.

12 *The Collected Poems of Langston Hughes*, ed. Arnold Rampersad (New York: Vintage Books, 1994), 5; Arthur Davis, "The Harlem of Langston Hughes's Poetry," *Phylon* 13, no. 4 (1952): 276; "Langston Hughes, Writer, 65, Dead," *New York Times*, May 23, 1967.

13 Langston Hughes, "My Adventures as a Social Poet," *Phylon* 8, no. 3 (3rd quarter, 1947): 205–12; Susan Duffy, *The Political Plays of Langston Hughes* (Carbondale: Southern Illinois University Press, 2000), 4; Margaret Larkin, "A Poet for the People," *Opportunity* 5 (March 1927): 84–85; Alain Locke, "Black Truth and Black Beauty: A Retrospective Review of the Literature of 1932," *Opportunity* 11 (January 1933): 14–18; *Proletarian Poetry in the United States: An Anthology*, ed. Granville Hicks and Michael Gold et al. (New York: International Publishers, 1935), 27.

14 Hughes, *Big Sea*, 51–56; Donald C. Dickerson, *A Bio-Bibliography of Langston Hughes* (Hamden, CT: Archon Books, 1972), 14. As late as 1952 Hughes considered "The Negro Speaks of Rivers" and "I, Too, Sing America" to be his most famous poems. In a letter to Arna Bontemps he suggested that they both be used in a recording of an anthology of Negro poetry being proposed by Folkways Records. See *Arna Bontemps–Langston Hughes Letters, 1925–1967*, ed. Charles H. Nichols (New York: Paragon House, 1990), 29.

15 Langston Hughes, "The Negro Speaks of Rivers," *Crisis* (June 1921): 7.

16 Letter from Langston Hughes to Jessie Fauset, January 18, 1921, Langston Hughes Papers, Beinecke Library, Yale University (hereafter LHP), Box 61, Folder 1163; letter from Jessie Fauset to Langston Hughes, June 18, 1924, LHP, the James Weldon Johnson Collection, Box 61, Folder 1164; Alain Locke, "The Weary Blues," *Palms* 4, no. 1 (1926); Onwuchekwa Jemie, *Langston Hughes: An Introduction to Poetry*

(New York: Columbia University Press, 1973), 103; Nathan Irvin Huggins, *The Harlem Renaissance* (New York: Oxford University Press, 1971), 66–67.

17 Rampersad, *Collected Works of Langston Hughes*, 1:9; Hughes, *Big Sea*, 266.

18 Langston Hughes, *Fine Clothes to the Jew* (New York: Alfred A. Knopf, 1927); Langston Hughes, *The Dream Keeper and Other Poems* (New York: Alfred A. Knopf, 1932), 51–59.

19 Langston Hughes, "Christ" and "Celestial Eye," LHP, Box 375, Folder 6232 and 6243.

20 Although Onwuchekwa Jemie, James A. Emanuel, and Mary Beth Culp offer analyses of religion in Hughes's poetry, Wagner's work is the most extensive. His expansive dissertation and the book upon which it is based offer penetrating critique and commentary and important social and literary contextualization. See Jean Wagner, *Black Poets of the United States: From Paul Lawrence Dunbar to Langston Hughes* (Urbana: University of Illinois Press, 1973); Jemie, *Langston Hughes*; James A. Emanuel, *Langston Hughes* (New York: Twayne, 1967); and Mary Beth Culp, "Religion in the Poetry of Langston Hughes," *Phylon* 48, no. 3 (1987): 240–45.

21 Rampersad, *Life of Langston Hughes*, 2:370. See also Culp, "Religion in the Poetry," 240.

22 Rampersad, *Life of Langston Hughes*, 1:63; Rampersad, Roessel, and Fratantoro, *Selected Letters of Langston Hughes*, xv; Leslie Catherine Sanders, "'I've Wrestled with Them All My Life': Langston Hughes's *Tambourines to Glory*," *Black American Literature Forum* 25, no. 1 (Spring 1991): 63.

23 "Hughes, Langston: Interview Notes, bms Am 2035 (64)," June 19, 1958, Jean Wagner Papers, Houghton Library, Harvard University.

24 Jemie, *Langston Hughes*, 90.

25 Benjamin E. Mays, *The Negro's God as Reflected in His Literature* (New York: Russell and Russell, 1938), 243.

26 Two studies on A. Philip Randolph and W. E. B. DuBois challenge the assertion that both men were agnostic and irreligious. Cynthia Taylor acknowledges that Randolph had a "complex relationship to African American religion" but disputes the notion that he was an "avowed atheist." Rather, Randolph's approach to religion covered a "wide spectrum," and he was, "in fact, a deeply religious man." Similarly, Edward J. Blum's portrait of DuBois shows that in his lifetime DuBois was considered a "Christ-like figure" and his words were "akin to scripture." His irreligiosity and atheism was a "mythical construction" by scholars, he contends, and DuBois was, rather, a "prophet" with "multiple religious selves" and was deeply engaged with the interconnection of religion and race. While my study differs from Taylor's and Blum's in some of their conclusions, I see us responding to similar historical and historiographical oversights on the role of religion in the lives of our respective subjects. See Cynthia Taylor, *A. Philip Randolph: The Religious Journey of an African American Labor Leader* (New York: New York University Press, 2006); and Edward J. Blum, *W. E. B. Du Bois: American Prophet* (Philadelphia: University of Pennsylvania Press, 2007).

27 James Weldon Johnson, *Along This Way*, (New York: Penguin Books, 1990), 155 and 413.

28 Zora Neale Hurston, *Dust Tracks on the Road: An Autobiography* (Philadelphia: J. B. Lippincott, 1942), 274–87.

29 Blum, *American Prophet*, 9; W. E. B. DuBois, ed., *The Negro Church: Report of a Social Study Made under the Direction of Atlanta University; Together with Proceedings of the Eighth Conference for the Study of Negro Problems. Held at Atlanta University, May 26th, 1903* (Walnut Creek, CA: AltaMira Press, 2003), ix.

30 Langston Hughes, "The Negro and the Racial Mountain," *Nation*, June 23, 1926, 692–94.

31 Rampersad, *Life of Langston Hughes*, 1:309.

32 Culp, "Religion in the Poetry," 241.

33 David E. Chinitz, *Which Sin to Bear: Authenticity and Compromise in Langston Hughes* (New York: Oxford University Press, 2013), 92; Donald B. Gibson, "The Good Black Poet and the Good Gray Poet: The Poetry of Hughes and Whitman," in *Langston Hughes Black Genius: A Critical Evaluation, ed.* Therman B. O'Daniel (New York: William Morrow, 1971), 78; Arnold Rampersad, introduction to Rampersad, Roessel, and Fratantoro, *Selected Letters of Langston Hughes*, xxv.

34 Rampersad, *Life of Langston Hughes*, 2:133 and 177.

35 Michael S. Sherry, *Gay Artists in Modern American Culture: An Imagine Conspiracy* (Chapel Hill: University of North Carolina Press, 2007), 17; Rampersad, *Life of Langston Hughes*, 2:177: Gene Lees, "The Gospel Gimmick," Randolfe Wicker Papers, Box 2, Printed Emphemera 1964 Folder, New York Public Library; Carl Bean, interview with the author, August 15, 2011, Princeton University.

36 Faith Berry, *Langston Hughes: Before and Beyond Harlem* (Westport, CT: Lawrence Hill, 1983), 43, 360.

37 Jeffrey Q. McCune Jr., *Sexual Discretion: Black Masculinity and the Politics of Passing* (Chicago: University of Chicago Press, 2014), 7–8.

38 In correspondence that stretched from 1921 to 1926, Andrzejewski poured out his heart to Hughes, informing his friend of nearly every detail of his life and the struggles he faced in college. The letters are tender and loving, and they speak of a time past that seemed to suggest that they had been physically intimate. Mostly, however, Andrzejewski complained about his job, his failure to achieve an acting career, and his inability to be a "real man." Letters from Sartur Andrzejewski to Langston Hughes, 1921–1926, LHP, Box 8, Folder 166; Rampersad, *Life of Langston Hughes*, 1:77; Berry, *Langston Hughes*, 49–50. I want to thank Jacob Dorman for pointing me to these letters and for engaging me in some vigorous conversations about Hughes and sexuality.

39 George Hutchinson, *Harlem Renaissance in Black and White* (Cambridge, MA: Harvard University Press, 1995), 512; Rampersad, *Life of Langston Hughes*, 1:92; Leonard Harris and Charles Molesworth, *Alain Locke: The Biography of a Philosopher* (Chicago: University of Chicago Press, 2008), 163–70.

40 Langston Hughes, "Little Ham," in Leslie Catherine Sanders, *The Collected Works of Langston Hughes: The Plays to 1942: "Mulatto" to "The Sun Do Move,"* vol. 5 (Columbia: University of Missouri Press, 2002), 196–265; Langston Hughes, "Blessed Assurance" drafts, LHP, Box 285, Folder 4671; Langston Hughes, "Seven People Dancing," *New Yorker*, June 6 and 13, 2016, 60–61; Deborah Treisman, "Discovering an Unpublished Story by Langston Hughes," *New Yorker*, May 30, 2016, 60–61. See also Sharyn Emery, "The Philadelphia Harlem Story: Langston Hughes's Screwy Play *Little Ham*," *Modern Drama* 55, no. 3 (Fall 2012): 373–85; Marlon Rachquel Moore, "Black Church, Black Patriarchy, and the Brilliant Queer: Competing Masculinities in Langston Hughes's *Blessed Assurance*," *African American Review* 42, nos. 3–4 (Fall/Winter 2008): 493–502.

41 Shane Vogel, *The Scene of a Harlem Café: Race, Sexuality, and Performance* (Chicago: University of Chicago Press, 2009), 107. Vogel has offered a most innovative intervention in the debate about Hughes's sexuality, arguing that the fault lies with attempts to substantiate it through limited understandings of what constitutes "archival" evidence and in limiting sexuality to a matter of "sexual object choice." He suggests, rather, that we consider the "alternative archive of queer practices" Hughes left, including his evasiveness about his sexuality, as sufficient "evidence" of his sexuality.

42 Isaac Julien, writer and director, "Looking for Langston," Sankofa Film and Video Productions, UK, 1989.

43 Adrienne Johnson Gosselin, "Beyond the Harlem Renaissance: The Case for Black Modernist Writers," *Modern Language Studies* 26, no. 4 (Autumn 1996): 37–45; Hutchinson, *Harlem Renaissance Black and White*, 1–31. See also Houston A. Baker Jr., "Modernism and the Harlem Renaissance," *American Quarterly* 39, no. 1 (Spring 1987): 84–97; James De Jongh, *Vicious Modernism: Black Harlem and the Literary Imagination* (New York: Cambridge University Press, 1990); James Smethurst, *The African American Roots of Modernism: From Reconstruction to the Harlem Renaissance* (Chapel Hill: University of North Carolina Press, 2011); *The Leroi Jones/Amiri Baraka Reader*, ed. Amiri Baraka, Imamu Baraka, and Villiam J. Harris (New York: Thunder's Mouth Press, 1991), 217.

44 For a historical analysis of the rise of religious liberalism in America, see Matthew Hedstrom, *The Rise of Liberal Religion: Book Culture and American Spirituality in the Twentieth Century* (New York: Oxford University Press, 2015); *American Religious Liberalism*, ed. Leigh E. Schmidt and Sally M. Promey (Bloomington: Indiana University Press, 2012); and Gary Dorrien, *The Making of American Liberal Theology: Imagining Progressive Religion, 1805–1900* (Louisville, KY: Westminster John Knox Press, 2001); and *The Making of American Liberal Theology: Idealism, Realism, and Modernity, 1900–1950* (Louisville, KY: Westminster John Knox Press, 2003).

45 "Let America Be America Again," in Rampersad, *Collected Poems of Langston Hughes*, 189. Hughes sent the poem to his literary agent at the time, Maxim Lieber, who considered it "magnificent." It was first published in *Esquire* and then

in Hughes's 1938 collection, *New Song*. See Rampersad, *Life of Langston Hughes*, 1:315–16.

46 Barbara Dianne Savage, *Your Spirits Walk Beside Us: The Politics of Black Religion* (Cambridge, MA: Harvard University Press, 2008), 16, 157.

47 Leigh E. Schmidt, *Restless Souls: The Making of American Spirituality from Emerson to Oprah* (New York: HarperSanFrancisco, 2005), 11; Richard Wightman Fox, "The Culture of Liberal Protestant Progressivism, 1875–1925," *Journal of Interdisciplinary History* 23 (Winter 1993): 646.

48 Albert J. Raboteau, *Slave Religion: The "Invisible Institution" in the Antebellum South* (New York: Oxford University Press, 1978), 92.

49 W. E. B. DuBois, *The Souls of Black Folk* (New York: Bantam Dell, 1989),142; E. Franklin Frazier, *The Negro Church in America*, and C. Eric Lincoln, *The Black Church in America* (New York: Schocken Books, 1974), 14, 115; *God Struck Me Dead: Voices of Ex-Slaves*, ed. Clifton H. Johnson (Cleveland: Pilgrim Press, 1969), 122.

50 David Hempton, *Evangelical Disenchantment: Nine Portraits of Faith and Doubt* (New Haven, CT: Yale University Press, 2008), 4.

51 Wagner, *Black Poets*, 385–474; "Poems of the Spirit," document sent to François Dodat, June 24, 1963, LHP, Box 383, Folder 6830; Leslie Catherine Sanders, "'I've Wrestled with Them,'" 63.

CHAPTER 1. NEW TERRITORY FOR NEW NEGROES

1 Langston Hughes, *The Big Sea: An Autobiography*, 2nd ed. (New York: Hill and Wang, 1993), 81.

2 Langston Hughes, *The Big Sea* (New York: Hill and Wang, 1940), 83.

3 Ibid., 224, 85. *Shuffle Along* was a major Broadway hit in the early 1920s. It ran for over five hundred shows and advanced the careers of Josephine Baker, Paul Robeson, and Florence Mills, whom Hughes adored. It was one of the first productions in the history of Broadway to be held in a white theater venue and to have interracial audiences. Many view *Shuffle Along* as the beginning of modern black theater. In addition to launching the careers of a number of black actors and musicians, the show also spawned some successful all-black musicals in the 1920s. James Weldon Johns saw the musical as a breakthrough in modern theater, and Loften Mitchell credited *Shuffle Along* for initiating the Harlem Renaissance. See James Weldon Johnson, *Black Manhattan* (New York: Atheneum Press, 1977), 186–89; Errol G. Hill and James V. Hatch, *A History of African American Theater* (Cambridge: Cambridge University Press, 2006); and Samuel A. Hay, *African American Theater: A History and Critical Analysis* (Cambridge: Cambridge University Press, 1994).

4 Arnold Rampersad, *The Collected Poems of Langston Hughes* (New York: Vintage Books, 1995), 312; originally published in *Hawk's Cry* (the base newspaper for the Tuskegee Army Airfield), August 18, 1945.

5 Arnold Rampersad, *The Life of Langston Hughes*, vol. 1, *1902–1941: I, Too, Sing America* (New York: Oxford University Press, 2002), 4. Hughes's mother's given

name at birth in 1873 was Carolina. Throughout her life, however, she often referred to herself as Caroline or Carolyn. Most people simply called her Carrie. *My Dear Boy: Carrie Hughes's Letters to Langston Hughes*, ed. Carmaletta M. Williams and John Edgar Tidwell (Athens: University of Georgia Press, 2013), 1.

6 Rampersad, *Life of Langston Hughes, 1*:7–8; Mark Scott, "Langston Hughes of Kansas," *Journal of Negro History* 66, no. 1 (Spring 1981): 1–9; Louis-Alejandro Dinnella Borrego, "From the Ashes of the Old Dominion: Accommodation, Immediacy, and Progressive Pragmatism in John Mercer Langston's Virginia," *Virginia Magazine of History and Biography* 117, no. 3 (2009): 214–49.

7 Jonathan Gill, *Harlem: The Four Hundred Year History from Dutch Village to Capital of Black America* (New York: Grove Press, 2011), 277.

8 *Washington Bee*, March 27, 1897; *Colored American*, September 24, 1898, August 13, 1898; *The Freeman*, June 12, 1897; and (Indianapolis) *Recorder*, November 4, 1899.

9 Henry Louis Gates Jr., "The Trope of the New Negro and the Reconstruction of the Image of the Black," *Representations* 24 (Autumn 1988): 136; *New Negro for a New Century*, ed. Booker T. Washington et al. (New York: Arno Press, 1969), 3.

10 Quoted in *The New Negro: An Interpretation*, ed. Alain Locke (New York: Albert and Charles Boni, 1925), 285; Gerald Early, "The New Negro Era and the Great African American Transformation," *American Studies* 49, no. 1/2 (Spring/Summer 2008): 14.

11 *Encyclopedia of the Harlem Renaissance, ed.* Sandra L. West and Aberjhani (New York: Checkmark Books, 2003), xviii.

12 Gregory Holmes Singleton, "Birth, Rebirth and the 'New Negro' of the 1920s," *Phylon* 43, no. 1 (1982): 23.

13 Holstein released a statement of his reasons for establishing the prizes: "Having been all my life a firm and enthusiastic believer in the creative genius of the Black Race, to which I humbly belong, *Opportunity's* Prize Contest to foster artistic expression among Negroes has been a source of breathless interest to me. I honestly think it will go far towards consolidating the interests of, and bridging the gap between the black and white races in the United States today, and particularly will it encourage among our gifted youth the ambition to scale the empyrean heights of art and literature." *Opportunity*, October 1925, 308; January 1928, 5. See also Eugene C. Holmes, "Alain Locke and the New Negro Movement," *Negro American Literature Forum* 2, no. 3 (Autumn, 1968): 63; Darryl Pinckney, "The Honorary Negro," *New York Review of Books*, August 18, 1988; Edward White, *The Tastemaker: Carl Van Vechten and the Birth of Modern America* (New York: Farrar, Straus and Giroux, 2015), 48.

14 *Opportunity* 3, no. 29 (May 1925).

15 Gene Andrew Jarrett, *Representing the Race: A New Political History of African American Literature* (New York: New York University Press, 2011), 74–75; Wayne Cooper, "Claude McKay and the New Negro of the 1920s," *Phylon* 25, no. 3 (1964): 297; Singleton, "Birth, Rebirth," 31; *Crisis* (May 1925); Gill, *Harlem*, 279.

16 Singleton, "Birth, Rebirth," 31.

17 Gunter H. Lenz, "Symbolic Space, Communal Rituals, and the Surreality of the Urban Ghetto: Harlem in Black Literature from the 1920s to the 1960s," *Callaloo* 35 (Spring 1988): 319–20; Jean Wagner, *Black Poets of the United States: From Paul Lawrence Dunbar to Langston Hughes* (Champaign: University of Illinois Press, 1973), 192.

18 Josef Sorett, "'We Build Our Temples for Tomorrow': Racial Ecumenism and Religious Liberalism in the Harlem Renaissance," in *American Religious Liberalism,* ed. Leigh Eric Schmidt and Sally M. Pomey (Bloomington: Indiana University Press, 2012), 190–206.

19 Sorett, "'We Build Our Temples,'" 193.

20 Robert Thomas Kerlin, *Negro Poets and Their Poems* (Washington, DC: Associated Publishers, 1923), 51; Countee Cullen, ed., *Caroling Dusk: An Anthology of Verse by Black Poets of the Twenties* (New York: Carol Publishing Group, 1993), x.

21 Clarence Taylor, *The Black Churches of Brooklyn* (New York: Columbia University Press, 1996); Carla Peterson, *Black Gotham: A Family History of African Americans in Nineteenth Century New York City* (New Haven, CT: Yale University Press, 2012), 283–344; *WPA Guide to New York City: Federal Writer's Project Guide to 1930s New York* (New York: Pantheon Books, 1982), 257; "Harlem Churches a Many Splendored Thing," *New York Amsterdam News*, February 18, 1956.

22 James Weldon Johnson, in Locke, *New Negro*, 301–11.

23 Arthur P. Davis, "The Harlem of Langston Hughes's Poetry," *Phylon* 13, no. 4 (1952): 283.

24 Michel de Certeau, *The Practice of Everyday Life* (Berkeley: University of California Press, 1984), 91; Benedict Anderson, *Imagined Communities: Reflections on the Origin and Spread of Nationalism* (New York: Verso, 2006), 6–7; Vivian Patraka, *Spectacular Suffering: Theater, Fascism, and the Holocaust* (Bloomington: Indiana University Press, 1999), 123.

25 The son of a barber from Massachusetts who came to New York seeking his fortune in 1899, Payton is most responsible for building what would become the greatest black community in the world, earning him the moniker "father of [the] Negro Community." He took full advantage of the opportunities provided by the racist restrictions in housing, a building boom and bust, and the expansion of Harlem as a viable residential neighborhood to build a successful real estate business and to amass a fortune. The historical record is mixed on Payton, however, as it is clear that his activities as a real estate developer had as much to do with financial gain as "uplifting the race." Ethnic historian Gilbert Osofsky sensitively intimated this, stating, "sometimes his activities as a businessman were less than exemplary." Harlem historian Jonathan Gill was more forthright: "Change came to Harlem less through goodwill than good business instincts," and Payton had a spate of those. But within a few years of establishing his office he was receiving praise for "doing an excellent business in New York City and vicinity" and supplying "all reliable parties with desirable homes, storerooms, and flats," as Gill further

noted. His shrewd, calculated, and, at times, dishonest tactics laid the principle groundwork for the territory of black Harlem. See "A Negro City in New York," *Topeka Plaindealer*, February 5, 1915; Osofsky, *Harlem*, 95; Gill, *Harlem*, 177.

26 Edwin G. Burrows and Mike Wallace, *Gotham: A History of New York City to 1898* (New York: Oxford University Press, 2000), 993.

27 The Jazz Age refers to the 1920s—also called the Roaring Twenties—when a transformation in American lifestyles developed around the culture of jazz music, a new musical genre created by black Americans and characterized by innovation and up-tempo. The Jazz Age was typified by modern styles of dress (particularly for women), a corresponding dance craze, and changes in speech patterns and social codes. It was a youthful and optimistic era that came to an abrupt end with the Great Depression. See Gary Dean Best, *The Dollar Decade: Mammon and the Machine in 1920s America* (Westport, CT: Praeger, 2003); Frederick Lewis Allen, *Only Yesterday: An Informal History of the 1920s* (New York: Harper Perennial Modern Classics, 2010) ; William Leuchtenburg, *The Perils of Prosperity, 1914–1932* (Chicago: University of Chicago Press, 1993); Paula S. Fass, *The Damned and the Beautiful: American Youth in the 1920s* (New York: Oxford University Press, 1979); and Ann Douglas, *Terrible Honesty: Mongrel Manhattan in the 1920s* (New York: Farrar, Straus and Giroux, 1996).

28 Hughes, *Big Sea*, 228.

29 "Five Points" refers to a notorious five-pointed intersection in Lower Manhattan, originally bounded by Orange, Cross, and Anthony Streets. Anthony (now Worth) ran in a northwestern direction, dividing one of the four corners of Orange and Cross into triangular blocks, creating a fifth point. See Tyler Anbinder, *Five Points: The 19th Century New York City Neighborhood that Invented Tap Dance, Stole Elections and Became the World's Most Notorious Slum* (New York: Free Press, 2010), 1; Edward Robb Ellis, *The Epic City of New York: A Narrative History* (New York: Basic Books, 2004), 231.

30 Burrows and Wallace, *Gotham*, 854; Gilbert Osofsky, *Harlem: The Making of a Ghetto: New York, 1890–1930* (Chicago: Ivan R. Dee Publishers, 1996),11; Terry Miller, *Greenwich Village and How It Got that Way* (New York: Crown, 1990), 198.

31 Cornelius William Willemse, *Behind the Green Lights* (New York: Knopf, 1931).

32 Burrows and Wallace, *Gotham*, 854; Osofsky, *Harlem*, 11, 48; Terry Miller, *Greenwich Village*, 198; Peterson, *Black Gotham*, 226; Willemse, *Behind the Green Light*.

33 Gill, *Harlem*, 101.

34 David W. Dunlap, "Vestiges of Harlem's Jewish Past," *New York Times*, June 7, 2002.

35 *WPA Guide*, 258; "Shifting Populations in Great Northern Cities," *Opportunity* (September 1928): 279; Philip Kasinitz, *Caribbean New York: Black Immigrants and the Politics of Race* (Ithaca, NY: Cornell University Press, 1992), 24; Gill, *Harlem*, 281.

36 Georgia Douglas Camp Johnson and Claudia Tate, *The Selected Works of Georgia Douglas Johnson* (Boston: G. K. Hall, 1997), xxi. See also *Black Women of the Har-*

lem Renaissance Era, ed. Lean'tin L. Bracks and Jessie Carney Smith (New York: Rowman and Littlefield, 2014), 135; "The New Negro as Revealed in His Poetry," *Opportunity* (April 1927).

37 Singleton, "Birth, Rebirth," 33; George Hutchinson, *Harlem Renaissance in Black and White* (New York: Belknap Press, 1997), 389.

38 For biographies on Locke, see Leonard Harris and Charles Molesworth, *Alain Locke: The Biography of a Philosopher* (Chicago: University of Chicago Press, 2008); and Russell J. Linnemann, *Alain Locke: Reflections on a Modern Renaissance Man* (Baton Rouge: Louisiana State University Press, 1982).

39 Locke, *New Negro*, ix; Harris and Molesworth, *Alain L. Locke*, 179.

40 Henry Louis Gates Jr., "The Trope of the New Negro and the Reconstruction of the Image of the Black," *Representations* 24 (Autumn 1988), 147.

41 A. Philip Randolph, "A New Crowd—A New Negro," in *Voices from the Harlem Renaissance*, ed. Nathan Irvin Huggins, 18–20 (New York: Oxford University Press, 1976).

42 Allen Dunn and George Hutchinson, "The Failure of the Harlem Renaissance," *Soundings: An Interdisciplinary Journal* (Winter 1997): 445–54; David Levering Lewis, "Dr. Johnson's Friends: Civil Rights by Copyright during Harlem's Mid-Twenties," *Massachusetts Review* 20, no. 3 (Autumn 1979): 501–19; David Levering Lewis, *When Harlem Was in Vogue* (New York: Penguin, 1997), xxviii.

43 Sorett, "'We Build Our Temples,'" 201; Christopher Buck, *Alain Locke: Faith and Philosophy* (Los Angeles: Kalimet Press, 2005).

44 Locke, *New Negro*, ix, xi.

45 Ibid., 4, 16.

46 Ibid., 7.

47 Jupiter Hammon, "An Evening Thought: Salvation by Christ, with penetential cries: Composed by Jupiter Hammon, a Negro belonging to Mr. Lloyd, of Queen's Village, on Long-Island, the 25th of December 1760" (Boston: Quaestiones, 1760).

48 Phillis Wheatley (Negro Servant of Mr. John Wheatley of Boston, in New England), *Poems of Various Subjects Religious and Moral* (London: A. Bell Bookseller, 1773), 18.

49 Reverdy Ransom, "The New Negro," *New York Amsterdam News*, January 3, 1923; on Ransom, see Annette Louis Gomez-Jefferson, *The Sage of Tawana: Reverdy Cassius Ransom, 1861–1959* (Kent, OH: Kent State University Press, 2003); and Calvin S. Morris, *Black Advocate of the Social Gospel* (Lanham, MD: University Press of America, 1990).

50 "Contest Awards: Holstein Prizes: Poetry," *Opportunity* 4 (May 1926): 156.

51 Cullen, *Caroling Dusk*, 145.

52 *The Book of Negro Poetry*, 2nd ed., ed. James Weldon Johnson (New York: Harcourt, Brace, 1931), 284. See Hughes, *Big Sea*, 219; *Arna Bontemps–Langston Hughes Letters, 1925–1967*, ed. Charles H. Nichols (New York: Paragon House, 1990), 454.

53 Cuney's faith journey culminated in a hermitic retreat from society, a rejection of his friends, including Hughes, and a subsequent re-emergence in order to defend the religious nature of his poetry. Hughes and Cuney had had a long relationship dating back to when they met by chance on a streetcar in Washington, DC, in 1925. Cuney happened to be reading the announcement of Hughes's forthcoming book, *The Weary Blues*, in the *Chicago Defender* and recognized Hughes from the accompanying picture. Enrolled at Lincoln University in Pennsylvania at the time, the place Hughes would later describe as "the ideal college for a poet," Cuney influenced Hughes to choose it over Howard University and most likely, along with Alain Locke, introduced him to Georgia Douglas Johnson's Saturday night literary salon. The two poets collaborated intermittently over the years until Cuney withdrew to live a contemplative religious life. Writing to lifelong friend Arna Bontemps in 1963, Hughes stated that Cuney had gone on a "religious kick and won't see sinners." Described by Countee Cullen as "at all times cool, calm, and intensely religious," Bontemps had also collaborated with Cuney and made his own mark on religious poetry during the Harlem Renaissance with such poems as "God Give to Men," "Golgotha Is a Mountain," and "Gethsemane." Cuney's self-imposed exile lasted for nearly a decade and he only re-emerged in 1971 to answer what he considered an insult to his work hurled by Georgia novelist John Oliver Killens. In an article on the Harlem Renaissance for *Black World*, Killens had characterized Cuney's religious poetry, particularly the poem "My Jesus" as "humorous," "idiomatic," and "irreverent." Cuney retorted that his religious poems may be "idiomatic," but they were never humorous or irreverent. He again disappeared from public life after the exchange, never to resurface, and died in New York City in 1976. See Cullen, *Caroling Dusk*, xiii; *Opportunity* (June 1925): 183; *Opportunity* (June 1926): 177; and John Oliver Killens, "Another Time When Black Was Beautiful," *Black World* 20, no. 1 (November 1970): 32; William Waring Cuney, "From Waring Cuney," *Black World* 20, no. 5 (March 1971): 98.

54 Mary Jenness, "The Negro Laughs Back," *Opportunity* 6, no. 8 (August 1928); *Opportunity* (December 1925): 357.

55 J. Harvey L. Baxter, "Paint Me a God," *Opportunity* 5 (March 1927).

56 Esther Popel, "Kinship," *Crisis* 3, no. 25 (January 1928).

57 Esther Popel, "Blasphemy—American Style," *Opportunity* 12 (December 1934).

58 Alfred H. Lloyd, *The Will to Doubt* (CreateSpace Independent Publishing Platform, 2015), preface, 1, 21.

59 Laurie Maffly-Kipp, *Setting Down the Sacred Past: African-American Race Histories* (Cambridge, MA.: Harvard University Press, 2010), 277–79.

60 See George S. Schuyler, "Black America Begins to Doubt," *American Mercury* (April 1932): 423–30.

61 See Judith Weisenfeld, *Hollywood Be Thy Name: African American Religion in American Film, 1929–1949* (Los Angeles: University of California Press, 2007).

62 Edwin E. Aubrey, *Journal of Negro Education* 8, no. 2 (April 1939): 226; Carter G. Woodson, *Journal of Negro History* 24, no. 1 (January 1939): 118–19; Josef Sorett,

Spirit in the Dark: A Religious History of Racial Aesthetics (New York: Oxford University Press, 2016), 2.

63 Randal Maurice Jelks, *Benjamin Elijah Mays: Schoolmaster to the Movement* (Chapel Hill: University of North Carolina Press, 2012); Benjamin E. Mays, *The Negro's God as Reflected in His Literature* (New York: Russell and Russell, 1938), 218, 15.

64 Mays, *Negro's God*, 126, 97.

65 Ibid., 19.

66 Ibid., 218.

67 Ibid., 233; W. E. B. DuBois, *Darkwater: Voices from within the Veil* (CreateSpace Independent Publishing Platform, 2012), 3, 12–14, 130–31.

68 Mays, *Negro's God*, 244.

69 Ibid., 3.

70 *My Soul's High Song: The Collected Writings of Countee Cullen*, ed. Gerald Early (New York: Anchor Books, 1991), 17, 57–58.

71 *Kelley's* (October 1922): 13; Countee Cullen, *Color* (New York: Harper and Brothers, 1925).

72 Cullen, *Caroling Dusk*, 179.

73 Countee Cullen, "Pagan Prayer," in Early, *My Soul's High Song*, 92–91.

74 Countee Cullen, *The Black Christ and Other Poems* (New York: Harper and Brothers, 1929), 77. See also James H. Smylie, "Countee Cullen's 'The Black Christ,'" *Theology Today* 38, no. 2 (July 1981): 160–73; Wagner, *Black Poets*, 343.

75 Mays, *Negro's God*, 208.

76 Walter Everette Hawkins, *Chords and Discords* (Boston: Richard G. Badger, Gorham Press, 1920), 33, 63, 67, 49, 55, 99, 100, 45, 29, 83.

77 Ibid., 99; Mays, *Negro's God*, 218.

78 Kelly Miller, "Watchtower," *New York Amsterdam News*, September 15, 1934, 8; Jon Michael Spencer, "The Black Church and the Harlem Renaissance," *African American Review* 30, no. 3 (Autumn 1996): 454; Mays, *Negro's God*, 238–39.

79 Mays, *Negro's God*, 239, 243.

80 James H. Snowden, "The Place of Doubt in Religious Belief," *Biblical World* 47, no. 3 (March 1916): 151–55; J. L. Schellenberg, *The Wisdom to Doubt: A Justification of Religious Skepticism* (Ithaca, NY: Cornell University Press, 2007); Christopher Lane, *The Age of Doubt: Tracing the Roots of Our Religious Uncertainty* (New Haven, CT: Yale University Press, 2011); Mays, *Negro's God*, 209.

81 Mays, *Negro's God*, 254–55.

82 Ibid., 18.

83 Langston Hughes, "Christians and Communists," LHP, "In Draft Form, Corrected Copy," Box 417, Folder 9177.

84 Ann Douglas, *Terrible Honesty: Mongrel Manhattan in the 1920s* (New York: Farrar, Straus and Giroux, 1996), 383; Langston Hughes, "Fascination of Cities," *Crisis* 31, no. 3 (January 1926): 138–40.

85 Langston Hughes, "Gospel Songs: From Kansas to Broadway," in Sanders, *Collected Works of Langston Hughes*, 8:406; letter from Langston Hughes to "Mrs. Smith," August 6, 1964, LHP, Box 148, Folder 2741.

86 Langston Hughes, *I Wonder as I Wander: An Autobiographical Journey* (New York: Hill and Wang, 1993), 297–98.

87 Wallace Best, *Passionately Human, No Less Divine: Religion and Culture in Black Chicago, 1915–1952* (Princeton, NJ: Princeton University Press, 2007), 102; Matthew J. Cressler, "Authentically Black and Truly Catholic: African American Catholics in Chicago from the Great Migration to Black Power" (PhD dissertation, Northwestern University, 2014), 82; LHP, Box 494, Folder 12490.

88 Wallace Best, "Everybody Knew He Was That Way: Chicago's Clarence H. Cobbs, American Religion and Sexuality during the Post WWII Period" (unpublished paper in possession of author); Langston Hughes, "New Subject for College Theses," *Chicago Defender*, June 7, 1958.

89 An itinerant preacher named Steamboat Bill was perhaps first to establish a storefront in Harlem during the early years of the Great Migration. Steamboat, described in Works Progress Administration (WPA) documents as "a picturesque old fashioned Negro Preacher," actually began as a street preacher who was often carted off to jail for disorderly conduct. "Long and lanky, of dark complexion," the fiery preacher was always immaculately dressed, "black swallow-tail coat and stiff white shirt," and eventually established his church on West 133rd Street. "Store Front Churches," Library of Congress, WPA Files, Box A857, Folder: "The Portrait of the Negro as an American, Chapter 5"; letter from Langston Hughes to Arna Bontemps, May 26, 1962," in Nichols, *Arna Bontemps–Langston Hughes Letters*, 447.

90 James Baldwin, *Fire Next Time* (New York: Vintage International, 1993), 32, 28; Jonathan L. Walton, *Watch This!: The Ethics and Aesthetics of Black Televangelism* (New York: New York University Press, 2009), 43.

91 "You Pray for Me: Elder Horn Latest Radio Exhorter Is Unusual Person: Evangelist Refuses Witchcraft Belief," *New York Amsterdam News*, October 13, 1934; "Radio Once Devil's Tool to Mother Horn—Now It's Blessing: Church of all Faiths Now Favorite on Air," *New York Amsterdam News*, October 31, 1936.

92 Langston Hughes, "Big Round World," in *The Return of Simple* (New York: Hill and Wang, 1995), 159.

93 Langston Hughes, "The Meaning of Faith: Cults," *Chicago Defender*, January 9, 1960.

94 "Langston Hughes, Tribute to Father Divine," *New York Post*, September 17, 1965.

95 Jon Butler, "Religion in New York City: Faith That Could Not Be," *U.S. Catholic Historian* 22, no. 2 (Spring 2004): 53.

96 Lewis, *When Harlem Was in Vogue*, 28; David W. Dunlap and Joe J. Vecchione, *Glory in Gotham: Manhattan's Houses of Worship: A Guide to Their History, Architecture and Legacy* (New York: City and Company Guide, 2000), 158; Craig D.

Townsend, *A Faith of Their Own: Black Episcopalians in Antebellum New York City* (New York: Columbia University Press, 2005), 8.

97   The Schomburg Center for Research in Black Culture, *The Black New Yorkers: The Schomburg Illustrated Chronology, 400 Years of African American History* (New York: John Wiley, 2001), 129.

98   St. Philip's Church, *Reaching Out: An Epic of the People of St. Philip's Church: Its First 170 Years* (New York: Custombook, 1986), 42, 39.

99   For the latest work to date on Adam Clayton Powell Sr., see Vernon C. Mitchell Jr., "Jazz Age Jesus: The Reverend Adam Clayton Powell, Sr. and the Ministry of Black Empowerment, 1865–1937," (PhD dissertation, Cornell University, 2014).

100 Adam Clayton Powell Sr., *Against the Tide: An Autobiography* (New York: R. R. Smith, 1938), 68.

101 Schomberg Center, *Black New Yorkers*, 171; Powell, *Against the Tide*, 72.

102 Adam Clayton Powell Sr., "The Church in Social Work," *Opportunity* (January 1923).

103 "Abyssinia [*sic*] Baptist Church—Unemployed Section and Adult Education," WPA, Federal Writers' Project (FWP) Files, Library of Congress; Lee A. Daniels, "The Political Career of Adam Clayton Powell: Paradigm and Paradox," *Journal of Black Studies* 4, no. 2 (December 1973): 118; Adam Clayton Powell Jr., *Upon This Rock* (New York: Abyssinian Baptist Church, 1949), 56–67.

104 Langston Hughes, "Let My People Go—Now!," LHP, Box 537, Folder 13189; "Simple Says, 'Black Is Basic,'" LHP, Box 414, Folder 8952; *Chicago Defender*, June 24, 1958.

105 Powell, *Upon This Rock*, 39.

106 *Ibid.*, 39–40.

107 Ibid., 44–45.

108 Genna Rae McNeil, Houston Bryan Roberson, Quinton Hosford Dixie, and Kevin McGruder, *Witness: Two Hundred Years of African-American Faith and Practice at the Abyssinian Baptist Church of Harlem, New York* (Grand Rapids, MI: William B. Eerdmans, 2014), 169.

109 Langston Hughes, "New Year's Resolutions," *Chicago Defender*, January 6, 1945.

110 Hughes compiled this collection to be performed with a "musical background." It is unclear if it ever was. In addition to "Projection of a Day (Desecration)," the poems "Alas! Alack!" and "Projection" were also included. The latter poem seems to have been an earlier version of "Projection of a Day (Desecration)." St. James was a rival denomination of elite status on 141st Street in Harlem, and 409 Edgecombe was one of the most exclusive addresses in the Sugar Hill area of Harlem, home to the likes of Thurgood Marshall and W. E. B. DuBois. The address on 133rd Street doubtless referred to one of the many speakeasies located on the street during Prohibition and after repeal. Known for interracial mixing, it was pejoratively dubbed "Jungle Alley." Langston Hughes, "Gospel and Religious Poems: For Performance with a Musical Background," Langston Hughes Collection, Schomburg Center for Research in Black Culture, New York Public Library, R-977, Reel 3, Series B.

111 Letters between Langston Hughes and Gwendolyn Jones, March 6, 24, and 29, 1962, LHP, Box 2, Folder 21; Helen Walker-Hill, *From Spirituals to Symphonies: African American Women Composers and Their Music* (Champaign: University of Illinois Press, 2007).

112 "Art, Religion, and Harlem's St. Philip's Church," *Chicago Defender*, April 18, 1963; LHP, Box 415, Folder 8992.

CHAPTER 2. POEMS OF A RELIGIOUS NATURE

1 Carla Kaplan, *Miss Anne in Harlem: The White Women of the Black Renaissance* (New York: Harper, 2013), 297; *Negro: An Anthology*, ed. Nancy Cunard (New York: Continuum, 1996), xxxi, xxxii, 3; letter from Nancy Cunard to Langston Hughes, n.d., Langston Hughes Papers Beinecke Library, Yale University (hereafter LHP), Box 49, Folder 920.

2 Lois Gordon, *Nancy Cunard: Heiress, Muse, Political Idealist* (New York: Columbia University Press, 2007), 163–64, 181; letter from Langston Hughes to Jean Wagner, April 2, 1958, LHP, Box 166; "8 Letters to Jean Wagner; 1958–1963," Jean Wagner Papers, Houghton Library, Harvard University.

3 "Poems of Langston Hughes on Religious and Biblical Themes, Some in the Manner of the Spirituals from Various Books and Unpublished Works of Langston Hughes," Jean Wagner Papers, Folder: "Hughes, Langston: Poems, bMs Am 2035 (66)"; hereafter cited as "Poems of Langston Hughes."

4 Naomi Madgett, *Journal of Negro History* 59, no. 3 (July 1974): 299–301; Ralph Willett, *Journal of American Studies* 8, no. 3 (December 1974): 404–5; Robert Bone quoted in Jean Wagner, *Black Poets of the United States: From Paul Laurence Dunbar to Langston Hughes* (Urbana: University of Illinois Press, 1973), xiv.

5 Wagner, *Black Poets*, xiv and xxii.

6 Robert Bone quoted in ibid., xvii.

7 Letter from Langston Hughes to François Dodat, August 18, 1964, LHP, Box 55, Folder 1038.

8 Wagner, *Black Poets*, 440.

9 Arnold Rampersad, "Langston Hughes's *Fine Clothes to the Jew*," *Callaloo* 26 (Winter 1996): 144.

10 Walt Whitman, introduction to 1855 edition of *Leaves of Grass*, ed. Malcolm Cowley (New York: Penguin Books, 1959), 12.

11 Rampersad, "Langston Hughes's *Fine Clothes*," 156; *Camden Evening Courier*, March 3, 1927; C. Glenn Carrington Papers, Emory University Manuscript, Archive, and Rare Book Library, Box 2, Folder 2.

12 Rampersad, "Langston Hughes's *Fine Clothes*," 156; *Chicago Daily News*, June 29, 1927; Karen Jackson Ford, "Do Right to Write Right: Langston Hughes's Aesthetics of Simplicity," *Twentieth Century Literature* 38 (Winter 1992): 437.

13 The relationship between Hughes and Baldwin had always been tense and never very friendly. Although Hughes commended Baldwin as one who wrote "beautifully," it is clear that he didn't always appreciate Baldwin's style or artistic choices.

After Hughes read Baldwin's first novel, *Go Tell It on the Mountain*, he confessed to his close friend and confidant, Arna Bontemps, that he felt it to be slow, "sleepy," and mostly inauthentic. "Baldwin over-writes and over-poeticizes in images way over the heads of the folks supposedly thinking them—often beautiful writing in itself—but frequently out of character—although it might be as the people *would* think if they *could* think that way." As far as Baldwin was concerned, Hughes lacked "discipline" as a writer. He famously stated in his 1959 review that Hughes's volume contained a great many poems that "a more disciplined poet would have thrown into the waste-basket." See *Arna Bontemps–Langston Hughes Letters, 1925–1967*, ed. Charles H. Nichols (New York: Paragon House, 1990), 302–3; and Henry Louis Gates Jr. and K. Anthony Appiah, eds., *Langston Hughes: Critical Perspectives Past and Present* (New York: Amistad Press, 1993), 37.

14 Gates and Appiah, *Langston Hughes*, 10; Onwuchekwa Jemie, *Langston Hughes: An Introduction to Poetry* (New York: Columbia University Press, 1977), 24.

15 In 1962 Hughes significantly revised "Angels Wings" in terms of its tone, cadence, and implication. He dropped the vernacular in favor of "standard English," which had the effect of further underscoring the contrast between the whiteness of the angels' wings and the speakers' wings mired by dirt. Purity and profanity emerge in a stark polarity. See LHP, Box 373, Folder 6082.

16 *The Book of American Negro Poetry*, 2nd ed., ed. James Weldon Johnson (New York: Harcourt, Brace, 1931), 31; James Weldon Johnson, *God's Trombones: Seven Sermons in Verse* (New York: Viking Press, 1927), 7–8; John Keeling, "Paul Dunbar and the Mask of Dialect," *Southern Literary Journal* 25, no. 2 (Spring 1993): 24–38; Lillian S. Robinson and Greg Robinson, "Paul Laurence Dunbar: A Credit to His Race?," *African American Review* 41, no. 2 (Summer 2007): 215–25; Gossie Harold Hudson, "Paul Laurence Dunbar: Dialect et la Negritude," *Phylon* 34, no. 3 (1973): 236–47.

17 On the socially constructed nature of "the folk," see Robin D. G. Kelley, "Notes on Deconstructing 'The Folk,'" *American Historical Review* 97 (December 1992): 1400–1408.

18 Ann Borden, "Heroic 'Hussies' and 'Brilliant Queers': Genderracial Resistance in the Work of Langston Hughes," *African American Review* 28, no. 3 (August 1994): 334.

19 U.S. Department of Commerce, Bureau of the Census, "Census of Religious Bodies," 1926, 69–70.

20 Langston Hughes, "Christ," LHP, Box 375, Folder 6243. Hughes substituted "po an' bowed" for "po' an' black" in the version published in *The Dream Keeper, and Other Poems* (New York: Alfred A. Knopf, 1932). For a historical exploration and analysis of Christ and color, see Edward J. Blum and Paul Harvey, *The Color of Christ: The Son of God and the Saga of Race in America* (Chapel Hill: University of North Carolina Press, 2014).

21 Tatha Wiley, *Original Sin: Origins, Developments, Contemporary Meanings* (New York: Paulist Press, 1989), 3–4. Helpful studies that cover cultural implications

as well as the theological include Alan Jacobs, *Original Sin: A Cultural History* (New York: HarperOne, 2001); Paula Fredriksen, *Sin: The Early History of an Idea* (Princeton, NJ: Princeton University Press, 2012); and Gary A. Anderson, *Sin: A History* (New Haven, CT: Yale University Press, 2009).

22 Richard Lingeman, *The Noir Forties: The American People from Victory to Cold War* (New York: Nation Books, 2012), x.

23 "Hughes, Langston: Poems," Jean Wagner Papers, Houghton Library, Harvard University. Box 383, Folder 6846.

24 "*The Dream Keeper* and Other Poems of Langston Hughes," Smithsonian Folkways Recordings, 1955.

25 Langston Hughes, *Selected Poems of Langston Hughes* (New York: Alfred A. Knopf, 1959), 17–29.

26 Barbara Garvey Jackson, "Florence Price, Composer," *Black Perspective in Music* 5, no. 1 (Spring 1977): 31–43. African American composer Hall Johnson also arranged "Feet o' Jesus," and the song has been performed by such artists as Sonya Gabrielle Baker and Amy Yovanovich.

27 Although "Black Prophetess" was never collected into a volume, it appears to be an early work of Sandburg, written at the time of the Chicago poems. The similarity in language and subject matter would indicate that Hughes did come across the poem at some point. E-mail correspondence with Paul L. Berman, June 1, 2009. See also Paul L. Berman, *Carl Sandburg: Selected Poems* (New York: Library of America, 2006).

28 Anne Elizabeth Carroll, *Word, Image, and the New Negro: Representations and Identity in the Harlem Renaissance* (Bloomington: University of Indiana Press, 2007), 111–12. In the Helen Sewell illustration for the poem in *The Dream Keeper,* the figure is prostrate as if in prayer. See Hughes, *Dream Keeper*, 48.

29 Langston Hughes, "Ma Lord," LHP, Box 380, Folder 6627.

30 Warren Street Baptist Church was the second of two black churches in Lawrence, Kansas, in the late nineteenth and early twentieth centuries. Despite some theological and programmatic differences, the two churches shared much in common and congregants interchangeably participated in the others' worship services and activities. Affiliated with the National Baptist Convention, the church became Ninth Street Baptist Church in 1945. See Denise Low and T. F. Pecore Weso, *Langston Hughes in Lawrence: Photographs and Biographical Resources* (Lawrence, KS: Mammoth, 2004), 41–43.

31 "First Lecture Notes—Written for My First Cross-Country Tour / 1931–1932," LHP, Box 479, Folder 11914.

32 Ibid.

33 "Ma Lord," recorded on "The Dream Keeper and Other Poems of Langston Hughes," Smithsonian Folkways Records, 1955.

34 Letter from Langston Hughes to François Dodat, June 18, 1963, LHP, Box 55, Folder 1038.

35 Letter from Pierre Seghers to Langston Hughes, April 18, 1963, LHP, Box 143, Folder 2669.

36 Letter from Langston Hughes to "Frcoi [*sic*] Dodat," June 1963, LHP, Box 383, Folder 6830; *Temples for Tomorrow: Looking Back at the Harlem Renaissance*, ed. Genevieve Fabre and Michel Feith (Bloomington: Indiana University Press, 2001), 326–27.

37 François Dodat, *La poésie de Langston Hughes* (Paris: Pierre Seghers, 1955), 7–9.

38 François Dodat, *Langston Hughes* (Paris: Pierre Seghers, 1964), 10.

39 Leigh E. Schmidt, *Restless Souls: The Making of American Spirituality from Emerson to Oprah* (New York: HarperSanFranscisco, 2005), 4.

40 Originally titling the poem "Terminal" when it was first published in *Opportunity*, Hughes changed it to "Pennsylvania Station" when it was reprinted in *Approach* in 1962. It had been announced that year that the massive structure would be demolished to make room for the proposed Penn Plaza and Madison Square Garden. The demolition was hugely controversial and elicited emotional responses from many New Yorkers. For a thorough account of the history of Penn Station, see Jill Jonnes, *Conquering Gotham: A Gilded Age Epic—The Construction of Penn Station and Its Tunnels* (New York: Viking Press, 2007).

41 Langston Hughes, "Encounter," LHP, Box 377, Folder 6363.

42 Hughes often revisited the theme of the tragic mulatto in his writing. From "Cross" he developed a short story, a play, and an opera. Renamed "Mulatto," the play opened on Broadway to unfavorable reviews on October 24, 1934. See Rampersad, *Life of Langston Hughes*, 1:104, 313.

43 Langston Hughes, "Crucifixion," LHP, Box 376, Folder 6283.

44 Langston Hughes, "Let All Men Pray," LHP, Box 379, Folder 6572.

45 Langston Hughes, "Simple Prays a Prayer," in *The Best of Simple* (New York: Hill and Wang, 1961), 6–7.

46 Langston Hughes, "Dust and Rainbows," LHP, Box 383, Folder 6845.

47 Wagner published "Not for Publication" as part of an appendix in "Le poètes Nègres des États Unis." See *Les poètes Nègres des États-Unis: Le sentiment racial et religieux dans la poésie de P. L. Dunbar à L. Hughes, 1890–1940* (Paris: Librarie Istra, 1963), 586. It appeared as "Bible Belt" in *The Panther and the Lash*.

48 Langston Hughes, "Each Soul Has Need" and "The Lord Has a Child," LHP, Box 377, Folder 6352, and Box 380, Folder 6610, respectively.

49 Langston Hughes, "Celestial Eye," LHP, Box 375, Folder 6227.

50 "It is beautiful and very well made." Letter from Langston Hughes to François Dodat, June 18, 1963, LHP, Box 55, Folder 1038. Arnold Rampersad, *The Life of Langston Hughes*, vol. 2, *1941–1967, I Dream a World* (New York: Oxford University Press, 2002), 380; letter from Langston Hughes to François Dodat, August 18, 1964, LHP, Box 55, Folder 1038; letter from Langston Hughes to Pierre Seghers, August 16, 1964, LHP, Box 55, Folder 1038.

51 Dodat, *Langston Hughes*, 62.

52 Ibid., 63–64.

53 Ryan James Kernan, "Lost and Found in Black Translation: Langston Hughes's Translations of French and Spanish Language Poetry, His Hispanic and Fran-

cophone Translators, and the Fashioning of Radical Black Subjectivities" (PhD dissertation, University of California, Los Angeles, 2007), 428.

54 François Dodat, "Situation de Langston Hughes," *Présence Africaine* n.s., 64 (1967): 50.

55 Kernan, "Lost and Found," 330.

56 Clayton Eshleman and Annette Smith, trans., *Aimé Césaire: Collected Poetry* (Berkeley: University of California Press, 1983); Lilyan Kesteloot, *Black Writers in French: A Literary History of Negritude*, trans. Ellen Conroy Kennedy (Washington, DC: Howard University Press, 1991).

57 "Interview with Langston Hughes," June 19, 1958, Jean Wagner Papers, Folder 8.

58 "Hughes, Langston: Interview Notes, bms Am 2035 (64)," June 19, 1958, Jean Wagner Papers; letter to Jean Wagner from Langston Hughes, April 12, 1963, Jean Wagner Papers, Folder "8 Letters to Jean Wagner, 1958–1963."

59 Wagner, *Black Poets of the United States*, 440n180. Hughes provides a note under the title of "Sunday Morning Prophecy" that drew attention to the contrast between the hellfire rhetoric of the preacher and his profane call for money. It read, "An old Negro minister concludes his sermon in his loudest voice, having previously pointed out the sins of the world."

60 Ibid., 192, 372.

61 Ibid., 440.

62 Robert Bone quoted in ibid., xvi.

63 Wagner, *Black Poets*, 438.

64 Ibid., 437–38.

65 "Hughes, Langston: Interview Notes," June 19, 1958, Jean Wagner Papers.

66 Ibid. Wagner signals his skepticism with a series of question marks placed after nearly every statement of Hughes regarding his antireligiosity.

67 "As to Gold Door Knobs: New Waldorf Astoria Contractors Deny They Have Been Ordered Yet," *New York Times*, July 3, 1930; "Waldorf Highest Hotel," *New York Times*, September 14, 1930; "Hotel Decoration in the Grand Manner," *New York Times*, September 27, 1931. See also Frank Farrell, *The Greatest of Them All: History of the Waldorf-Astoria* (New York: K. S. Giniger, 1982); Ward Moorehouse III and Gregory Minahan, *Waldorf-Astoria* (Bloomington, IN: Xlibris, 2005).

68 Hughes did not include the "Christmas Card" section of "Advertisement for the Waldorf-Astoria" in *The Big Sea* (see 320–21); Shulman, *Power of Political Art*, 330n32. "Oscar at the Waldorf" was a real person, Oscar Tschirsky, who for many years was the hotel's famous maître d'hôtel.

69 Haywood Patterson, *Scottsboro Boy* (New York: Doubleday, 1950); Dan T. Carter, *Scottsboro: A Tragedy of the American South* (Baton Rouge: Louisiana State University Press, 1969; David Aretha, *The Trial of the Scottsboro Boys* (Greensboro, NC: Morgan Reynolds, 2008); James R. Acker, *Scottsboro and Its Legacy* (Westport, CT: Praeger, 2008).

70 Langston Hughes, "Brown America in Jail," *Opportunity* 10 (June 1932); "The Town of Scottsboro," *New Masses* 7 (February 1932); "Scottsboro," *Opportunity* 9

(December 1931). Hughes published "Scottsboro Limited" as an attempt to raise money for the Scottsboro Defense Fund. See Robert Shulman, *The Power of Political Art: The 1930s Literary Left Reconsidered* (Chapel Hill: University of North Carolina Press, 2000), 248.

71 Rampersad, *Life of Langston Hughes*, 1:225.

72 *Charlotte News*, December 8, 1931.

73 "Protest on Hughes, Contempo, Recalls Similar S.C. Case: Governor Won't Take Action on Chapel Hill Magazine," *Atlanta World*, December 18, 1931; *Charlotte Observer*, December 9, 1931; Rampersad, *Life of Langston Hughes*, 1:225.

74 James A. Emanuel, *Langston Hughes* (New York: Twayne, 1967), 97.

75 Jemie, *Langston Hughes*, 114.

76 Hugh T. Murray Jr., "Changing America and the Changing Image of Scottsboro," *Phylon* 38, no. 1 (1977): 82; William J. Maxwell, *New Negro, Old Left: African American Communism between the Wars* (New York: Columbia University Press, 1999), 141.

77 Wagner, *Black Poets*, xv, 440n180.

78 Ibid., 192.

79 Ibid., 440.

80 Ibid., 443.

81 Ibid., 320, 322, and 339.

82 Ibid., 248.

83 Shulman, *Power of Political Art*, 303.

CHAPTER 3. "CONCERNING 'GOODBYE CHRIST'"

1 Matthew Avery Sutton, *Aimee Semple McPherson and the Resurrection of Christian America* (Cambridge, MA: Harvard University Press, 2007), 245–47; Arnold Rampersad, *The Life of Langston Hughes*, vol. 1, *1902–1941: I, Too, Sing America* (New York: Oxford University Press, 2002), 390. Berlin originally wrote "God Bless America" in 1918 but revised it in 1938.

2 "My Adventures as a Social Poet," in *Good Morning Revolution: Uncollected Social Protest Writings by Langston Hughes*, ed. Faith Berry (New York: Lawrence Hill, 1973), 140.

3 "Minister Flays Evangelist Aimee; Upholds Hughes' 'Goodbye Christ,'" *Chicago Defender*, January 4, 1941; "Evangelist Aimee Ruins Langston Hughes' Lunch," *Chicago Defender*, November 30, 1940; Rampersad, *Life of Langston Hughes*, 1:390.

4 Rampersad, *Life of Langston Hughes*, 1:252.

5 Langston Hughes, "Goodbye Christ," *Negro Worker* 2, nos. 11–12 (November–December 1932): 32. The poem has appeared in two forms since it was first published in 1932, as "Goodbye Christ" and "Goodbye, Christ." The comma does not exist in the original version and it is not clear when or why it began. It has been quite common to include the comma, however, and even Hughes was known to do so. I have chosen not to include the comma in deference to the original version except for instances when it appears with that structure in a quote.

6 James Edward Smethurst, *The New Red Negro: The Literary Left and African American Poetry* (New York: Oxford University Press, 1999).

7 Morris Dickstein, *Dancing in the Dark: A Cultural History of the Great Depression* (New York: W. W. Norton, 2009), 154–72; Cary Nelson, *Repression and Recovery: Modern American Poetry and the Politics of Cultural Memory, 1910–1945* (Madison: University of Wisconsin Press, 1991).

8 Hughes's one-act play, *Scottsboro Limited*, gave an interpretation of the event by depicting the southern culture that made it possible. The play had communist overtones and ended with the raising of a red flag and the singing of the "Internationale." See Hugh T. Murray Jr., "Changing America and the Changing Image of Scottsboro," *Phylon* 38 (1977): 82–83; Richard Jackson, "The Shared Vision of Langston Hughes and Black Hispanic Writers," *Black American Literature Forum* 15 (August 1981): 91; Dan T. Carter, *Scottsboro: A Tragedy of the American South* (Baton Rouge: Louisiana State University Press, 1969).

9 John L. Garner, "African American in the Soviet Union in the 1920s and 1930s: The Development of Transcontinental Protest," *Western Journal of Black Studies* 23 (1999); Mark Solomon, *The Cry Was Unity: Communists and African Americans, 1917–36* (Jackson, MS: University Press of Mississippi, 1998), 174; "Louise T. Patterson: Last Survivor of the Harlem Renaissance," *New York Times*, September 19, 1999. Louise Thompson became better known as Louise Thompson Patterson after her marriage to William L. Patterson in 1940. However, since a significant amount of her interaction with Hughes occurred before her marriage and for the sake of consistency, I refer to her only as Louise Thompson.

10 Rampersad, *Life of Langston Hughes*, 1:241.

11 Homer Smith, "Prejudice Finds No Sanctuary: Doors of Opportunity Stand Open for People of All Races and Faiths: Langston Hughes and Wayland Rudd Are Examples," *Chicago Defender*, March 4, 1933.

12 Rampersad, *Life of Langston Hughes*, 1:244; *Chicago Defender*, August 13, 1932; Faith Berry, *Langston Hughes: Before and After Harlem* (Westport, CT: Lawrence Hill, 1983), 156; Verner D. Mitchell and Cynthia Davis, *Literary Sisters: Dorothy West and Her Circle, A Biography of the Harlem Renaissance* (New Brunswick: Rutgers University Press, 2012), 139; Langston Hughes, *I Wonder as I Wander* (New York: Hill and Wang, 1993), 70; "Louise Patterson on Langston Hughes," transcript of interview, October 18, 1985, for the film *Dream Keeper*, Louise Thompson Patterson Collection, Box 18, Folder 6, Manuscript, Archives, and Rare Books Library, Emory University.

13 Charles A. Moser, "Mayakovsky and America," *Russian Review* 25 (July 1966): 242–56; George Annenkov and William Todd, "The Poets and the Revolution: Blok, Mayakovsky, Esenin," *Russian Review* 26 (April 1967): 129–43; Alexander Mikhailov and Nancy Tittler, "At the Feet of a Giant (Arguments about Mayakovsky)," *New Literary History* 23 (Winter 1992): 113–32.

14 Berry, *Before and After Harlem*, 159.

15 "Good-Bye Christ: Langston Hughes's Sacrilegious Poem Published in Red Magazine, in January," *Baltimore Afro-American*, December 31, 1932.

16 Dickstein, *Dancing in the Dark*, 81; Rampersad, *Life of Langston Hughes*, 1:247; Langston Hughes, *The Big Sea* (New York: Hill and Wang, 1993), 76.

17 Rampersad, *Life of Langston Hughes*, 1:247; "Louise Patterson on Langston Hughes," Louise Thompson Patterson Collection, Box 18, Folder 6.

18 *American Communism and Black Americans: A Documentary History, 1930–1934*, ed. Philip S. Foner (Philadelphia: Temple University Press, 1991); Mark I. Solomon, *Red and Black: Communism and Afro-Americans, 1929–1935* (New York: Garland, 1988).

19 "Something Rotten in U.S.S.R.," *Pittsburgh Courier*, October 15, 1932.

20 Three members of the group, Wayland Rudd, Lloyd Patterson, and Homer Smith remained in Russia permanently. See Hughes, *I Wonder as I Wander*, 101–7.

21 Homer Smith, "Prejudice Finds No Sanctuary: Doors of Opportunity Stand Open for People of All Races and Faiths: Langston Hughes and Wayland Rudd Are Examples," *Chicago Defender*, March 4, 1933.

22 This version of "Goodbye Christ" circulated in 1948. It was apparently printed in *Reader's Digest* and made its way into the hands of the leadership of the Federal Council of Churches. Olive Lindsay Wakefield, one of Hughes's strongest supporters in the aftermath of "Goodbye Christ," distributed it as a means to demonstrate that it was a "clear example of the thinking of the extreme left group of the early days of the Depression" and not an example of Hughes's current thinking or political position. See "Goodbye Christ," Langston Hughes Papers, Box 166, Folder 3044, Beinecke Library, Yale University (hereafter LHP).

23 Joyce Moore Turner, *Caribbean Crusaders and the Harlem Renaissance* (Urbana: University of Illinois Press, 2005); David Levering Lewis, *When Harlem Was in Vogue* (New York: Penguin Books, 1997), 56. When Huiswood died in 1961, Hughes stated in a letter to Arna Bontemps that Huiswood was "the guy who first published Goodbye Christ in Holland [it was Germany, actually]—without my knowledge or permission and where copyright laws prevail not—so started all the hullabaloo that continued right up to Mills College now." See *Arna Bontemps–Langston Hughes Letters, 1925–1967*, ed. Charles Nichols (New York: Paragon House, 1990), 411.

24 Henderson was by all accounts an enigmatic preacher. His conservative response to Hughes and "Goodbye Christ" belied a theologically and socially progressive agenda for which he was known and often attacked. His home was once bombed and his outspokenness prompted the white ministers of Atlanta to ask that he leave town for his own safety: "They didn't want a hothead to kill him." Henderson finally agreed and in 1937 left for California with his wife and four children. Elva T. Foster (longtime member of Wheat Street Baptist Church), interview with the author, July 15, 2007, Atlanta.

25 J. Raymond Henderson, "Atlanta Minister Takes Writer to Task about Book: Decries Such Expressions as 'Christ Had His Day, but It Is Over; Bible a Fictitious

Story of Christ; Christ in the Way," *Pittsburgh Courier*, January 14, 1933; J. Raymond Henderson, "Rev. J. R. Henderson Claims Prof. Tolson Misses the Point," *Pittsburgh Courier*, February 11, 1933.

26 Melvin Beaunorus Tolson, "Langston Hughes' Goodbye Christ a Challenge and Warning—Tolson," *Pittsburgh Courier*, January 28, 1933; Robert M. Farnsworth, *Melvin B. Tolson, 1898–1966: Plain Talk and Poetic Prophesy* (Columbia: University of Missouri Press, 1984), 36–39; Melvin B. Tolson, *The Harlem Group of Negro Writers*, ed. Edward J. Mullen (Westport, CT: Greenwood Press, 2001), 57–67; Rampersad, *Life of Langston Hughes*, 1:309; Rampersad, "The Poetry of the Harlem Renaissance," in *The Colombia History of American Poetry*, ed. Jay Parini and Brett C. Millie (New York: Columbia University Press, 1993), 470.

27 Reverend D. Ormande Walker, "Cleveland Pastor Defends Hughes' Contention," *Pittsburgh Courier*, April 8, 1933.

28 Tolson, "Challenge and Warning—Tolson," January 28, February 4 and 11, 1933.

29 J. Edward Hines Jr., "Louisiana Writer Claims Many Are Puzzled by Poem: Thinks Rev. Henderson Has Made Time Attack and Professor Tolson a Unique Defense," *Pittsburgh Courier*, February 18, 1933.

30 James Oliver Slade, "Atlanta Professor Defends Hughes' Good Bye Christ: Claims Poet Shows That If the Church in the U.S.A. Is Christ, Then Christ's Time's Out," *Pittsburgh Courier*, February 25, 1933; Edward Taylor, "Man-Handled Religion: Langston Hughes' Conception of Religion Perfectly Logical," *Pittsburgh Courier*, March 11, 1933.

31 The *Pittsburgh Courier* added the lines "go ahead now" either by editorial mistake or flourish. Nancy Cunard published the poem in its original version in her 1934 anthology. See *Negro: An Anthology*, ed. Nancy Cunard (New York: F. Ungar, 1996), 264.

32 Calvin S. Morris, *Reverdy C. Ransom: Black Advocate of the Social Gospel* (Lanham, MD: Universal Press of America, 1990); Donald A. Drewett, "Ransom on Race and Racism: The Racial and Social Thought of Reverdy Cassius Ransom—Preacher, Editor and Bishop in the African Methodist Episcopal Church, 1861–1959" (PhD dissertation, Drew University, 1988); Reverdy C. Ransom, *The Pilgrimage of Harriet Ransom's Son* (Nashville: Sunday School Union, n.d.); Terrell Dale Goddard, "The Black Social Gospel in Chicago, 1896–1906: The Ministries of Reverdy C. Ransom and Richard R. Wright, Jr.," *Journal of Negro History* 84 (Summer 1999): 227–46; Ralph Luker, "Missions, Institutional Churches and Settlement Houses: The Black Experience, 1885–1910," *Journal of Negro History* 69 (Summer–Autumn 1984): 101–13.

33 Bishop Reverdy C. Ransom, "The New Negro," *New York Amsterdam News*, January 3, 1923.

34 Bishop Reverdy C. Ransom, "All Hail to Christ: A la Langston Hughes," *Pittsburgh Courier*, March 25, 1933. Ransom also published "All Hail to Christ" in the April 1933 edition of *Voice of Missions*.

35 Ibid.

36 D. DeWitt Turpeau Jr., "Father Forgive," *Pittsburgh Courier*, April 8, 1933.

37 Bishop E. E. Bennett, "Forgive Him Christ," *Baltimore Afro-American*, February 4, 1933.

38 "Thoughtful People Losing Confidence in the Church, Rev. Powell Tells Baptists: Declares Baptists Lost Big Opportunity in Failure to Take More Active Part in Scottsboro Case—Says Church Must Arrange to Meet Present Day Trends," *Pittsburgh Courier*, July 15, 1933.

39 W. H. R. Powell, "Claims Times Have Changed; Church Is Challenged: Points Out That Negro Church Leadership Is Defective in Vision along Main Lines—Lacking in Seriousness of Purpose," *Pittsburgh Courier*, November 18, 1933; "Claims Church Is Challenged: Church Leadership Defective of Vision; Lacking in Seriousness of Purpose—Must Present United Front," *Pittsburgh Courier*, November 25, 1933; "Witness to Civil Rights History: The Essays and Autobiography of Henry W. Powell" (document in possession of author).

40 Ibid.

41 "New Challenge—Talley," *Pittsburgh Courier*, December 2, 1933; M. A. Talley, "Church Faced by New Challenge Says Dr. Talley," *Pittsburgh Courier*, December 23, 1933. The quote "Harlot of the Nations" is from the book of Revelation, chapters 17 and 18.

42 "Can Religion Stage a Comeback? 'Doubtful,' Says L. M. King: People Too Disillusioned, St. Mark Pastor Tells Local M. E. Clergy," *Baltimore Afro-American*, September 24, 1932.

43 Bishop E. D. W. Jones, "Bishop Jones Says Christmas Should Usher in a New Religion: Zion Prelate Urges Denominationalism and Heaven Philosophy Be Cast Aside for a Religion of Brotherhood and the 'Everlasting Now,'" *Baltimore Afro-American*, December 24, 1932.

44 R. W. Tryne, "Is the Church Losing Ground?," *Pittsburgh Courier*, December 16, 1933; Bishop Wilber P. Thirkield, "The Peril of the Negro Church," *Opportunity* (July 1933); *Pittsburgh Courier*, January 1, 1933.

45 "Report Shows Negro Church Is Largely Self-Supporting: Intensive Study by Two Sociologists Reveals that Church Is Only Institution Negro Can Really Call His Own," *Pittsburgh Courier*, February 25, 1933.

46 Rudolf Bultmann, "Protestant Theology and Atheism," *Journal of Religion* 52, no. 4 (October 1972): 332.

47 James Oliver Slade, "Atlanta Professor Defends Hughes' Good Bye Christ: Claims Poet Shows that If the Church in the U.S.A. Is Christ, then Christ's Time's Out," *Pittsburgh Courier*, February 25, 1933.

48 John Julius Norwich, *Absolute Monarchs: A History of the Papacy* (New York: Random House, 2011), 438. See also Frank J. Coppa, "Pope Pius XI's 'Encyclical' *Humani Generis Unitas* against Racism and Anti-Semitism and the 'Silence' of Pope Pius XII," *Journal of Church and State* 40, no. 4 (Autumn 1998): 775–95.

49 Langston Hughes, "Gandhi Is Fasting," in *The Collected Works of Langston Hughes*, vol. 3, *The Poems: 1951–1967*, ed. Arnold Rampersad (Columbia: University of Missouri Press, 2001), 287.

50 I am greatly indebted to Anne Monius of Harvard Divinity School for this insight on Gandhi and his popular perception during the early years of his activism.

51 Hughes, *Big Sea*, 275–78. Becton's murder remains unsolved and there is uncertainty as to what motivated his killing. Initial reports suggested that the two white assailants who carjacked him in front of the Broadway Athletic Club in Philadelphia, where he was holding revival meetings, wanted to steal that evening's receipts. They also wanted to halt the inroads Becton was making among the city's black poor, who were giving large sums of money to the evangelist during his meetings, money they believed would otherwise go to them through a number of illegal and racketeering operations they ran. Nearly twenty years after the assassination, an official police report suggested an entirely different motive for Becton's murder. It contended that a rival of Becton's, "Sweet Daddy Grace," was responsible for the hit because Becton was contemplating a permanent move into Grace's territory, which would threaten the success of his church, the United House of Prayer. According to the report, Grace had baptized one of the assailants. See "Faith in Flux," a paper by Danielle Sigler presented at the American Association of Religion, November 2005 (paper in possession of author); "Evangelist Shot after Abduction in Own Motor Car," *Philadelphia Inquirer*, May 22, 1933; Robert Bruce Nugent, "On Harlem," in *Gay Rebel of the Harlem Renaissance: Selected Writings of Richard Bruce Nugent*, ed. Thomas Wirth (Durham, NC: Duke University Press, 2002), 154; "Police Link Daddy Grace with Gang-Style Murder," *Color* (September 1952).

52 Daniel Mark Epstein, *Sister Aimee: The Life of Aimee Semple McPherson* (New York: Harcourt Brace Jovanovich, 1993), 252. See also Edith Blumhofer, *Aimee Semple McPherson: Everybody's Sister* (Grand Rapids: W. B. Eerdmans, 1993); and Matthew Avery Sutton, *Aimee Semple McPherson and the Resurrection of Christian America* (Cambridge, MA: Harvard University Press, 2007).

53 Langston Hughes, "Let's Get It Straight: Poet, a Little Confused about All the Fuss Made over a Poem He Wrote over 10 Years Ago, Does a Little Explaining for Those Just Getting around to It," *Chicago Defender*, January 11, 1941.

54 Ibid.

55 Letter from Langston Hughes to James Emanuel, September 19, 1961, LHP, Box 59, Folder 1123.

56 Hughes, "Let's Get It Straight." Hughes reproduced the ideas in "Let's Get It Straight" in another piece written for the *Pittsburgh Courier* the same year. See "Hughes Says 'Good-Bye' to Good-Bye Christ': Famous Poet Gives Retort, Courteous and Explanatory, to Critics of His 'Anti-Christ,'" LHP, Box 428, Folder 9537.

57 Arnold Rampersad, *The Life of Langston Hughes*, vol. 2, *1941–1967: I Dream a World* (New York: Oxford University Press, 1988), 8.

58 Letter from Langston Hughes to Matthew Crawford, February 4, 1941, Matthew Crawford Papers, Box 19, Emory University Manuscript, Archives, and Rare Book Library.

59 Ibid.; letter from Langston Hughes to Louise Thompson, January 6, 1941, Louise Thompson Patterson Papers, Box 17, Emory University Manuscript, Archives, and Rare Book Library.

60 *Letters from Langston: From the Harlem Renaissance to the Red Scare and Beyond*, ed. Evelyn Louise Crawford and MaryLouise Patterson (Oakland: University of California Press, 2016), 10–11; "Louise Patterson on Langston Hughes: New York Center for Visual History Interview, October 18, 1985, New York City," transcript, Louise Thompson Patterson Papers, Box 18, Item 6, Emory University Manuscript, Archives, and Rare Book Library.

61 Glen Jeansonne, *Gerald L. K. Smith: Minister of Hate* (Baton Rouge: Louisiana State University Press, 1997); "Detroit Fascists Picket Langston Hughes Talk," *Chicago Defender*, April 24, 1943.

62 "Hughes, Langston: Concerning 'Goodbye, Christ,'" Jean Wagner Papers, Houghton Library, Harvard University; LHP, Box 291, Folder 4753, "Concerning 'Goodbye, Christ,'" drafts, typescript, and carbon, corrected, and mimeograph, 1941–1961.

63 Letter from Langston Hughes to Joseph McCarthy, March 22, 1953, LHP, Box 109, Folder 2030.

64 David K. Johnson, *The Lavender Scare: The Cold War Persecution of Gays and Lesbians in the Federal Government* (Chicago: University of Chicago Press, 2006).

65 Federal Bureau of Investigations (FBI) files, "Langston Hughes," file number 100–151–39.

66 Hoover published the essay, "Secularism—A Breeder of Crime" without any reference to "Goodbye Christ" but argued, "Communism is secularism on the march." Communism was "the mortal foe of Christianity. Either it will survive, or Christianity will triumph, because in this land of ours the two cannot live side by side." See *The Christian Faith and Secularism*, ed. J. Richard Spann (New York: Abingdon-Cokesbury Press, 1948), 180–89. See also William J. Maxwell, *F. B. Eyes: How J. Edgar Hoover's Ghostreaders Framed African American Literature* (Princeton, NJ: Princeton University Press, 2015); and Curt Gentry, *J. Edgar Hoover: The Man and His Secrets* (New York: W. W. Norton, 1991); letter from J. Richard Spann to Langston Hughes, May 13, 1948, LHP, Box 213, Folder 3601; letter from Langston Hughes to J. Richard Spann, May 24, 1948, LHP, Box 213, Folder 3601.

67 *Executive Sessions of the Senate Permanent Subcommittee on Investigations of the Committee on Government Operations*, vol. 2, 83rd Cong., 1st sess., 1953 (Washington, DC: U.S. Government Printing Office, 2003), 975.

68 His meeting before the PSI was not the first time Hughes had been called before government officials on suspicion of being a Communist or of sympathizing with Communist causes. Stopping in Tokyo en route back to the United States after nearly a year in the Soviet Union, Hughes was called before Japanese police and

government officials to explain why he had stopped first in China. Hughes had met many people in China who were vocal in their opposition to Japan's aggressive moves toward China. The interrogation lasted an entire afternoon, after which Hughes was told that he was "persona non grata" in Japan and ordered to leave immediately. See Hughes, *I Wonder as I Wander*, 263–73.

69 Cohn was one of the principle characters in Tony Kushner's 1993 Pulitzer Prize–winning play and subsequent TV miniseries, "Angels in America," a "fantasia" about the early AIDS crisis. Cohn was depicted as a self-hating gay man who was in denial about his sexuality and attempted to hide his AIDS diagnosis before his death in 1984. For a full description of Cohn's professional life, see Nicholas Van Hoffman, *Citizen Cohn: The Life and Times of Roy Cohn* (New York: Doubleday, 1988).

70 *Executive Sessions*, 2:976–980; Nicholas von Hoffman, *Citizen Cohn* (New York: Doubleday, 1988), 155–18.

71 David E. Chinitz has written the fullest account of Hughes's appearance before McCarthy and the PSI, and his book contains the complete transcripts of both sessions, including the one of the public session, which was only released in 2003. See David E. Chinitz, *Which Sin to Bear: Authenticity and Compromise in Langston Hughes* (New York: Oxford University Press, 2013), 110–44, 179–218.

72 Rampersad, *Life of Langston Hughes*, 2:214–15.

73 "Closing Testimony of Langston Hughes, Poet and Author, Before the Senate Committee on Permanent Investigations on Thursday, March 26, at Washington, D.C. with Senators McCarthy and McClellan, as taken from a radio broadcast," LHP, Box 482, Folder 12201.

74 Langston Hughes, "Freedom's Plow: A Radio Poem," LHP, Box 377, Folder 6414.

75 The play "The Sun Do Move" was inspired by famed Negro preacher John Jasper's classic sermon of the same title. Hughes maintained a lifelong fascination with Jasper as well as with black "folk" preaching. Hughes often used the phrase "de sun do move" when remarking about improbable occurrences or unexpected instances of racial progress. This was the subject of a *Chicago Defender* article he wrote in 1954, "In Racial Matters in St. Louis, De Sun Do Move." Hughes's lifelong friend Arna Bontemps was aware of Hughes's fascination with Jasper and wrote Hughes in 1961 to tell him that he had recently discovered a picture of Jasper, something Hughes had never seen. See Christopher C. De Santis, *Langston Hughes and the Chicago Defender: Essay on Race, Politics, and Culture, 1942–1962* (Urbana: University of Illinois Press), 65–66; and Nichols, *Arna Bontemps–Langston Hughes Letters*, 422.

76 "Closing Testimony of Langston Hughes, Poet and Author, Before the Senate Committee on Permanent Investigations on Thursday, March 26, at Washington, D.C. with Senators McCarthy and McClellan, as Taken from a Radio Broadcast," LHP, Box 482, Folder 12201.

77 Chinitz, *Which Sin to Bear*, 142.

78 Hughes was enormously grateful to Reeves for his legal services, writing to him several times after the hearing to settle business matters and to express his thanks.

"No words—and certainly no money . . . could in any sense express to you my gratitude," he wrote. As late as 1959, Hughes was still recalling to him "how you once 'saved my life.'" Letter from Langston Hughes to John Sengstacke, April 3, 1953, LHP, Box 43, Folder 776; letters to Frank Reeves, March 29, 1953; April 8, 1953; and March 30, 1959, LHP, Box136, Folder 2525.

79 *Executive Sessions*, 2:982.

80 Rampersad, *Life of Langston Hughes*, 1:375; letter from Langston Hughes to Matthew Crawford, February 12, 1941, Matthew Crawford Papers, Box 19. See also Crawford and Patterson, *Letters from Langston*.

81 Letter from Langston Hughes to Harold Blake, November 23, 1961, LHP, Box 291, Folder 4745; "Prayer for the Mantle-piece," copied to Gerald S. Pratt, LHP, Box 382, Folder 6846; letter from Langston Hughes to Sister Rose Veronica, February 18, 1963, LHP, Box 291, Folder 4754.

82 LHP, Box 213 Folder 3601.

83 Letter from Fern Worthington to Langston Hughes, September 20, 1961, LHP, Box 213, Folder 3601.

84 Letter from Raymond Konkle to Langston Hughes, February 27, 1963, LHP, Box 213, Folder 3601.

85 Rampersad, *Life of Langston Hughes*, 2:8.

86 "Minister Flays Evangelist Aimee; Upholds Hughes' 'Goodbye, Christ,'" *Chicago Defender* January 4, 1941.

87 Letter from J. B. Simmons to Langston Hughes, January 29, 1946, LHP, Box 213, Folder 3601.

88 Hughes, "Draft Ideas," LHP, December 3, 1964, found in Rampersad, *Collected Works*, 8:408.

CHAPTER 4. MY GOSPEL YEAR

1 Letter from Langston Hughes to Arna Bontemps, July 1956, in *Arna Bontemps-Langston Hughes: Letters, 1925–1967*, ed. Charles H. Nichols (New York: Athena, 1990), 344.

2 Letter from Langston Hughes to Carl Van Vechten, November 16, 1958; letter from Carl Van Vechten to Langston Hughes, September 20, 1958; letter from Carl Van Vechten to Langston Hughes, October 30, 1958, in *Remember Me to Harlem: The Letters of Langston Hughes and Carl Van Vechten, 1925–1964*, ed. Emily Bernard (New York: Knopf, 2001), 287, 302, 303.

3 Letter from Langston Hughes to Alex Bradford, October 13, 1962, Langston Hughes Papers (hereafter LHP), Box 22, Folder 453, Beinecke Library, Yale University.

4 Clarence Taylor, *Black Churches of Brooklyn* (New York: Columbia University Press, 1994).

5 "The Gospel Glow," LHP, Box 537, Folder 13181; *New York Amsterdam News*, October 13, 1962.

6 "Introducing Mahalia Jackson," LHP, Box 310, Folder 5047.

7　Liner notes, "My Lord What a Mornin'," Harry Belafonte, RCA Records, 1960.

8　The cover letter Hughes sent to publishers along with *Prayers around the World* expressed an emphatic ecumenical intent. "These prayers cover the major religions of the world. They range from the primitive and pagan, Buddhist, Confucian, Hebrew, Catholic, and Protestant to contemporary prayers in poetic form by such poets as Robert Frost, Carl Sandburg, James Weldon Johnson, and T. S. Elliot." LHP, Box 335, Folder 5453; Arnold Rampersad, *The Life of Langston Hughes*, vol. 2, *1941–1967: I Dream a World* (New York: Oxford University Press, 1988), 306.

9　Dave Hepburn, "Producers Make Changes, Hire Langston for TV Show," *New York Amsterdam News*, October 27, 1962.

10　Rampersad, *Life of Langston Hughes*, 2:327.

11　Leslie Catherine Sanders, "'I've Wrestled with Them All My Life': Langston Hughes's *Tambourines to Glory*," *Black American Literature Forum* 25, no. 1 (Spring 1991): 68, 54.

12　*The Collected Works of Langston Hughes: Gospel Plays, Operas, and Later Dramatic Works*, vol. 6, ed. Leslie Catherine Sanders (Columbia: University of Missouri Press, 2004), 342.

13　Sanders, *Collected Works*, 6:281.

14　Keith Byerman, "'I Did Not Learn Their Name': Female Characters in the Short Fiction of Ralph Ellison," *American Studies* 54, no. 3 (2015): 101. See also Carolyn W. Sylvander, "Ralph Ellison's *Invisible Man* and Female Stereotypes," *Negro American Literature Forum* 9, no. 3 (Autumn 1975): 77–79; Yolanda Pierce, "The Invisible Women in Ralph Ellison's *Invisible Man* (1952)," in *Women in Literature: Reading through the Lens of Gender*, ed. Jerilyn Fisher and Ellen S. Silber (Westport, CT.: Greenwood Press, 2003); Alan W. France, "Misogyny and Appropriation in Wright's *Native Son*," *Modern Fiction Studies* 34, no. 3 (Fall 1988): 413–23. By contrast, women were numerous, prominent, and multidimensional in the fiction of James Baldwin. See Trudier Harris, *Black Women in the Fiction of James Baldwin* (Knoxville: University of Tennessee Press, 1985); and Jacqueline E. Orsagh, "Baldwin's Female Characters—A Step Forward?," in *James Baldwin: A Critical Evaluation*, ed. Therman B. O'Daniel (Washington, DC: Howard University Press, 1977), 56–68.

15　Joyce A. Joyce, "Hughes and Twentieth-Century Genderracial Issues," in *A Historical Guide to Langston Hughes*, ed. Steven C. Tracy (New York: Oxford University Press, 2003), 120.

16　Ibid., 126.

17　Michael W. Harris, *The Rise of the Gospel Blues: The Music of Thomas Andrew Dorsey* (New York: Oxford University Press, 2004).

18　Shane White, Stephen Garton, Stephen Robertson, and Graham White, *Playing the Numbers: Gambling in Harlem between the Wars* (Cambridge, MA: Harvard University Press, 2010), 72–76.

19　Langston Hughes, *Tambourines to Glory* (New York: Hill and Wang, 1970), 172.

20 *Five Plays by Langston Hughes*, ed. Webster Smalley (Bloomington: Indiana University Press, 1963), 251.

21 Nick Salvatore, *Singing in a Strange Land: C. L. Franklin, the Black Church, and the Transformation of America* (Champaign: University of Illinois Press, 2006); Lerone A. Martin, *Preaching on Wax: The Phonograph and the Shaping of Modern African American Religion* (New York: New York University Press, 2014).

22 Sanders, *Collected Works*, 6:342.

23 Langston Hughes, "Gospel Singing: When the Spirit Really Moves," *New York Herald Tribune*, October 27, 1963; Rampersad, *Life of Langston Hughes*, 2:344.

24 Smalley, *Five Plays*, 184.

25 Ibid., 184.

26 Langston Hughes, "Poets of Song," *Chicago Defender*, August 28, 1965. For the history of Chicago's importance in the development of black gospel music, see Robert M. Marovich, *A City Called Heaven: Chicago and the Birth of Gospel Music* (Champaign: University of Illinois Press, 2015); Robert Darden, *People Get Ready!: A New History of Black Gospel Music* (London: Bloomsbury Academic, 2005); and Michael W. Harris, *The Rise of the Gospel Blues: The Music of Thomas Andrew Dorsey in the Urban Church* (New York: Oxford University Press, 1992).

27 *Tambourines to Glory: Gospel Songs by Langston Hughes and Jobe Huntley*, recorded by the Porter Singers, October 3, 1958, LHP, Box 539, Folder 13230.

28 "Character Notes," in Sanders, *Collected Works*, 182.

29 "Author's Note," in Smalley, *Five Plays*, 184.

30 Langston Hughes, *The Big Sea* (New York: Hill and Wang, 1993), 228.

31 "8 Letters to Jean Wagner, 1958–1963," bms Am 2035 (12), Jean Wagner Papers, Houghton Library, Harvard University.

32 R. Glenn Carrington Papers, Moorland Spingarn, Howard University, Box 17, Folder: "Hughes, Langston Correspondence, H–Z). See also LHP, Box 220, Folder 3684.

33 Eileen J. Lawless, "Writing the Body in the Pulpit: Female-Sexed Text," *Journal of American Folklore* 107 (Winter 1994): 56; Wallace Best, "'The Spirit of the Holy Ghost Is a Male Spirit': African American Preaching Women and the Paradoxes of Gender," in *Women and Religion in the African Diaspora: Knowledge, Power, and Performance*, ed. R. Marie Griffith and Barbara Dianne Savage, 101–27 (Baltimore: Johns Hopkins University Press, 2006).

34 Jervis Anderson, *This Was Harlem: 1900–1950* (New York: Farrar, Straus and Giroux, 1981), 348; *Harlem U.S.A.*, ed. John Henrik Clarke (New York: Seven Seas Books, 1964), 14.

35 L. Alex Swan, "The Harlem and Detroit Riots of 1943: A Comparative Analysis," *Berkeley Journal of Sociology* 16 (1971): 75–93; Günter H. Lenz, "Symbolic Space, Communal Rituals, and the Surreality of the Urban Ghetto: Harlem in Black Literature from the 1920s to the 1960s," *Callaloo* 35 (1988): 309–45.

36 Sandburg's poems on prostitutes and prostitution are found in the "Shadows" section of his *Chicago Poems*. See Penelope Niven, *Carl Sandburg: A Biography* (Fort Washington, PA: Eastern National Publishing, 2001), 29.

37 *The Collected Poems of Langston Hughes*, ed. Arnold Rampersad and David Roessel (New York: Vintage Books, 1994), 258, 33, 120.

38 Rampersad, *Life of Langston Hughes*, 1:22; Hughes, *Big Sea*, 18. See also Sanders, "I've Wrestled with Them," 69.

39 Hughes, *Tambourines to Glory* (1970), 150.

40 Sanders, *Collected Works*, 6:317, 344.

41 Langston Hughes, *Tambourines to Glory* (New York: Broadway Books, 1986), 110.

42 Hughes, *Tambourines to Glory* (1986), 59.

43 Hughes likely read Emerson because Emerson had a direct influence on Walt Whitman. A nineteenth-century poet, philosopher, and Unitarian minister, Emerson developed his notion of "self-reliance" in one of his most famous essays, published with that title in 1841. Emerson called each individual to forsake conformity and imitation in order to rely solely on their own instincts and intuitions as their divine right as human beings. "Trust thyself: every heart vibrates to that iron string," he wrote, "nothing is at last sacred but the integrity of your own mind." Ralph Waldo Emerson, "Self-Reliance," in *Self-Reliance and Other Essays* (New York: Dover, 1993), 19–38.

44 Sanders, *Collected Works*, 6:302.

45 Hughes, *Tambourines to Glory* (1970), 2.

46 Howard Thurman, *Jesus and the Disinherited* (Boston: Beacon Press, 1976), 112.

47 Hughes, *Tambourines to Glory* (1970), 47.

48 Langston Hughes, *The Gold Piece: A Play that Might be True*, *Brownies' Book* 2, no. 7 (July 1921). See also Donald C. Dickerson, "Langston Hughes and the *Brownies' Book*," *Negro History Bulletin*, December 1, 1968.

49 Smalley, *Five Plays*, ix–xii.

50 Ibid., x–xi.

51 Berry, *Before and Beyond Harlem*, 64.

52 Craig R. Prentiss, *Staging Faith: Religion and African American Theater from the Harlem Renaissance to World War II* (New York: New York University Press, 2013), 5.

53 Rampersad, *Life of Langston Hughes,* 1:63.

54 Sanders, *Collected Works*, 5:538, 570, 573.

55 Langston Hughes, *The Sun Do Move: A Music-Play*, National Activities— Publications Department, International Workers Order, 1943. Copy found in Littauer Library, Social Sciences Program, Harvard University. See also Sanders, *Collected Works*, 5:591.

56 C. Eric Lincoln and Lawrence Mamiya, *The Black Church in the African American Experience* (Durham, NC: Duke University Press, 1990), 6.

57 Langston Hughes, "Church, Theatre, and Gospel Songs," *Chicago Defender*, July 5, 1947.

58 Ibid. For a full exploration of the career and significance of Tharpe, see Gayle Wald, *Shout Sister Shout!: The Untold Story of Rock-and-Roll Trailblazer Sister Rosetta Tharpe* (Boston: Beacon Press, 2008).

59 Robert Sheldon, *New York Times*, April 18, 1962; Langston Hughes, "God, War, and Swing," *Chicago Defender*, June 5, 1943.

60 Langston Hughes, "Gospel Singers and Gospel Swingers Are Gone, Says Simple, Gone!," *Chicago Defender*, November 25, 1953; Sanders, "I've Wrestled with Them," 67.

61 Langston Hughes, "Church, Theatre, Gospel Songs," *Chicago Defender*, July 5, 1947.

62 Langston Hughes, "Gospel Singers: New Asset to American Theater," *Dramatist Bulletin* (April 1963), LHP, Box 302, Folder 4956; R. Glenn Carrington Papers, Moorland Spingarn, Howard University, Box 19, Folder: "Hughes, Langston Writing by—Gospel Singers."

63 Langston Hughes, "Gospel in the Theatre/Musica Biblica nel Teatro," LHP, Box 536, Folder 13154.

64 Hughes, *Tambourines to Glory* (1970), 61.

65 Rampersad, *Life of Langston Hughes*, 1:380–81.

66 Langston Hughes, "Gospel in the Theatre/Musica Biblica nel Teatro," LHP, Box 536, Folder 13154.

67 Langston Hughes, "Poets of Song," *Chicago Defender*, August 28, 1965.

68 "Off Broadway" is the term used to designate venues with smaller seating capacities than regular Broadway theaters.

69 Hughes and Bontemps letters, July 26 and 29, 1956, respectively, in Nichols, *Arna Bontemps–Langston Hughes Letters*, 344–45.

70 The United Arts Guild (New Haven, CT) Brochure of Production of "Tambourines," LHP, Box 539, Folder: "Tambourines to Glory."

71 Letter from Langston Hughes to James Baldwin, July 25, 1953, in Sanders, *Collected Works*, 5:2; Paine Knickerbocker, "Broadway Adventure by Langston Hughes," *San Francisco Chronicle*, February 20, 1961; D. Evans, "Langston Hughes: The Poet as Playwright: A Love-Hate Relationship," *Afro-Americans in New York Life and History* 19, no. 2 (1995).

72 Letter from Langston Hughes to Bontemps, December 13, 1959, in Nichols, *Arna Bontemps–Langston Hughes Letters*, 390.

73 Letter to Langston Hughes from Bontemps, November 9, 1959, in ibid., 388–89.

74 Letter from Langston Hughes to Bontemps, August 2, 1960, in ibid., 402.

75 Letter from Langston Hughes to Clara Ward, March 25, 1958, LHP, Box 167, Folder 3063.

76 The letter from Clara Ward to Langston Hughes is undated, but Hughes's response was on April 17, 1962. LHP, Box 167, Folder 3063. For more on Clara Ward, see Willa Ward-Royster (as told to Toni Rose), *How I Got Over: Clara Ward and the World-Famous Ward Singers* (Philadelphia: Temple University Press, 1997).

77 Karen Chilton, *Hazel Scott: The Pioneering Journey of a Jazz Pianist from Café Society to Hollywood to HUAC* (Ann Arbor: University of Michigan Press, 2008), 187–88; *New York Amsterdam News*, October 22, 1960.

78 Letter from Hughes to Bontemps, August 26, 1960 ("4 A.M."), in Nichols, *Arna Bontemps–Langston Hughes Letters*, 402.

79 Rampersad, *Life of Langston Hughes*, 2:322.

80 Letter from Langston Hughes to Frank Mitchell, September 28, 1960, LHP, Box 113, Folder 2156. Hughes and Mitchell had been friends for over thirty years at the time of the letter.

81 United Arts Guild brochure, LHP, Box 539, Folder: "Tambourines to Glory."

82 Rampersad, *Life of Langston Hughes*, 2:322.

83 Ibid., 2:322.

84 Poppy Cannon White, "Too Late—Too Soon," *New York Amsterdam News*, November 23, 1963; letter from Murray D. Morrison to Langston Hughes, November 1, 1963, LHP, Box 220, Folder 3684.

85 Letter from Anna Arnold Hedgeman to Langston Hughes, November 4, 1963, LHP, Box 220, Folder 3684.

86 Letter from Jan Meyerowitz to Langston Hughes, November 22, 1963, LHP, Box 113, Folder 2129.

87 Letter from James Emanuel to Langston Hughes, November 15, 1963, LHP, Box 59, Folder 1124.

88 Letter from David Litt to Langston Hughes, October 26, 1963, LHP, Box 220, Folder 3684.

89 Letter from Elmer Rice to Langston Hughes, October 3, 1956, LHP, Box 136, Folder 2536.

90 Letter from Mary Douglas to Langston Hughes, June 14, 1959, LHP, Box 220, Folder 3684.

91 Letter from Joan C. Jackson to Langston Hughes, January 23, 1961, LHP, Box 220, Folder 3684.

92 Sanders, *Collected Works*, 6:283, 336.

CHAPTER 5. CHRISTMAS IN BLACK

1 Anthony Heilbut, interview with the author, New York City, July 23, 2011; "New Fields Found by Gospel Singers," *New York Times*, February 18, 1962. Sheldon further reported that Kramer was convinced that gospel was positioned for a mass breakthrough of popularity such as had just been experienced by rock and roll. "There are signs," Kramer claimed "of another revolution in the popular music field, along gospel lines."

2 Arnold Rampersad, *The Life of Langston Hughes*, vol. 2, *1941–1967: I Dream a World* (New York: Oxford University Press, 2001), 345. Hughes had become acquainted with Steward in the 1940s, discovering that she "can move your soul." See *Chicago Defender*, July 5, 1947.

3 *The Collected Works of Langston Hughes: Gospel Plays, Operas, and Later Dramatic Works*, vol. 6, ed. Leslie Catherine Sanders (Columbia: University of Missouri Press, 2004), 353. Kasi Lemmons directed a movie version of *Black Nativity* in

2013, starring Forrest Whitaker, Angela Bassett, Jennifer Hudson, and Tyrese Gibson.

4 Joseph McLaren, "From Protest to Soul Fest: Langston Hughes's 'Gospel Plays,'" *Langston Hughes Review* 15, no. 1 (1997): 51; Rampersad, *Life of Langston Hughes*, 2:347.

5 For the definitive analysis of *The Green Pastures*, see Judith Weisenfeld, *Hollywood Be Thy Name: African American Religion and American Film, 1929–1949* (Berkeley: University of California Press), 2007. See also Nick Aaron Ford, "How Genuine Is *The Green Pastures*?," *Phylon* 20, no. 1 (1959): 67–70; Doris B. Garey, "*The Green Pastures* Again," *Phylon* 20, no. 2 (1959): 193–94; and Curtis J. Evans, "The Religious and Racial Meanings of *The Green Pastures*," *Religion and American Culture* 18, no. 1 (2008): 59–93.

6 Kenneth Tynan, "Telling It on the Mountains," *Observer*, August 19, 1962.

7 William Sonnega, "Beyond a Liberal Audience," in *African American Performance and Theater History: A Critical Reader*, ed. Harry J. Elam Jr. and David Krasner, 81–82 (New York: Oxford University Press, 2001).

8 The cards were printed with "Carol of the Brown King" on them in 1954. "Carol of the Brown King Cards, 1954," Langston Hughes Papers (hereafter LHP), Box 375, Folder 6227, Beinecke Library, Yale University.

9 Amy Helene Kirschke, *Aaron Douglas: Art, Race, and the Harlem Renaissance* (Jackson: University of Mississippi Press, 1995), 78–79. Douglas shared a philosophy in common with Hughes regarding black art and artists. In a spirit that would be echoed in Hughes's 1926 manifesto, "The Negro and the Racial Mountain," Douglas made his own declaration to Hughes a year earlier. "Your problem, Langston, my problem, no our problem is to conceive, develop, establish an art era. Not white art painted black. . . . Let's bare our arms and plunge them deep through laughter, through pain, through sorrow, through hope, through disappointment, into the very depths of the souls of our people and drag forth material crude, rough, neglected. Then let's sing it, dance it, write it, paint it. Let's do the impossible. Let's create something transcendentally material, mystically objective. Earthy, Spiritually earthy. Dynamic." Letter from Aaron Douglas to Langston Hughes, December 21, 1925, LHP, Box 56, Folder 1057.

10 Langston Hughes, "Christmas Time," "The Christmas Story," LHP, Box 375, Folder 6227.

11 Langston Hughes, "Christmas Comes But Once a Year and Now It Is Almost Here," November 20, 1953, LHP, Box 411, Folder 8715.

12 Langston Hughes, "Memories of Christmas," from "A Christmas Sampler," LHP, Box 29, Folder 4739.

13 Langston Hughes, "Christmas Song," from "A Christmas Sampler," LHP, Box 29, Folder 4739.

14 Langston Hughes, "Poems for Christmas," from "A Christmas Sampler," LHP, Box 29, Folder 4739.

15 Langston Hughes, "Christmas with Christ," from "A Christmas Sampler," LHP, Box 29, Folder 4740.

16 "Coeds to See Play by Langston Hughes Jan. 7," *Chicago Defender*, December 23, 1961.

17 "Black Nativity Files, 1961–1980," New York Public Library, Performing Arts Library, Box 2. The words were scratched out in blue ink presumably by Kramer and did not appear in the final version, nor did the "Mrs. Waddy" character.

18 Barbara Meyer (Griner), interview with author, February 12, 2012; "O, Come, All Ye Faithful," *Chicago Defender*, December 22, 1963.

19 Heilbut interview, July 23, 2011; Griner interview, February 12, 2012.

20 "No-Good Shepherd," LHP, Box 285, Folder 4657.

21 "Black Nativity (A Gospel Song-Play) by Langston Hughes, Proposal and Libretto for a Joyous Christmas Time Television Special," *Black Nativity* files, New York Public Library, Performing Arts Library, Box 1: "Black Nativity—Proposed Libretto." All quotations from *Black Nativity* are from this edition, hereafter cited in the text by act number.

22 See Katherine Hankey, *Old, Old Story* (New York: American Track Society, 1866), 6.

23 "Langston Hughes Yule Play Uses Gospelers," *Afro-American*, December 23, 1961; *Black Nativity*, original cast recording liner notes, Veejay Records, 1962.

24 Calvin McClinton, *The Work of Vinnette Carroll, an African American Theatre Artist* (Lewiston, NY: Edwin Mellen Press, 2000), 77.

25 Tynan, "Telling It on the Mountains"; *Black Nativity* liner notes; "Play Warm Version of Yule Story Woven into Folklore," *Philadelphia Tribune*, August 7, 1965.

26 Peter Guralnick, *Dream Boogie: The Triumph of Sam Cooke* (New York: Little Brown, 2005), 374–75, 389; "Gospel Songs of 'Black Nativity' Offer New Trend in U.S. Music," *Chicago Defender*, December 24, 1962; Barbara Griner, interview with the author, February 3, 2012.

27 "Black Nativity. . . . How It Happened," document found in the Barbara F. Meyer (Griner) Collection. Document and collection in possession of the author.

28 Hughes, "Gospel in the Theatre."

29 Letter from Gary Kramer to Langston Hughes, October 5, 1961, LHP, Box 98, Folder 1842.

30 "Co-Sponsor Replaced," *New York Times*, December 13, 1961; Rampersad, *Life of Langston Hughes*, 2:347.

31 Kramer's ouster was vicious, abrupt, and nasty. Santangelo took the lead. Hughes further reported to Searchinger that Santangelo had not only ousted Kramer from the show but also barred him and any of his associates from the theater. He would not be sold tickets or allowed in the theater on opening night. Hughes had been standing nearby when some of Kramer's friends attempted to buy tickets but were refused.

32 Letter from Langston Hughes to Arno Bontemps, February 16, 1962, in *Arna Bontemps–Langston Hughes Letters, 1925–1967*, ed. Charles H. Nichols (New York: Paragon House, 1990), 452.

33 "Correspondence and Memos on Black Nativity, 1962–1963," *Black Nativity* files, Box 1.

34 Letter from Marion Searchinger to Barbara Griner, November 27, 1962, LHP, Box 143, Folder 2668.

35 Jennifer Dunning, *Alvin Ailey: A Life in Dance* (Reading, MA: Addison-Wesley, 1996), 142–43.

36 According to the *Shubert Theatre Playgoer* (New Haven, CT), it was Santangelo who changed the name of the song-play. *Shubert Theatre Playgoer*, November 18–23, 1963, 21, LHP, Box 535, Folder 13151.

37 *New York Post*, December 3, 1961.

38 Alvin Ailey with Peter Bailey, *Revelations: The Autobiography of Alvin Ailey* (Seacaucus, NJ: Carol Publishing Group, 1995), 47.

39 "2 Quit 'Black Nativity,'" *New York Times*, December 4, 1961.

40 "'Black Nativity' Will Play Lincoln Center," *New York Amsterdam News*, December 8, 1961; *New York Post*, December 3, 1961.

41 Carmen de Lavallade, interview by phone with the author, September 16, 2013, Princeton University.

42 Ben L. Martin, "From Negro to Black to African American: The Power of Names and Naming," *Political Science Quarterly* 106 (1991): 83–107.

43 McClinton, *Work of Vinnette Carroll*, 79.

44 Arnold Rampersad, *The Life of Langston Hughes*, vol. 1, *1902–1941: I, Too, Sing America* (New York: Oxford University Press, 2002), 343; Tom Feelings, "Black Artist," *Negro Digest* (September 1967).

45 Langston Hughes, "That Word Black," in *Langston Hughes: The Return of Simple*, ed. Akiba Sullivan Harper, 146–48 (New York: Hill and Wang, 1994).

46 Letter from Langston Hughes to Waring Cuney, December 21, 1953, LHP, Box 39, Folder 924.

47 Rampersad, *Life of Langston Hughes*, 2:347.

48 Anthony Heilbut, *The Gospel Sound: Good News and Bad Times* (New York: Simon and Schuster, 1971); Horace Clarence Boyer, *How Sweet the Sound: The Golden Age of Gospel* (Washington, DC: Elliott and Clark, 1995). See also Barbara J. Kukla, *Swing City: Newark Nightlife, 1925–1950* (New Brunswick, NJ: Rutgers University Press, 2002).

49 Letter from Alex Bradford to Langston Hughes, March 27, 1965, LHP, Box 22, Folder 453.

50 Madeline Bell, Skype interview with the author, February 14, 2012.

51 Heilbut, *Gospel Sound*, 157.

52 Carl Bean, telephone interview with the author, New York City, January 31, 2012.

53 "Black Nativity . . . How It Happened," Barbara Meyer (Griner) Collection.

54 McClinton, *Vinnette Carroll*, 26.

55 Letter from Vinnette Carroll to Langston Hughes, September 21, 1962, LHP, Box 42, Folder 725.

56 Letter from Langston Hughes to Vinnette Carroll, September 16, 1962, LHP, Box 42, Folder 725.

57 McClinton, *Vinnette Carroll*, 18.

58 Anthony Heilbut, interview with the author, New York City, July 23, 2011. Carroll exclaimed that Bankhead "is wonderful in the play . . . such discipline." Letter from Vinnette Carroll to Langston Hguhes, November 17, 1963, LHP, Box 57, Folder 1085.

59 Heilbut interview, July 23, 2011; Bean interview, January 31, 2012.

60 "Miss Vinnette Carroll, Today's Woman," *New York Amsterdam News*, December 22, 1962.

61 Ibid. Barbara Griner not only insisted that Carroll was a lesbian but that she had been in a "long term relationship with Cicely Tyson, who broke it off at some point." For Griner, Carroll was "masculine" in appearance and had a deep and "resonate" voice. Barbara Meyer (Griner) interview, New York City, July 19, 2011.

62 Both Griner and Heilbut confirm this, but also suggest that Carroll shared the same view as her parents.

63 Letter from Vinnette Carroll to Langston Hughes, September 2, 1962, LHP, Box 42, Folder 725.

64 Heilbut interview, July 23, 2011.

65 McClinton, *Vinnette Carroll*, 13.

66 "Gospel Abroad," *Newsweek*, September 3, 1962.

67 Letter from Vinnette Carroll to Langston Hughes, August 19, 1962, LHP, Box 42, Folder 725.

68 "Theatre: 'Black Nativity,'" *New York Times*, December 12, 1961.

69 John Beaufort, "A Joyful Noise on 41st Street," *Christian Science Monitor*, December 16, 1961.

70 Anthony Heilbut, e-mail correspondence with the author, August 7, 2013.

71 Barnes, Jennifer, *Television Opera: The Fall of Opera Commissioned for Television* (Rochester, NY: Boydell Press, 2003); Bernard Holland, "Gian Carlo Menotti, Opera Composer, Dies at 95," *New York Times*, February 2, 2007.

72 "'Black Nativity' Gets Ovation as It Begins Run in London," *New York Times*, August 15, 1962.

73 *Chicago Defender*, August 21, 1962; letter from Vinnette Carroll to Langston Hughes, September 21, 1962, LHP, Box 42, Folder 725.

74 Letter from Langston Hughes to Marion Searchinger, September 5, 1962, LHP, Box 143, Folder 2668; "An International Hit Returns to New York Christmas Week," *New York Times*, November 25, 1962; Anthony Heilbut, e-mail correspondence, August 8, 2013.

75 Milton Shulman, "Religion Put to a Hot Jazz Beat," *Evening Standard* (London), August 1962.

76 Herbert Kretzmer, "Religion This Way Goes with a Swing," *Daily Express* (London), August 1962.

77 Excerpts from Eugenie Soderberg's review of *Black Nativity* in *Stockholms-Tidningen*, Sweden, January 2, 1962," LHP, Box 285, Folder 4664; "Nativity with a Swing," *Times of London*, August 15, 1962.

78 "Tidings of Great Joy," *Daily Mirror*, August 15, 1962.

79 Shulman, "Religion Put to a Hot Jazz Beat," *Evening Standard* (London), August 1962.

80 "Nativity Hottest," *Chicago Defender*, December 4, 1962.

81 Barbara Griner interview, February 3, 2012; "Philharmonic Hall Books Hughes Play," *New York Times*, November 21, 1962. See also "'Black Nativity' Comes Back," *Chicago Defender*, November 26, 1962.

82 "'Black Nativity' Will Play Lincoln Center," *New York Amsterdam News*, December 8, 1962; Jesse H. Walker, "Theatricals," *New York Amsterdam News*, December 8, 1962.

83 Letter from Hughes to Bontemps, December 29, 1962, in Nichols, *Arna Bontemps–Langston Hughes Letters*, 451.

84 *Black Nativity* income statements, LHP, Box 523, Folder 12975.

85 Phyl Garland, "'Black Nativity'—A Joyful Sound to the Lord," *Pittsburgh Courier*, December 22, 1962.

86 Jesse H. Walker, "Theatricals," *New York Amsterdam News*, February 16, 1963; *Chicago Defender*, December 10, 1963.

87 Melvin Maddocks, "Joyous Gospel Song Play," *Christian Science Monitor*, December 26, 1962.

88 "'Black Nativity' to Be Broadcast over WIND Here on December 24," *Chicago Defender*, December 17, 1962.

89 Letter from Hughes to Bontemps, January 14, 1963, in Nichols, *Arna Bontemps–Langston Hughes Letters*, 453.

90 Edgar A. Wiggins, "Nativity Takes Paris; Ellington Catches Show," LHP, Box 285, Folder 4664.

91 Sanders, *Collected Works*, 6:356.

92 Letter from Tony Buttitta to Langston Hughes, March 29, 1965, from Salerno, Italy, LHP, Box 37, Folder 661.

93 Letter from Viv Campbell to Langston Hughes, n.d., LHP, Box 41, Folder 706. The letter was sent between the Spoleto engagements and April 19, 1963, when she and Elmer saw the show in Zurich.

94 Letter from Elmer Simms Campbell to Langston Hughes, April 19, 1963, LHP, Box 41, Folder 706.

95 "Black Christmas: Translation of an Article," November 7, 1964, LHP, Box 285, Folder 4664.

96 Everett Helm, "Africa Comes to Berlin," *Christian Science Monitor*, October 12, 1964.

97 "Foes Seek to Bar Negro Poet's Play," *New York Times*, November 28, 1963.

98 Ibid. For more on Cantwell, see John T. McGreevy, *Parish Boundaries: The Catholic Encounter with Race in the Twentieth Century Urban North* (Chicago: University of Chicago Press, 1998).

99 "Black Nativity," *Chicago Defender*, December 2, 1963; "Foes Seek to Bar Negro Poet's Play," *New York Times*, November 28, 1963; "Poet Langston Hughes Is Target of Letter Writing Drive in Chicago," *Philadelphia Tribune*, December 3, 1963; "Smear Campaign Fails to Scuttle Chi Opening of 'Black Nativity,'" *Philadelphia Tribune*, December 10, 1963; "'Nativity' Outlasts Smear Campaign," *Afro-American*, December 14, 1963.

100 Letter from Thomas A. Dorsey to Langston Hughes, January 20, 1964, LHP, Box 55, Folder 1053.

101 *New York Telegraph and Sun*, December 26, 1961.

102 Letter from Mrs. Eleanor Owens to Langston Hughes, December 13, 1962, R. Glenn Carrington Papers, Moorland Spingarn, Howard University, Box 17, Folder: "Hughes, Langston Correspondence, H–Z.

103 *Call and Post*, December 1962.

104 Earl Calloway, "The Artist's Circle," *Call and Post*, January 11, 1964; "Youth Discuss Black Nativity," *Call and Post*, March 2, 1963.

105 Lillian S. Calhoun, "Confetti: Top of the Town," *Chicago Defender*, December 5, 1963. Lillian Calhoun (1923–2006) was a pioneering African American journalist from Chicago. She began her career in Detroit in the 1940s working for a monthly magazine targeted at black readers. Moving to Chicago in 1959, Calhoun worked as fine arts editor for the *Chicago Defender*, where she also explored civil rights issues in her "Confetti" column. Having served as a reporter for *Ebony* and *Jet* magazine, Calhoun joined the newsroom of the *Chicago Sun Times* in 1965, becoming the first black woman to do so.

106 Louise Peacock, "About 'Black Nativity,'" *Call and Post*, January 19, 1963.

107 Louise Davis Stone, "'Black Nativity' Makes a Joyful Noise unto Chicago," *Chicago Defender*, December 4, 1963.

108 Letter to Langston Hughes from Carl Van Vechten, January 29, 1962, in *Remember Me to Harlem: The Letters of Langston Hughes and Carl Van Vechten, 1925–1964*, ed. Emily Bernard (New York: Knopf, 2001), 318; "Comment on 'Black Nativity': Excerpt from a letter to a London friend written by a prominent New York psychiatrist, January 1962," LHP, Box 285, Folder 4660.

109 "Excerpt from a Letter to Langston Hughes from Florence Graham of Boston, Mass., January 16, 1963," LHP, Box 285, Folder 4660.

110 Letter from Carl Van Vechten to Langston Hughes, January 29, 1962, in Bernard, *Remember Me to Harlem*, 318.

111 "Langston Hughes Musical Opens in London," *Chicago Defender*, August 21, 1962.

112 Sanders, *Collected Works*, 6:354.

113 Ibid.

114 Ibid.

115 Paule Marshall, "People and Places in the Life of a Writer: An Homage to Mr. Hughes," Alaine Locke Lectures, Harvard University, April 19, 2006. See also Paule Marshall, *Triangular Road: A Memoir* (New York: Basic Books, 2009), 1–34.

116 Alice Walker, "Turning into Love: Some Thoughts on Surviving and Meeting Langston Hughes," *Callaloo* 41 (Autumn 1989): 665, 663, respectively.

117 Rampersad, *Life of Langston Hughes*, 2:410.

118 Langston Hughes, *The Panther and the Lash* (New York: Vintage Books, 1992), 16, 37, 38.

119 Warren Burdine, "Let the Theatre Say 'Amen,'" *Black American Literature Forum* 25, no. 1 (Spring 1991): 76.

120 Madeline Bell interview, February 14, 2012.

121 Heilbut interview, July 23, 2011; e-mail correspondence from Anthony Heilbut, November 13, 2016; "Rites Set for Princess Stewart," *Chicago Defender*, February 18, 1967.

122 Griner interview, February 3, 2012.

CONCLUSION

1 Arnold Rampersad, *The Life of Langston Hughes*, vol. 2, *1941–1967: I Dream a World* (New York: Oxford University Press, 2001), 424–25.

2 "Last Rites," R. Glenn Carrington Papers, Moorland-Spingarn, Howard University, Box 17, Folder: "Hughes, Langston Funeral and Memorial Service."

3 Langston Hughes, "Funeral," LHP, Box 377, Folder 64224; Rampersad, *Life of Langston Hughes*, 2:425; "The Ashes of Langston Hughes Return in Ancient Rite," *New York Times*, February 2, 1991; "Ashes of Langston Hughes Buried under Artwork in Harlem's Schomburg Center," *Jet*, February 25, 1991. As a part of the ceremony, the poets Maya Angelou and Amiri Baraka danced on a cosmogram in celebration of Hughes being returned to "the ancestors."

4 Margaret T. G. Burroughs, "Langston Hughes—February 1, 1902–May 22, 1967," *Free Lance: A Magazine of Poetry and Prose* 11, no. 2 (1967): 1–4.

5 "First Memorial Tribute to Langston Hughes," Langston Hughes Collection, Schomburg Center for Research in Black Culture, New York Public Library, R-977, Reel 3, Series B.

6 "Christians and Communists," LHP, n.d., in draft form, corrected copy, Box 417, Folder, 9177.

7 Langston Hughes, *The Big Sea* (New York: Hill and Wang, 1993), 204–5. See Lewis Browne, *This Believing World: A Simple Account of the Great Religions of Mankind* (New York: Simon Publications, 2001).

8 James H. Snowden, "The Place of Doubt in Religious Belief," *Biblical World* 47, no. 3 (March 1916): 151–55; J. L. Schellenberg, *The Wisdom to Doubt: A Justification of Religious Skepticism* (Ithaca, NY: Cornell University Press, 2007); Christopher Lane, *The Age of Doubt: Tracing the Roots of Our Religious Uncertainty* (New Haven, CT: Yale University Press, 2011).

9 Langston Hughes, "The Meaning of Faith: Personal," *Chicago Defender*, January 23, 1960.

10 John B. Cobb Jr. and David Ray Griffin, *Process Theology: An Introductory Exposition* (Philadelphia: Westminster Press, 1976), 7; "Process Thought: A Contempo-

rary Trend in Theology," in *Process Theology: Basic Writings by the Key Thinkers of a Major Modern Movement*, ed. Ewert H. Cousins (New York: Newman Press, 1971), 25; Alfred North Whitehead, "God and the World," in ibid., 93; Roland Faber, *God as Poet of the World: Exploring Process Theologies* (Louisville, KY: Westminster John Knox Press, 2008), 8.

11 Hughes, "Meaning of Faith."

12 Arnold Rampersad, *The Life of Langston Hughes*, vol 1, *1902–1941: I, Too, Sing America* (New York: Oxford University Press, 2002), 47.

13 Hughes, "Meaning of Faith."

14 Ibid.

INDEX

Abyssinian Baptist Church, 60–65, 155, 182

African Methodist Episcopal (AME) Church: AME Zion (SC), 129; Bethel AME (Baltimore), 130; Mother AME Zion (Harlem), 60; St. James AME (Cleveland), 224; St. Luke AME (Lawrence, KS), 1–5, 74–76, 81, 168, 234, 238, 241n6

Ailey, Alvin, 205–208

"All Hail to Christ: A la Langston Hughes" (Ransom), 124–125, 149

Alter ego. *See* Semple, Jesse B.

Anderson, Marion, 79, 147. *See also* Music: gospel

"An Evening Thought: Salvation By Christ" (Hammon, 1761), 41

Apollo Theater. *See* New York City: Apollo Theater

Bailey, Pearl, 152, 181–182. *See also* Music: jazz

Baker, George. *See* Father Divine

Baldwin, James, 58, 72, 181, 255–256n13, 269n14

Baxter, J. Harvey L., 44

Bean, Carl, 15–16, 211, 213

Becton, Dr. George W., 120, 133–134, 159, 234, 265n51. *See also* "Goodbye Christ"

Bell, Madeline, 192–193, 211, 229

Bennett, Bishop E. E., 126–127, 131. *See also* "Forgive Him Christ"

Bethune, Mary McLeod, 20

"Big-Eyed Buddy Lomax" (character), 160, 189. See also *Tambourines to Glory*

Birdie Lee (character), 161, 169, 181–182. See also *Tambourines to Glory*

Bishop, Hutchens Chew, 60–61

Black and White (film), 114–119

Black Christ, 3, 41, 44, 50–51, 93, 96, 100, 103–105, 193–203, 221–222, 229, 256n20; "The Black Madonna," (Rice); 43; Black Mary, 43; "Carol of the Brown King," 65, 86, 197; "Paint Me a God," 44. *See also* "The Black Christ" (Cullen); *Black Nativity*

"The Black Christ" (Cullen), 50–51

Black Nativity (Hughes), 3, 15, 25–26, 154, 158, 178, 191–230, 273–274n3, 275n17; "Wasn't It a Mighty Day?," 191–192, 204, 206. *See also* Works of Langston Hughes

"Blasphemy—American Style" (Popel), 44–45

Blues. *See* Music: blues

Bonds, Margaret, 6, 65

Bone, Robert, 37, 69, 105

Bontemps, Arna, 15, 221, 233, 251n53; in correspondence with Langston Hughes, 57, 152, 180–182, 218, 220, 242n14, 251n53, 255–256n13, 262n23, 267n75

Bradford, Alex, 154, 164; and the Bradford Singers, 191–193, 202, 208–211, 223, 229. *See also* Music: gospel

Broadway. *See* New York City: Broadway

Brooks, Gwendolyn, 231–232

Burroughs, Margaret T. G., 233

Buttitta, Anthony, 102–104, 220–221

ABOUT THE AUTHOR

Wallace D. Best is Professor of Religion and African American Studies, and Associate Faculty Member of History at Princeton University.